CARE
FOR THE SOUL

Exploring
the Intersection
of Psychology
& Theology

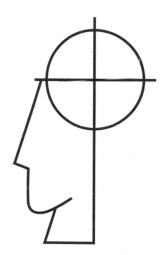

EDITED BY
Mark R. McMinn &
Timothy R. Phillips

InterVarsity Press
Downers Grove, Illinois

InterVarsity Press
P.O. Box 1400, Downers Grove, IL 60515-1426
World Wide Web: www.ivpress.com
E-mail: mail@ivpress.com

InterVarsity Press® is the book-publishing division of InterVarsity Christian Fellowship/USA®, a student movement active on campus at hundreds of universities, colleges and schools of nursing in the United States of America, and a member movement of the International Fellowship of Evangelical Students. For information about local and regional activities, write Public Relations Dept., InterVarsity Christian Fellowship/USA, 6400 Schroeder Rd., P.O. Box 7895, Madison, WI 53707-7895, or visit the IVCF website at <www.intervarsity.org>.

Scripture quotations, unless otherwise noted, are from the New Revised Standard Version of the Bible, copyright 1989 by the Division of Christian Education of the National Council of the Churches of Christ in the USA. Used by permission. All rights reserved.

Every effort has been made to acquire permission for material quoted in this book. The authors will be pleased to rectify any omissions in future editions if notified by copyright holders.

Cover illustration: Roberta Polfus

ISBN 0-8308-1553-8

Printed in the United States of America ∞

Library of Congress Cataloging-in-Publication Data

Care for the soul : exploring the intersection of psychology & theology / edited by Mark
R. McMinn and Timothy R. Phillips.
    p. cm.
    Includes bibliographical references.
    ISBN 0-8308-1553-8 (pbk. : alk. paper)
    1. Pastoral counseling—Congresses. 2. Pastoral psychology—Congresses. 3.
    Christianity—Psychology—Congresses. 4. Bible—Psychology—Congresses. I. McMinn,
    Mark R. II. Phillips, Timothy R. (Timothy Ross) 1950-2000
BV4012.2 C284 2001
261.5'15—dc21

00-054445

P	20	19	18	17	16	15	14	13	12	11	10	9	8	7	6	5	4	3
Y	19	18	17	16	15	14	13	12	11	10	09	08	07	06	05	04		

Dedication

As a historical and systematic theologian Dr. Timothy R. Phillips, coeditor of this book, was keenly aware of the pervasive brokenness of our world. Since the Fall of humankind—when sin corrupted a perfect creation—we have suffered with sickness and travail, and have yearned for our spiritual home where we will finally be able to experience the width, length, height and depth of God's love (Ephesians 3:18). Tim lived and taught this theology, quietly struggling against the cancer in his own body as he helped his students know God. On September 27, 2000, we lost a valued faculty member, friend and colleague. Sandy Phillips lost a faithful husband. Aaron and Caleb lost a loving father. Tim's death, like his fifty years of life, revealed a man of integrity and goodness. We miss him.

Mark R. McMinn, *Wheaton College, coeditor*

Tim Phillips embodied the best of what one could hope for in a Christian theologian and faculty member. He possessed, or more accurately was possessed by, a pure and passionate love for Jesus Christ, and a desire to have his life marked by simple obedience to his Lord and Savior. From this flowed his incredible discipline, strength, courage, servant's heart, compassion, sacrificial spirit and integrity. Added to the mix were a brilliant mind and superb training. Tim Phillips enriched all of us around him, students, colleagues and friends.

Stanton L. Jones, *provost of Wheaton College, author of chapter two*

Losing Tim Phillips has been a blow not only to his growing family but to his colleagues and students now deprived of a gentle, faithful and patient teacher. His dedication to opening theology to constructive conversation with other disciplines and to fostering fruitful discussion among evangelical and nonevangelical scholars was a blessing to the theological community. His legacy, as illustrated by this book, should not be allowed to perish, for unless theology engage the world in which we find ourselves, it will languish. May his family find comfort in the honor he brought to God, the academy and the church.

Ellen T. Charry, *Princeton Theological Seminary, author of chapter five*

Tim Phillips was one of the most deeply dedicated and hard-working teachers and scholars at Wheaton College, a man of high integrity, both intellectual and personal. He is sorely missed.

Robert C. Roberts, *Baylor University, author of chapter six*

My good friend and close colleague Tim Phillips spent an adult lifetime (cut short by the adversary) studying God as he has revealed himself in Jesus Christ, and inspiring others to do the same. What made his work so beneficial for the kingdom is that he deeply loved both the object of his study and those who wanted to join him in getting the study right.

Dennis L. Okholm, *Wheaton College, author of chapter seven*

From Tim's work I was always reminded of the importance of maintaining a Christ-centered faith, not simply a God-centered faith.

Michael W. Mangis, *Wheaton College, author of chapter eight*

I admired the congruence between what Tim believed and how he lived. That he died as well as he lived is a tribute to his faith in the God of Jesus Christ. We will miss him, even as we give thanks for his life.

L. Gregory Jones, *Duke University, author of chapter eleven*

It was appropriate that Tim's final lecture on September 20, 2000, addressed the topic of the inspiration of Scripture, for he devoted his life as scholar-teacher to upholding the authority of the Bible as God's Word.

Richard Schultz, *Wheaton College, author of chapter twelve*

We thank God for the gift to us of Tim's life, knowing that here was one in whom we saw the righteousness of Jesus shine like the dawn.

Myrla Seibold, *Bethel College, author of chapter fourteen*

I appreciated Tim Phillips's obvious passionate love for God, his careful Christ-centered approach to evangelical theology and his gentle pastoral manner.

Stephen K. Moroney, *Malone College, author of chapter fifteen*

Contents

Introduction

PSYCHOLOGY, THEOLOGY & CARE FOR THE SOUL

Mark R. McMinn

A CONTEMPORARY ADVERTISEMENT FOR A LUXURY CAR READS, "IT GETS INTO YOUR soul, not your pocketbook." For a car with a $45,000 price tag, this claim is disputable, but the advertisers persist because they understand that the soul is marketable. Contemporary book titles offer *Chicken Soup for the Soul, Penguin Soup for the Soul* and *Duck Soup for the Soul; The Soul of Sex; 100 Ways to Keep Your Soul Alive; Acupressure for the Soul; Chocolate for the Woman's Soul;* a *Flight Manual for the Soul;* and *Animal Guides for the Soul.* We have soul music, soul food and soul mates. A quick visit to Amazon.com yields thousands of book titles containing the word *soul.* There is legitimate reason to question whether today's resurgence of soul language reflects a Christian understanding of persons. Under the grip of modernity, in the midst of our fascination with stimulus-response connections and scientific formulations of psychoanalysis, the concept of the soul was often reduced to irrelevant historical lore. But as the empiricism and rationalism of modernity fade into the pluralism of postmodernity, there is renewed interest in the soul—even though there is little agreement about what the soul is.

One could argue that modernity itself brought about this interest in the soul. After all, in modern times the study of the soul—psyche—emerged as a highly visible discipline—psychology—that continues to attract thousands of new graduate students each year. Ellen Charry, in her contribution to this volume, describes the twentieth century as the "psychological century." And the discipline of psychology was dominated by the clinical and counseling subdisciplines where the care of the psyche is explored in great detail. How can we claim that we lost the soul in a time when psychology experienced enormous growth in interest? The answer, like the question, lies in the epistemological assumptions of modernity. In order to achieve respect as a science, the study of psychology in the past century often neglected the religious traditions that shaped the understanding of the soul before the Enlightenment.[1] Somehow we misplaced the soul even as we developed a thriving science of the psyche. Several contributors to this book note that the notion of soul was usurped by modernity's notion of self. And in relegating the care of selves to secular scientist-practitioners, we lost some critical aspects of caring for the soul.

With the changing winds of postmodernity swirling around us, we stand at a crossroads pondering the value and limits of science, the role of theological traditions and the boundaries of spirituality. Now that we can conceive of the material world as an aggregate of subatomic particles and build microscopes powerful enough to see the building blocks of creation, how do we understand the connections that bind atoms, molecules, cells, organisms, communities, cultures and societies together? Now that we have scientifically validated ways to treat panic attacks and psychopharmacological interventions for clinical depression, how do we make sense of the soul's journey through the "valley of the shadow of death" (Ps 23:4 NASB) or the "dark night?"[2] After the end of a century that knew more mass destruction than any other, how is the perversion and aggression of the human soul cured?

Modernity's psychology may have something to offer Christians who are interested in caring for souls. Thoughtful Christian psychologists contributed many of the chapters in this volume. But the central premise behind this book—and behind the conference that inspired it—is that care for the soul must also draw from the rich theological and ecclesiological traditions of the past and present. Our task is to explore the intersection of theology and psychology.

Care for the Soul or the Cure of the Soul?

This book grew out of a Wheaton Theology Conference titled "The Cure of the Soul: Exploring the Intersection of Theology and Psychology." The conference, which was cosponsored by the Wheaton College departments of Bible/theology and psychology, brought together leading theologians, philosophers and psychologists who are interested in the relationship between psychology and theology.

The title of the book, *Care for the Soul,* was changed only slightly from the conference title, "The Cure of the Soul." The *u* in *cure* was replaced with an *a.* The implications of this change are bigger than one letter. A number of psychologists at the conference expressed discomfort with the grandiosity implied in "The Cure of the Soul." Surely curing the soul is not the job of psychologists. Psychologists treat the soul by easing suffering, helping people in emotional pain to reclaim meaning and purpose and encouraging people to see themselves, others and the world more

---

[1]Allen E. Bergin, "Psychotherapy and Religious Values," *Journal of Consulting and Clinical Psychology* 48 (1980): 95-105; Stanton L. Jones, "A Constructive Relationship for Religion with the Science and Professional of Psychology: Perhaps the Boldest Model Yet," *American Psychologist* 49 (1994): 184-99.

[2]John of the Cross, *Dark Night of the Soul* (New York: Doubleday, 1990).

accurately. In short, psychologists care for the soul. The cure of the soul, most Christian psychologists would suggest, is God's work and is beyond the scope of mainstream psychological interventions.

The book title *Care for the Soul*, which is more comfortable for the psychologist contributors, may raise offsetting tensions among many theologians. Yes, evangelical Christian theology is about caring for the soul, but it is more interested in exploring the cure of the soul through the confession of sin and through the redemption found in Jesus Christ.[3] A throng of psychologists has emerged to care for the soul, but the message of evangelical Christian theology offers a cure for the broken soul.

So even the title of this book reflects some of the implicit tensions found at the intersection of theology and psychology. These tensions are not new—many scholars have explored them over the past several decades.[4] Fortunately, many of these same scholars are willing to stand at these crossroads and carefully evaluate the soul, helping to forge a Christian psychology that considers the rich traditions and doctrines of the past as well as the dynamic intellectual climate of the present.

Whether the goal is to care for the soul or to cure it, we must first vigorously consider the soul. In chapter four Jeffrey Boyd articulates this need in his passionate call for us to return to a theological understanding of the soul. Considering the soul is the shared task of psychology and theology, and it is the focus of this book.

Standing Together, but Not Too Close

If the task of considering the soul is shared, the approach to the task is not. Contributors to this volume have diverse backgrounds, perspectives, areas of scholarly interest and academic preparation. Indeed, one of the great values of this book is its multidisciplinary focus. Chapters have been contributed by philosophers, theologians, Bible scholars, clinical psychologists, developmental and social psychologists and biblical counselors. During the days of the conference and as we were compiling the pages of this book, we all stood together to look at the soul. And then we returned to our own professional worlds, having been privileged to hear and learn from one another.

One challenge of interdisciplinary work is learning when to emphasize our areas of commonality and when to emphasize our distinct and sometimes disparate perspectives. In *The Prophet* Kahlil Gibran advises two lovers to "stand together yet not too near together." A book such as *Care for the Soul* requires Christian psychologists, theologians and biblical counselors to stand together; each contributor has important perspectives to offer as we look at the soul. Yet each discipline has dis-

---

[3]Dennis L. Okholm and Timothy R. Phillips, eds., *More Than One Way? Four Views on Salvation in a Pluralistic World* (Grand Rapids, Mich.: Zondervan, 1995).

[4]See, for example, Paul C. Vitz, *Psychology As Religion: The Cult of Self-Worship* (Grand Rapids, Mich.: Eerdmans, 1977); Jay E. Adams, *Competent to Counsel* (Grand Rapids, Mich.: Baker, 1970).

tinct methods and bodies of knowledge that should not be quieted by the other disciplines.

Psychologists and counselors who are interested in the soul need theologians. Ellen Charry makes this point well in her chapter: psychology's contemporary view of persons is often missing a theologically responsible anthropology. Dennis Okholm in his chapter on anger and Robert Roberts in his chapter on Pauline psychotherapy illustrate the resources theologians and philosophers can offer contemporary mental health practitioners. And as Richard Schultz points out in his chapter, Christian mental health professionals often need the help of Bible scholars to properly handle Scripture.

As uncommon as it is to bring psychologists and theologians together for a book such as this, it is even less common to bring together biblical counselors and Christian psychologists. Since the publication of the seminal works of Jay Adams[5] on the one hand, and Gary Collins,[6] John Carter and Bruce Narramore[7] on the other, biblical counseling has stood apart from Christian psychology. Each approach has its own training institutions and regimens, leaders in the two fields have often been critical of one another (fairly and unfairly), and each group has sometimes resorted to hyperbole when describing the other. Some biblical counselors have misrepresented Christian psychologists by asserting that they uncritically accept the worldview assumptions implicit in contemporary psychological theories. Some Christian psychologists have misrepresented biblical counselors by accusing them of holding a simplistic view of sin.

The dispute between the biblical counselors and the Christian psychologists has often been confusing to Christians who are trying to make sense of their Christian mental health alternatives. And the unfortunate combative rhetoric between biblical counselors and Christian psychologists has been worsened by extremist Christian authors—most of whom are not themselves biblical counselors—who have added fuel to the fire by attacking Christian psychologists, collectively and personally, in their best-selling books. One author bemoans "Christians who turn from God and His word to psychotherapies for help with depression forsake 'the fountain of living waters' to drink from the polluted and unsatisfying and even harmful 'broken cisterns, that can hold no water' (Jer 13)."[8]

In response to a series of these vitriolic antipsychology books written in the

---

[5]Adams, *Competent to Counsel*. See also Jay E. Adams, *The Christian Counselor's Manual* (Grand Rapids, Mich.: Baker, 1973).

[6]See, for example, Gary R. Collins, *How to Be a People Helper* (Santa Ana, Calif.: Vision House, 1976); and his *Christian Counseling: A Comprehensive Guide* (Waco, Tex.: Word, 1980).

[7]John Carter and Bruce Narramore, *The Integration of Psychology and Theology: An Introduction* (Grand Rapids, Mich.: Zondervan, 1979).

[8]Dave Hunt, *Beyond Seduction* (Eugene, Ore.: Harvest House, 1987).

1970s and 1980s, a well-known Christian psychologist with theological training wrote the book *Can You Trust Psychology?* In it he gave cautious affirmation to some aspects of psychology, and he did so in a balanced and fair manner.[9] For a time it seemed possible that the battles might cease, or at least abate. Then in 1993 a pastor and biblical counselor answered with his book *Why Christians Can't Trust Psychology.*[10] It was more balanced than some of the earlier antipsychology books, but its publication made it clear that resolution had not been reached. Given this heritage of disagreement and conflict, it is a monumental step forward to have both groups represented among the contributors to this volume.

Evangelical theologian Millard Erickson suggests that "our approach to the problems of society will . . . be governed by our view of sin."[11] Christian psychologists and biblical counselors have disagreed about the role of sin in human problems. Biblical counselors have emphasized the devastating effects of sin that turns us away from a loving God and draws us instead toward idols of the heart. To care for the soul, then, we must confront the idols that impede us from experiencing God's rich grace and blessing. Christian psychologists have tended to emphasize faulty learning patterns, unhealthy relationships during formative years and incorrect thinking as the source of problems. They have valued many contributions of modernity's psychology while attempting to integrate psychology and theology. Of course this dichotomy is not as simple as it seems. Both groups see sin as a problem, and both look at faulty learning patterns, unhealthy relationships and incorrect thinking. The difference is primarily one of epistemological priorities. Biblical counselors place relatively more emphasis on special revelation and therefore on sin, and Christian psychologists typically spend more time and energy studying general revelation.

Both the biblical counselors and the Christian psychologists have legitimate points. Some of the discoveries of psychology are very useful for relieving human suffering. Stanton Jones uses treatment for childhood autism as an example in chapter two. Biblical counselors are correct in identifying sin as the fundamental human problem—this is emphasized in several chapters of this book. As Philip Monroe, a graduate of the biblical counseling program at Westminster Theological Seminary and of the doctoral psychology program at Wheaton College, points out in his chapter, Christian psychologists have sometimes failed to look carefully at the effects of sin in and around the lives of those they serve.

As tempting as it is for us to avoid conflict by announcing, "We're both saying the same thing, just with different words," biblical counselors and Christian psy-

[9]Gary R. Collins, *Can You Trust Psychology?* (Downers Grove, Ill.: InterVarsity Press, 1988).
[10]Ed Bulkley, *Why Christians Can't Trust Psychology* (Eugene, Ore.: Harvest House, 1993).
[11]Millard J. Erickson, *Christian Theology* (Grand Rapids, Mich.: Baker, 1985), p. 563.

chologists are not saying the same things. Certainly there are points of agreement, but there are crucial differences as well. Our premise in organizing the conference and editing this volume is that both biblical counselors and Christian psychologists have something to offer in discussions of the soul.

Standing at the Intersection

The book begins as the conference began, by looking at the different perspectives presented by a biblical counselor and a Christian psychologist. The first chapter, authored by David Powlison, calls into question the core assumptions of contemporary psychotherapists, including many Christian psychotherapists. Care for the soul, Powlison concludes, should lie primarily within the domain of the church. As a faculty member at the Christian Counseling and Educational Foundation (CCEF) and editor of the *Journal of Biblical Counseling*, Dr. Powlison devotes his full-time attention to the task of equipping the church to care for the soul.

Stanton L. Jones, author of chapter two, recognizes the danger of uncritically accepting contemporary psychotherapy. He articulates an "apologetic apologia" for the thoughtful integration of psychology and theology. Jones suggests that there is a strategic place for well-trained Christian psychologists in today's mental health care environment. As founder of the doctoral program in clinical psychology (and currently provost) at Wheaton College, Dr. Jones has invested many years in establishing a training environment for the type of thoughtful integration he describes.

The scholarly interchange evident throughout these first two chapters provides important context for the remainder of the book for at least three reasons. First, both Powlison and Jones find reason to be concerned about the mainstream contemporary practice of psychology. Collectively these chapters call us to critically evaluate the role of psychology in the care of souls. The integration movement, with its commendable purpose of blending responsible psychology with sound Christian theology, has sometimes led people to false and harmful conclusions about human experience, human relationships, and God. Too often Christian psychologists are guilty of pasting a spiritual veneer on a secular view of persons. Ellen Charry describes it this way: "Even if some therapists are beginning to recognize that some clients bring spiritual resources with them that can be called upon in the therapeutic process, it still sees these as additional resources of support for a basically secular self."[12] Most of the contributors agree that the current practice of Christian psychology is not what it can and should be.

Second, both Powlison and Jones address theological systems in their analyses, reminding us that understanding souls was the work of spiritual and theological leaders long before the advent of contemporary psychology. Any psychology that is perceived to categorically replace earlier forms of soul care should be viewed sus-

---

[12]Ellen T. Charry, "Theology After Psychology," in this volume, pp. 126-27.

piciously by people who are committed to exploring the intersection of theology and psychology. Effective soul care needs sound Christian theology.

Third, the areas of disagreement between Powlison and Jones illustrate the diversity of the opinions expressed throughout this volume. Particularly intriguing is their discussion of the church as the source of soul care. Should Christians turn primarily (or even exclusively) to the church for help with the struggles and challenges of life, or is there a proper place for Christian members of the helping professions to complement the work of the church? The tension of differing viewpoints is not unique to the chapters authored by Powlison and Jones. Areas of disagreement will be seen throughout this volume. Note the similarities and differences between L. Gregory Jones's and Myrla Seibold's views of forgiveness, and between Brett Webb-Mitchell's and Cynthia Neal Kimball's views of developmental psychology in church life. We have not attempted to avoid controversy by compiling a volume with like-minded contributors; we have not even selected a collection of essays with which we as editors completely agree. Rather, we trust the process of scholarly disagreement as something that can be used to strengthen the body of Jesus Christ—the church—and help it to grow.

Standing Boldly

The authors of chapters three to five call Christians to assert themselves in reclaiming the right to soul care. Guiding people to greater emotional health and maturity is a theological and religious task as well as a psychological task. This can be argued historically, philosophically, pragmatically and ecclesiologically.

From a historical perspective, soul care was once primarily the domain of the church and clergy, but it was wrestled away during modern times, and it has largely been relegated to a secular profession where religious values are often ignored[13] or even criticized.[14] Though postmodernism has softened psychology's blows against religion,[15] a therapeutic culture has emerged in which individuals consider themselves "free of the obligations of truth and the claims of ethical ideals." "In a therapeutic culture," Lundin writes, "there is no room for a Christian conception of truth and the ethical life."[16] This book helps put our therapeutic culture in a broader historical context and thereby causes us to consider ways of reclaiming the care of souls as a theological endeavor.

---

[13]Bergin, "Psychotherapy and Religious Values"; but for some recent changes in this regard, see P. Scott Richards and Allen E. Bergin, *A Spiritual Strategy for Counseling and Psychotherapy* (Washington, D.C.: American Psychological Association, 1997); also see Edward P. Shafranske, ed., *Religion and the Clinical Practice of Psychology* (Washington, D.C.: American Psychological Association, 1996).

[14]Albert Ellis, *The Case Against Religion: A Psychotherapist's View* (New York: Institute for Rational Living, 1983).

[15]Jones, "Constructive Relationship."

[16]Roger Lundin, *The Culture of Interpretation* (Grand Rapids, Mich.: Eerdmans, 1993), p. 6.

Philosophically, it is necessary to understand the theological and religious dimensions of soul care in order to embed the work of psychotherapists and counselors in a context of meaning. Browning argues that although many psychotherapists do not recognize that their work has a moral framework, psychotherapy always involves a moral framework.[17] To whatever extent mainstream psychology has failed to articulate its moral context, it has made itself irrelevant and formless. Grappling with the interface of theology and psychology gives us opportunity to consider the metaphysical dimensions of soul care.

Pragmatically, it is fascinating to observe that although psychologists are less religious than the general public, the majority of people seeking psychological help still prefer that their religious values be considered.[18] Those seeking care for their souls typically recognize a spiritual dimension to their lives. Tragically, it is often the professional care provider who fails to understand the importance of spiritual factors.

Ecclesiologically, the church needs models of human development, mental health and intervention that share a common foundation of faith. We cannot assume that a model developed in a particular context will necessarily translate to a church setting. For these reasons and more, it is fitting and timely for Christians to boldly assert the relevance of theology and religion in soul care.[19]

In chapter three Brett Webb-Mitchell critiques the church's uncritical acceptance of cognitive development theories, making his argument on pragmatic and ecclesiological grounds. He calls instead for a spiritually informed metaphor of pilgrimage. In chapter four Jeffrey Boyd notes that we rarely even talk about the soul any more, at least not in ways that promote an accurate understanding of God and ourselves. Boyd offers a historical and philosophical analysis of Christians' acquiescence to the secular mental health industry. In chapter five Ellen Charry argues that theological anthropologists have lost their voice amid the overwhelming presence of contemporary secular psychology. We have become selves instead of souls, as Boyd also suggests. Charry calls theologians to step up to the task of contributing to the care for and cure of souls. Together, these three chapters provide important arguments for being theologically grounded as we consider contemporary understandings of mental health.

Standing on the Promises
If modernity wrestled soul care away from the church because of wide-scale epistemological changes—people were looking to science rather than to ecclesiastic authority for truth—postmodernity has ushered in suspicion of all epistemologies. This has caused a sort of pluralistic rootlessness in which various truth claims are

[17]Donald S. Browning, *Moral Context of Pastoral Care* (Philadelphia: Westminster Press, 1976).
[18]See Stephen Quackenbos, Gayle Privette and Bonnel Klentz. "Psychotherapy: Sacred or Secular?" *Journal of Counseling and Development* 63 (1985): 290-93; also see Richards and Bergin, *Spiritual Strategy*.
[19]Jones, "Constructive Relationship."

accepted so long as they are not imposed on other people. The good news for Christians who are interested in soul care is that postmodernism has made religion a legitimate factor for psychotherapists to consider, thus opening the door for religious forms of psychotherapy. As a result, we have seen a proliferation of Christian inpatient and outpatient mental health facilities and church-based counseling centers. Also, the postmodern "hermeneutic of suspicion" provides opportunity for Christian scholars to recognize that even perfect truth must be interpreted by fallen humans. (Michael Mangis describes this in chapter eight, and David Williams alludes to it in chapter sixteen.)

The bad news for Christians is that truth claims from Christian scripture and church tradition are often viewed as old-fashioned and irrelevant. Many postmoderns fail to realize that we all have truth claims—even the claim that there is no absolute truth is a truth claim. Thus a significant challenge for Christians interested in soul care is to respond prudently to the opportunities and correctives provided by postmodern views of the person while clinging tenaciously to the truth claims of the Christian faith and the rich heritage of church history.

Chapters six to ten provide resources for people who are serious about building a psychology upon firmly established theological truth claims. Robert Roberts uses the apostle Paul's New Testament writings as a basis for soul care. Dennis Okholm and Michael Mangis explore the works of the desert fathers and the ascetic theologians and relate their findings to the contemporary assumptions and practices of psychotherapists. A careful look back at church history causes us to question some of the assumptions of modern psychology and the newer-is-better mindset that makes us prone to accept uncritically the contemporary claims of secular psychologists.

Philip Monroe draws upon Puritan theology to articulate the relevance of personal sin as a cause of psychological discomfort. Hamartiology (the theology of sin) is a central theme throughout this volume—it is addressed by Powlison, Stanton Jones, Charry, Gregory Jones, Moroney and others. Deborah van Deusen Hunsinger sets forth a theoretical framework in which the norms and values of Christian theology and contemporary psychology may be clearly distinguished yet serve the needs of the person seeking help. She conceives of the relationship between these diverse disciplines by following the logic of the relationship between the two natures of Jesus Christ as determined at the Council of Chalcedon.

Looking Both Ways
When we stand at the crossroads, as we did for the several days of the Wheaton Theology Conference and for the many months required to compile this volume, it is important to look both directions. We should ask both how theology can help psychology reclaim the soul and how psychology can contribute to theology and the Christian life. The final two sections of this volume address these questions.

First, theology has much to offer Christian psychology. L. Gregory Jones provides an illustration of this in his chapter on forgiveness. Psychologists have recently become interested in forgiveness and a recent Templeton Foundation grant program for the study of forgiveness promises to propel psychological understandings of forgiveness even farther, but Christian communities have been practicing and discussing forgiveness for many centuries. Can we really disconnect the act of forgiveness from Christian communities and theology without losing its essence? Forgiveness is more than a therapeutic technique.[20] Chapters twelve and thirteen on the importance of sound hermeneutics offer theological resources for psychology. In chapter twelve Richard Schultz critiques the hermeneutics often used by Christian therapists when approaching the wisdom literature of the Old Testament and offers suggestions for sound interpretation of that literature. In chapter thirteen Bryan Maier and Philip Monroe team up to articulate the importance of sound biblical hermeneutics for the Christian counselor.

If we are looking both ways, we must also recognize psychology's potential contribution to theology and Christian living. The final four chapters of this volume address this need. Myrla Seibold offers psychological observations about the forgiveness process—observations that will be controversial but that may provide a corrective to perspectives that Christian communities sometimes advocate when they interpret and apply forgiveness. Stephen Moroney provides social-psychological evidence of our tendency to overvalue our own perspectives and opinions, then offers biblical argument for accurate perceptions of self and others. Moroney's chapter would make excellent required reading for students who are taking an introductory course on hermeneutics. Next, David Williams demonstrates the importance of perception research for understanding the philosophy of knowledge and its theological implications. Finally, Cynthia Neal Kimball presents a developmental analysis of family brokenness, offering insights from developmental psychology regarding the role of Christian community in promoting family health.

The Road Ahead

In the twenty-fifth-anniversary issue of the *Journal of Psychology and Theology*, Tisdale, Thelander and Pike observe that "we have the opportunity to begin a new era in integration."[21] If we are to most effectively minister to souls, this new era should not be characterized by psychologists and theologians huddling in their respective professional circles. We need creative and productive dialogue. We need to explore the intersection of psychology and theology. This book is intended to be one step in that direction.

Like the scholarship presented in this book, the study of the relationship between

---

[20]Katheryn Rhoads Meek and Mark R. McMinn, "Forgiveness: More Than a Therapeutic Technique," *Journal of Psychology and Christianity* 16 (1997): 51-61.

[21]Theresa C. Tisdale, Scott E. Thelander and Patricia L. Pike, "We Press On Toward the Goal: Introduction to the 25th Anniversary Issue, Part 1," *Journal of Psychology and Theology* 25 (1997): 3.

psychology and theology should be multifaceted, employing various foci and methods of inquiry. It calls for at least four strategies involving psychological methods, theological systems and Christian spirituality.[22] They are interdisciplinary dialogue, intradisciplinary application, faith-praxis integration, and personal formation.

Interdisciplinary dialogue allows the Christian helper to place the work of counseling or psychotherapy within a well-articulated moral framework informed by theology, history, culture and faith. It calls for a critical appraisal of metaphysical and epistemological assumptions. For example, many secular doctoral training programs in psychology continue to rely almost exclusively on modernist, scientific ways of knowing. The designers of these programs seem to be unaware that the scholarship that contributes to an understanding of contemporary psychology goes back far beyond modernity and provides a foothold from which we must sometimes question the truth claims of science.

A well-known researcher recently wrote an article in a mainstream psychology journal titled "In the Final Analysis, It's the Data That Count."[23] The author appears to mean that the quantitative data of science will set us free from the uncertainties of our intellectual pondering. The presuppositions behind such a title are simply not consistent with the more inclusive scholarship found among other academic disciplines, such as theology. Effective soul care requires interdisciplinary dialogue that allows for theological as well as scientific ways of knowing. Interdisciplinary integration is bidirectional. Psychology can be helpful to theology, as van Deusen Hunsinger, Williams and others discuss. And the contributions of social science are not limited to clinical or counseling psychology. This volume, for example, includes contributions from people who are interested in clinical, social, perceptual and developmental psychologies.

Whereas interdisciplinary dialogue requires the tough-minded work of weaving together truths from various disciplines, intradisciplinary application calls us to apply these truths within the work of a single profession. The best scholars, those who are most capable of erudite interdisciplinary dialogue, are not always the best practitioners. Imagine sitting with a sobbing person who tells you, "All my life I've been a good person, but people criticize and reject me anyway." Knowing about the Pelagian or antinomian heresies may provide important grounding for you as a Christian who is interested in soul care, but it will not guarantee that you will respond effectively. It might not be helpful to refer to Augustine's *Confessions* or Calvin's *Institutes* and to discuss total depravity at a moment such as this. So what words would you select? How would those words be received by the distraught

---

[22]Steve Bouma-Prediger, "The Task of Integration: A Modest Proposal," *Journal of Psychology and Theology* 18 (1990): 21-31; Everett L. Worthington Jr., "A Blueprint for Intradisciplinary Integration," *Journal of Psychology and Theology* 22 (1994): 79-86.

[23]Peter E. Nathan, "In the Final Analysis, It's the Data That Count," *Clinical Psychology: Science and Practice* 4 (1997): 281-84.

person? These are the questions of intradisciplinary application.

Gary Collins wrote in the *Journal of Psychology and Theology* of that publication's treatment of integration: "I suspect that relatively few pastors or full time professional care givers find the articles to be of practical help in their counseling work. It would be helpful to see more of an applied perspective in this publication. . . . How do we do integration? What skills and methods are involved?"[24] A decade later Worthington noted that Collins's call for practical integration methods had not produced much change.[25] Creating these practical methods is appropriate work for those who are interested in care for the soul.

Intradisciplinary application brings the best of psychology and theology into the clinical practice of soul care (however that might be defined). Charry makes this point eloquently and directly: "We theologians have abandoned the practitioners, and we should be ashamed. Perhaps it is not too late to begin repairing the damage."[26] Those who are interested in intradisciplinary application will find a number of these chapters, written by both psychologists and theologians, fascinating. Seibold's and Gregory Jones's chapters on forgiveness will make clinicians think carefully about their application of forgiveness principles in clinical work. Contributions from Neal, Stanton Jones, and Powlison will cause us to contemplate the most effective context for therapeutic interventions. Mangis and Moroney call us to critically evaluate the role of self-deception—something that happens in virtually every counseling session. In many of the chapters the authors implore therapists to consider the implications of personal sin in understanding themselves and those with whom they work.

Yet another type of dialogue between psychology and theology, what Bouma-Prediger labels *faith-praxis integration*, addresses the need for Christian action.[27] Long ago Aristotle described *praxis* as action based on an ideal of what is right. Just as Christians value orthodoxy, true teaching, so we should also value orthopraxy, true and faithful action. Writing to Jewish Christians, James poses daunting questions about faith-praxis integration:

> What good is it, my brothers and sisters, if you say you have faith but do not have works? Can faith save you? If a brother or sister is naked and lacks daily food, and one of you says to them, "Go in peace; keep warm and eat your fill," and yet you do not supply their bodily needs, what is the good of that? So faith by itself, if it has no works, is dead. (Jas 2:14-17)

The task of soul care calls us to pursue the integration of faith and praxis—psychology that is delivered with a passion for Christian ministry in a world that is plagued by inequitable distribution of wealth and opportunity.

---

[24]Gary R. Collins, "Moving Through the Jungle: A Decade of Integration," *Journal of Psychology and Theology* 11 (1983): 2-7.
[25]Worthington, "Blueprint for Intradisciplinary Integration."
[26]Ellen T. Charry, "Theology after Psychology," this volume, p. 134.
[27]Bouma-Prediger, "Task of Integration."

Henri Nouwen writes:

The danger is that instead of becoming free to let the spirit grow, future ministers may entangle themselves in the complications of their own assumed competence and use their specialization as an excuse to avoid the much more difficult task of being compassionate. The task of Christian leaders is to bring out the best in all people and to lead them forward to a more human community; the danger is that their skillful diagnostic eye will become more an eye for distant and detailed analysis than the eye of a compassionate partner. . . . More training and structure are as necessary as more bread for the hungry. But just as bread given without love can bring war instead of peace, professionalism without compassion will turn forgiveness into a gimmick.[28]

Thus faith-praxis integration requires a thoughtful balancing of scholarship and action. Compassion that is uninformed by thoughtful scholarship can lead to uninformed or even harmful human interventions, especially in postmodern times, when any therapist's truth claim is considered to be personally valid merely because it is a truth claim. Scholarship that is uninformed by compassion can be irrelevantly or recklessly applied when we are dealing with hurting people. Integrating scholarship with human compassion is one challenge of soul care facing Christian communities in the coming millennium.

Many of the chapters in this volume are action oriented. For example, Seibold's chapter on forgiveness has implications for faith-praxis integration. She suggests that the people who are most likely to be hurt are the powerless members of society, and that the standard Christian views on forgiveness are often determined by people in positions of relative power. In her chapter on family brokenness, Kimball challenges some long-standing teachings regarding the proper use of power by Christian parents.

Finally, personal formation emphasizes the helper's character formation and therefore the helper's capacity to participate in meaningful and healing interpersonal relationships. Sol Garfield, a leading psychotherapy researcher, has recently argued that the therapist is a neglected variable in psychotherapy research.[29] According to Garfield and others writing in the same journal issue, the personal qualities of the therapist affect the outcome of therapy. It is reasonable to assume that the personal qualities of Christian ministers affect their capacity for soul care. People who help others with spiritual formation have been shaping the character of Christian ministers for many centuries. Their collective wisdom can contribute much to the personal and professional development of Christian psychologists.

When Christian spirituality is carefully bounded by responsible theology, people experience grace that goes beyond the intellect. This experiential integration is an essential part of Christian soul care. A Christian helper who ministers to a agitated client who is in a manic state, all the time remaining calm and continually relying

---

[28]Henri J. M. Nouwen, *Ministry and Spirituality* (New York: Continuum, 1996), p. 135.
[29]Sol L. Garfield, "The Therapist as a Neglected Variable in Psychotherapy Research," *Clinical Psychology: Science and Practice* 4 (1997): 40-43.

on God, is exploring the intersection of practical theology and psychology.

In the opening line of his best-selling book *The Celebration of Discipline,* Richard Foster observes, "Superficiality is the curse of our age."[30] It can be argued that superficiality is also becoming the curse of contemporary mental health care. With the advent of ubiquitous biological interventions, managed health care and now a new list of empirically validated treatment procedures advocated by the American Psychological Association, professional psychology has moved toward shorter, technique-based interventions and away from more relational approaches to healing. People who believe that relationship with Christ is the very center of Christian experience also recognize that this salvific relationship changes everything—including relationships with people we serve. If good soul care is simply a matter of dispensing the proper treatments at the proper time, then there is little need for personal formation. If, on the other hand, good soul care requires the helper's spiritual vitality, self-awareness and relational sensitivity, then personal formation has everything to do with Christian soul care.

This is not a simple matter. Spiritual strategies in psychotherapy are so easily turned into techniques, and a passion to know God is exchanged for a quest to know oneself. Van Deusen Hunsinger writes:

> Empirical studies have been published that show a positive correlation between the use of prayer and physical and emotional healing. Some people consider such studies to be a good apologetic for prayer, and some have been convinced enough by the studies to engage in daily prayer for the sake of its practical benefits. But the real focus and purpose of prayer as the means of intimate communion with God has been lost. Everything has been turned upside down. Instead of God being at the center of our lives, our emotional or mental health occupies the center.[31]

Personal formation requires more than learning spiritual techniques. It is a humble journey with God at the center. In his chapter exploring contemplative theology and psychoanalytic psychology, Mangis presents a compelling argument that the personal formation of the helper is an essential component of effective soul care. Character matters when we are selecting and training people who will be involved in caring for souls.

This volume explores the intersection of psychology and theology, an intersection that is not simple. It is an intersection affected by rich theological and ecclesiological traditions, by the ravages and wonders of modernity's psychology, and by the character qualities of today's ministers and communities of faith. We trust that this book will foster dialogue among the pastors, theologians, psychologists, biblical counselors, educators and students who are involved in caring for souls.

---

[30]Richard J. Foster, *Celebration of Discipline: The Path to Spiritual Growth* (San Francisco: HarperCollins, 1988), p. 1.

[31]Deborah van Deusen Hunsinger, "An Interdisciplinary Map for Christian Counselors: Theology & Psychology in Pastoral Counseling," this volume, p. 230.

1
QUESTIONS AT THE CROSSROADS

The Care of Souls &
Modern Psychotherapies

David Powlison

The epoch of a great revolution is never the eligible time to write its history. Those memorable recitals to which the opinions of ages should remain attached cannot obtain confidence or present a character of impartiality if they are undertaken in the midst of animosities and during the tumult of passions; and yet, were there to exist a man so detached from the spirit of party or so master of himself as calmly to describe the storms of which he has been a witness, we should be dissatisfied with his tranquility and should apprehend that he had not a soul capable of preserving the impressions of all the sentiments we might be desirous of receiving.[1]

W E LIVE IN THE EPOCH OF A GREAT REVOLUTION. CONSIDER THAT IN 1955 BELIEVing Protestants had no comprehensive models of counseling. Theological conservatives had no educational programs to train pastors or other Christian workers in face-to-face care for souls. Christian bookstores stocked no books on the problems of everyday life and the processes of change. No evangelical, fundamentalist, Pentecostal, or reformed leaders were known for their skill in probing, changing, and reconciling troubled and troublesome people. Practical theology concerned itself with preaching, missions, education, evangelism, liturgical activity, church government and administration. Good things all! Discipleship programs taught doctrine, morals and devotional activity. Good things all! But what was the quality of corporate wisdom for comprehending the

---

[1]William Duane, an American historian writing in 1798 about the French Revolution as its events continued to unfold, cited in Richard N. Rosenfeld, *American Aurora* (New York: St. Martin's, 1997), p. 11.

dynamics of the human heart? How rich was human self-understanding? How well did the church analyze the destructive and practice the constructive in human relationships?

What does change look like, think like, feel like, act like, talk like? How does change proceed? What sustains sufferers and converts sinners? No systematic analysis of care for the soul grappled with the particulars of how souls needed cure and might find it. In 1955 the churches that took God at his word had little to say about counseling. At that time the most recent significant counseling work from a conservative theological standpoint predated the Civil War. Without a well-developed practical theology of change and counseling—and without the institutions, books and practitioners to embody and communicate it—churchly resources were reduced to religious forms in abstraction from systematic understanding: a prayer, a Bible verse, a worship service, a banished demon, a creed, a testimony, an exhortation, a commitment. Should these fail, there was no option but referral out to the secular experts.[2]

The counseling vacuum among evangelicals was inversely proportional to the counseling plenum in the surrounding culture. The twentieth century witnessed the birth and proliferation of the modern secular psychologies, and of the mental health professions that mediated such theories into lives. Secular institutions teamed up with the mainline churches that were part product and part co-author of the emerging therapeutic culture. Modern forms of self-knowledge were psychological, or social, or somatic, or psychosocial, or psychosomatic, or psycho-social-somatic. In other words, intrapersonal, interpersonal and bodily phenomena pointedly did not exist vis-à-vis God. Religious beliefs, practices and experiences might be privately engaging and meaningful, but the God of the Bible was insignificant for objectively explaining and addressing the human condition.

We humans were not made and sustained; our diverse sufferings did not exist in a context of meaningfulness; we were not accountable, observed and evaluated; we were not pursued and redeemed. "God" was an objectively weightless concept with respect to the human psyche; the weighty things in our souls had to do with other things. Evangelicals might have objected to the secularity of the modern and modernist worldview, but they were not doing more than a rudimentary job of

---

[2]I am not implying that the living God does not sustain and transform his chosen people through times when our ability to systematically articulate his ways is weak. The grassroots wisdom of godly people far exceeds what is written in both secular and Christian counseling books. Plain folks, without a whisper of counseling training, will often size up others insightfully and communicate to them the honey and light of timely biblical wisdom. They will read a best-selling counseling book and comment, "I liked *xyz,* but *abc* didn't seem right to me." Their discernment—not analysis, but instinct—is frequently profound. God does sustain his own, but where our articulated understanding of truth is defective we become vulnerable to deviant and distracting theories for which we pay a price in confusion and harm. A well-systematized biblical counseling model will not transcend grassroots wisdom, but will express, encourage and defend such wisdom.

offering an alternate analysis and cure. Knowledge and skill to conduct patient, probing, remedial conversation had become the province of secularists and liberals.[3]

The Counseling Revolution

But a revolution has occurred in the past forty years, a counseling revolution. Evangelicals have begun to counsel, to write about counseling and to educate counselors. They have written bestsellers and have founded thriving graduate programs and counseling centers. Everyone agrees that a serious defect needs serious repair: confused, suffering and wayward people need more than a verse and a prayer. But as in most revolutions, those who agree heartily about the need for change disagree profoundly about the changes needed. Countless gradations and variations exist, but in broad strokes two parties have emerged in the counseling revolution.

One group has developed in the footsteps of Clyde Narramore and along the lines of Fuller Seminary's Graduate School of Psychology. Its core intellectual agenda can be characterized this way: wise counseling requires that evangelical faith be carefully integrated with the theories, therapeutic methods and professional roles of the modern psychologies. A movement of evangelical psychotherapists has arisen to tackle this intellectual and educational task and to address the counseling needs of the church.

The other group has developed in the footsteps of Jay Adams and along the lines of the Christian Counseling and Educational Foundation's pastoral training at Westminster Seminary. Its core intellectual agenda can be characterized this way: wise counseling recognizes that the Bible mandates development of a comprehensive pastoral theology that is distinct from prevailing cultural paradigms. A movement of biblical counselors has arisen to tackle this intellectual and educational task and to address the counseling needs of the church.[4]

Passions have been tumultuous, and serene impartiality has been impossible, even suspect and undesirable. How can a thoughtful person remain indifferent when the issues at stake are so momentous? The well-being, self-understanding and

---

[3]For a description of how liberal-psychological pastoral theology eclipsed conservative-soteriological pastoral theology, see E. Brooks Holifield, *A History of Pastoral Care in America: From Salvation to Self-Realization* (Nashville: Abingdon, 1983). For a description of how secular mental health professions subordinated mainline pastoral care, see Andrew Abbott, *The System of Professions: An Essay on the Division of Expert Labor* (Chicago: University of Chicago Press, 1988).

[4]Brief descriptions of this revolution—from varying points of view—can be found in Jay E. Adams, *Lectures on Counseling* (Grand Rapids, Mich.: Zondervan, 1975, 1976, 1977); Donald Capps, "The Bible's Role in Pastoral Care and Counseling: Four Basic Principles," *Journal of Psychology and Christianity* 3, no. 4 (1984): 5-15; George M. Marsden, *Reforming Fundamentalism: Fuller Seminary and the New Evangelicalism* (Grand Rapids, Mich.: Eerdmans, 1987). An extended treatment of the issues raised in the last two paragraphs is found in my "Competent to Counsel? The History of a Conservative Protestant Anti-Psychiatry Movement" (Ph.D. diss., University of Pennsylvania, 1996).

practice of real people, the people of God, both corporate and individual, is at stake. Our ability to love and address those outside of Christ is at stake. God's glory in this therapeutic culture is at stake. How can we know and do what we need to know and do in order to care for souls?

This essay is no attempt at dispassionate history. My commitments and convictions will be obvious in what follows. I believe that the church needs above all else a comprehensive pastoral theology, something worthy of the name *systematic biblical counseling.* But I am no triumphalist. I am as interested in the remaining agenda as I am in the extant accomplishments of people whom I think are on the right track. And I am keenly sympathetic to many of the concerns and intentions that energize people with whom I must fundamentally disagree. No one will "arrive" until we all arrive. And arriving is not just a matter of bare truth. Truth, love, skill and institutional structure must all grow to the same stature. That is our Lord's call in Ephesians 4.

Finding a Workable Taxonomy

Christ's call for us to walk and talk worthy of his calling creates an immediate problem of terminology for all of us. Participants in the counseling revolution sharply disagree about how things ought to be run, and this is not merely bickering between ideologues over inconsequential matters. None of us should be indifferent about the existence of vastly disparate conceptions of the faith and practice of Christ's people. People have staked education, careers, reputations, institutions and ministries on significantly differing points of view about what is true and what is needed for the health of the church. But how do we talk about the conflict constructively? How can we fairly characterize the different sides in the current counseling wars so that matters are clarified and not muddied? How do we speak the truth in love and in pursuit of a just peace, rather than exacerbating quarrels and perpetuating self-serving caricatures?

Psychology bashers or psychoheretics? Unfortunately, when the so-called psychology bashers and psychoheretics square off it produces an effect like loud static in a public address system. God's children are rarely edified by scathing words. When we look at each group through the other's language, both groups appear shamefully disreputable. Reckless and factious language fails the test of constructive, gracious, gentle speech to which God calls us and by which he will examine us (Eph 4:15, 29; 2 Tim 2:24-26; Mt 7:1-5). There are some true bashers and heretics around. But provocative language and sweeping generalizations usually provoke, nurture and justify the worst tendencies in human nature, rather than furthering the outworking of our redemption.[5]

---

[5]Eric L. Johnson, "A Place for the Bible in Psychological Science," *Journal of Psychology and Theology* 20 (1992): 346-55. Johnson comments insightfully on the communication breakdown caused by posturing and polemics. Of course, we must generalize if we are to speak in any context wider than private conversation. I will generalize in this essay. But I hope to do so in a constructive way.

I suspect that most of us are brothers and sisters who are to be dealt with gently. We are ignorant and wayward, beset with weakness (Heb 5:2), and many well-intended believers on both sides of the debate are more clumsy than perverse. Our sin makes us clumsy thinkers, clumsy practitioners, clumsy theologians, clumsy exegetes, clumsy cultural analysts. We all get pigheaded, shortsighted and stuck in those forms of error that contain partial truths. All error has a perverse logic, but we may hold to errors and semitruths without being wholly perverted people. May God make us more skillful—together.

The Bible-believing church has been woefully weak in caring for souls in the twentieth century. Christ would have us do some serious maturing in individual and collective wisdom. Maturing is hard, slow work, and it is made slower because the issues at stake are so momentous. The sower of discord and falsehood is always active in hindering the church from growing up toward real wisdom about humanity's ailment and redemption. But the Sower of love and truth is willing to work amid the tumult of passions and over the long haul: over decades, lifetimes and centuries. Biblical wisdom does not spring full grown from the head of Zeus. It is born small and grows through many trials and missteps by the sustaining grace of God toward the fullness of the mind of Christ.

So-called psychology bashers—those who believe in the sufficiency of Scripture for generating a comprehensive counseling model—do fundamentally disbelieve the modern psychologies, taking them to be systematic counterfeits and pretenders in the final analysis. They believe that the Bible fiercely resists syncretism. But they still claim that something can be learned from the psychologies: wrong does not mean stupid; error must borrow elements of truth to be plausible; God often allows observant and persuasive error to expose lacunae, crudities and distortions in his own children's thinking and practice. That Scripture is sufficient does not mean that the Bible is exhaustive or that its message is accessed and communicated only through proof texts. All application of Scripture demands that we engage in a theological and interpretive task. Good, true, faithful theology is closely grounded in the text, but often says a somewhat different thing than the text says because it speaks to a different set of questions.[6] Face-to-face ministry must use the Bible in the same way; ministry is not simply a matter of inserting proof texts into conversation. All ministry demands sensitivity and flexibility in response to the varying conditions of those to whom one ministers.[7]

---

[6]A good summary of the difference between biblicism and *sola scriptura* can be found in John Frame's "In Defense of Something Close to Biblicism: Reflections on *Sola Scriptura* and History in Theological Method," *Westminster Theological Journal* 59 (1997): 272-80.

[7]At the most rudimentary level, the Bible itself teaches us that ministry does not always lead out with a Bible verse. We read in Acts 13:14-41 that Paul cited and applied specific chapter and verse with a timeliness that created an uproar of interest among his hearers. In Acts 14:8-

Though one might find some exceptions, so-called psychology bashers are not anticounseling. Most of them work to develop and practice loving and effective care for souls as the alternative to secular or quasi-secular psychotherapy. The debate is not about whether or not to counsel; the debate is about what sort of counsel to believe and what sort of counseling to do.

So-called psychoheretics—those who believe that Scripture does not intend to be sufficient for generating a comprehensive counseling model—do see an essential role for the secular psychologies. Psychological disciplines offer some sort of necessary truth; the psychological professions offer some sort of necessary and valid practice. But the so-called psychoheretics still claim that the Bible must provide the final authority. That Scripture is not sufficient does not mean that the Bible is irrelevant or that it ought to be subordinated to secular psychologies, but that the Bible itself mandates looking and learning from outside. The Bible itself resists biblicism.

Though one might find exceptions, "heretics" are not out to swallow the camel of secularity and foist it on an unsuspecting church. Most of them work to critique the secularity of the modern psychologies and to screen out what seems to fail the test of Scripture. Why do they become psychologists? Glaring defects in the church's current understanding and practice are the main reason they expend time and effort to do hard study of human beings. In this culture, that often means to study psychology. Where else does one gain the permission and acquire the discipline to gaze steadily into the complications and miseries of the soul? Where else do defective relationships come under scrutiny? Where else can one be taught to probe the details of life as it is lived, and then to offer timely and patient aid? Theological and pastoral training typically do not look closely enough or get hands-on enough to engender case wisdom and a patiently probing counseling process.[8]

Theologizers or psychologizers? Polemical language tends to subvert understanding and godliness by superheating the conversation. We could describe the "bashers" and "heretics" more calmly as theologizers and psychologizers, respectively,

---

18 we see that he gained entry by performing a loving action, vigorously identified with his hearers, then discussed everyday human experiences, weaving in biblical truth without specific citation. In Acts 17:16-34 we read that Paul began by talking about some observations that had given him pause. He went on to cite his listeners' own poets and philosophers, the "psychologists" of that day, co-opting their words to proclaim Jesus, to call his listeners to a change of mind and to awaken lively concern about the day when our lives will be weighed in the balance. How did Paul know the difference? Case wisdom. He had come to know people through his diverse experience in applying the singular message of the Bible.

[8]The introductory chapters of Stanton L. Jones and Richard Butman, *Modern Psychotherapies: A Comprehensive Christian Appraisal* (Downers Grove, Ill.: InterVarsity Press, 1991) and of David Powlison, ed., *Counsel the Word: A Selection of Readings from the Journal of Biblical Counseling* (Glenside, Penn.: CCEF, 1997) capture the differences in emphasis between the insufficiency and sufficiency points of view.

but these terms, too, quickly become misleading.

Those who pursue a systematic pastoral theology claim to speak about psychological experience; they interpret the case-study realities of life as it is lived through the lens of biblical categories. Their view of theology is that it is about the interior and horizontal dimensions no less than the vertical.

On the other side, those who pursue an integration of theology and psychology or a dialogue between Christianity and psychological theory claim to do theology. They seek to unfold the implications of the doctrine of common grace with respect to intrapersonal and interpersonal problems, and with respect to the methods of addressing such problems. Secular disciplines are fit subjects for theological inquiry, and the stuff of psychology does not necessarily wholly overlap the Bible. They also view their practice as a communication of God's grace to people whose church experiences have often nurtured legalism and dishonesty. Where the church has been brusque, they aim to offer an incarnation of grace, a generous and accepting attitude in which trust can flourish. So both parties claim to be both theological and psychological.

Pastoral counselors or psychologists? How about using occupational categories to characterize the contemporary debate? Is this simply a turf war between pastors and psychotherapists? It is clear that the pastoral counselors strongly value the ministry and consider the local church significant for both authority and mutuality. It is equally clear that the psychologists strongly value licensure for professional identity and because it makes possible insurance reimbursements, and they resist coming under ecclesiastical jurisdiction. But one cannot draw lines in the sand regarding occupational titles.

The "pastoral counselor" group includes many people with training, experience and credentials in the field of mental health: psychologists of various sorts, psychiatrists, neurologists, psychiatric nurses, social workers, physicians, graduate students, former psychology majors.[9] They know the psychologies from the inside—and think them pervasively flawed and finally impotent. The Bible and theology probe the human heart far more graphically, make better sense of life as it is lived and bring the living power of Christ to turn lives upside down.

On the other side, the "psychologist" group includes thousands of people with ecclesiastical training, experience and credentials: pastors, elders, deacons, seminary graduates and professors, lay counselors, graduates of pastoral counseling programs and members in good standing of local churches. They know and believe their faith from the inside—but all too often find the operative faith and practice of their ecclesiastical training and setting to be ignorant, peremptory and pat. Psychology, despite

---

[9]I am among this number. I majored in psychology as an undergraduate, then worked for four years in psychiatric hospitals, intending to go on to graduate school in clinical psychology. My conversion to Christ rerouted me to seminary.

obviously bumbling the closer it gets to ultimate issues, validates neglected dimensions of human experience, prompts intellectual curiosity, and encourages patient pursuit of both self-knowledge and case wisdom. In sum, neither ecclesiastical nor mental health experience offers a predictable guide to the issues.

Biblical counseling or Christian counseling? What about the names the groups have largely adopted for themselves: biblical counseling (as in *Journal of Biblical Counseling*) and Christian counseling (as in American Association of Christian Counselors [AACC])? Each group finds the other's self-designation objectionable. The label *biblical counseling* seems to imply that whatever its advocates believe and do comes with the authority of the Bible, and that any other form of counseling is unbiblical. Similarly, the label *Christian counseling* seems to imply that whatever its advocates believe and do is distinctly Christian, not a maybe/maybe-not activity that *Christians-who-counsel* do, and perhaps do in ways at odds with their professed faith. The terms *biblical* and *Christian* are precisely what is at stake and what is up for debate in the present tumults.

Here is a further dilemma: In the landscape of Christian counseling, it has become harder to keep the parties straight because they seem to have moved closer together in the past ten years. The psychotherapists have apparently moved the greater distance, but those building on the Jay Adams model have also significantly developed. The Christian counselors were more explicitly biblically oriented in the nineties than they were in the seventies and eighties. Gary Collins and Larry Crabb are only the most visible exemplars of how the evangelical part of the evangelical psychotherapist's dual identity is no longer a professional embarrassment.

A more holistic view of human nature has emerged among evangelical psychotherapists. Some still attempt to separate "spiritual" problems from "psychological, emotional, relational and mental" problems, attempting to validate their professional existence and to define their activity as something qualitatively different from care for the soul. But many at the leading edge of the profession see that the divide between "spiritual" and "psychological" problems is artificial and problematic. Advocates have been won for John Calvin's foundational insight that true self-knowledge and knowledge of the true God are interchangeable perspectives. This more holistic outlook has affected evangelical psychotherapists' professional self-image. Increasingly, Christian counselors seek to express an explicitly Christian identity by defining their work of counseling as care for the soul or eldering or ministry for Christ that must be closely linked to the church. The Christian counselors have come to sound more like the pastoral counselors and pastoral theologians who follow Jay Adams.

Meanwhile, the biblical counselors have also changed. Their writing now evidences a broader scope of concerns and concepts than it did in the early seventies. They have supplemented, developed or even altered many aspects of Adams's initial model. They are paying a great deal of attention to (1) intrapersonal dynamics such as motivation, self-evaluation, belief and self-deception; (2) the impact of and responses to various kinds of suffering; (3) the compassionate, flexible, probing and patient aspects of counseling methodology; (4) nuances in the interaction between Christian faith and the modern psychologies; (5) the practicalities of marital and familial communication; and (6) the causes and treatment of so-called addictions.[10] The biblical model of counseling is now more detailed and comprehensive regarding a number of "psychological" matters.

So the psychologists seem more biblical and the biblical counselors seem more psychological. What does this apparent convergence mean? Are the parties heading toward a rapprochement or toward a more profound collision? Or are they moving toward an as-yet-unimagined realignment?

I believe that the two visions are still fundamentally incompatible. But I also believe that our current situation is ripe for a fresh articulation of the issues. Half-truths and good intentions—all too easily corrupted by posturing, tunnel vision and parochial ignorance—can appear in a very different light when they are seen within a more comprehensive call and truth. I hope that we, the body of Christ, can identify where ideas and practices are fundamentally incongruent. Such incongruities ought to be openly identified and debated, so that the church can evaluate positions and choose wisely. We may also find places of unexpected congruence that bid us to cross or to realign current party lines. After all, we serve the living God who masters history to his glory and our welfare. He will not leave his children bedraggled by ignorance, incompetence, quarrels and confusion. In the rough-and-tumble of our gropings after him, in our uneven hearing and partial seeing, he manages to triumph in and through us.

VITEX or COMPIN? So what taxonomy should we use? I suggest that we use language that is minimally prejudicial and maximally descriptive of the sticking point. The core question turns on the intent and scope of Scripture, the nature of theological work and the degree of significance attached to what the church can appropriate from the world.

I will speak of VITEX and COMPIN as the two fundamentally different tendencies. Acronyms are dull? All the better! Though these terms sound like something from Jurassic Park, I hope their very oddity and connotative flatness will aid discussion by damping the excesses of passion. VITEX asserts that psychology must make

---

[10]Articles, reviews and bibliographies in the *Journal of Biblical Counseling* provide an entry point into the literature. One regrettable aspect of the debates in print is that evangelical psychologists continue to cite only Jay Adams's earliest works *Competent to Counsel* (Grand Rapids, Mich.: Baker, 1970) and *The Christian Counselor's Manual* (Grand Rapids, Mich.: Baker, 1973), seemingly unaware of twenty-five years of development. Two introductions to recent developments are David Powlison, "Crucial Issues in Contemporary Biblical Counseling," *Journal of Pastoral Practice* 9, no. 3 (1988): 53-78; and David Powlison, ed., *Counsel the Word.*

a VITal EXternal contribution to the construction of a wisely Christian model of personality, change and counseling. COMPIN asserts that there are COMPrehensive INternal resources within the Christian faith for the construction of a wisely Christian model of personality, change and counseling. VITEX asserts that while biblical faith and practice give us controls to evaluate outside input, it does not give enough detail to constitute a model. COMPIN asserts that while the psychologies may stimulate and inform, they are unnecessary for the constitution of a robust model.[11]

There are three crucial questions whose answers over the coming years will define the intellectual, methodological and institutional characteristics of evangelical counseling, characteristics that will ultimately be shaped either by a VITEX or a COMPIN vision. The three questions, around which a host of subquestions cluster, have to do with epistemology, motivation theory, and social structure. First, what knowledge really matters for understanding and helping people? Second, how do we fundamentally understand people? Third, how should we educate, license and oversee counselors in order to deliver the goods?

Epistemological Priorities

What knowledge really matters for understanding and helping people? Evangelical counselors have been deeply divided over epistemology. On the one hand, VITEX is interested in "integrating" Christianity and psychology because secular psychology makes a vital contribution to Christian counseling. Christians can learn constitutive things from what the world has to offer in the social and behavioral sciences. Christians can participate in psychological research and in the mental health professions. But as honest evangelicals, VITEX advocates want Scripture to exert final and functional authority.

On the other hand, COMPIN is interested in the sufficiency of Scripture for informing and defining counseling ministry because resources internal to the Christian faith are comprehensively about what counseling is about. Scripture is suffi-

---

[11]Though a sharp social divide has existed between integrationist psychologists (approximately VITEX) and biblical counselors (approximately COMPIN), my definition muddies that divide a bit, adding some immediate twists and nuances. For example, at Wheaton College Stan Jones's and Richard Butman's *Modern Psychotherapies* is a classic articulation of VITEX. But Robert C. Roberts's *Taking the Word to Heart: Self and Other in an Age of Therapies* (Grand Rapids, Mich.: Eerdmans, 1993) comes within a millimeter of COMPIN. Intending to "mitigate the Christian captivity to psychology," Roberts says that "a Christian psychology would not *have* to be pursued in dialogue with secular psychology" (p. 14). Among the work of popular evangelical psychologists, the genial eclecticism of Gary Collins and James Dobson exemplifies VITEX, but Larry Crabb's epistemology since the mid-1980s has been explicitly COMPIN. Obviously, clearer categories never solve all vexatious questions, though they may help focus discussion. For example, the adjectives *vital* and *comprehensive* are ambiguous and their appropriateness is debatable. The concrete implications need to be fleshed out.

cient, not in that it is exhaustive, containing all knowledge, but in that it rightly aligns a coherent and comprehensive system of counseling that is radically at odds with every a-theistic model. Christians can offer a distinct alternative to what the world has to offer. Christians can revitalize their own distinctive shepherdly and mutual ministries. But as honest observers and thinkers, COMPIN advocates want to gain what knowledge they can, both theoretical and applied, from the social sciences and other fields.

But both sides tend to talk past each other. VITEX discredits itself to COMPIN ears by sounding epistemologically naive and syncretistic. "All truth is God's truth" is an epistemological truism without bottom-line value, exactly like "All lies are the devil's lies." The real question is how to tell the difference, which throws us back into the crucible: we need to define the source of significant and reliable knowledge. Furthermore, the actual products of VITEX thinking have usually self-admittedly been—in the name of general revelation—rewarmed and baptized versions of secular theory.[12] As much as thoughtful VITEX would like to dissociate itself from the egregious offenses of Christianized pop psychology, the two groups tend to sound like "birds of a feather."

On the other side, COMPIN discredits itself to VITEX ears by sounding biblicistic, obscurantist and anti-intellectual. Sufficiency stumbles too easily into pat answers, legalism and triumphal separatism. What anyone *says* the Bible says is not self-evident; it must be subjected to serious scrutiny and criticism. "The Bible says" ought to engender hard thought, close observation and careful discussion—not freeze our minds, end the conversation and close our eyes to life as it is lived. Furthermore, in the name of biblical authority, the actual products of COMPIN thinking have too often self-admittedly been reversions to moralism, pietism and exorcism.[13] As much as thoughtful COMPIN would like to dissociate itself from the egregious offenses of those who engage in biblicistic quick fixes and ranting, it tends to sound like a bird of the same feather.

The church's counseling has been locked in stalemate. How can we break through to fresh ground? To break the stalemate I propose that we significantly reframe the epistemological debate. We should ask ourselves what our epistemo-

---

[12]Stan Jones and Richard Butman frame *Modern Psychotherapies* with criticisms of the shallowness and sloppiness of many Christianized psychologies (pp. 29ff., 415).

[13]In fact, Jay Adams opened *Competent to Counsel* not by criticizing psychology but by criticizing the Bible-believing church's impoverishment in counseling: he does not consider "read the Bible, pray, yield, or cast out a demon" adequate either as a reflection of Scripture or as a way to meet human need. His *Insight and Creativity in Christian Counseling* (Grand Rapids, Mich.: Zondervan, 1982) was an extended critique of the tendency of biblical counselors to fall into a cookbook mentality. I critiqued the demon-deliverance movement as a reversion to superstition and animism in the name of biblical counseling in David Powlison, *Power Encounters: Reclaiming Spiritual Warfare* (Grand Rapids, Mich.: Baker, 1995).

logical priorities should be. This question has a double reference. First, what episte-mological priorities are expressed by the Bible? Second, what priorities do we need in our time and place, both for the church's welfare and for the therapeutic culture to which the church is called to bear witness? I believe that both the model of Scripture and the needs of our times yield the same answer:

■ Our first priority must be to articulate positive biblical truth, a systematic practi-cal theology of those things that our culture labels "counseling issues." A systematic theology of care for the soul will wed conceptual, methodological and institutional elements.

■ Our second priority must be to expose, debunk and reinterpret alternative mod-els to biblical care for souls, whether secular or religious.

■ Our third priority must be to learn what we can from defective models; we should be stimulated and informed by those with whom we disagree and whom we aim to convert.

If we keep these priorities in their proper order, the church will thrive, both in our ministries to each other and as a light to the world. Does the Bible itself model this particular ordering of priorities? Yes. This is one of those questions whose answer enjoys an embarrassing abundance of supporting material.

The first priority: articulating biblical truth and developing a systematic theology of care for the soul. Biblical confirmation of the first priority is unmistakable. God's primary revelatory purposes are neither to criticize nor to adopt what floods the cultural surround. He is different, holy. He aims to proclaim, teach and model something distinctive. The Bible's positive message both is and is about counseling. In content, method and institutional locus the Bible overflows with counseling instructions and implications, not just in proof-texts, but in the whole body of Scrip-ture.

We begin with how we even define counseling. Counseling is not fundamentally a professional helping activity in which an identifiably competent party intention-ally offers aid to an identifiably distressed party in a formalized structure (such as weekly one-hour sessions on a fee-for-service basis). Given the culture's profes-sionalized definition, the Bible seems relatively insufficient—even utterly silent—on the subject of counseling. But if counseling is about the tongue, and wise or foolish companions, and master-disciple relationships, and one-anothering, and the truth or lie that speaks in the heart, and ministry of the Word of life, then the Bible brims over. Relatively formal, private counseling only applies and extends the practical truth and knowledgeable love that ought to characterize both informal relationships and public ministry. Counseling, whatever its formal or informal status, is either foolish (reorienting us away from God) or wise (reorienting us to God). We need, first and foremost, to learn our own paradigm.

The second priority: exposing, debunking and reinterpreting alternative models. The Bible conducts a running border war with multiform error. Idolatries and lies, false teachers and "the world" are like viral pathogens that endlessly mutate. False-hood is always new and creative, yet it always plays variations on the same old themes. Sinful human beings instinctively think about life as if there were no living God, no weighing of our lives in his eyes, and no need for a savior. Human beings assiduously construct God substitutes and truth substitutes, other meanings of life, other ways of making life work. Theories about our lives are like our lives: they reflect our instinct for evading reality.

Sin exerts a systematic distorting effect. The Bible teaches us how to see and expose sin and error. Most ungodliness is not unusually vile. It is so utterly com-monplace that we miss it. In our day, it includes the pervasive assumptions every secular psychology makes about what happens in the human heart. Secular psy-chologists cannot help the godlessness of their view of the psyche and relationships because a secular psychology is the cultural product of a godless person. Theories systematize and rationalize the unbelief of those who create and embrace those theories. Because the wisdom of the world has always been foolishness, the Bible conducts a secondary polemic in order to defend and clarify the truth and to pro-tect people from plausible falsehoods. This argument does not arise from paranoid irascibility. The Redeemer is conducting an invasion, and he critiques theories in order to convert people to a better truth. The second priority, criticism, is one logi-cal implication of the first priority, articulating biblical truth.

The third priority: learning what we can from defective models. We can learn from everything around us. The Bible freely co-opts surrounding cultures as one aspect of God's redemptive, transformative working. God's servants interact with what is around them linguistically, politically, religiously, economically, artistically, educationally, agriculturally, militarily. Knowing the truth, and critiquing error, we appropriate lots of things. But from the standpoint of fundamental model building, such learning plays a distinctly tertiary role. Because we are tainted by sin, God often uses perceptive error to reprove his people and to make us get to work to refine our understanding of his truth. God's redemptive revelation is constitutive, but counterbiblical theories may be provocative. And extrabiblical knowledge—of ourselves and our world—is the grist with which biblical truth works continually to extend the range and depth of understanding. We learn, critique, reinterpret, con-vert, apply. We traffic in the extrabiblical constructively when we know what we ought to know that reorients and controls our view.

This is God's world, so everything, even if it intends to efface God, bears wit-ness to God—if it is viewed through biblical eyeglasses. The Bible freely traffics in the extrabiblical, in the creation, in fallen cultural products, in the terminology of contemporary falsehoods that God is attacking. But God always interprets or rein-terprets. He is imperial. Biblical truth provides a corrective to our view. For exam-ple, the formal structure of Deuteronomy is modeled on ancient Near Eastern political treaties, but what God appropriates he radically reworks. Some Old Testament proverbs are formally identical to older Egyptian sayings, but they mean something fundamentally different when they are embedded in the context of Yahweh-fearing proverbs from what they meant when embedded in a context of superstition, animism and idolatry.

The writers of the Bible never feared secular education. Moses was educated in all the learning of the Egyptians (Acts 7:22); God gave Daniel and his friends knowledge and intelligence in every branch of Chaldean literature and wisdom (Dan 1:17); Paul was a man of great learning (Acts 26:24). But Moses, Daniel and Paul interpreted life through God's redemptive grid. Paul could quote with favor an "anthropologist" who studied life in Crete (Tit 1:12) and could weave the words of Greek literati into his argument in Athens (Acts 17:28). Where the living, speaking, seeing, acting God rules, his servants move freely into the culture of their time and place. The Bible gives no warrant for Christians to be intellectual isolationists, biblicistic, cut off from culture and speaking a private language to our own kind.

Fallen though it is, this world is God's stage of redemption. But appropriation of culture should always be subordinated first to a clear-eyed grasp of God's truth, and second to a keen-eyed skepticism about fallen alternatives. Paul obviously learned a great deal from his culture. But he did not learn the living, systematic truth he proclaimed from sterile and deviant substitutes; rather, the truth he proclaimed radically reworked those substitutes.[14]

Applying the three priorities to the needs of our culture. The Bible itself models what I have termed the primary, secondary, and tertiary priorities. What then are the needs of our culture? I believe the same priorities apply. First, both the confused church and the benighted culture need, more than anything else, positive biblical truth pointedly applied. We need to understand and practice our own distinctive psychology. We need to understand and practice our own distinctive care for souls. If we do not know well the peculiar wisdom of our own truth, we do not act as light in the current darkness, but as second-rate disciples of that darkness. Truth is the best thing we can offer.

Second, we need a penetrating critique of contemporary sources of confusion and darkness. Secular alternatives for understanding and caring for souls need careful exposure and pointed challenge. Priorities one and two will enable us to build up and protect the people of God. They will also enable a telling and timely proclamation of Christian truth to a psychologized culture. We believe and do differently from the world around us.

---

[14]All that I have said about appropriating, working with and learning from what is around us is no less true of what is within us. We make our own experience normative only to our peril. Experience is not autonomous, self-interpreting or self-interpreted, except in sin's delusion. The truth of the mind of Christ (priority one) critiques us (priority two) and remakes us, folding and reinterpreting all of life's learning and experience (priority three) into God's pattern and story (priority one).

Finally, the call to develop our model by interacting with contemporary error is a distinctly tertiary priority. Their successes can certainly reprove us and help us to our areas of ineptitude and ignorance more clearly—as long as we do not become so persuaded that we counterconvert. Their observations of what makes human life go or not go can sometimes inform us—if we radically reinterpret them from within our worldview. At every point, the first priority must be first; the second, second; the third, third.

Implications of getting our priorities straight. The process of getting our priorities straight generates a host of implications and applications in three areas: psychological research, the church's ability to evangelize psychologized people, and the appropriation of historical theology.

First, the necessity of reordering our priorities does not mean that it is wrong to closely study psychological, relational, and counseling processes. Exactly the opposite. Psychological study that submits itself to God's truth becomes part of the joyous outworking of the church's first priority. When we believe in the sufficiency of Scripture, we face a vast practical-theological task, not a search for a proof text for every problem. Adopting a frankly biblical worldview, we should get about the business of hard, fruitful study in subordination to the mind of Christ.

Jonathan Edwards's *Treatise Concerning Religious Affections* is a model of empirical study constrained by biblical presuppositions. His was not positivist science pretending to neutrality; it was not narrow biblicism closing its eyes to the very phenomena that need study and interpretation; it was not a borrowing of secular thinking, thinly glossed with Christian words. Rather, it was a theological labor to develop systematic biblical understanding. But Edwards looked at only one slice of human life, albeit a significant slice. Who will do equivalent work regarding the multitude of significant counseling issues we face today? A hundred Edwardses could write a hundred equally masterful books, and a systematic practical theology of counseling would not yet be finished.

In the very generality and universality of God's revelation, the Bible invites systematic inquiry. The writers of the Bible intended to provide eyeglasses that enable all vision, not an encyclopedia that contains all facts. For example, Galatians 5:19-21 says that the manifest nature of the lifestyle of sin is "obvious." Paul then gives fifteen representative examples, closing with "and the like," thus providing an inexhaustible research agenda. Of course, Paul does not pretend to be methodologically or theoretically neutral. The "works of the flesh" are sinful, and they arise causally from various "lusts of the flesh"; both desire and doing should be morally evaluated. So we know a priori that such behaviors are not fundamentally products of enculturation, psychosocial trauma, unmet needs, a syndrome identified in the DSM-IV, or a somatic disease process. Each of the items on the Galatians 5 list—"interpersonal conflict," "substance abuse," "dysphoric emotions" and "sexual disorders"—invites extensive research to flesh out biblical understanding.

What about problems, like those labeled "eating disorders," that do not appear on the representative list in Galatians 5? "Obvious" (and research will unpack the details to show the how and why). Fear and anxiety are not on the list? "Obvious." The countless faces and voices of self- and other-deception? The many forms of self-righteousness and self-pity? The psychological and interpersonal complexities of people pleasing? "And the like." There is work to be done in cultivating a biblical view; a biblical view cultivates wide-ranging knowledge.

Our doctrine must control our study, and our study must flesh out our doctrine. Psychological study is a direct implication of the sufficiency of Scripture and of getting our first priority right. We study psychology best not by submitting ourselves to the world's deviant psychologies, but by looking at the world with the view of our own systematic biblical understanding. If we want to understand people so that we can help them, we undertake a task in practical theology.

Second, powerful evangelism to psychologized people is another direct implication of getting priorities straight. If we are begging from them, they will never see their own need. If we have the true riches and a corresponding critique of their poverty, we have something they will want.

I believe that several aspects of the contemporary psychological culture make the time ripe for the church to display its goods. In this post-Kuhnian, postmodern climate, confidence in positivistic scientific methodology for the social sciences has waned. The underpinnings of psychology as neutral truth have been kicked out. The age of confident model building, of the Grand Unified Theory (G.U.T.), has faded. Microtheories and eclecticism are the order of the day. Despite the brave face psychologists attempt to put on it, these tendencies register epistemological skepticism and despair. All of this creates an opportunity for the church to get about business and stand up with our own counseling model.

We have the G.U.T.—the work in progress of a systematic practical theology of counseling. As practitioners in the mental health professions increasingly rationalize themselves by their licensed control over turf, rather than by any defensible truth or claims of efficacy, the church will doubtless suffer intimidation, lawsuits, legal restrictions, and so forth. But the fundamentally nonprofessional character of biblical wisdom shines with particular poignancy in such a world of brazen self-interest. We need not care much about licensure, accreditation, and third-party reimbursement schemes. The state does not license the church to believe and do what we need to believe and do, and it cannot stop us. Counseling is not primarily a profession according to our G.U.T. Instead, it is a lifestyle. It is character, wisdom, every word out of our mouths, walking worthy of our calling. It is serving up the message of life to the ignorant and wayward, to the afflicted and dying, to the redeemable, to ourselves.

As Christians get our priorities straight, wonderful things happen. We become distinctively wise, able to help our own with our own resources. We begin to shine into a world in which people realize, when they are honest, that mental health professionals are groping in the dark. We have something positive to offer our world: truth, love and power in the exact areas in which people are most concerned and most confused. Our critique becomes more than sectarian intransigence. Our message becomes more than religious mumbo jumbo for and from religious people. Our message is about life as it is actually lived, experienced, motivated and evaluated—for every human being.

Third, our labors will result in something the world has not yet seen. We can appreciate the achievements of theologians, philosophers, and pastors who have alerted us to the historic resources of the Christian faith. Exemplary texts include Thomas Oden's series Classical Pastoral Care, Robert Roberts's *Taking the Word to Heart*, Tim Keller's "Puritan Resources for Biblical Counseling," Paul Griffiths's "Metaphysics and Personality Theory" and Dennis Okholm's "To Vent or Not to Vent?"[15] The intellectual revival of the works of long-departed practical theologians offers a healthy corrective to the subjection of evangelical faith to various contemporary psychologies, and it reasserts positive Christian wisdom about the nature of persons, relationships, and the activities we call counseling.

But we must not forget the call to do fresh theological work. It is not enough to recover what has been long forgotten or obscured regarding human nature and counseling; it is not enough to appropriate the fruits of historical theology for present edification. Yes, Augustine's *Confessions* is a marvel of insight into the myriad ways in which sin disorders our loves and grace reorders them. Yes, Edwards's *Treatise Concerning Religious Affections* is a masterpiece of empirical study conducted under the authority of Scripture. Yes, Gregory the Great and William Baxter collated vast wisdom. But the questions these writers address are not all universal; they are also significantly dated. Our generation must—and will—break new ground. Positive formulations of fresh theological work will enable us to criticize our Christian past discerningly. Not all earlier practical theologies were created equal. Not all are equally worth resurrecting. We must appropriate the best and forsake the worst, and that demands fresh criteria for judgment. Our task is always fresh: "A theology that does not build on the past ignores our debt to history and naively overlooks the fact that the present is conditioned by history. A theology that relies on the past evades the demands of the present."[16]

None of our forebears hammered out fidelity to Christ within a culture in which

---

[15]Paul J. Griffiths, "Metaphysics and Personality Theory," in *Limning the Psyche: Explorations in Christian Psychology,* ed. Robert C. Roberts and Mark R. Talbot (Grand Rapids, Mich.: Eerdmans, 1997), pp. 41-57; Timothy J. Keller, "Puritan Resources for Biblical Counseling," *Journal of Pastoral Practice* 9, no. 3 (1988): 11-44; Thomas C. Oden, *Pastoral Counsel,* Classical Pastoral Care (Grand Rapids, Mich.: Baker, 1987); Robert C. Roberts, *Taking the Word to Heart;* Dennis Okholm's "To Vent or Not to Vent?" appears in this volume.

[16]John Murray, *Collected Writings* (Edinburgh: Banner of Truth, 1982), p. 9.

an omnipresent mental health establishment attempts to define and meliorate human nature. The church's care for souls has never before faced such stiff, organized, and persuasive competition. This has arisen under the sovereignty of God, so that we might expect and pursue fresh wisdom.

Robert Roberts was hesitant to suggest that we expect a radically Christian counseling model to emerge internally, from within the Christian faith:

> A Christian psychology would not *have* to be pursued in dialogue with secular psychology—at least not if the psychologist in question were Augustine, or Kierkegaard, or Saint John of the Cross. But I can think of two reasons why we more ordinary Christian thinkers are well advised to do our psychology in dialogue with important secular psychologists.[17]

Perhaps Roberts rightly fears our presumption and incompetence, our lack of intellectual and practical stature. I grant that our psychology will emerge in some sort of interaction with the psychologies that are around us—and with everything else we experience culturally. But such dialogue should not be a matter of advice, policy or necessity. For one thing, the dialogue with secularity has most often been unprofitable. It has largely resulted in counseling models that are recapitulations of and capitulations to secular forms of thinking and practice. The dialogue may make a tertiary contribution, but our primary call is to dialogue with the Bible and with lives as they are lived. Let us work explicitly from our own foundation.

Roberts may be right that no solitary and extraordinary genius will arise among us. Perhaps because care and counseling are fundamentally tasks of corporate wisdom, our Lord will be pleased to raise up something better: a corporate Augustine, a hundred Augustines, a hundred thousand Augustines, for the task that faces us. Perhaps many Christians will tackle the same massive intellectual and practical project: to construct "systematic biblical counseling" for the beginning of the third millennium anno Domini. After all, the Bible offers unique and superior wisdom, not only for extraordinary people, but also for ordinary people (see Ps 119:98-100; 1 Cor 1—2). Our problem is not so much a matter of talent, but a matter of corporate vision and will.

If our counseling model arises from Scripture, it will explicitly cohere with long-formulated Christian orthodoxy and orthopraxy. It has often been said regarding the relationship of Old Covenant to New Covenant that "the new is in the old concealed; the old is in the new revealed." The same is true of theological progress. A systematic pastoral theology for the twenty-first century will cohere with historic orthodoxy, yet will break open new light and new power. Our concepts will probe the depths of the human heart and map the diversity of individual and cultural differences. Our methods will deliver the goods that comfort the disturbed and disturb the comfortable, converting all into the image of Jesus. Our institutional structures

---

[17]Roberts, *Taking the Word to Heart*, p. 14.

will be ecclesiastically rooted vehicles of the ministry of the Word, combining pastoral authority and mutual encouragement.

Systematic biblical counseling will break fresh ground theologically, practically and institutionally. For example, our understanding of the Christian life will be radically transformed as we deliver progressive sanctification out of its religious closet—a sector of religiously colored experiences, doctrines, morals and activities—and work out the renovation of our humanity in daily life and in our social existence. We might barely recognize the radical new forms that church, ministry and piety will take when Ephesians 4 and Hebrews 3:12-14; 4:12-16; 10:19-25 come into their own—and yet those forms will be utterly familiar.

When our priorities become tangled. What happens when our priorities become tangled? People who elevate the tertiary priority—learning from defective models—to first priority find themselves subtly or overtly psychologized, and they promulgate faulty reasoning and practice throughout the body of Christ. Those who overweigh the significance of secular psychology "learn" more than they bargained for. We tend to undergo a wrong-way conversion, becoming anesthetized to the God-centered realities playing out in the human psyche. We begin to reason godlessly about behavior, mood, relationships, motives, cognition and so on. The scope of Christian faith becomes constricted, its significance restricted to a "spiritual" sector. However unwittingly, we allow conceptual categories from personality theory or self-help or medicine, the authority of the latest research studies, the well-socialized and tacit assumptions of mental health professionals, and the necessities of licensure and accreditation to permeate thought and practice. All of this works in concert to unnerve faith. The Bible becomes an ancillary and supportive text, a source of proof texts in the worst sense. Christian faith and biblical citation are pressed to rationalize ideas that are intrinsically alien to the mind of God. Only when our first priority is first will we truly think and act in ways that transform our culture, those we counsel and ourselves.

People who major in the secondary priority—exposing, debunking and reinterpreting alternative models—create a different problem for the body of Christ. Criticism without the rich, growing edge of the first priority is unpalatable and unedifying. When we major in criticism, we become polemicists rather than agents of redemption. Sometimes polemicists excuse their loveless rough edges by appealing to the demands of truth. But they lose more than they realize. When love is lost, truth is also lost. Biblical truth loses its scope, balance, depth, applicability, savor and growing edge when the second priority seizes center stage. The positive theological task that is the need of our age becomes obscured. Caricatures of truth and discernment replace the realities. Words that are not constructive, timely and grace-giving are rotten, whatever their formal likeness to Christian content (Eph 4:29). To lose charity, tenderheartedness, sympathy and generosity is always to simultaneously pervert the redemptive nature of biblical revelation. Narrowed truth may bristle enough to defend one city wall, but it is not good enough to conquer the world.[18] Only when our first priority is first do we Christians have a robust, radiant and sensible alternative in our hearts and in our mouths, something good to offer those we critique, those we counsel and ourselves.

The church must transcend the misplaced priorities and fruitless posturing of much of the current debate between VITEX and COMPIN. The tertiary priority must be submitted to the call to pursue the primary and secondary priorities. The secondary must be submitted to the primary, and then the implications of the tertiary must be spelled out. When we get our priorities straight, the shift will invigorate both the secondary and the tertiary to function as they ought, and will produce a buoyant intellectual and practical confidence for both counseling ministry and evangelism. Our ability to understand ourselves, to counsel our own, and to reach the world with our distinctive truth is at stake.

Our Theory of Motivation

What is wrong with people, and how can we make it right?

At the center of every view of human nature is a theory of motivation, and the logical end of every theory of motivation is a proposed solution. The various answers to the question "Why do we do what we do?" provide synopses of the various schools of thought. Each definition of the core problem is then a signpost to the cure for the soul that the respective theory proposes. Everyone agrees that something is wrong with us. The big questions are always "Why?" and "What can be done about it?"

If your brain chemistry is unhinged, then you need chemical reengineering. If you are fixated at a particular point on the hierarchy of needs, then the needs at that level must be met for you. If your drives have been conditioned to take you in unacceptable directions, then you need to be redirected and reconditioned.

If your spirit is dead while your soulishness is too lively, then you need God's Spirit to release your spirit to master your soul. If you are wounded, then you need healing. If you search for meaning while believing and doing meaningless things, then you need the courage to embrace something meaningful.

If this is a bad-star day for people born under your zodiac sign, then you need to stay home today. If you feel bad about yourself, then you need reasons to have more self-confidence. If you were born into a miserable existence because of previous bad karma, then you need to produce good karma in hopes of getting something better next time around.

If your self-talk is self-defeating, then you need a motivational speech and a dose of stoic philosophy. If you are mentally ill, then you need to find the right medicine to make you well. If you are lazy, then you need more self-discipline. If

---

[18]For a stimulating discussion of matter and manner in defending the faith, see John Frame, "Scripture and the Apologetic Task," *Journal of Biblical Counseling* 13, no. 2 (1995): 9-12.

your problem is just a guy-thing or a woman-thing, then you need to affirm the quirks that make you hard to live with. If you have been oppressed by society, then you need to stand up for your rights.

If you are fleeing from acknowledging unacceptable impulses, then you need to stop and look in the mirror. If a demon of anger has staked out turf in your soul, then you need to get it ejected. If you have psychic voids created by disappointing object relations, then you need to find ways to understand your personal history and redirect your longings. If you are compensating for your inferiority complex, then you need to learn to accept yourself realistically and do something worthwhile.

Everyone in the supermarket of ideas knows that something is wrong with people. But what is it? Everyone in the supermarket of cures wants to do something to make it better. But what gives the life that is life indeed? Different views of the soul's ailments will logically produce different cures for the soul. Wrong views of any disease always bring with them wrong remedies. The right view brings the right remedy.

So what is the problem? The three-word description that Christians have harvested from the Bible is "sin and misery." The remedy? The two-word solution that Scripture sows into our lives is "Jesus Christ." The seven words that encompass our response are "Christ's grace enabling repentance, faith and obedience." God is in the business of turning folly and misery into wisdom and felicity. How is this theological shorthand relevant to the problems that counselors of all stripes address daily? How do basic Christian diagnostic categories map onto the details of interpersonal conflicts, unpleasant emotions, misdirected lives, twisted cognitions, chaotic cravings, compulsively escapist behaviors, sufferings at the hands of others, somatic afflictions, devilish temptations and sociocultural lies? This is simply a twenty-five word elaboration of "sin and misery." One could further elaborate any counseling-related topic or subtopic into book length without ever needing to slip into another set of categories. Similarly, God's solution, the wise felicity of grace, can, must and will be elaborated, tailored and nuanced as it is worked into our lives.

The holy grail after which counseling theories ultimately aspire is redemption from what ails us, a cure for the diagnosed problem. In the Bible's comprehensive view, redemption must engage both inward and outward aspects of the person, and it must engage both the individual and the community. The renewing of our hearts (making our cognitive, emotional and volitional processes fruitful), the renewing of our manner of life (transforming individual behavior), the renewing of our community (transforming corporate relationships), and the renewing of our bodies (the resurrection from the dead) all go together. In biblical language, such comprehensive renewal is "wisdom and felicity." It is the goal of God's counseling.

The psychology of Jesus. The writers of the Bible portray and intend to create such wisdom at every turn. We are taught and shown a tremendous amount about the psychology of Jesus; this is a centerpiece for understanding. We know how Jesus thought, felt, chose, acted and spoke. We know not only how he related interpersonally, but also how he related individual identity to community. We know how he interpreted and responded to suffering and how he located individual life in the larger flow of history. In what terms did his psychic life transpire? How did he interpret? What did he want? How did he understand himself? When we consider the psychology of Jesus, we learn how the human soul is intended to work, and hence we have the standard from which to make diagnoses of defection and distortion.

We witness the psychology of Jesus not only in the Gospels, but also in Psalms, Proverbs and the books of the prophets, which also give expression to how he works both intrapsychically and interpersonally. When we witness how Jesus works and thinks, what emerges as the central drama, the pivot of human existence? What threads through every emotion, cognition, action, relationship, suffering? Our souls play out a drama of evil and good, sin and righteousness, fall and redemption, false and true, misery and felicity, folly and wisdom, deafness and hearing, stupor and wakefulness, death and life. We play out this drama vis-à-vis God at every moment; in every choice; in every nuance of cognition, emotion and volition; in every detail of lifestyle. Our psychological, behavioral, social and somatic existence plays out on the stage of history, and a day of reckoning is coming.

We also learn about psychopathology, the madness in our hearts. From a biblical point of view, one of the leading characteristics of sin's psychopathology is that we repress awareness of the moral, theological and historical terms in which the drama of our psyches is cast.[19] This is a stunning psychology. People with problems in living, people who seem to function in healthy ways, and the psychological models that attempt to make sense of things are equally sick. They all repress the truth.

The psychology of Jesus is multifaceted. The psalmist is simultaneously sinner and sufferer, par excellence. The proverbist is simultaneously wise and keenly aware of remnant folly, par excellence. The prophet lives simultaneously in the moment and in the larger flow of history, par excellence. In each case, individual identity and community identity are interwoven. What cure is there for what ails us? The steadfast love of Yahweh is the only hope for deliverance from both sin and suffering. We all know this. These things lie on the surface of Scripture, and they

---

[19]Psalms 10, 14 and 36 are but a few examples of how the thought processes of the sinful psyche are analyzed. The repression of God and of our historical embeddedness and accountability are prominent themes. Only a biblical psychology reveals how significant this is; fallen psychologies manifest the repression.

constitute the depths of Scripture. They deconstruct and reconstruct the human soul. They are so familiar and so "religious" that we barely hear them. We barely hear their shocking implications for our conceptual and applied psychology.

What does this mean for our model of counseling? Jesus owned the psalms, proverbs and prophets as the voice of his experience and emotion, the content of his cognitive process, and the framework of his action. They articulate what human life is about. The fully honest, fully human person thinks, feels and reacts in the ways that the psalmist, the proverbist and the prophet do. These writings record the categories of consciousness and action of the only fully conscious and seeing man who ever lived. They record the categories through which the gaze of the Searcher of hearts thoroughly searches our lives. One sees in the Bible the normatively wise human psychology. It is so radically God-centered that we can barely see it as a psychology or as the true psychology. It sounds like theology, not psychology. But in the Bible the nitty-gritty of human psychology is portrayed as pervasively theological.

One sees in the Bible many portrayals of the normally foolish human psychology. This is utterly familiar stuff—dysfunctions and healthy functions of relationship, emotion and cognition; the Lego pieces with which every false psychology plays; the descriptive case-study data. But it all looks shockingly different when we see it with a biblical gaze, when we see it against the diagnostic backdrop of the normative psychology of God fearing. Jesus experienced life as he counseled others to experience life: the issues of life as it is lived are specifically sin and misery, specifically gracious deliverance and specifically the felicitous wisdom of repentance, faith and obedience. There is no "religious" sector of life. Such sectoring is one of the commonplace machinations of sin's logic that flies in the face of reality.

Why belabor this point? I wish I could belabor it better, less impressionistically, more radically! What the Bible communicates to us about God's gaze on the psyche and on relationships is so odd that even to glimpse it turns our whole notion of psychology and counseling inside out, upside down and backward. God gives a radically "other" explanation and agenda. Contemporary counseling models— including "Christian" models—do an extremely poor job of reflecting and communicating what life is really about. They are weakest where they claim to be strongest. We are immersed in decidedly bad psychologies, in gross misinterpretations of human existence.

By definition a personality theory ought to help counselor and counselee alike to accurately understand what is going on within and between persons. By definition a counseling model claims to help us reorient to reality, to know what to do to fix things. But what should we make of models that essentially and consistently evade reality? That misdefine the basic problem? That suppress the major Player in human psychological, relational and somatic existence? That suppress the historical conditions—past, present and future—that qualify human existence? That redefine the dynamics of our God-dealing hearts by expunging God? That redefine the basic solution that is so radically a Person? That redefine the desired human response that is so radically interpersonal? A model that does not move within the categories of human experience that Jesus himself moved in, and by which God himself looks at life, will fundamentally disorient and misguide those who embrace it. A counseling model offers a map of reality, an interpretive framework. The Bible's reality map sets the goal of all valid counseling conducted in the consciousness and lifestyle of Jesus. We witness and listen in on the normative subjectivity and intersubjectivity.

Thinking covenantally. The psychology of Jesus has enormous implications for our theory of motivation. First of all, the dynamics of human intention and desire cannot be defined in purely psychological terms (or psychosocial terms, or psychosocial-somatic terms). Motivational dynamics do not operate simply within or between persons. The human heart has to do with God. So when the Bible describes the desires that obviously play within our souls and rule our lives, it does not speak of them as hard-wired psychological or physiological givens—as needs, instincts, drives, longings or wishes. It speaks of our desires as morally freighted vis-à-vis God, as moral-covenantal choices: we are ruled either by cravings of the flesh or by repentance, faith and obedience to God's desires. Our desires are tilted one way or the other, either toward the true God or toward the host of idols that we fabricate both collectively and individually. Our mastering desires are relationally and morally qualified.

Similarly, when the Bible describes the beliefs, assumptions and inward conversations that so obviously play within our souls and shape our lives, it does not speak of them in neutral fashion as mere cognitive functions—as self-talk, schemata, conscious or unconscious content, memory, attitude, imagination or worldview. Such things not only occur *coram Deo*, they actually have to do directly with God. Our mental life operates either for or against God: lies and unbelief contend with truth and faith. In the Bible people whose self-talk operates as if there were no God—and hence no ongoing and eventual moral evaluation by God—are described in vividly moral terms: they are fools, wicked and proud. People who talk in their hearts in the light of God are also described in vividly moral terms: wise, righteous, after God's own heart. Our mastering beliefs are relationally and morally qualified.

In the same way, when the Bible describes the self-evaluating capacities that play within our souls and so powerfully determine us, it does not speak of them as intrapsychic entities—as self-esteem, self-image, self-worth, self-love, self-confidence, inferiority complex or identity. Our evaluative and self-knowing capacity registers human-before-God realities. The conscience, or "eyes," by which we evaluate ourselves either expresses our self-will ("in my own eyes," pride) and our subjection to the opinions of others ("in others' eyes," fear of other people)—or it expresses and is informed by God's evaluative criteria ("in God's eyes," *coram Deo*, the fear of the Lord). Self-evaluation is not intrinsically an autonomous, intrapsychic function. It only acts that way when sin operates to suppress God-awareness. Our mastering conscience is relationally and morally qualified.

In sum, the human heart—the answer to why we do what we do—must be understood as an active verb with respect to God. If you climb inside any emotional reaction, any behavioral choice or habit, any cognitive content, any reaction pattern to suffering, you ought to hear and see active verbs at work. Love God or anything else. Fear God or anything else. Want God or anything else. Need God or anything else. Hope in God or anything else. Take refuge in God or anything else. Obey God or anything else. Trust God or anything else. Seek God or anything else. Serve God or anything else. The Bible's motivation theory shouts from every page—but it does not look like a motivation theory to those whose gaze has been bent and blinded by sin's intellectual logic. How can we learn to think and see psyche and behavior covenantally?

Consider this analogy. The Bible's psychology is like a hyperpsychosocial theory. Psychosocial theories embed psychic functions in social realities. The Bible's motivation theory is a psychosocial theory on steroids. A covenantal-relational analysis of the human heart adds a pervasive and determinative dimension to which encapsulated-psyche theories and interhumanly psychosocial theories are utterly oblivious. No one else in the modern world is able or willing to say what the church can and must say: that human beings are radically sin-sick. This is what explains human behavior. No secular theory can say this, because no secular theory can see this, because no secular theory wants to see this. Care for the soul must address this ailment or else it is prescribing painkillers for cancer; it is whistling in the dark while a deadly, unseen corruption festers and an imminent, unrecognized destruction approaches.

Christ cures sin-sickness. Where sin abounds, grace superabounds. One small but significant part of the cure is that he reveals his own psychology to us and demonstrates how these are the realities that operate in our souls. When we get straight how the active heart works vis-à-vis God, then the grace of Jesus maps straight onto human need. The good news of Jesus refuses to be relegated to a religious sector of life. It is the explicit need of the psychologically honest and the clear seeing. All other psychologies—whether formulated into personality theories or merely lived out in the workings of individual idiosyncrasy—traffic in myth, lie and perverted speculation.

The Bible locates the core motivational dynamic in covenantal space, not in psychological, physiological or psychosocial space. What God sees in us mocks the paradigm and content of the encapsulated psyche that most of the older psychologies posited. It mocks the social psyche of many of the newer psychologies. It mocks the epiphenomenal psyche of the empty organism posited by behaviorists, medicalists and sociobiologists. The intricacies of behavior, emotion, forgetting and remembering, attitude and cognitive processes specifically come out of the heart. This is not simply a vague, religiously toned generalization. What people do with the living God plays out into the details. In other words, our core psychological problem is sin. Sin operates specifically here and now, not generally back then and there.

Distortions in the definition of sin. Sin is the problem, but people find it difficult to make the core of Jesus' view useful in developing a counseling model because there are several common distortions in the working definition of sin.[20]

First, people tend to think of sins in the plural, as consciously willed acts in which one was aware of and chose not to perform the righteous alternative. Sin, in this popular understanding, refers to matters of conscious volitional awareness of wrongdoing and the ability to do otherwise. This view of sin infects many Christians and almost all non-Christians. It has a long legacy in the church under the label *Pelagianism,* one of the oldest and most instinctive heresies. The Bible's definition of sin certainly includes the high-handed sins in which evil approaches full volitional awareness. But sin also includes what we simply are and the perverse ways we think, want, remember and react.

Most sin is invisible to the sinner because it is simply how the sinner works, how the sinner perceives, wants and interprets things. Once we see sin for what it really is—madness (Eccles 9:3) and evil intentions (Gen 6:5) in our hearts, when we see that sin means we have no fear of God in our eyes (Ps 36:1), when we see that we are slaves to various passions and pleasures (Tit 3:3)—then it becomes easier to see that sin is the immediate and specific problem that all counseling deals with at every moment, that it is not a general and remote problem. The core insanity of the human heart is that we violate the first great commandment. We will love anything except God unless our madness is checked by grace.

People do not tend to see sin as applying to relatively unconscious problems, to the deep, interesting and bedeviling stuff in our hearts. But God's descriptions of sin often highlight the unconscious aspect. Sin—the desires we pursue, the beliefs we hold, the habits we obey as second nature—is intrinsically deceitful. If we knew we were deceived, we would not be deceived. But we are deceived unless we are awakened through God's truth and Spirit. Sin is a darkened mind, drunkenness,

---

[20]Sin's very logic produces these distortions in the view of sin, for sin is elusive and evasive. If I were to add another section to this article, I would discuss the interplay of situational variables and our sins in a cursed, redeemable world. The Bible is crystal clear about the ways in which God's sovereign and immediate purposes play out in our reactions to being sinned against, to diverse somatic problems, to sociocultural conditioning, to the devil, to suffering, to misery, to temptation and so forth. There are many fine Christian books on suffering and on God's purposes in suffering (topics about which the psychologies are ignorant); I will leave the reader to those sources.

animal-like instinct and compulsion, madness, slavery, ignorance, stupor. People often think that to define sin as unconscious is to remove human responsibility. How can we be culpable for what we do not sit down and choose to do? But the Bible takes the opposite tack. The unconscious and semiconscious nature of much sin simply testifies to the fact that we are steeped in it. Sinners think, want and act sinlike by nature, nurture and practice. All psychological processes are sin-kinked. That is their most interesting and significant aspect diagnostically.

The tendency to see sin as behavioral and fully volitional carries enormous implications for counseling. When people see sin only as willed actions, they must invent other categories to cover the blind chaos, insanity, confusion, compulsion, impulsivity, bondage and fog that beset the human soul. A person who is grappling with the chaos of the human condition must be suffering from emotional or psychological problems, demons, mental illness, addiction, inner wounding, unmet needs and longings, adjustment reactions, or some DSM-IV syndrome. A few people, the consciously bad people, can then be usefully described as sinners. Everybody else might commit a few sins: "Of course, we're all sinners." But that is a weightless comment. The weighty action typically occurs deeper inside the person; it operates beneath or beside those occasional, undefined, generic sins.

If a certain problem happens occasionally and is presumably under conscious control, then it is sin. But if the problem happens a lot and is driven by blind compulsion, then it is presumably something else; it is only remotely sin. When the deacon gets drunk and sleeps with his secretary, he sins. But when the drunkard and pornography habitué succumbs, he suffers alcoholism and sexual addiction. When a normal mother feels anxiety about her children and pressures them to perform, she ought to repent of her worry and domineering and learn to trust God. But when someone who is a walking nervous breakdown feels wracking anxiety about everything and manipulates everyone, he or she suffers neurosis or codependency or borderline personality or an adjustment reaction. Such thinking swings a wrecking ball into the church's ability to think about counseling the way Jesus thinks about it. If we have a psychologically astute gaze, we will discern how sin plays out in people's problems—and in the things they do not think are problems. False psychologies obscure what the true psychology sees.

The modern psychologies are wrong about psychology. Their perceptive descriptions of certain features of human existence may be challenging and informative, but their theoretical gaze always blinkers out significant data. That gaze always distorts the very things seen most acutely and cared about most intensely. It always fabricates significant data because what is seen is an artifact of the way of seeing. Sin blinds while preserving the illusion of seeing.

As far as secular psychologists know themselves, they want to understand and help people. But they are committed to defining the core, causal problem as anything except sin. Imagine a group of detectives examining a murder scene. The criminal has left countless clues. An hour before the crime he had been making loud threats in a restaurant. He dropped his business card at the scene of the crime. He stood in front of a surveillance camera that took a picture every three seconds. He left fingerprints everywhere, including on the gun, which he left beside the body and which he had purchased three days earlier. He made a credit-card call on the victim's telephone moments after the crime. He was collared running away from the scene wearing blood-spattered clothes. Under questioning he is extremely agitated and alternates between contradictory excuses and sharp cries of remorse. But imagine further that the detectives are committed to finding some other culprit, any other culprit—because they themselves are accomplices to the murder. All of the evidence will be processed through a grid of intentions that forbids the truth. Secularity cannot help noticing the clues that scream out "sin," even as it cannot help rationalizing away the true interpretation.

A further problem almost invariably accompanies a defective view of sin. When we think of naming problems "sin," we tend to react in one of two ways. One reaction is to punish sin. We become moralistic and condemning, morbidly curious about others' failings, morbidly depressed about our own failings. When we assume a punitive stance toward sin and assume that others do the same, then calling something "sin" necessarily involves condemnation of self or others. We all know, however, both by Scripture and instinct, that those who would help others need to love them, and that those who would find help need to know love. In the interest, then, of bringing sweet necessities—grace, kindness, gentleness, patience, acceptance, tender solicitude and sympathetic understanding—we must come up with categories other than sin. The unexamined and ultimately bizarre logic of this reaction is that we assume that we can be Christlike toward others and ourselves only if we define a problem as something other than sin—as a psychological problem, a mental illness or an addiction.

People who would understand a problem as sin must presumably be punitive. But how curious it is that Jesus, whose gaze was utterly conditioned by the sin analytic, brought grace and kindness! In fact, to be conscious that sin is the problem is the only way to experience grace for oneself and then to love as Jesus loved. When we know ourselves accurately, we become recipients of spectacular grace that we are able to give away freely and patiently. Because he knew his own sins and God's grace, the high priest was able to "deal gently with the ignorant and wayward" (Heb 5:2; cf. Heb 4:12—5:3). May we learn to know and do likewise.

The second reaction is to excuse sin. We euphemize, whitewash, re-label, evade, rationalize and blame. We get defensive about ourselves and we try to excuse others. This strategy is at work throughout the modern psychologies. It is part of their allure that they pretend to reflect deep and determinative knowledge about the human soul, yet they evade the essential problem of the soul. But when we know grace, we have no reason not to look in the mirror frankly and no reason not to help others look in the mirror. Indeed, we look in the mirror so that our hearts might be remade as we shout with exultation.

The Bible is crystal clear about all these things. This is Theology 101 applied remedially to contemporary bad psychologies in the interests of a sound psychology. These are the *ABC*s of a biblical theory of why we do what we do and what we should do about it. These concepts appear nowhere in any secular model, and rarely with any profundity in Christian counseling models. Instead we find counterfeits, abstractions of human existence ripped out of their true theistic context.

Let me pose a series of questions to the VITEX community, the community of people who believe that psychology must make a vital external contribution to the construction of a wisely Christian model of personality, change and counseling. Why do the models of Christian counseling that have been proposed over the past forty years fail to teach the biblical theory? Why does one or another secular theory of human motivation almost inevitably control the Christian counseling theory at the punch line, where counseling engages the details of life as it is lived? In particular, why have "need" theories that define significance, love and self-esteem as the standard needs been so prominent when they are so alien to the gaze of God and the psychological experience of Jesus? Why has the most typical, and apparently the most vital, external contribution of psychology been secular motivation theory, the very thing that wrenches human life out of its true context and drains psychological experience of its essential characteristics? Why do integrationist theories fail to take seriously the specific, omnipresent nature of sin as the chief and most immediate problem in the hearts of those we counsel?

VITEX has paid lip service to sin, treating it generally and placing it in the remote background. But where is the hard work and clear thinking that shows exactly how sin, specifically and in the here-and-now, underlies those dysfunctions and dysphorias that plague those we counsel? Why do the current Christian counseling models have such a hard time portraying the gospel of a sin-bearing and wisdom-giving Savior as intrinsic, vivid, logical and immediately relevant? Why do Christian counselors so often override the biblical view of the active heart by considering suffering (socialization, trauma, unmet needs, biochemistry and genetics) to be determinative and causative? Why do Christian counseling models fail to recognize, mention or make clear God's immediate and sovereign purposes in suffering? Why do they treat sin vaguely while they consider other factors to be deeper, more significant and more interesting for both theory development and therapeutic attention? Why aren't counselors who call sin "sin"—searching the heart and bringing patient grace—credited with bearing such mercy and grace, both personally and from Christ?

The conservative church has often been touched by Pelagianism or semi-Pelagianism, which has, in some circles, fed moralism and tendencies toward punitive harshness. In other circles, it has encouraged a flight to other explanations for what is deep in the human heart. But the comprehensive Bible and a faithful, systematic practical theology for caring for souls corrects all such defects by bringing amazing grace to sin-sick souls.

Educating, Licensing and Overseeing Counselors

How should help be organized?

When we get our epistemological priorities straight, our understanding of diagnosis and care radically changes. Those same reordered priorities also bring radical implications for institutional structure. So far in this essay I have concentrated on epistemological and conceptual concerns. But some readers will have noticed that a concern about social structure has been simmering on the back burner. For example, in describing the VITEX position, I described not only the vital external contribution of theory and knowledge from secular disciplines, but also participation in the mental health professions. This easy segue from epistemology to the sociology of professional practice needs to be analyzed rather than assumed to be self-evident. Institutional structure is not the same thing as epistemology.

Evangelicals' earliest rationalization for psychotherapeutic professionalism utilized trichotomist anthropology: If human nature can be divided into body, spirit and soul, then we need the doctor to treat the body, the pastor to treat the spirit and the psychologist to treat the soul. Though it is highly dubious both theologically and logically, some Christians still buy the argument. Subsequent rationalizations for professional practice have more often tended to use theoretical epistemology: If we can learn something about people from secular disciplines, then mental health professionals can provide leadership in care for the soul. That epistemology is equally dubious both theologically and logically—an intellectual sleight of hand—but it has been frequently accepted without examination.

We need to ponder and discuss two sets of questions. The first set of questions asks: What ought to be the social structure of counseling if we are to please the Shepherd of the sheep? How should care for souls be organized? What institutional structures ought to be in place to equip and oversee those who do face-to-face ministry? How should grassroots counseling be delivered? What credentials and characteristics define leadership or professionalism in the care of souls? How should the faith and practice, the concepts and methods of our counseling be both enriched and regulated so that we grow and stay faithful to God?

The second set of questions asks: What is the viability and validity of our current institutional arrangements? What are the implications for the church of Christ when its designated or presumed experts in the care of souls are state-licensed, fee-for-service mental health professionals who lack organic linkage to ecclesiastical oversight? What are the implications for the church of Christ of its current lack of crucial institutional structures that are necessary for caring for souls?

These questions are structural. They are matters of the sociology of pastoral care, of biblical ecclesiology, of the role and function of professions and social institutions. Our epistemological foundation, the Bible, addresses not only ideas and practices, but also social structure. Does the Holy Spirit intend that we develop a normative social institution for caring for souls? The answer is yes. The church— as the Bible defines it—contains an exquisite blending of leadership roles and mutuality, of specialized roles and the general calling. It is the ideal and desirable institution to fix what ails us.

During the past forty years a new ministry role has emerged in the body of Christ: that of the professional psychotherapist. In the 1950s there were perhaps six main categories of full-time Christian workers: pastors, missionaries, chaplains, school teachers, parachurch evangelism and discipleship workers, and medical personnel. *Christian psychotherapist* would have been an oxymoron, rather like *Christian Mormon,* for reasons that had to do both with conceptual framework and social structure. But in the past thirty years the vocation of state-licensed psychotherapist has become viable and popular for Christians who want to help people. Christian psychotherapists have rapidly become a seventh category of full-time Christian workers—sort of. The relationship between church and autonomous profession remains uneasy; it will always be uneasy. That uneasiness arises from a structural contradiction that cannot be effaced.

I am not saying, by the way, that there is no place for various sorts of Christian workers other than pastors, missionaries, and the rest. I am not saying that there is no place for institutional innovation in the church or in parachurch structures, or for development of specialized ministries. I am not saying that there is no place for people with particular gifts, training and experience in caring for souls. What I am saying is that state-licensed professionalization of the care of souls is not a desirable direction. A care-for-souls profession operating autonomously from the church is an anomaly.

The explicit intellectual rationale for integrating secular psychology and Christian faith has most often been epistemological: secular science can make a vital contribution to Christian thinking about human nature and change. But the social effect of importing psychotherapeutic professions has been at least as significant as the intellectual effect of importing psychological ideas. And the VITEX community has historically ignored efforts to bring the question up for discussion. For example, Jay Adams repeatedly challenged the evangelical psychotherapy community on ecclesiological and professional grounds, but he was repeatedly rebutted by psychologists on epistemological grounds. When the psychologists ritualistically charged that Adams had adopted an against-psychology position epistemologically, denying common grace and general revelation, they skirted the fact that Adams was most often exercised about the sociology of professions, not about epistemology.

In fact, Adams's formal epistemology is a rather typically reformed transformationist or integrationist position regarding the observations and ideas of secular disciplines. He denied the necessity of the ideas of secular disciplines for constructing a systematic pastoral theology, but he affirmed their potential usefulness when appropriated in the context of a Christian worldview. Epistemologically Adams is a radical Christianizer of secularity, not a biblicistic xenophobe.[21] But Adams was sharply against psychology when it came to giving state-licensed and secularly trained mental health professionals the reins for face-to-face care of souls.[22]

The evangelical counseling community has only apparently been locked in an epistemological stalemate between the VITEX and COMPIN positions. The underlying reality is more complicated—and more social. I suggest that "common grace" has often served as a symbolic resource by VITEX to evade discussion of the implications of professionalization. I also suggest that rhetoric about the church has often served as a symbolic resource by COMPIN to evade discussion of the actual state of the church regarding care of souls. We must look at and address both what ought to be and what is, bringing the two together to design solutions.

What ought to be. The church is in trouble when its designated experts in the care of souls are mental health professionals who owe their legitimacy to the state. Caring for souls is a decidedly pastoral function in the broadest and deepest sense of the word. It is deeply problematic to operate as if the Word of God is useful, necessary and sufficient for public ministry—preaching, teaching, worship, the sacraments—but that training and credentialing in secular psychology are necessary for private ministry. In the Bible the same truths that address crowds address individuals. A preacher no more needs a Ph.D. in public speaking than a counselor needs a Ph.D. in psychology. Graduates of psychology programs should not have the right and the honor to teach the church about the human condition. Fee-for-service psychotherapeutic professionals should not have the right and the honor to practice the care of souls. They have the wrong knowledge base, the wrong credentials, the wrong financial and professional structure.

According to the Bible, caring for souls—sustaining sufferers and transforming sinners—is a component of the total ministry of the church, however poorly the contemporary church may be doing the job. There is no legitimate place for a semi-

---

[21]See Adams, *Christian Counselor's Manual,* pp. 71-93; and Jay E. Adams, *Lectures on Counseling* (Grand Rapids, Mich.: Zondervan, 1973), pp. 31ff. See extended discussion of Adams's views of psychology in chapter seven of David Powlison, "Competent to Counsel? The History of a Conservative Protestant Anti-Psychiatry Movement" (Ph.D. diss., University of Pennsylvania, 1996). Adams's transformationist attitude toward culture is most apparent in his attitude toward medicine. He is less interested in and more suspicious of the social sciences, but he never denies that we can learn from anyone anywhere. In *The Christian Counselor's Manual* (p. 80), he even cited a swami favorably!

[22]Jay E. Adams, *More than Redemption: A Theology of Christian Counseling* (Phillipsburg, N.J.: Presbyterian & Reformed, 1979), pp. ix-15; Jay E. Adams, "Counseling and the Sovereignty of God," *Journal of Biblical Counseling* 11, no. 2 (1993): 4-9.

Christian counseling profession to operate autonomously from ecclesiastical jurisdiction and in subordination to state jurisdiction.[23] The Lord whose gaze and will
the Bible reveals lays claim to the care of souls. If counseling is about understanding and resolving the human condition, if it deals with the real problems of real
people, if it ever mentions the name Jesus Christ, then it traffics in theology and
care for souls. It ought to express and come under the church's authority and
orthodoxy.[24]

Psychotherapists are "ordained" by the state, not by the church. From the
church's standpoint they are lay persons, not professionals. They attempt exceedingly significant and delicate work in people's lives in a dangerously autonomous
way, without guidance or checks from the church that has responsibility for those
people's lives. However sincere the beliefs and intentions of individual practitioners, however close the thought of particular individuals may be to biblical thinking,
the problem is structural. A hugely influential profession is operating by claiming
title to the most personally intimate and weighty aspects of caring for souls:
addressing identity confusion, disordered motivation, distortions of functional
beliefs, broken relationships, responses to suffering, compulsive sins and so on. In
effect, functional authority over the souls of Christ's sheep is being granted to a
semisecular, unaccountable parapastorate. This invites trouble.

Christian counseling is out of control doctrinally. It lacks regulative ideas and
regulative structures, though the Bible clearly gives both. The integration of psychology has provided carte blanche for "every man did what was right in his
own eyes" (Judg 17:6). One can arise as a leader in the Christian counseling
world with little more than an apparently sincere profession of faith, an

---

[23]It is not necessarily wrong for Christians to work within the secular mental health system if
they can do so without being forced to communicate false ideas, diagnostically and
prescriptively, to those they counsel. Sometimes in God's common grace, Christians are given
great freedom within an ostensibly secular setting. But Christians in such settings must realize
that when they are barred from mentioning sin and Christ, they can only describe problems,
but they cannot accurately diagnose them; they can only suggest the outward shell of
solutions, but they cannot get to the deep issues that plague the heart. Christians in such
settings are still free to know people, to love them and to provide various outward mercies,
but they are limited to being relatively superficial and moralistic in the content of their
counsel. Unfortunately, in my observation, well-meaning Christians in mental health settings
typically are far more profoundly socialized and enculturated than they realize. They fail to
recognize that they are working in a radioactive zone, and they absorb faulty diagnostic,
explanatory and treatment models without knowing that they have done so.
[24]I do not mean that there is not a carefully circumscribed place for parachurch, specialized
ministries. Parachurch ministries can often serve useful auxiliary roles beyond what a
particular local church might be able to do. But people working in parachurch ministries need
to remember that those ministries are barely legitimate and ought to exist only when they
genuinely and consciously serve the interests of the community whose mature functioning
will put them out of business. Autonomous psychotherapeutic professionalism competes,
rather than serves, those community interests.

advanced secular degree and authorship of a book.

We must face the question of professionalism, of the social structure for delivering counseling care. Creedal standards must also be formulated to guide and constrain the content and the theory of private counseling. For example, a counselor's motivation theory will align the entire interpretive endeavor toward truth or error. Christian counselors currently mediate every motivation theory, however contradictory to Scripture. Nothing besides the good faith and reputation of individuals is protecting evangelical psychotherapists—and pastoral counselors—from importing serious error into the church regarding care for souls. Sadly the flimsiness of current protections shows. The mind of the church about counseling is being shaped, and largely misshaped, by Christians of presumably good intentions who have their primary education and their professional identity outside of the church they claim to serve.

Psychotherapeutic professionalism is rooted in a defective institutional structure. Some leaders have expressed hope that they will eventually form a Christian version of state licensing boards so that Christians can qualify and accredit fellow Christian psychotherapists. But that would only bump the problem back a step. Those who claim expertise to teach and counsel others would still not be significantly accountable to the church and to orthodoxy for their faith and practice. To replicate an inherently defective social structure within the body of Christ is no solution.

What is. We have looked at what ought to be and at the failure of mental health professions to match up to the structures enjoined by the Bible. But what is the state of the church regarding care for souls? It is not enough for those who believe in COMPIN to proclaim, "The church, the church, the church!" That sounds good, and it has biblical warrant. But the church does not have institutional structures in place to deliver the goods. Functional autonomy and the potential for confusion and error are problems not only of mental health professionalism; within the church itself care for souls operates with almost identical autonomy and with almost identical potential for theological and practical trouble.

Let me give a concrete example of the problem. I am part of the Presbyterian Church in America (PCA). One of the leaders in our congregation, A. J., is pursuing ordination. In order to be ordained in the PCA, to be recognized as competent to lead the people of God pastorally, A. J. will be tested in many significant areas. His personal character must match the requirements for Christian maturity and seasoned fidelity to Christ. He must complete examinations in Bible knowledge, in theology proper (the study of God), in soteriology (the study of salvation), in exegesis (the ability to get at what the Bible says), in church history, in church government, and in preaching.

But what about care for souls and counseling? A. J. will not be examined on what he believes about and how he practices ministry to individuals. He will present no case study of a disintegrating marriage or of a church member who binges and purges. There is no tradition of wisdom for the care of souls into which A. J. has been systematically discipled. There is no institutional system—creedal, educational, credentialing or supervisory—to help him think as biblically about counseling as he does about preaching and evangelism. His views on counseling will be matters of opinion and conscience. He can believe what he wants to about counseling as long as he is able to profess the right answer to the technical theological question about sanctification.

Imagine, then, that A. J. must deal with a troubled church member named Roger. Roger is emotionally volatile; he is given to fits of rage, bouts of depression and pervasive restlessness and anxiety. His is estranged from others, and his work history is spotty. As a pastor in the PCA, A. J. could take any one of many fundamentally different approaches to Roger. Perhaps he could send Roger to a Minirth-Meier New Life Clinic, where he would be put on a course of Prozac and taught the principles of *Love Is a Choice*. Perhaps A. J. could counsel Roger according to Larry Crabb's late-1980s *Inside Out* model, teaching him to explore his pain and disappointment with primary caregivers in order to refocus his deep longings for relationship onto the Lord. Or he could send Roger to a secular psychiatrist to get Prozac to level his moods.

A. J. could attempt to identify demons of anger and cast them out of Roger. He could send Roger to a secular psychologist for cognitive-behavioral retooling that would inculcate stoic rationalism in Roger rather than leading him to a relationship with the living Savior. A. J. could give Roger a course of study in basic Christian doctrines or a concentrated dose of a particular doctrine or a Navigators 2:7 study. A. J. need not believe in counseling at all, but might assert that sitting under the preaching of the word, participating in corporate worship and cultivating a more consistent devotional life will be sufficient to cure what ails Roger. Or A. J. might seek to counsel Roger according to the thought forms and practices of biblical counseling as best he understands them, perhaps incorporating components of the various other approaches. In any case A. J. will choose what Roger will receive. And no one will teach, question, supervise or discipline A. J. about that choice.

Five needs. How can this problem be remedied? Let me identify five needs. First, the church needs wisdom in the face-to-face care of souls. We cannot practice, teach or regulate what we do not know how to do or think. Much of the plausibility of the VITEX position arises not from its intellectual characteristics but from the practical reality that the church has been poor in understanding and enabling the processes of change. We must articulate wisdom conceptually, we must incarnate it institutionally, and we must become skillful methodologically. Let us think institutionally: When people are troubled or troublesome, who will help them? Where will be the location of that aid? How long will it last? What forms of help will be offered? All ministry costs money. How will help be funded? I believe that the COMPIN position will sound increasingly plausible as mature biblical counseling characterizes the grassroots practice and structures of the church of Jesus Christ.

Second, we need creedal standards for the care of souls, or at least a widely recognized corpus of practical theological writing. A system of practical theology is something to which we can subscribe, toward which we can aim educationally, on the basis of which we can be supervised and challenged regarding our faith and practice. Our current understanding of faith and practice does not include views of counseling (except by extension and application from historical formulations that generalize about the nature of ministry, about human nature and about progressive sanctification). Our understanding of faith and practice must be extended to include personality theory, counseling methodology, the dynamics of change and delivery systems for the care of souls.

Third, we need educational institutions that are committed to the Bible's distinctive model for understanding persons and change. For many years seminaries taught virtually nothing substantive about progressive sanctification or the particulars of hands-on, case-wise, heart-searching, life-rearranging care for souls. In the past twenty years institutions have stampeded to create counseling programs and departments, but the results are very spotty in terms of consistent biblical thinking. Christian colleges typically have a department of psychology. But neither seminaries nor colleges typically teach concepts that significantly differ from those that are taught at secular institutions. Most institutions give a junior version of secular theory and methods or prepare students for graduate education in mental health fields or make students "ordainable" through state licensing entities. Few teach students how to understand and counsel people in ways that are harmonious with the Bible's vision for the care of souls.

Fourth, we need determination of proficiency in caring for souls to become part of the church's qualifying procedures that recognize fit candidates for ministry. Licensure, ordination and accreditation usually occur on two levels. One level, ordination, qualifies the pastoral leadership. For pastors skill in counseling individuals, couples and families must become as important as doctrinal fidelity and skill in speaking to crowds. The second level qualifies members of local churches to function in grassroots ministry under the authority of pastors and elders. Here is where most skilled counseling, whether formal or informal, will occur. Most psychotherapists are laypersons—not professionals—ecclesiastically, whatever their secular credentials. Are they willing to submit their theories, methods and structures to the church's professional oversight, to subscribe to a distinctly Christian model of persons and change?[25]

---

[25]The typical professional self-image of Christian mental health practitioners is that they are at the top of the pyramid of wisdom, competency and legitimacy; that pastors are at midlevel; and that laypersons are at the bottom. In the biblical image true pastors are at the top of the pyramid, and laypersons of all sorts function under the pastors' oversight. This biblical image must define our corporate task. Psychotherapeutic professionalism is at odds with that task, and each increment of progress in our task will mean a further repudiating and abandoning of professionalistic social structures as defective, redundant and counterproductive.

Fifth, we need ecclesiastically grounded supervisory structures for the care of souls. The secular mental health professions usually offer continuing education, case supervision and discipline for moral offenses (breach of trust in sexual, financial or confidentiality matters). The church has often offered continuing education in the form of books, seminars and doctoral programs, and it has often offered discipline for moral or doctrinal offenses. But the care of souls tends to drop through the cracks; it is an optional activity with optional beliefs and practices. Case supervision and case discussion are clear needs within local churches. Ecclesiastical supervision ought to extend to the faith and practice of the care of souls, both in local churches and at higher ecclesiastical levels. It matters what theories and ideas are being mediated to counselees. A secular psychotherapist can freely adopt any of many theoretical orientations—behavioral, cognitive, psychodynamic, existential, somatic and so on—or can hold theory loosely and can function multimodally. The church does not believe in such theoretical diversity but aims to refine its doctrine to cohere with the gaze of God revealed in the Bible.

Current ecclesiastical structures, functions, standards and competencies are far removed from what I am proposing. Perhaps it sounds ludicrous even to propose that the church get a grip on the care of souls. Counseling is renegade from God and truth within the culture; counseling is a runaway from the church within the church. But without such wisdom of doctrine, practice and social structure, we as the people of God court trouble. In the previous section we considered the prevalence of secular motivation theories in the care of souls. Such ideas would not last five minutes if they were examined in a decent systematic theology class on human nature. But the shoe fits on the other foot, too. The current state of most ecclesiastical forms, theoretical development and definitions of ministry for the care of souls would not last five minutes in a secular counseling class on how to go deep and hang in for the long haul with a troubled person. In the Bible we have a social model the secular world would kill for. It seamlessly joins specialized competency with community and peer resources. But in the extant church, both the defined specialists on the soul and the community of care often fall woefully short of biblical understanding and competency.

Those who rightly tout the centrality of the church face a dilemma because the church has few structures that facilitate and regulate the hands-on care of souls. What if the intellectual and structural defects of secularity among psychotherapists are mirrored by the intellectual and structural defects of religiosity among pastors and other Christian workers? It is fine to call Christians to practice and seek care of souls in submission to the local church. But the church needs to become something to come under.

The intellectual leading edge of VITEX—What things can we learn from the disciplines of psychology?—has masked a serious defect in the social structure for delivering counsel. To orient face-to-face care for soul toward the mental health professions is fundamentally, even disastrously, wrong-headed. At the same time the commitments of COMPIN—my own commitments—toward church-oriented counseling ministry are decades from significant institutional realization.

What must we do now? Jesus calls us to row our boat in the right direction, however far away the destination seems. He is committed to completing us together in the maturity of his wisdom. Ephesians 4 gives us both our modus operandi and our goal. I hope this very article is one small case of "speaking the truth in love" (Eph 4:15 NASB) in the direction of perfecting the collective wisdom, love and power of the people of God. We must each labor to disassemble autonomous professionalism rather than further assembling it. We must each labor to make our professed loyalty to the church a significant reality rather than a hollow profession of good intentions.

Conclusions

I am firmly committed to the point of view I have labeled COMPIN. I do not think that the VITEX epistemological priorities can equip us to understand and help people. We need our own robust, comprehensive theory—our own paradigm—to guide our interaction with the "human documents" entrusted to our care. We need our own paradigm to guide interaction with the secular models that "read" and attempt to "edit" those documents in ways significantly different from God's reading and editing. Our paradigm must become incarnate institutionally. We need a fresh practical theology of the care of souls. This is a corporate work in progress, an agenda, a presuppositional gaze that seeks to be faithful to the Word of our Redeemer. It coheres with orthodox theology about God, about persons and about the inworking and outworking of grace. It is distinctly different conceptually and structurally from the world's counseling models. It recognizes historical defects in the Bible-believing church's understanding of human nature and defects in its proposed remedies, but it does not let that recognition rationalize a flight from biblical resources.

I propose no return to pietism, moralism or exorcism, let alone sacerdotalism, doctrinalism or any other easy reassertion of a "spiritual" sector of life. I am not inviting us to inhabit some windowless, sectarian hovel. I have sought to describe a large house with wide-open doors and with picture windows revealing all of life, a habitation in which all God's people can thrive. I hold no bias against Christians who have mental health credentials and education, but they must grasp that there is no inherent bias in their favor either. And they must overcome a certain justifiable suspicion because their education and credentials have prepared them not for the care of souls but for a different care, a different wisdom.[26] When it comes to the care of souls, the question for Christian mental health professionals, just as for Christians who have ecclesiastical credentials and education, is: Do you think and

---

[26]Roberts's *Taking the Word to Heart* is provocative in this regard.

practice in fidelity to the mind of God? Both in the local church and at higher ecclesiastical levels, only biblically wise people should qualify to counsel other people.

Counseling ought to cohere intellectually and structurally with all other forms of the church's ministry: worship, preaching, teaching, discipleship, child rearing, friendship, evangelism, mercy works, missions and pastoral leadership. Counseling ought to operate within the same worldview and with the same agenda as all ministry for Christ. I hope that what I have proposed, general though it is, merits the adjectives *biblical* and *Christian*. My recommendations are a creation forged from the Word of God for our time and place, for our questions, for our tumults. I have attempted to sketch faithful answers to burning contemporary questions. They are questions about which the church stands at a crossroads. We cannot go just any way, or both ways, or every which way, except to our harm. We could go bad ways, lurching either into sectarianism or into compromise. But I hope that I have mapped the good way forward. I hope that I have described for our times nothing less than "the building up of the body of Christ; until we all attain to the unity of the faith, and of the knowledge of the Son of God" (Eph 4:12-13 NASB).

This essay began with a comment about the difficulty of finding and keeping one's bearings amid the tumults and animosities that gust during times of great revolution. It is worth closing on the note of clear confidence with which Paul closes 1 Thessalonians. One day we who love Christ will be collectively conformed to final wisdom: "May God himself, the God of peace, sanctify you through and through. . . . The one who calls you is faithful and he will do it" (1 Thess 5:23-24).

2

AN APOLOGETIC APOLOGIA FOR THE INTEGRATION OF PSYCHOLOGY & THEOLOGY

Stanton L. Jones

THIS CHAPTER IS A DEFENSE OF THE INTEGRATION OF PSYCHOLOGY AND CHRIStian faith, but it is an ambivalent defense because the utilization or incorporation of secular psychological thought into the life of the twentieth-century church has not had an unambiguously positive effect. One could even argue that on balance twentieth-century psychology has had more of a negative than a positive effect on the work of the church and the advance of the gospel. Nevertheless, my understanding of the issues does not allow me to mount anything less than a defense of integration, properly understood. Thus, this is an apologetic defense of integration, an apologetic apologia.

A critic of integration and defender of the traditional pastoral care methods of the church against any encroachment by psychology might well present the following illustrative scenario and challenge: A Christian man confessing adultery comes to a pastoral counselor, consumed with guilt and the resultant depression, anxiety and mental preoccupation. Where does the pastoral counselor turn for help? Is there any reason for the pastoral counselor to depart from the classic interventions of compassionate and humble listening; confrontation over sin; consolation, comfort and companionship in despair; receiving of confession, assurance of pardon, and reconstruction of that man's life in accord with proper virtues of self-control, fidelity, respect for life and so forth? Why depart from that tradition to offer what secular psychology would offer in such a case? I would argue, along with my friend David Powlison, that the pastoral counselor should not abandon that rich and biblically grounded tradition.[1]

---

[1]Such a response begs the question of whether psychology might have a minor contribution to make to proper understanding and intervention in such case. In such a case, though, the contribution will be minor.

But consider a contrasting scenario: The parents of a eighteen-month-old son note a stable pattern in their child's behavior. He rejects affection, has failed to develop language, and manifests bizarre, stereotypic behaviors such as rocking and repetitive self-stimulation. Because they have taken an undergraduate introductory psychology course, the parents know about childhood autism and about the behavioral treatment program for the disorder that was developed by O. Ivar Lovaas.[2]

Lovaas's treatment program is grounded in the explicitly materialistic and deterministic worldview of radical, Skinnerian behaviorism.[3] Yet it indisputably works better than any other approach. If their diagnosis of autism is accurate and their son does not receive such treatment, he faces a better than 90 percent likelihood of life-long institutionalization. With this treatment, however, their young son has a 50 percent chance of being indistinguishable from normal children by his teen years, and he has a less than 20 percent likelihood of life-long institutionalization. How in the name of compassion, reason and stewardship could a Christian willfully disregard such a treatment approach? How can a pastoral counselor who knows of Lovaas's treatment hide such knowledge from parents or counsel them to not avail themselves of the treatment? I would argue that you cannot, or that if you do you are either callous and hard of heart or you are a great fool, or both.

Some have decided, based on circumstances like those in the first scenario, to advocate a policy of utter and absolute nonengagement with secular psychology. But the second scenario, I would argue, invalidates an absolutistic stance against the cautious utilization of secular psychology. Logic tells us that any absolute claim is invalidated by a single contrary case. Just as the gay-affirming claim that change of the homosexual condition is impossible is invalidated by the demonstration of even a single case of change (and such cases abound),[4] this second scenario tells us that we may not responsibly hold the view that Christians are morally obligated to shun secular psychology. Some would try to wriggle out of the implications of this, arguing that such findings of clear effectiveness are rare in psychology, that such phenomena as autism are rare, but they would just be avoiding the point: the establishment of *any* circumstance in which utilization of secular psychology is right undermines the view that Christians are morally obligated to shun secular psychology.

We are then left with a *strategic* question: How do we handle the field of secular psychology appropriately, in a manner most honoring to God and most edifying to his body, the church? I call this a strategic question because it is question of wis-

---

[2]O. Ivar Lovaas, "Behavioral Treatment and Normal Educational and Intellectual Functioning in Young Autistic Children," *Journal of Consulting and Clinical Psychology* 55 (1987): 3-9.
[3]See Stanton L. Jones and Richard Butman, *Modern Psychotherapies: A Comprehensive Christian Appraisal* (Downers Grove, Ill.: InterVarsity Press, 1991).
[4]Stanton L. Jones and Mark A. Yarhouse, *Homosexuality: The Use of Scientific Research in the Church's Moral Debate* (Downers Grove, Ill.: InterVarsity Press, 2000).

dom and not of absolute prohibitions and easy answers.

The strategic concerns are considerable. I share the opinion of many critics of psychology that too many of our churches are benighted by their seduction into a primarily psychological conception of their mission as a *therapeutic* mission. They have lost their centeredness on Christ. They have lost a sense of the transcendent meaning of life, of the depth of our sinfulness and our need for grace and mercy, of our Lord's demand for our obedience, of God's claim on the transformation of our minds and hearts and behavior. These are grave losses, but all together they do not justify the utter abandonment of secular psychology; rather, they occasion a strategic response of caution, discretion and tentative engagement. Why don't they signal that we need to utterly abandon psychology? Because our God is a God of truth.

In this chapter I will outline some major theological choice points that will influence where we come out on these strategic decisions. I will presume, rather than argue, that these choice points are not matters of core or salvific doctrines (except as I specify otherwise), but are points on which Christians may legitimately disagree. I refuse to label as heroics those who disagree with me on these strategic matters.

In the body of this paper I will presume, rather than argue for, the following three orienting assertions:

■ First, psychology as a discipline has something of value to offer God's people.

■ Second, the nearly complete domination of people helping today by secular psychological understandings of the person is a regrettable state of affairs.

■ Third, in this difficult debate we should avoid simple dualisms (such as "you must choose Jesus or Freud") with all scrupulousness unless it can be clearly shown that they are valid dualisms. One example of a valid dualism is the assertion that salvation is by Christ and no other. Some dualisms are valid but require a nuanced understanding. Paul's admonition to beware of "philosophy and empty deceit, according to human tradition, according to the elemental spirits of the universe, and not according to Christ" (Colossians 2:8 NRSV) sets up a dualism, but certainly not one that is easily or necessarily understood to mandate nonenrollment in Wheaton College philosophy courses.

What then are the theological issues around which we must mold our strategic response to secular psychology?

Revelation

Question 1: Does Scripture provide an exhaustive account of what we need to know about helping people, and can we know anything of value from psychology to aid us in that task?

General versus special revelation. Romans 1 is the pivotal text for distinguishing between general and special revelation. Paul depicts God as allowing humanity, both redeemed and unredeemed, to see clearly enough to understand part of the truth. This testimony is consonant with the spirit of the proverbs, the creation narrative and other texts that communicate the presumption that with their native capacities humans can come to know rightly some things about their world and themselves. But it is critical to note that in this passage Paul seems to presume that general revelation, valid and valuable as far as it goes, is never clear or extensive enough to ground saving, or salvific, knowledge of God. According to Romans 1 the knowledge produced via general revelation is enough to convict, but it is not enough to save; we cannot reason ourselves to a saving knowledge of God.

Is nonsalvific knowledge trivial or antagonistic to true faith? Christian orthodoxy has never included an argument to that end. Anyone who has ever pursued any education has lived in a manner inconsistent with the claim that nonsalvific knowledge is antagonistic to faith. Does secular psychology, as a possible route to helpful general knowledge, necessarily make salvific claims and hence discredit itself? Most secular psychologists do not make such claims, and neither do Christians who wish to utilize secular psychology in the service of the church. Knowledge that comes by general revelation can be of enormous value, but we must make crucial decisions about how much to value it, and we must understand that it is never saving knowledge, never knowledge that heals the breach in our relationship with God.

The scope of special revelation. The scope of special revelation is a fear-inducing topic, but it must be faced directly. I trembled to find that I was being held up as one of the prototype integrationists in conflict with biblical counseling in Powlison's insightful writings.[5] In particular, Powlison critically highlighted a quote from *Modern Psychotherapies,* a book I wrote with Richard Butman, calling it one of the clearest statements of the limits of revelation. I want to stand by that quote:

> The Bible is thus an essential foundation for a Christian approach to psychotherapy and is very relevant to this field. Nevertheless, while the Bible provides us with life's most important and ultimate answers as well as the starting points for knowledge of the human condition, it is not an all-sufficient guide for the discipline of counseling. The Bible is inspired and precious, but it is also a revelation of limited scope, the main concern of which is religious in its presentation of God's redemptive plan for his people and the great doctrines of the faith. The Bible doesn't claim to reveal everything that human beings might want to know.[6]

To properly understand the point of this quote, it is crucial to understand what we mean by "the discipline of counseling." Throughout the book we clearly aimed toward Christian engagement in and with the mental health fields; we did not mean that the Bible is insufficient as a foundation for pastoral counsel. Our book might inform a thoughtful pastoral counselor, but not in the way it is meant to inform the

---

[5]David A. Powlison, "Competent to Counsel? The History of a Conservative Protestant Anti-Psychiatry Movement" (Ph.D. diss., University of Pennsylvania, 1996). This dissertation was in the History and Sociology of Science program.

[6]Jones and Butman, *Modern Psychotherapies,* p. 27.

Christian who is becoming a psychologist or psychiatrist.

When I write of the scope of special revelation, I am referring to the thorny problem captured in this simple question: For how many of humanity's disorders are we given clear and exhaustive guidance in Scripture for their resolution? How do we understand the scope of special revelation with regard to human ills? By way of analogy, the knowledge of how to extend life by fabricating insulin and administering it to diabetics is a great good. Yet this knowledge did not come directly via special revelation, and it is not necessary to salvation. God allowed untold millions of diabetics in ages past to die earlier than they would have if insulin had been available to them, and I trust that through God's sovereign will their ultimate states were justly and compassionately established even though they did not have the extended life they might be afforded today, and even though they had to endure sufferings they would not have to endure today in the West. I trust in this in light of such crucial passages as 2 Peter 1:3-4:

> His divine power has given us everything needed for life and godliness, through the knowledge of him who called us by his own glory and goodness. Thus he has given us, through these things, his precious and very great promises, so that through them you may escape from the corruption that is in the world because of lust, and may become participants of the divine nature.

This passage causes me to believe that Christian persons who in years past died prematurely by today's standards missed nothing essential to life and godliness. Yet I also believe—perhaps paradoxically—that it is a great good that we are able to extend such lives today.

The core point here is that the Scriptures present us with saving knowledge of our Lord and Savior, and of everything necessary for a fruitful and good life in him. Yet just as modern medicine produces something good that complements and supplements the saved life that God holds out to us in the Scriptures, so also may psychology. A person may struggle with periodic crippling depression like Martin Luther and Charles Spurgeon did and still bring great glory to God and live a full and good life. Nevertheless, it would be a great good to eradicate that depression. It is not a clear purpose of scripture to present solutions for every complex and debilitating psychological condition. Neither does secular psychology present many sure-fire cures, but it does represent a sustained attempt to shed light on these conditions through the application of fallen human wisdom.

Much of the debate we are engaged in today hinges on this one crucial question: Does the corpus of the canonical text of the Bible contain everything necessary to develop a systematized view of all counseling processes? The Scriptures were written to respond to the current concerns of real people, and the pastoral letters of the apostles, in particular, were written to meet the needs of real people. When I offer advice to a group of graduate students about how to develop a particular skill that I am deemed to manifest or at least to know something about, I sculpt the advice around a general case, but I do not mean that that advice can be extended to every case. My wife, Brenna, and I have written books on sex education in the Christian family,[7] and in them we omitted references to many populations and left many specialized cases untouched. The general validity of our advice is not thereby destroyed or falsified. In Scripture we have guidance that is inspired by God and is perfect; it is utterly inerrant in all that it teaches. But it is the question of what it teaches that is at issue.

Further, though the Scriptures were originally targeted to particular groups of people, its guidance is of enduring relevance to us today. I have staked my professional life on this claim of enduring relevance as I have argued for the continuing moral relevance of the ancient prohibitions on homosexual behavior.[8] But the prohibition on homosexual behavior leaves me largely uninformed about the causes of homosexual tendencies or about how I should respond beyond giving general guidance to stay celibate and pursue sanctification. I do not mean to demean or trivialize the Scriptures by making such a statement. I presume that our loving and good God gave us precisely the information he judged essential and sufficient for us to acknowledge our own sinfulness and to pursue holiness. But there is no virtue in stopping at that point if helpful knowledge on this and other pressing problems can be obtained by means of a cautious engagement with the field of psychology.

We must deal also with the issue of whether it is possible to develop a unified model of Christian counseling through diligent Scripture study and theological reflection. Mine has been cited as a primary example of the pessimistic view on this matter. I am pessimistic, but I want my view to be rightly understood. I am not at all pessimistic that compelling Christian models (plural) can be developed, nor am I pessimistic that a compelling outline of intervention can be developed from Scripture alone in numerous specific cases of pastoral care. Adultery should be dealt with by moral disapproval, confrontation over sin, repentance, absolution, and constructive improvement of the marriage; we do not need modern psychology to tell us that this is what is needed, and indeed much of modern psychology does not know it yet.

We can achieve Christian models, but not one single Christian model. As Christians we have historically failed corporately to arrive at one way of viewing anything beyond the most sketchy outline of core doctrine and moral teaching. The manner in which the various Christian or biblical counseling models tend to mutate and evolve over time suggests there is a family of possible Christian views on a great number of matters related to the counseling enterprise.

---

[7]See the five-book series God's Design for Sex (Colorado Springs, Colo.: NavPress, 1993, 1995).
[8]Stanton L. Jones, "The Loving Opposition: Speaking the Truth in a Climate of Hate," *Christianity Today* (July 19, 1993): 18-25; Jones and Yarhouse, *Homosexuality*.

We are more likely to achieve consensus when an issue in counseling is close to core doctrine (such as the need for repentance for sin), to an understanding of our common moral failings or to matters of general or common concern in the body of Christ (such as matters of the fundamental ordering of our life together in families and churches). But I think it pleased God to leave us with something to discover about the most effective way to deal with the disorders that are less common and less related to core doctrine.

I will use a brief example to make my point crystal clear. The Scriptures address the matter of anxiety in numerous places. Any Christian struggling with anxiety would be foolish not to make a systematic study of these passages and to live out the realities they prescribe. But I contest the claim that these verses constitute the entire corpus of knowledge needed for addressing every variant of anxiety. For the more extreme and debilitating conditions such as obsessive-compulsive disorder and posttraumatic stress disorder, the scriptural revelation forms the frame within which we engage in the best thinking we can muster to address the problem—and we may use psychological theory and research, as well as the physiological, to do this.

There is one further reason for tolerating some degree of latitude in our formulation of the Christian distinctiveness of our understanding of persons. I believe that Scripture teaches that we humans are rational, relational, made for dominion and purposeful work, sinful, lost, emotional, sexual, embodied, responsible, culpable and spiritual, and we exhibit a whole host of other characteristics as well. How I organize and prioritize these legitimate dimensions of humanness will shape in quite different ways my vision of what it means to be a human being and what it takes to correct disorder in my being.

If as a Christian scholar I am not always striving to bring my understanding of my subject matter into conformity with biblical revelation, I am an unfaithful servant and deserve admonishment for my error. But I am wary of an overscrupulosity that demands closure where closure is not ours to achieve. Trying to do Christian psychology involves difficulties rather like trying to do systematic theology does, but even more so—we are trying to make sense of the disparate elements of scriptural truth, presented in different genres in different ages by different authors addressing different situations and concerns. In doing so we necessarily go beyond scripture itself, and we necessarily, whether wittingly or unwittingly, add our own understandings to make it all gel.

Doing Christian psychology is a worthy task to take on, but we must always do it with caution, tentativeness and a scrupulous and recursive return to the fundamental Word that we have received from God—the Word of the Scriptures. Here I agree with many of my critics: Much of what passes for integration reflects slavish devotion to the fads of today's psychological thought and is little transformed by the eternal Word. That is a problem to be corrected, but it is not an invalidation of the venture.

Anthropology

Question 2: Are human beings, and is the sin that afflicts us, of such a nature that interventions grounded in human wisdom and effort can add anything constructive to our state?

The unitary character of human nature. Whether we accept the dualistic distinction between body and soul, the trichotomous distinction among body, soul and spirit, or some other delineation of the various components of human nature, our essential nature is found in the unity of those constituent elements. On this I agree with H. D. McDonald[9] and others. First Corinthians teaches a vitally important truth: that we will be reembodied at the end of time. The doctrine of the resurrection of the human body is a powerful testimony to our essentially unified nature.

This emphasis on unity ultimately defeats those attempts to partition intervention in human problems that argue that pastoral counsel deals with spiritual problems, psychology with emotional and mental problems, and medicine with physical problems. Sexual addiction is a spiritual, moral, emotional, behavioral and probably physiological disorder, and it should be dealt with in a unified fashion. I agree with many critics of the integrationist Christian psychotherapy movement that all human problems are spiritual and moral problems.[10] I believe that every failing I have is a moral and spiritual failing. Where those critics often lose me is when they fail to recognize that those problems are not therefore *only* moral and spiritual problems.

Our recognition of the fundamentally unified character of human existence does not, however, demand utterly unified intervention methods. Unity of impact in the life of a person receiving counsel can be achieved even if multiple professionals serve the same person, and even if the components of the problem are dealt with sequentially. We do not have to understand unity in an overly simplistic manner. This recognition gives me the freedom to intervene in the complex reality that the person presents to me without using a rigid formula—for example, a formula that dictates that I must love and support but not confront the person.

Often, intervention in one dimension of a problem opens up the possibility of dealing with other aspects of the problem without the need for the counselor to guide the process to make sure that all the "right" dimensions of the problem are dealt with. One of the last clients I saw in clinical practice was a man who began without prompting to consider his failings as a husband and father—after I had responded empathetically to his concerns about the incredible work stress he was under. But there are others who must be guided toward recognizing the unified nature of their problem by being confronted in some manner with its missing

---

[9]Hugh Dermot McDonald, *The Christian View of Man* (Westchester, Ill.: Crossway, 1982).
[10]This is as true for childhood autism as it is for an apparently random birth defect—even such problems are the result of the fallen order, and pose a spiritual challenge to the afflicted person and those around him or her.

dimensions, be they moral, spiritual, relational or behavioral.

Merely recognizing our unified nature begs the question of how best to address the complex unity that counselees present to us. We may not be able for any number of reasons to address every facet of their concern, but we must ensure that our interventions do not permanently blind them to the other aspects of their problem. Psychological interventions should not be used in a way that leaves counselees permanently blinded to the spiritual and moral dimensions of their problems, and "biblical counseling" interventions should not be used in a way that leaves counselees permanently blinded to the psychological and emotional dimensions of their problems.

Hamartiology.[11] How we understand sin is crucial. There are more complexities here than I can begin to unpack or understand. Sin is act and yet sin is state. Sin is a diagnosis of my moral state and yet it is an active agent and a purposive force in my life. Sin can be as narrow as a willful violation of a clear moral rule or as broad as missing the mark set for us all by Christ our Lord.

All truly Christian pastoral care and all truly Christian psychotherapy takes sin seriously. But what does taking sin seriously mean?

Penthouse magazine is not frequently an outlet for ecclesiastical news. Nevertheless, the December 1996 issue of the raucously pornographic men's magazine contained a documented exposé of a purported clerical homosexual and transvestite sex ring in the Episcopal Diocese of Long Island, New York. A number of clergy, the *Penthouse* article claimed, had regularly cruised Latin America, had lured young men to Long Island with promises of good jobs, and had then entrapped the men in sexual servitude, even involving them in group homosexual orgies in a parish church sanctuary. *Penthouse* printed irrefutable photographs of one priest engaging in homosexual activities with a young male partner.

In his official response to the *Penthouse* story, the accused priest denied many of the more grotesque allegations and the allegations of illegal activity.[12] He also repented of an interesting, uniquely psychological catalog of sins—of having let himself be used by others, of being self-deceived, of letting infatuation blind him to the reality of how nasty his young homosexual partner was, of not realizing that age-disparate relationships cannot work, of the indiscretion of letting himself be photographed having sex, and of embarrassing his church. Curiously, though, he never repented of sexual sin. When I read the priest's reply, it struck me that these patterns of experiencing infatuation, of being used, of being indiscreet and so forth were part of the constellation of sin afflicting this man. The problem with his reply was not that he identified these problems, but that in his presentation they were cut

---

[11]Hamartiology is the doctrines regarding and the systematic theological examination of the nature of sin.

[12]The statement was released by the Episcopal Diocese of Long Island via the Internet.

off from their essential connection to rebellion against God, to idolatry of the flesh, to disobedience and lasciviousness.

Many of the patterns that psychotherapists identify as central to human dysfunction are part of what it means to be enslaved to sin. But if those psychological understandings are not wedded to a deep understanding of our condition before a righteous and loving God, they fail to be fully diagnostic of our true condition. This takes me back to my core point about dualisms—it is not sin *or* low self-esteem, sin *or* narcissism, sin *or* disordered conditioned reactions. Rather, sin is manifested in and incorporates each of those possibilities and more.

In my own avoidance of conflict throughout much of my life I see an inadequate learning history, complicated dynamics in my relationship with my mother, skills deficits and many other problems. But I see all of those problems as sin. Behind and around all of those problems is an unwillingness to trust God, a rebellious embrace of dishonesty, and many other more traditional sins. It is not either-or. The way we formulate our understanding of the nature and meaning of sin will profoundly shape the way we view the possibility of integration. We must clarify how we understand sin, and we must do so in a way that well reflects the complexity of the human condition, that reflects at the deepest levels the core narrative of the Christian tradition regarding sin as moral failing and rebellion against God.

Gradations of good and evil. For evangelistic purposes we often refuse to make distinctions about the relative severity of sins. "Lust is as bad as fornication," we say; "and coveting is the same as theft." In terms of making an accurate diagnosis of our depravity, one sin *is* as bad as another. I do not need to commit theft to prove I am a thief; garden variety covetousness is all it takes. Any sin at all is sufficient to destroy my claim that I merit salvation from God.

But evangelism is not our only purpose, and if we insist rigidly that all sins are the same, we are at odds with our Protestant heritage or at least the Reformed part of it. The Westminster Larger Catechism makes distinctions among sins of different gravity based on visibility in the church and putative maturity of the person sinning, the degree of vulnerability of the persons sinned against, the degree of damage done and the number of people hurt, and a number of other factors.[13] In this view adultery is worse than lust, and adultery committed by an elder is worse than adultery committed by a new convert.

Bringing an unbeliever to a saving knowledge of Jesus Christ is the highest good we can aspire to, but it is not the only good. If certain persons are resistant at a certain time to coming to a saving knowledge of Christ, is it a good thing to act in such a way as to diminish in their lives the influence of violence, or substance abuse or hatred and bitterness? I would argue that it is. This is similar to asking whether it is good to bring medical advances as part of the missionary endeavor, or whether it is

---

[13]Questions 150 and 151.

good to challenge such evils as child sacrifice, widow burning, cannibalism or female circumcision. When we reduce substance abuse or alleviate the clinical depression that causes a woman to neglect her children, we are reducing the evil impact of sin in a person's life even when we do not bring that person to Christ.

The bondage of the will. Some people who are of a conservative theological persuasion state as a matter of fact that the unregenerate cannot change because their will is dead, enslaved to sin. Aside from the empirical reality that non-Christian people do sober up and snap out of depression every day, this assertion is worth a quick glance theologically.

What is the practical relevance of the Reformation doctrine of the bondage of the will? At its core the bondage of the will means that we are not free to choose the perfect good and thus achieve our own salvation. We cannot choose not to sin. The bondage of the will does not mean, however, that we must reject a priori the possibility that the unregenerate can change meaningfully. We can help the unregenerate to change meaningfully, and in a moment I will argue that this is a good thing.

On the other hand, Christian mental health workers must constantly guard against contributing to the illusion that temporal change, change in this life, however substantial it may be, somehow addresses the most meaningful questions in life. When I have counseled people who seem to have no spiritual quickening at all, I have finished my work with them by trying to balance a sense of celebration for the changes they have made with a strong message that any positive change is only a reminder of how broken they are and how much they need to address the ultimate questions in life. Indeed, once counselees have been strengthened by resolving immediate and painful concerns, I have charged or burdened them with a greater accountability to seek out those higher questions. Whether such messages are effective may be debatable, but psychotherapy does not have to result in cozy complacency that further distances the counselee from God.

Soteriology

Question 3: Are the tools of psychology that integrationists appropriate able to contribute to God's redemptive work in human life and in the world?

When we discuss soteriology, the doctrines related to salvation, we encounter thorny questions about God's redemptive activity among his people and in the world. I am thinking broadly in terms of the full scope of God's redemptive work in all of creation. There are two critical questions here: Is it legitimate to help believers with the tools of secular psychology as appropriated and modified by the thoughtful Christian integrationist? Is it legitimate to help those who are not Christians with those same tools?

I will start with two assertions. First, it is the Lord Jesus Christ who saves; salvation is to be found in and through him and no other. Second, in certain psychological systems competing claims of "salvation" (as understood within those systems) are made that contrast with the claims of the Christian gospel. Humanistic psychology and radical behaviorism function as comprehensive metaphysical systems that explain all of life. Pretensions to offer ultimate answers to ultimate concerns must be contested wherever we encounter them. Each grand personality and psychotherapy system is a mixed bag, a complicated amalgam of worldview, personality theory, practical wisdom, astute observation, empirical results and so forth. Wherever religious and other metaphysical claims are found in one of these systems, they do not obviate the possible utility or truthfulness of other claims of that system any more than the rabidly antireligious claims of an atheistic scientist render false all other claims and assertions he or she might make about scientific fact.

Religious and metaphysical claims warn us to be cautious, nothing more. Caution is critical, however. Mental health professionals who are immersed in profoundly secular ways of viewing persons, including themselves, and do not receive refreshment and sustenance from a deep and sustaining faith life can experience a steady erosion of the caution that keeps them centered on the gospel.

Allow me to pose two fundamental questions about healing, emotional healing in particular. First, is healing God's first priority? I am deeply concerned by a growing trend among believers. The American church is becoming consumed with the therapeutic relevance of everything. Christians are always asking "Will this make me feel better?" rather than "Is this true?" or "Will this bring God glory?" Some people who criticize this trend denigrate the importance of healing relative to the need for saving knowledge of Christ and sacrificial obedience to God's revealed will.

I share these concerns, but I'm not sure whether we are framing the question correctly when we ask whether healing is God's first priority. On the face of it the answer would appear to be no, but is our God limited to one interest in people? Such a view might be valid if salvation were merely the awarding of eternal life after this life, but it is more than that. Salvation involves the drying of every tear, the healing of every wound, the mending of every imperfection, and the establishment of true shalom—not the absence of conflict, but the presence of perfect well-being. If God is interested in all of those things on an eternal scale, why would he not be interested in them here and now? And if our eternal life begins here and now, why would his redemptive work not begin the healing and restoration process now? God's redemptive work is universal in scope; he aims to wipe away all traces of sin from his creation even though not all sin and imperfections will be eradicated in this life, as Paul's thorn in the flesh serves to remind us. So I am forced to conclude that healing is one of God's concerns.

This leads to the second question: Will temporal healing brought about by human intervention disrupt God's use of suffering in bringing people to Christ? In this area psychology should be appropriately criticized for its pragmatism, because God can be glorified in suffering, just as he can be glorified in weakness and persecution. But quietism toward suffering has never been understood as the first Christian response.

This is one point on which Christianity contrasts with Buddhism, which looks at suffering as illusory and ultimately insignificant. Even Paul implored the Lord to remove his thorn in the flesh, and he only stopped pleading when God spoke directly to him. We must be careful in drawing lessons from the healing work of Christ on earth. Still, if suffering were the primary means by which he draws people to himself, then it is remarkable that he offered healing often with no direct connection to transformation. Do we have any reason to think that individuals are able to turn to Christ in the midst of suffering in a way that they are not able to do as that suffering is alleviated? Suffering is not the only tool God uses to bring people to himself.[14]

Is psychology as a discipline or psychotherapy as a profession an appropriate venue for the "cure" of souls?[15] I would deny that it is, when the phrase *cure of souls* is taken literally. Psychotherapy may grow into the cure of souls, but it ceases be psychotherapy in the process. Still, this does not obviate the validity of the discipline of psychology or the profession of psychotherapy. Why? Because the proper goals of psychology and psychotherapy are too modest to qualify for the august title, "cure of souls."

What then are proper goals of psychological intervention? They include overcoming a pathological fear of men or women, defeating a crippling phobic reaction, de-escalating the patterns of violence in a marriage that is out of control, and other focal human concerns. In dealing with such problems, we should be contributing to the *care* of the soul, and in the process we may be clearing away the garbage that is forestalling the ultimate *cure* of that soul. People have come to me who want their souls cured, and I have typically disabused them of the notion that that is a goal of our psychotherapeutic work. I have directed them to their personal relationship with God, to their church, to a pastor. But I have told them as a fellow believer that I would be proud to help them overcome obstacles that impede God's work in their life and to encourage them as they strive for an ultimate cure of the soul.

But what about helping people who have no interest in the cure of their souls, who profess no faith whatsoever? Jay Adams says that "man cannot be helped in any fundamental sense apart from the gospel of Jesus Christ."[16] On the basis of this and

---

[14]I will not go into the unfathomable complexities in the question of suffering's role in the spiritual maturation of the individual and the church. It seems vital, however, to steer a middle path between two unacceptable extremes. On the one hand, it is unacceptable to argue that suffering is the tool that God uses so uniformly to bring his children to himself that we are forced to adopt complete passivity toward practical interventions to diminish suffering—the response that is historically more characteristic of Buddhists than of Christians. On the other hand, it is unacceptable to argue that suffering has no utility at all (or that suffering is not a valued tool that God uses often) for bringing God's people closer to himself.

[15]The topical focus of the conference that was the origin of the papers in this book was on the "cure of souls." To claim to be about the *cure* of souls would seem a slightly more audacious one than to be committed to the *care* of souls.

[16]Jay E. Adams, *Competent to Counsel* (Grand Rapids, Mich.: Baker, 1970), p. 68.

similar statements, I believed for years that Adams would never work with non-Christians. He seems profoundly ambivalent and hence confusing on this point, sounding in much of his work as if no significant work at all should be attempted with non-Christians. But just a few pages after this statement, he offers a remarkably good rationale for helping people who exhibit no responsiveness to the gospel. He follows the argument of the Westminster Confession that virtuous or improved behavior, though in accord with the virtues and commendatory behavior described in Scripture, does not please God and does not help a bit in terms of salvation. Nevertheless, he argues that when people are helped to change their actions for the better, they bring honor to God and do that which contributes to the triumph of the good in human life.[17]

In other words, improvements in the human condition that fall short of bringing salvation still contribute to God's glory. When we hold together a faltering marriage and resolve the bitterness ingrained there, when the alcoholic man curbs his drinking and eschews violence, when the panic-disordered individual is able to return to productive employment, in these situations and more God is honored and his good work advanced. Consequently, we might even have reason to suspect that his Holy Spirit is at work in the process.

Is it sufficient then to do good but never attempt to share directly the good news of salvation in Christ? David Powlison quotes two psychologists who stated that there is an "implicit evangel in psychotherapy. . . . The psychotherapist does not have to state explicitly, 'Believe in the Lord Jesus and you will be saved.' . . . The message of the gospel is carried by the grace with which the therapist treats his/her client and by the implicit value system of the therapist."[18] Like Powlison, I couldn't disagree more. To assert this is to argue that all good is gospel, and that is simply not the case. I can offer no more convincing refutation than to say that Jesus did not do it that way. This goes right back to the general revelation issue—it is good to do good, but doing good cannot bring salvation. Still, we must grapple with hard issues such as institutional constraints, the imposition of values, discernment and wisdom, transference and timing to discern if and when a psychotherapist should direct a client toward the ultimate curer of souls.

We are doing good when we help people, even when they are not brought to a saving relationship with Jesus Christ. If we truly care for the souls we are touching, however, we will want them to experience every good—and the highest good—in their lives, and thus we will directly or indirectly point them toward the Great Physician and to the church as a place of growth in grace.

Ecclesiology
Question 4: Is it legitimate for Christian persons to work outside of the ordained

---

[17]Ibid., pp. 69-73
[18]David Powlison, "Competent to Counsel?" p. 321.

ministry of the church in attempting to contribute positively to human welfare?

A recent student play at Wheaton College was a powerful and thought-provoking depiction of depravity and grace. An almost psychotic moment of self-mutilation was a critical turning point in the life of the main character, a woman of mean origins trying to escape a life of frustration, anger, rebellion and crime. In a fruitful discussion that followed the play, faculty and students talked about the fact that God is capable of using anything, *anything*, toward his redemptive ends. I thought back over the horrific things that God has used redemptively in the lives of clients I have worked with, and indeed in my own life. But I was troubled by the discussion, and it was not until hours later that I understood my discomfort. I realized that while God may use any means he chooses as a vehicle of his grace, that does not free us to recommend that a counselee can blithely choose any path in life and expect to encounter grace. The fact that God *may* infuse grace into the darkest moment should not form a basis for indifference toward our counselee's plan to move steadily into darkness. Grace may surprise us by appearing in unusual places, but we must not conduct our lives carelessly, thinking we will trip over and fall into grace no matter where we step.

The church is a locus of healing and of all of God's redemptive work. God loves the church. God may use any means to work his redemptive will, and yet we should expect him to work in special and unique ways through the ministry of the church. This means that we should labor to facilitate his redemptive work in the church.

I am therefore sympathetic and supportive of the desire to strengthen the effectiveness of pastors and lay-people involved in spiritual nurture in the church. Pastors may indeed learn something from the careful integrative work of Christian psychologists, counselors, psychiatrists, social workers and others. But who should guide and direct the pastoral work of the church? Its first resource should be deep learning from the Scriptures and from the historic teaching of the church. Further, I applaud a return to the pastoral counseling tradition of the great counselors of the church, such as that being led by Thomas Oden today.[19] While some conservative Christian critics may want to stamp out what we do here in the department of psychology at Wheaton College—and indeed in all integration efforts of this college—I do not want to stamp out any effort to better empower effective biblical counselors for the whole body of Christ.

I once talked with a trusted Christian friend and skilled psychologist about his gut reaction to the work of Neil Anderson of Freedom in Christ Ministries, which is committed to breaking bondage to sin and the work of Satan.[20] His response was simple. He said, "I pray for the effectiveness of his ministry and support his work. It doesn't work with everyone, however, and a fair number of my clients have walked away from his ministry without their core concerns being resolved. I rejoice in

[19]Thomas C. Oden, *The Care of Souls in the Classic Tradition* (Philadelphia: Fortress, 1984); see also Oden's four-book series Classical Pastoral Care (Grand Rapids, Mich.: Baker, 1995).
[20]One of Neil Anderson's works is *The Bondage Breaker* (Eugene, Ore.: Harvest House, 1990).

being able to help a fair number of those who walk away discouraged, doubting and deeply troubled by their failure in that ministry. I try to help them in a way that strengthens their faith and commitment to Christ." That colleague's response was a model of how psychology can serve as a helpful adjunct to the church rather than competing with and superseding the church.

Ecclesiology refers to our doctrines of the church—its proper ordering, staffing, governance and so forth. Jay Adams embraces a strict ecclesiology that leads him to be negative about nonordained counselors. I suppose it was on that basis that he told me during our only meeting, which lasted about one minute, to "drop out" of the study of clinical psychology.

The doctrine of the priesthood of all believers has been used to generate a lot of mischief over the centuries. I am cautious of stretching it too far. But if we may gain knowledge of the human condition through the Scriptures and also through fallen human reason, and if humans can be helped, genuinely helped, by human interventions that may be aided by the work of the Holy Spirit, then perhaps there is a legitimate role for Christians in the mental health fields, one in which they may legitimately see their work as ministry in the name of Christ—in a sincere and meaningful way, and not merely as a self-serving justification or marketing gloss.

I urge a modest role for psychology in direct partnership with the church, to work with the unusual problems, those that are intractable to the usual means of grace and growth that are available in the church. I also urge a role for Christian mental health professionals to work with people outside of the church, people who merit compassionate care by methods consistent with biblical revelation and administered by individuals who have their ultimate cure in mind and want to help move them toward that end. To fill either of these roles, we integrationists need to be scrupulous in our efforts to do all that we do in a manner consistent with God's Word, in a manner truly submitted to God for transformation and purification. Much of what the integrationists have produced in writing, speaking and practice is flawed, but I doubt that it is as distorted, as depraved, as some critics of psychology make it out to be.

Conclusion

There is a range of acceptable positions on these important issues. It is vital that we avoid paralyzing dualisms such as the "psychological way versus the spiritual way" or "the Bible or the couch." Critics of integrationism render a great service when they call those trying to do integration to be faithful to their first love. Our Lord demands and deserves our first loyalty, a loyalty that is pure, and the church should be strengthened and not weakened by the work of Christian mental health workers.[21]

---

[21]For further study see Gary Collins, *The Biblical Basis of Christian Counseling for People Helpers* (Colorado Springs, Colo.: NavPress, 1993), and also, to a lesser extent, Jones and Butman, *Modern Psychotherapies*.

3

LEAVING DEVELOPMENT BEHIND & BEGINNING OUR PILGRIMAGE

Brett Webb-Mitchell

Happy are the people whose strength is in you, whose hearts are set on the pilgrims'
way. (PS 84:5 AUTHOR'S TRANSLATION)

W ITH LITTLE FANFARE OR DISCUSSION, A SILENT AGREEMENT WAS MADE IN
the church that modern theories of human developmental psychology will determine many of the church's practices. The theories are but the most recent embodiment of the European Renaissance and Enlightenment, and they shape all matters
of practice in a congregation's life. Developmental theories inform our decisions
concerning who can or cannot perform certain roles in worship, and which people
can or cannot participate in church life. The theories arrange the entire format and
understanding of the what and how of education in the church.

Evidence of Human Developmental Psychologies in the Church

For an example of the way in which the developmental theories script our lives in
a congregation, consider Jenifer, now a seminarian, who has worshiped for most of
her life in the mainline Protestant church where she was baptized. She spent her
first years in the nursery during worship because the adults believed she wasn't old
enough to understand the abstract concepts of worship, like the concept of God. In
her preschool years Jenifer went to Sunday school, then to the first twenty minutes
of "big people's" worship, and then spent another forty minutes in children's
church, where she was left to color in her coloring books.

In third grade, having completed the necessary years in children's church, Jenifer was allowed to spend a full hour in worship. More important was the next milestone in third grade: she received her personalized Bible, which was presented to

her during a special ceremony during worship.

When Jenifer was in fifth grade, the next milestone was negotiated: she became an acolyte. She was at the age at which children are deemed capable of lighting and snuffing out candles in the sanctuary before and after worship. However, not all the children were given these Warholian fifteen minutes of fame as an acolyte. Jenifer writes:

> A friend of my same age, Tony, was held back in school, so he did not reach the acolyte phase until a year later. Tony was an acolyte a year after the rest of us had graduated to sitting on the back pew and we did not consider it "cool" for Tony to still be an acolyte. My sixth grade year I went to confirmation class during Sunday school because I had finally reached the stage in which I was ready to become a member of the church. I was rewarded with a nice certificate for completion of this stage.[1]

Jenifer survived the next few years in the church's educational program. She successfully negotiated the youth stage when she was old enough to meet in the church on Sunday nights for games with the youth group. She led worship on youth Sunday and attended administrative board meetings in the church as the youth representative. She was set free from the church's educational programs in college, just when her identity was being formed.

> College was a time to develop outside the church. I was pushed out of the church and thrown into young adulthood without support from the church. It was expected that I would get by just fine using the influence that the church had on my "developmental years." One could use the skills . . . learned during this time when [I] would [come] back to run the church as an adult.[2]

Jenifer's life in the church was narrated by the script of developmental psychology. It is the same script that is used by the modern American educational system, as well as other American institutions. In this case Jenifer was successful according to the developmental schema, while Tony, her friend, was not. Because he was held back a year in public school, he was held back a year in responsibilities in the church.

Why was Jenifer to spend time in children's church rather than adult worship when she was in preschool? We read this prescription in the United Methodist Church curriculum for ages three and four: "All children are individuals with their own names, identities, backgrounds and experiences. . . . All children need opportunities to explore the meaning of life, what God is like, and how persons relate to one another and to God." Below this description is written: "As you read this, think of each child in your class and how you can nurture his or her growth in a godly way." Then there is a list of various areas of development under each of several headings. Under "Physical Development" is "short attention spans"; under "Mental

---

[1] Jenifer Copeland, "Generic Development," final paper for Human Development in the Church at Duke Divinity School, Durham, N.C., May 6, 1997.
[2] Ibid.

Development" is "learning to identify colors, sizes and shapes (Piaget)"; under "Social Development" is "enjoying playing side by side with other children (Erikson)"; and under "Religious Development" is "Can develop a sense of belonging at church (Fowler)."[3]

While the above material is implicitly based on developmental theories, consider Kenneth Garland's article that is used by some Protestant churches. Garland describes a young person in the church through this Piagetian focus: "Teenagers are mentally creating what Piaget referred to as a 'Created Reality' against which all new and incoming information and data will be tested. They need guidance which will help them develop this 'Created Reality' from a Christian perspective." Later, using Erik Erikson's work, Garland writes about the primary "identity formation" issues facing many young people in their "psycho-social developmental tasks": "As Erikson saw it, the major task of the teenager is the formation of a secure ego identity which includes all of one's perceptions and feelings about self. Failure to reach this ego identity led to what Erikson called identity/self-diffusion, which means that the teenager has a lack of personal definition, commitment, and a loss of a sense of togetherness."[4]

When these developmental descriptors are placed in curricula used by many churches, developmental theory not only becomes a prescription for how children and youth are to behave, but also provides constructs for our perceptions of what a child or youth is.

If developmental psychologies determine who may or may not participate in many activities of a church, they also determine who may or may not participate in the very life of a church. For example, in a large Protestant mainline church, a mother, Sandra, wanted to attend worship along with her twelve-year-old son Steven, who was cognitively disabled with an IQ of 40, had cerebral palsy and a speech disorder, and was confined for much of the day in an adaptive wheel chair. Sandra brought Steven's Individualized Education Plan (IEP) to show us the behavioral goals for Steven in the wheelchair.

> When Sandra asked the Director of Christian Education (DCE) and I, then a youth minister, what should Steven do during worship, we gave Sandra an answer, simultaneously. I suggested that we move pews and try to arrange a place where Steven could better see and hear what was occurring during worship. Meanwhile, the DCE suggested that the nursery school would be a welcoming place for Steven. Sandra, hearing the discrepancy in our response, called a halt to our deliberations since we were confusing her. We had two different visions of what we would do, based solely on our assumptions about worship. For the DCE, worship was something someone

---

[3]M. Franklin Dotts, *Invitation: Bible Studies for Ages 3-4, Teacher Manual: Living as God's People* (Nashville: United Methodist Publishing House, 1993), p. 8.
[4]Kenneth Garland, "The Christian Education of Youth," in *Foundations of Ministry,* ed. Michael Anthony (Wheaton: Victor, 1992), p. 162.

did, leading one to consider what one gets out of worship. For me, the issue was that Steven is present *with* us in worship, not because of what he cannot do, but because of whose he is. Steven reminds us that we worship God because of whose we are: one of God's children. It is a matter of ontology.[5]

Each of these examples shows a way in which developmental theories not only are present in church but also, and more seriously, determine our practices in church, crafting the way we perceive one another and God. In the first story we see how developmental theory tells us who can and cannot participate in leadership of worship in a church. In the second story we see that developmental theories construct our understanding of one another, providing self-fulfilling prophecies regarding what is normal or abnormal in terms of what a person ought to be able to do and when, according to one's age and stage. In the third story developmental theories dictate not only who can lead in worship, but who can attend worship.

Human developmental theories are not theologically neutral, nor is their advancement in the life of the church necessarily a good for Christ's body. For according to these theories we are not first and foremost God's children, created in God's image. Instead, we become the sum of our many divided and disparate developmental categories. We are our psychosexual, cognitive, psychosocial, moral or faith developmental portrait, depending on which developmental theory is used. Each theory is inextricably connected to certain assumptions both about the self, our relationship with one another and the means by which we grow, and about the particular ends to which we are growing. These assumptions may be contrary to, if not antagonistic toward, the practices of the church.

This leads me to consider this question: What would the education mission of the church look like if we were to consider crafting Christians into Christ's pilgrim people rather than into isolated individuals struggling through the categories of the divided self as they become more mature?

In response to this question I will begin by critiquing theories of developmental psychology not as objective fact but as one story embodying certain philosophical ideals of the British and French Enlightenment movements, which are in many cases antithetical to the gospel. Second, I will examine how these theories promote an agenda that emphasizes individualism over community, opposition rather than obedience to authority, and emotivism and mental acuity over virtue and character, duty and responsibility. They dichotomize the mind-body relationship, with emphasis on a narrow definition of *mind,* instead of understanding that a person is a fusion of mind, body and spirit in Christ. These theories also promote a certain kind of natural religion over Christianity, reinforming a certain kind of universalist concern and claim in contrast to a particular context over specific lives. Third, I will consider what it would it look like to be Christ's pilgrim people. How do the prac-

---

[5]Brett Webb-Mitchell, *Unexpected Guests at God's Banquet* (New York: Crossroad, 1994), p. 8.

tices and the associated rhetoric of pilgrimage provide an alternative to developmental psychologies? Christians understand themselves to be on a pilgrimage, as Christ's body accompanied by Christ, in journey to Zion.

Traces of the Enlightenment in Developmental Psychologies

In critiquing developmental psychologies, I begin with this presumption: developmental psychologies are a storied system for constructing a human being. The system works well for those who believe in the universal, secular rationality of the modern world, whose telos is progress as constructed by social scientists. The system works less well for some Christians.

The idea that developmental psychologies are a *storied* system, a story among many stories, comes from Julian Rappaport, who rightly observes that a writer of stories (like Kafka) may say as much about alienation as would a social scientist (e.g., a psychologist). Both the storyteller and psychologist provide one way, not the only way, of viewing life. Rapport writes, "Does Shakespeare's literature say any less about us than Freud or Skinner? The choice [of] methods [for] understanding lies in a leap of faith to science, religion, art or some other system [or story]. Once the leap is made, each has its own logic. Today, most psychologists believe in science."[6] Developmental psychologies are but one storied system among many in understanding human beings and human growth.

What is the purpose of stories in general, of the storyteller, of the specific story that is told? First, the stories of a community not only hold us together, as Barry Lopez states. More importantly, the stories of a community like the church make it possible for people to know the good that we share in common. In other words, the primary story of a community gives the gathering a sense of unity and purpose. Alasdair MacIntyre argues that our very understanding of a "self" resides in the "unity of a narrative which links birth to life to death as narrative beginning to middle to end."[7] In addition, our understanding of life between birth and death is narrated by the very stories of a community in which we belong and have our being. Our conversations and our human actions embody the community's story.

Second, the very stories by which we dream, remember, anticipate, hope, despair, believe, doubt, plan, revise, criticize, construct, gossip about, learn, hate and love are not of our own making. MacIntyre writes that in stories we are both actor and coauthor. We do not design our own narratives. Rather, we play the leading role in one story, and we play subordinate roles in other stories, either constraining or being constrained by other actors.[8]

---

[6]Julian Rappaport, *Community Psychology* (New York: Holt, Rinehart & Winston, 1977), p. 28.
[7]Alasdair MacIntyre, *After Virtue: A Study in Moral Theory,* 2nd ed. (Notre Dame, Ind.: University of Notre Dame Press, 1984), p. 205.
[8]Ibid., pp. 211, 213.

In the story of developmental psychology, people like Freud, Piaget, Erikson, Kohlberg, Fowler and Lev Vygotsky, and the philosophers whom they read, like Plato, Comte, Descartes and Kant, are all storytellers. These storytellers designed powerful stories that diagram human action and are based on a philosophical and social movement, the Enlightenment. Neil Postman argues:

> Because this suggests that an author has given a unique interpretation to a set of human events, that he or she has supported his or her interpretation with examples in various forms, and that his or her interpretation cannot be proved or disproved but draws its appeal from the power of its language, the depth of its explanations, the relevance of its examples, and the credibility of its theme. And all of this has an identifiable moral purpose. The words "true" and "false" do not apply here in the sense that they are used in mathematics or science. For there is nothing universally or irrevocably true or false about these interpretations. There are no critical tests to confirm or falsify them. There are no postulates in which they are embedded. They are bound by time, by situation, and above all by the cultural prejudices of the researcher. Quite like a piece of fiction.[9]

And what is the story that is being told by these storytellers? This is the third concern: the story that is told. In this case, it is the story of developmental psychologies embodying the philosophical ideals of the Enlightenment. Some modern social scientists would have us believe that what they present is more than a story, indeed, that what they present is irrefutable knowledge based on objective facts and confirmed by empirical proof. But what they present is based on the ideals of the Enlightenment.

Our modern worldview is narrated by the norms of the eighteenth-century British and French Enlightenment. It was believed that individuals must make their own way in this world without the benefit of fixed referents or traditional philosophical or theological moorings. Ours is a world in which knowledge is continually changing, in which meaning can no longer be anchored in a specific teleological view of history.[10] Zygmunt Bauman writes that what we consider "modern" is fueled by the Enlightenment, which has made ours the era of unadulterated individualism that is limited solely for tolerance, has a minimalist morality and thwarts self-examination every time it comes up in conversation.[11]

I will focus on five characteristics of the Enlightenment that are embodied in the theories of developmental psychologists: individualism, opposition to authority, the centrality of the mind, natural religion and universalism.

Individualism. Prior to the Enlightenment, Renaissance humanism gave us the individual. No longer was a person connected to a village, to its past or its tradi-

---

[9]Neil Postman, *Conscientious Objections* (New York: Vintage, 1992), p. 13.
[10]Jean-François Lyotard and Fredric Jameson, in Stanley Aronowitz and Henri Giroux, *Postmodern Education* (Minneapolis: University of Minnesota Press, 1991), p. 60.
[11]Zygmunt Bauman, *Postmodern Ethics* (Cambridge: Blackwell, 1993), pp. 2-3.

tions. Each person was disconnected from a community greater than herself, and her idea about who she was came from the particular social identity that she inherited.[12] We were now unique individuals, able to think for ourselves, disconnected from the past and free to choose which circumstances we would be slave to. Our lives no longer needed to follow anyone else's script. We were free to do as we chose. A man was bold enough to be himself.

According to this new view of a human being, in which I am the center of the universe where I live, the individual does not exist purely for God's sake, or for the sake of others for that matter. MacIntyre captures the bravura of this individualistic stance well. He observes one social feature of individualism in the new understanding: "I may biologically be my father's son; but I cannot be held responsible for what he did unless I choose implicitly or explicitly to assume such responsibility."[13] We can delight in the life that we are living at the moment, in the existential here and now, and we are able to disentangle ourselves from past and future. No longer are parameters that are set by a community necessary. The sky is the limit of human achievement.

The subject of most developmental psychologies is the self as primarily an individual tangentially interrelated with that individual's context.[14] From Piaget to Fowler the author of life is the individual who pokes and prods the context in which she lives. Fowler describes this kind of individualism well in his "Individualtive-Reflective Faith" stage, in which the young person, all alone, must resolve the tension between being an individual and being defined by a group.[15] This individual is the primary actor, the solitary meaning maker who acts on the world with the purpose of keeping a certain balance, or equilibrium, with outside forces.

For Piaget, the individual maintains equilibrium through the formulaic machinations of adaptation, which equals assimilation plus accommodation. This structure of adaptation makes it possible for us to grow or develop. Even the word *develop* is taken from the modern biological sciences; we are like a plant that grows or evolves over time.[16] According to Piaget, such growth in the individual is a result of the individual negotiating several forces independently: "Development = Physical maturation + Experience with the physical environment + Social experience + Equilibration."[17] These four forces work on me, causing me, the individual, to

[12]MacIntyre, *After Virtue*, p. 220.
[13]Ibid.
[14]I understand that for Vygotsky and Luria culture is of equal importance with the growth of the child.
[15]James Fowler, *Stages of Faith* (San Francisco: Harper & Row, 1980), p. 182.
[16]Sharon Parks, herself a developmental psychologist, criticizes human developmental theory because of its concept of human beings growing like plants (see Mary Boys, *Educating in Faith* [San Francisco: Harper & Row, 1989], p. 174).
[17]Patricia Miller, *Theories of Developmental Psychology*, 3rd ed. (New York: W. H. Freeman, 1993), p. 75.

grow—whether I like it or not. After all, this is a social Darwinistic model: survival of the fittest, adapt or die.

Opposition to authority. MacIntyre understands rightly that in this modern construct of individualism we live under the claim that we must be free from moral responsibility to others to be truly human: "I may legally be a citizen of a certain country; but I cannot be held responsible for what my country does or has done unless I choose implicitly or explicitly to assume such responsibility." Thus, because I am a modern white male, the slavery of the nineteenth century does not involve me. I never owned a slave.[18] Being free from my country's legacy, I am able to stand in opposition to my country in the present as well. I have responsibility for knowing its story more fully before I oppose its current action. This is, after all, a matter of personal choice or preference.

This opposition to authority is largely based on emotivistic appeals. MacIntyre defines *emotivism* as the belief that all moral judgments are nothing more and nothing less than expressions of preference, "expressions of attitude or feeling, insofar as they are moral or evaluative in character." Moral judgments are based on how I feel or what I like in relationship to other people and events. What is good or bad, right or wrong, is dependent solely on what I, the individual, feel is good or bad, right or wrong.[19] Emotivism underwrites our capacity to oppose authority that we don't like, to oppose the authority of someone who does something we do not feel good about. For example, most theories based on developmental psychology pigeonhole the people they call adolescents: adolescents are people who rebel against the authority of the parent or guardian at a certain stage as a normal part of development. Mary Pipher writes:

> Adolescence is currently scripted in a way that builds in conflict between teenagers and their parents. Conflict occurs when parents try to protect daughters who are trying to be independent in ways that are dangerous. Teenagers are under great social pressure to abandon their families, to be accepted by peer culture and to be autonomous individuals.
>
> Girls this age often no longer want to be touched by their parents. They grimace and pull away with a look of alarm when their parents approach. . . . It's a way of stating "I need space to be my own person."[20]

The centrality of the mind. This individual who has the capacity for opposing authority, whether the authority of the state or authority in the home, has certain inherent rational abilities that lead to a clear line of reasoning. The Enlightenment in France was celebrated as the Age of Reason. Most of the philosophers of the Enlightenment had great faith in human reason, and human reason was always

---

[18]MacIntyre, *After Virtue*, p. 220.
[19]Ibid., p. 12.
[20]Mary Pipher, *Reviving Ophelia: Saving the Selves of Adolescent Girls* (New York: Ballantine, 1994), p. 65.

proved correct by the new sciences, including the social sciences.

The faculty responsible for the heightened awareness of reason and rationality was the mind. Descartes gave expression to a dualistic understanding of body and soul that continues to bind our lives. He assumed that "ego" is the mind by which I am what I am, and by which I know that I am distinct and exist only in a tenuous relationship with the body. Our minds within the body serve us like the pilot of a vessel. Dale Martin writes that the mind and body are joined together in a certain unity, otherwise the mind would not be able to experience pain. But all of these sensations of hunger, thirst and pain are nothing more than confused modes of thinking arising from the union or fusion of mind and body. Therefore, on the one side there is body, matter, nature and the physical. On the other side there is soul or mind, the supernatural and the spiritual or psychological. There has been a complete separation of mind from body, a mechanical view of the body and volitional view of the mind, that has served science, both natural and social, to this day.[21]

Roughly, the focus of Jean Piaget's principal scientific concern is the theoretical and experimental investigation of the qualitative development of intellectual or cognitive structures. His study of intelligence, or cognitive development, set apart Piaget's work from that of other child psychologists. Furthermore, understanding the development or ontogenetic change of one's mental structure is valuable in its own right.[22] A person's intelligence is constantly being transformed, "yet within the schema of equilibrium, during early childhood from simple sensorimotor or practical intelligence to thought itself . . . all of reality is constructed with the self as the model."[23] For Piaget our entire lives are dependent on both the structure and the process of cognitive development. The cognitive processes are the functional invariants: organization and adaptation. Patricia Miller writes that these invariants function in essentially the same way throughout development, "but their relationship changes. For example, assimilation and accommodation become both more differentiated and more in balance, (via equilibration)."[24] This is all performed by the mind.

Natural religion. With the mind the individual could now prove, through various philosophical arguments, mathematical formulations or computer programs, the existence of God.[25] Questions about the existence of God could be answered through reason rather than through dependence on biblical descriptions of faith. A

---

[21]Dale Martin, *The Corinthian Body* (unpublished manuscript, Duke University, Durham, N.C.), p. 6.

[22]John Flavell, *The Developmental Psychology of Jean Piaget* (New York: D. Van Nostrand, 1963), pp. 15-16.

[23]Jean Piaget and David Elkind, *Six Psychological Studies* (New York: Random House, 1968), pp. 7, 22, 29.

[24]Miller, *Theories of Developmental Psychology,* p. 81.

[25]For an entertaining novel that explores this assumption, read John Updike's *Roger's Version* (New York: Knopf, 1986).

Pelagian strain has emerged in our relationship to God because we are now the initiators of the inquisition, and God is, in the words of C. S. Lewis, waiting in the dock for our judgment. God has become a philosophical proof to be figured out and controlled rather than the acknowledged Lord of creation.

According to the philosophers of the Enlightenment, Christianity needed to be stripped of irrational dogmas or doctrines, of so-called myths and superstitions. God was to be known through nature and through natural, rational laws, not through the mysterious and supernatural. Deism emerged: God was given credit for creating the world, or worlds, ages ago, but was not readily known or needed in the present.

In developmental psychologies the God of Abraham and Sarah, of Jesus and Paul, is often reduced to a psychological phenomenon or to a figment of our imagination according to object relations theory. Ana-Maria Rizzuto writes that Sigmund Freud "charmingly describes how he found himself reversing the well-known text in Genesis, 'God created man in his own image,' into 'Man created God in his.' "[26] For Piaget, God is a projection of a child's understanding of the parent. "The child begins by attributing the distinctive qualities of the divinity—especially omniscience and almightiness—to his parents and thence to men in general. Then, as he discovers the limits of human capacity, he transfers to God, of whom he learns in his religious instruction, the qualities which he learns to deny to men."[27]

Erik Erikson did not focus on God, but he did discuss religion:

> The parental faith which supports the trust emerging in the newborn, has throughout history sought its institutional safeguard (and on occasion, found its greatest enemy) in organized religion. Trust born of care is, in fact, the touchstone of the *actuality* of a given religion. All religions have in common the periodical childlike surrender to a Provider or providers who dispense earthly fortune as well as spiritual health; some demonstration of man's smallness by way of reduced posture and humble gesture; the admission in prayer and song of misdeed, of misthoughts, and of evil intentions; fervent appeal for inner unification by divine guidance; and finally, the insight that individual trust must become a common faith, individual mistrust a commonly formulated evil, while the individual's restoration must become part of the ritual practice of many, and must become a sign of trustworthiness in the community.[28]

While Marx branded religion as opium for the masses, developmental psychologies have reduced religion, including Christianity, to free, voluntary social movements that are practical sources of support for what people do. Or as Freud said in twisting Genesis 1:27, we create God in the image of ourselves. Christianity becomes one more religious system, relative to and equal to any other world reli-

---

[26]Ana-Maria Rizzuto, *The Birth of the Living God* (Chicago: University of Chicago Press, 1979), p. 13.

[27]Jean Piaget, *The Child's Conception of the World* (Totowa, N.J.: Littlefield, Adams, 1979), p. 268.

[28]Erik Erikson, *Childhood and Society,* 2nd ed. (New York: W. W. Norton, 1963), pp. 250-51.

gion like Hinduism and Islam, part of a grand scheme that is narrating and thus constructing what it means to be a human being in light of belief in some mythological higher source. For religion is created out of our natural need for a power greater than our own.

Universalism. Universalism claims that it is the nature of humans that we all create religions, with gods or goddesses who tell us what to do and what not to do.

Universalism is a perception of certain features of the world, not of the world itself. Stanley Aronowitz and Henri Giroux, citing the work of Jean-François Lyotard, note that modernity is the acceptance of one, grand, universal narrative that embraces a metaphysical philosophy, a universal rule of reason or logic, as a foundation for all human affairs.[29] Bauman described this universal rule as "the order of things that would replace slavery to passions with the autonomy of rational beings, superstition and ignorance with truth, tribulations of the drifting plankton with self-made and thoroughly monitored history-by-design."[30]

Assuming that there is a universal rule of reason, of logic, by which all human beings operate, Aronowitz and Giroux point out that this rule informs our educational theory and practice (e.g., developmental psychology).[31] For example, developmental psychologies have a universal feel because the modern world has articulated them as universal. It appears that everyone has it, does it and is doing it.

Consider the feeling of universalism in something called a culture, which is key to Lev Vygotsky's contextual approach to human development. *Culture* is one of those terms that everyone has a feeling is universally understood in the same way. Vygotsky advanced the idea that a child, the people around him and the social context he is in are somehow fused in an activity: "The social-cultural-historical context defines and shapes any particular child and his experience. At the same time, children affect their contexts."[32] This is unlike many other theories of human development that focus on the child or the adult alone, and that look for causes of behavioral change within the individual rather than in the context. Vygotsky directs our attention to the fusion of child and culture.

Yet here is the problem: while other developmental psychologies promote universal categories of a child and of developmental stages, Vygotsky does a similar thing with culture and context. For example, Urie Bronfenbrenner, a student of Vygotsky, proposes an ecological psychology that depicts our environment as a system of nested structures, from immediate face-to-face interaction with people—a "microsystem"—to an all-encompassing cultural belief system—the "macrosystem," which is an umbrella to microsystems, mesasystems and exo-

---

[29]Aronowitz and Giroux, *Postmodern Education*, p. 60.
[30]Zygmunt Bauman, *Life in Fragments* (Cambridge: Blackwell, 1995), p. 24.
[31]Aronowitz and Giroux, *Postmodern Education*, pp. 57-69.
[32]Miller, *Theories of Developmental Psychology,* p. 375.

systems.[33] Vygotsky and Bronfenbrenner define culture as "shared beliefs, values, knowledge skills, structured relationships, ways of doing things (customs), and symbol systems (such as spoken and written language). Culture also includes physical settings (such as buildings and highways) and objects (such as tools, computers, television, and art)."[34] This definition of culture is a universal declaration. One can take this generalized, universal description and apply it to any context and call it a culture. The church is a culture; the synagogue is a culture; the temple is a culture; the farmer's market in Carrboro, North Carolina, is a culture. We live in and among many cultures.

This is the story of developmental psychologies, which is underwritten by and is an embodiment of the narrative of the Enlightenment. Developmental psychologists share in common the universal modernist ideals that stress the capacity of individuals to think critically with their minds, to be their own authority figures, and to choose when to oppose or agree with those in authority, depending on their feelings.

Herein lies a critical problem for Christians. At best, developmental psychologies relegate the practices of the church, in which we know God, to the role of serving human beings in achieving various stages of development. At worst, the church is a relic of a bygone era. We are known in this world by our stage of development. It is clear that because educational theory and practice are strongly wedded to the language of modernism, the focus is on the individual to think critically, to act responsibly socially, making the world of the Enlightenment a place of reason and freedom, or in the words of B. F. Skinner, a world beyond freedom and dignity in which God and the culture of the church are ancillary players.

But what if the church is not a relic of a bygone era, an ancillary player or merely a culture? Continuing the argument that developmental psychology is just one story and taking Rappaport's argument seriously—that there are ways of constructing our understanding of reality and of being human other than developmental theory—I now propose another story. This one is based on the gospel story, in which the rhetoric and practices of the church, like pilgrimage, matter.

The Possibility of Pilgrimage

Why pilgrimage? The practice of pilgrimage has roots in the Old and New Testaments, as well as in the story of Christians as a pilgrim people. In the Old Testament, in Exodus, we read that the people of Israel were taken out of slavery and set upon a pilgrimage, a sojourn, for forty years, wandering in the wilderness toward a "land of milk and honey." The psalmist writes: "Happy are the people

---

[33]See Urie Bronfenbrenner, *The Ecology of Human Development* (Cambridge, Mass.: Harvard University Press, 1979).

[34]Miller, *Theories of Developmental Psychology,* p. 377.

whose strength is in you, whose hearts are set on the pilgrims' way" (Ps 84:5 my translation).

In the New Testament, in Luke 2:41, we read that the children of Israel would take pilgrimages and travel to holy places to worship Yahweh during Passover. The writer of 1 Peter, concerned about the practices of the chosen people as pilgrims, admonishes them: "Beloved, I urge you as aliens and exiles to abstain from the desires of the flesh that wage war against the soul" (1 Pet 2:11).

In the days of the early church, people went on pilgrimages because of the possibility of incarnation, the hope of witnessing the physical presence of Christ in a present time and place. And people still go on pilgrimages today for that reason.[35] Victor and Edith Turner outline five characteristics of medieval Christian pilgrimages. First, it is believed that all pilgrimages were made to places where miracles had once happened, were continuing to happen and might happen again. The wine had turned into blood in Ovieto, Italy; visions of and healings by the Virgin Mary had taken place at Lourdes; a local patron saint had appeared at a nearby chapel or grotto. People understood that going to a cathedral or shrine was their hotline to God.[36]

> What is interesting is that the pilgrim couldn't make the assumption that a miracle *would*, of course, occur. The pilgrim was *not* to expect any corporeal remedy to a problem. However, if a miracle did occur, it was attributed to God's grace, through the mediation of the pilgrim's devoted saint. And there was a panoply of saints that one could turn to in hopes of obtaining a miracle.[37]

Second, the purpose of the pilgrimage was to get out and away from a place in which there were the occasions of sin that make up so much of the Christian's experience of life. In John Bunyan's *Pilgrim's Progress*, the pilgrim, "Christian," is leaving the City of Destruction for the gate that leads to the Celestial City because the City of Destruction is the place in which one will "sink lower than the Grave, into a place that burns with Fire and Brimstone."[38] Chaucer records tales of medieval pilgrims, simple people who traveled from the ends of every shire in England, "to see the holy, blissful martyr [St. Thomas à Becket], who helped them when they were sick."[39]

---

[35]F. L. Cross and E. A. Livingstone, *The Oxford Dictionary of the Christian Church* (New York: Oxford University Press, 1978), p. 1091.

[36]Victor Turner, and Edith Turner, *Image and Pilgrimage in Christian Culture* (New York: Columbia University Press, 1978).

[37]In Frank McCourt's autobiography *Angela's Ashes* he tells the story of his mother's birth on New Year's Day. The saints are asked to be present in this most difficult delivery. The faithful begin with St. Gerard Majella, patron saint of expectant mothers, but the baby does not come quickly enough. They switch to praying to St. Ann, patron saint of difficult labors, but still the child does not emerge. Then they pray to St. Jude, patron saint of desperate cases, who finally helps (New York: Scribner, 1996), p. 14.

[38]John Bunyan, *The Pilgrim's Progress* (New York: Penguin, 1987), p. 12.

[39]Geoffrey Chaucer, *Canterbury Tales* (New York: Bantam, 1982), p. 3.

Because pilgrims were leaving places in which they had occasion to sin and going to another place in hopes of a miracle, namely salvation, they understood that the pilgrimage was not an escape into enjoyment. This leads to the third characteristic of medieval pilgrimage: in the hazards met along the way pilgrims were performing a kind of penance for their sins. Hazards like robbers and fresh, unpredictable troubles represented and released the pilgrim from the ills of sins associated with home. The journey was one in which the Almighty tested one's mettle or character. To this end, the pilgrim was an initiate entering into a new, deeper level of existence, more so than the pilgrim had known or been accustomed to in everyday life. After completing the pilgrimage, a person was not expected to be the same as before. To this end, the journey is the thing (i.e., the ultimate, not penultimate, experience).

Fourth, the pilgrim was never alone. Knowledge of the pilgrimage site was shared by pilgrims who have already been to the place. Along the journey, the pilgrim met people, whether during times of rest or on the march itself. Chaucer's pilgrims in *Canterbury Tales* are a community of Christians who go together on the pilgrimage.

Fifth, pilgrims left a certain place and went to a certain destination, though they may not have known what to expect at the point of arrival. There was a telos to the journey, a purpose, an aim. For Moses, it was Canaan; for Bunyan's pilgrim it was the "City beyond the Wicket Gate." For Chaucer's pilgrims it was Canterbury Cathedral, to worship at the place where St. Thomas à Becket was martyred. Pilgrimage was an act of an entire community or of a lone traveler in search of community. Pilgrims sought a relationship with God in which they would be irrevocably changed.

Human developmental psychologics present a universal paradigm for charting how a person will change over time, becoming more of a disconnected self or individual in a multistage sequence that is determined by the story of modernity and disregards context. Christian pilgrimage is different from the developmental psychology path because it takes place on a particular pathway among a particular community that is greater and older than an individual and is constituted and guided by a specific story, the gospel of God. In Christian pilgrimage one strives to be less oneself and to be more like Christ, who is our reason for living. In order to proceed on the journey in and as Christ's community, in a life together, we will be called to be obedient to an authority that is greater than ourselves, namely God in Christ. Along the journey we grow in our understanding of what it means to be the mind, body and spirit of and in Christ. God, who created us, is our alpha and omega. His Spirit is with us in the beginning and in the end of our journey, in our pilgrimage with and in Christ. Every step on our journey adds to what we know about whose we are. Every step reveals that there is no end to what we know, or what is known, about God and about our lives in God.

Five characteristics of Christian pilgrimage shape our daily lives as Christians. To help us to understand better how Christian pilgrimage is different from the path of developmental psychologies, I will discuss those characteristics using Scripture, the stories of Dorothy Day and St. Augustine, *Pilgrim's Progress*, and Wendell Berry's essays.

Community and its story. While developmental psychologies embrace the rhetoric of individualism, pilgrimage embraces the practice of community. All pilgrimages involve a community, whether the pilgrim is leaving from a community of people, is traveling with a community, or is meeting others on the way, thus creating or discovering a new community. Those who do not participate in the pilgrimage know community in the sharing of stories from the pilgrimage. They discover that they have experiences in common with the pilgrims. As Christians we know whose we are because the community of Christian faith into which we are born and baptized tells us first. And in the Eucharist, as we are "remembered" into the body, we are reminded that we are members of the one body of Christ (Rom 12:5).

In the body of Christ I am continually reminded that I am no longer a self; rather, in the words of Paul, I am in Christ. For the old self has died, and I have risen with and am in Christ. There is no more self. Because I am in Christ, I am inextricably part of and in relationship to others who make me a brother, a father, an uncle, a husband, a friend, a pastor and a teacher. The web of relationships and its accompanying roles and functions names, shapes, disturbs and quiets life around me. To Richard Rodriguez, in Christ's body I am related to the Puritans and the Roman Catholics of the eighteenth-century American colonies, to the runaway slaves and the slave owner, the suffragettes of the nineteenth century. I am related to people whom I have never seen and whose presence I know merely as a "cloud of witnesses." We are but the most recent beneficiaries, the latest link in the chain of people who preceded us.[40]

This sense of the community's claims on my life is best articulated in the baptismal vow which initiated me into the practices of the living community of Christian faith: for in baptism, I claim that Jesus knows me first, and through Jesus, do I know myself. According to the sacrament of baptism of the Presbyterian Church (USA): "You are a child of the covenant, you have been sealed by the Holy Spirit in Baptism, and marked as Christ's own forever. . . . You have been received into the one holy catholic and apostolic church through baptism. God has made you a member of the household of God, to share with us in the priesthood of Christ."[41] No longer does a person *have* a life; one is now understood to be part of a life that is greater than oneself, namely, the life of Christ in the household of God, which extends beyond our limited knowing.

---

[40]Richard Rodriguez, "On Borders and Belonging: A Conversation with Richard Rodriguez," *Utne Reader* (March-April, 1995): 78.

[41]*Book of Common Worship* (Louisville: Westminster John Knox, 1993), p. 414.

John Calvin writes that we grow into our understanding of baptism, rather than having already received an explanation of it and having comprehended it. "If they happen to grow to an age at which they can be taught the truth of baptism, they shall be fired with greater zeal for renewal, from learning that they were given the token of it in their first infancy in order that they might meditate on it throughout life."[42] In one of the prayers that may be prayed at a funeral, a service of witness to the resurrection, we say, "We thank you for your servant, whose baptism is now complete in death."[43]

The Eucharist reminds us of what was publicly proclaimed at our baptism. Consider the story of Dorothy Day, in which individualism was conquered by community. In *The Long Loneliness* Day offers community as the answer to the loneliness of individualism. "That was the social answer to the long loneliness. . . . The living together, working together, sharing together, in loving God and loving our brother, and living close to him in community so we can show our love for Him."[44]

In and as Christian community we find that the most significant thing is knowing we are not alone. What is most important about Christian community is the love found in community; our very faith, writes Day, in love that has been tried through fire. "We cannot love God unless we love each other, and to love we must know each other. We know Him in the breaking of the bread, and we know each other in the breaking of bread, and we are not alone any more. Heaven is a banquet and life is a banquet too, even with a crust, where there is companionship."[45]

Day's eloquent telling of her life story, her "confession" as she calls it, is so important in this discussion because Day had tried earnestly to live the modern life of individualism, She was the kind of rebel who sought community in communism and in early-twentieth-century American feminism. Day was a thoroughly modern woman. She knew abortion, gave birth out of wedlock and became a single parent. Then she encountered Peter Maurin, whose practices of devotion appealed to her sensibilities, giving her the vision of community with Christ's love at the heart of it. It was community in which "love is an exchange of gifts" and people could show their love for each other in simple, practical, down-to-earth ways. "If the love was not there in the beginning, but only the need, such gifts made love grow," writes Day.[46]

Finally, Paul makes it clear that in terms of the individual's growth in Christ's body, it is God, not the individual, who gives all growth: "I planted, Apollos watered, but God gave the growth. So neither the one who plants nor the one who

[42]John Calvin, *Institutes of Christian Religion,* ed. John McNeill (Philadelphia: Westminster Press, 1960), 4.16.21.
[43]*Book of Common Worship,* p. 921.
[44]Dorothy Day, *The Long Loneliness* (New York: Harper & Row, 1981), pp. 224, 243.
[45]Ibid., p. 285.
[46]Ibid., p. 225.

waters is anything, but only God who gives the growth." We possess neither our own lives nor the lives of others. Our lives are God's possessions, for "we are God's servants, working together; you are God's field, God's building" (1 Cor 3:6-11). This is a rich description of the Christian community's efforts to understand our place in God's world in matters of growth.

Obedience to authority. While developmental psychologies construct a time in a person's life to oppose authority, usually "adolescence," pilgrimage teaches us the importance of obedience to authority. In order to get from the beginning point of the journey to the telos of the quest, the pilgrim needs to be obedient to the authoritative knowledge of the pilgrimage that is held by those who had been on the pathway. Trouble looms when the pilgrim opposes or resists the authority of those who have already trod the road. The pilgrim who forgets or abuses knowledge about the journey faces tremendous problems ahead. Pilgrims need to be taught obedience to authority rather than opposition to it.

Jesus' conversation with Peter provides an example. "Jesus said to Simon Peter, 'Simon son of John, do you love me more than these?' He said to him, 'Yes, Lord; you know that I love you.' Jesus said to him, 'Feed my lambs' " (Jn 21:15). This interchange was repeated twice. Why did Jesus keep asking Peter? " 'Very truly, I tell you, when you were younger, you used to fasten your own belt and to go wherever you wished. But when you grow old, you will stretch out your hands, and someone else will fasten a belt around you and take you where you do not wish to go.' (He said this to indicate the kind of death by which he would glorify God.) After this he said to him, 'Follow me' " (Jn 21:18, 19).

Jesus was clearly telling Peter to no longer oppose and ignore the authority of his instructions, as he had done before when he emotionally denied Jesus three times before Jesus' death. Peter was charged to follow Jesus' instructions to the point of death, even death on a cross. Jesus was shaping the very character of Peter, calling forth such virtues as constancy and perseverance of faith. Peter was to learn that to follow Jesus, to obey Jesus by doing what he was told, to "feed my sheep," would not necessarily feel good.

John Calvin writes that because God is merciful and all holy, he requires of us obedience, not as a way to garner salvation, but because of salvation. In the light of God's grace we see how far we are from conforming to God's will in our lives. When we worship God and hold forth in our lives that only God is good, when we are obedient to such truth, we show our willingness to conform to the requirements of God's will. Calvin quotes St. Augustine, who writes that "obedience that is paid to God [is] sometimes the mother and guardian of all virtues, sometimes their source."[47]

The importance of obeying the authority of the story and the storyteller, which is

---

[47]Calvin *Institutes* 2.8.5.

the church, in Christian pilgrimage is displayed in Bunyan's *Pilgrim's Progress.* Christian gets lost for the first time when he forgets the story of where he is from and where he is going. It is clear that the story and remembrance of it do not yet have authority in his life. When Help asks Christian how he fell into the Slough of Despond, Christian tells him, "Fear followed me so hard, that I fled the next way, and fell in." Help gives Christian a hand to get him on his way. He sets him on solid ground and bids him go on his way.[48]

We are mindbodyspirit in Christ. Modernity has made the claim that "mind" is central to being human. Descartes says, "I think, therefore I am." William Poteat writes against the Cartesian paradigm of mind-body dualism, which "conceptually estranges thought about our minds from thought about our bodies." He hangs mind and body together in the awkward creation of a different concept of "mindbodily rootedness." Poteat is attempting to mix together our uses of such concepts as reason, logic, body and mind. He believes that language is claimed first by the sinews of our bodies, followed by the rhetorical engagement with the world, with meaning.[49]

In a pilgrimage, more is wandering than one's mind. In part, to borrow Poteat's rhetoric, a pilgrimage is a journey that is known by mindbodiliness. Christian pilgrimage involves more than mental or cognitive acuity and development. It involves more than psychosocial developments à la Erikson, though relationships are necessary. It involves more than moral judgments according to Kohlberg's or Gilligan's definition of justice or care, though God's justice and care are necessary. It involves more than Fowler's humanly constructed faith, though faith as a gift given by God's grace, known in the performance of a life in which Christian faith matters, is necessary.

Christian pilgrimage is an act of the mindbodyspirit of a person in and as part of a particular community; a community that is of a specific time and place but includes the communion of all the saints as well. This is where the miracle of Christian pilgrimage lies: Christian pilgrimage is not an act of the mind, body and spirit of the individual person; rather, it is the transformation of the self by the grace-full power of the Holy Spirit. It is celebrated at our baptism, in which not our mind, body and spirit, but the mindbodyspirit of Christ is our life. In other words, a pilgrimage involves our entire life in and as the body of Christ. It is a coordination of our transformed will, desire and habits, which must be employed in order for us to travel on the journey.

Augustine understood that he was not alone in this pilgrimage. God walked with him: "You have walked everywhere at my side, O Truth, teaching me to seek and what to avoid, wherever I laid before you the things that I was able to see in this world below and asked you to counsel me."[50] Augustine knew that he was not the

---

[48]Bunyan, *Pilgrim's Progress*, p. 11.
[49]William Poteat, *A Philosophical Daybook* (Columbia: University of Missouri Press, 1990), pp. 2-3.
[50]Augustine, *Confessions* (New York: Penguin, 1979), p. 248.

creator of his own understanding of truth; God alone was his truth.

Augustine's conversion was clearly more than an act of his human rational intellect or self-willed control of his mind or body. Instead, his life was being narrated
by a force, a power stronger and other than his own. When he heard the words
"Take and read," Augustine was overcome by a flood of tears, and he marked the
place of Romans 13:13-14 with his finger. Augustine acknowledges that he was con-
verted to God, "so that I no longer desired a wife or placed any hope in this world
but stood firmly upon the rule of faith, where you had shown me to her (his
mother) in a dream so many years before."[51] No longer was Augustine in control of
his life and destiny. Instead, he lived his life to the one good God.

God in Christ. While developmental psychologies encourage us to embrace as a
"higher source" a deist God created by philosophers during the Enlightenment,
Christians understand that they are creatures created in the image of the Creator
God.[52] In pilgrimage, the telos, the point of the journey, defines the method of the
journey and the journey itself. If we had no hint of where and what the telos was,
there would be no reason for the journey. Even if the telos is the journey itself, that
must be articulated. The telos defines the rest of the mission; it is the raison d'être
of the journey.

For developmental psychologists the final stage defines the rest of the stages; all
the previous stages lead up to the climax of the final stage. For example, Piaget's
highest stage of achievement is formal operations in which the child is able to
move "from the plane of concrete manipulation to the ideational plane, where
expression is in some kind of language (words, mathematical symbols, etc.), without the support of perception, experience, or even faith."[53] Erikson's final stage is
ego integrity versus despair. Ego integrity is "an emotional integration which permits participation by followership as well as acceptance of the responsibility of
leadership."[54]

Fowler's highest stage of faith development is universalizing faith, in which we
are involved in "decentration from self" as we "rest our hearts" on "centers of value
that confirm our identities and confer significance on our sense of selfhood. . . . We
become attached to causes, persons, institutions, possessions, and the like precisely
because they seem to promise to ground us in worth."[55]

At the height of its development, the self constructed by developmental psychol-

---

[51]Ibid, pp. 178-79.
[52]Developmental psychologist Sharon Parks goes so far as to put *God* in quotes. For while
"God" may function as the center of life for Christians, "God" is not necessarily the "ultimate
value" of all people. See Sharon Parks, *The Critical Years* (New York: Harper & Row, 1986),
p. 17.
[53]Piaget, *Six Psychological Studies,* pp. 62-63.
[54]Erikson, *Childhood and Society,* p. 269.
[55]James Fowler, *Becoming Adult, Becoming Christian* (New York: Harper & Row, 1984), p. 69.

ogists is still mortal and isolated. The question for theologians is whether we want people to grow to be more human than they already are. Or do we desire people to grow into an understanding that as Christ's followers we are like Christ, that as members of Christ's body we are different from mere individual human beings? Paul writes that we die to self because "we know that our old self was crucified with him so that the body of sin might be destroyed, and we might no longer be enslaved to sin. . . . But if we have died with Christ, we believe that we will also live with him" (Rom 6:6, 8). We have been raised from the dead not only with Christ but into Christ and Christ alone, who has become and is our mind, body and spirit: "For just as the body is one and has many members, and all the members of the body, though many, are one body, so it is with Christ. For in the one Spirit we were all baptized into one body—Jews or Greeks, slaves or free—and we were all made to drink of one Spirit" (1 Cor 12:12-13).

As members of Christ's body we are like Bunyan's Christian, headed from the City of Destruction to the Celestial City. Beyond the gate was the City that "shone like the Sun, the Streets also were paved with Gold, and in them walked many men, with Crowns on their heads, Palms in their hands, and golden Harps to sing praises withal."[56] Christian and Hopeful were led into the Celestial City, having survived the rigors of their journey, while Ignorance was bound hand and foot and led away.

The key for Christian throughout the journey was keeping his eyes on the Celestial City, and this objective was held in tension with the knowledge of where he had came from, the City of Destruction. Every time he had doubts, he would find himself stuck along the way or headed toward one kind of chaos or another. What mattered most was the vision before him: God.

Clearly what matters most is which god determines the purpose or end of the journey. For developmental psychologists like Piaget, Erikson and Fowler, a god is an idea of a continuously refurbishing self who becomes more civilized and accommodating to differences in this world as the years roll on, then dies. The self has a growing ability to rationalize away differences. The grandiosity of the self at the pinnacle of each of these sets of stages is that, more than anything else, the self is tolerant of differences.

This is in contrast with the end of members of Christ's body. As members of Christ's body we experience a deep knowing and an unquenchable yearning that direct our fragile lives toward the City of God. In salvation's story, death is not our end, but resurrection.

A particular people of a particular God: A kind of universal. Developmental psychologists present their theories as if they were universal. For example, consider Vygotsky's claims regarding a universal construction of culture. Contextualists are informed by modernity as they argue for a universal definition of *culture* that is

---

[56]Bunyan, *Pilgrim's Progress*, p. 101.

able to describe anything that calls itself a culture in the broad sense. But the very act of defining *culture* is problematic. The concept of culture is itself context. It is culturally dependent, and there is no universal agreement about what culture is.

In the modern anthropological sense, *culture* is not new. Kathryn Tanner points out that in Latin *culture* means the care and tending of crops or animals. In the age of Goethe, *culture* became a synonym for the more usual German term *Bildung*. A cultured person was a person with education, a member of what was then the new German middle class. *Kultur* was applied to a social group in Germany. It was used to describe a person who had attained the highest achievements of society. In France, *culture* was not only a way to describe a certain person, but was synonymous with civilization itself, representing "the means by which problematic differences in ways of life among the various classes of French society could ultimately be overcome in the interest of social order and unity." In Britain there was high culture and low culture. High culture was a "principle of social reform and national rejuvenation [that] might save the nation from the mechanistic and leveling effects of industrialization and democracy."[57]

In human development terms, what does a culture actually do? Does a culture continually change, evolving through time and eliciting change among the people in the culture? Or does a culture seek equilibrium and find harmony by not changing, by maintaining a status quo existence, causing those who are not in sync with the culture to either quickly adapt or die? Do people make a culture? Or does culture make the person? Is there a universal categorization of culture?

Zygmunt Bauman argues that modernity's claims of universalism have slipped, and that modernity now makes the meeker claim of being global. Globality means that "everyone everywhere may feed on McDonald's burgers and watch the latest made-for-TV docudrama." Previously the universal rule of reason was managed by the adjudication of philosophers, but in globality chaos and contingency, the wild beasts of spontaneity, are back.[58]

Wendell Berry, living in and writing from the context of his neighborhood, his farm, his desk and his church, takes globality down one more notch. To Berry, community is a particular place in a particular time and a particular physical setting. In "a common dependence on a common life and a common ground . . . community is . . . placed, its success cannot be divided from the success of its place, its natural setting and surroundings: its soils, forests, grasslands, plants and animals, water, light, and

---

[57]Kathryn Tanner, *Theories of Culture* (Minneapolis: Fortress, 1997), pp. 3-24. *Culture* is widely used by Christians as well, as if we knew what we were talking about. We have H. Richard Niebuhr's *Christ and Culture* (New York: Harper & Row, 1951); and Lesslie Newbigin's definition of *culture* in *Foolishness to the Greeks* (Grand Rapids, Mich.: Eerdmans, 1986), p. 3, in which culture is simply understood as "the sum total of ways of living developed by a group of human beings and handed on from generation to generation. Central to culture is language." This definition of *culture* is broad and nonspecific enough to fit any kind of social grouping, human or not human, as long as it has a language.
[58]Bauman, *Postmodern Ethics*, p. 24.

air."[59] According to Berry, Christians are bound by, connected to and dependent on God in Christ, through relationships with one another in the church. Each community is different because one is in Ireland and another in Port William, Kentucky; so each church is more than just another culture. Berry indicts the church for caving in to bland, generalized Christianity, for failing to appreciate our heritage. He offers the example of church architecture. "Most modern churches look like they were built by robots without reference to the heritage of church architecture or respect for the place; they embody no awareness that work can be worship."[60]

Berry's insight helps in our criticism of developmental psychologies because in community we may know a sense of health or wholeness. Berry writes:

> The word "health," in fact, comes from the same Indo-European root as "heal," "whole," and "holy." To be healthy is literally to be whole; to heal is to make whole. I don't think mortal healers should be credited with the power to make holy. But I have no doubt that such healers are properly obliged to acknowledge and respect the holiness embodied in all creatures, or that our healing involves the preservation in us of the spirit and the breath of God.[61]

What is the opposite of wholeness or health? Disease, which makes us conscious not only of the state of our health but also the division of our bodies into separate parts, distinct cogs labeled cognitive, psychosocial, psychosexual, moral and spiritual as if we were machines.

In sum, the telos is what matters in our understanding of what development is. The telos describes both the process of growth and the context of such maturation. For developmental psychologists the telos is a refurbishing and recycling of the self, which becomes more civilized and accommodating to all kinds of differences in the world as the years roll on. Individuals can negotiate these differences because they are capable of rationalizing away bothersome particularities of other people's lives. This is in stark contrast to the telos for members of Christ's body. Our telos is to grow into the head of the church, which is Christ. Our end is not a completed self, but resurrection.

Conclusion

In Chinua Achebe's masterful novel *Things Fall Apart,* Okonkwo, an Igbo tribesman, and his thick, complex, nuanced life, fall apart, leading to suicide at the end of the story. The British commissioner in that part of Africa, who is in large part complicit in Okonkwo's death, first sees Okonkwo as a man who has killed a messenger and later has hanged himself. This would make an interesting read. But later, as the commissioner thinks more about Okonkwo's death, there is a painful simplification of this once-rich story. The commissioner writes, "One could almost

---

[59]Wendell Berry, *What Are People For?* (San Francisco: North Point, 1987), p. 192.
[60]Wendell Berry, *Sex, Economy. Freedom and Community* (New York: Pantheon, 1993), p. 112.
[61]Wendell Berry, *Another Turn of the Crank* (Washington, D.C.: Counterpoint, 1995), pp. 86-87.

write a whole chapter on him. Perhaps not a whole chapter but a reasonable paragraph, at any rate. There was so much else to include, and one must be firm in cut-
ting out details." Achebe explains that "he had already chosen the title of the book,
after much thought: *The Pacification of the Primitive Tribes of the Lower Niger.*"[62]

Developmental psychologies often do what the commissioner did with
Okonkwo's life story: distort, reduce and simplify life, with all its rich complexities
and ever-changing nuances, to a single set of stages, categories or descriptive levels
that shapes how we see ourselves and one another. In their construction of human
beings and their growth, developmental psychologies often fail to capture the
unpredictable, changing, growing, fluid and dynamic life stories that transcend the
boxlike structure of stages or levels of development. A human life cannot be
divided into cognitive life, psychosocial life, moral life and spiritual life.[63]

We should consider being human in terms of the body of Christ (and the politics of
this particular body). For as we consider what it is to be human in this context, if we
consider the actions of the body of Christ before we consider our body, mind and
spirit, we may come to understand or perceive ourselves and one another differently as
we grow "with a growth that is from God" (Col 2:19). This is why the rhetoric and practice of Christ's body on a pilgrimage are so intriguing. Pilgrimage connotes a movement—journeying toward the telos of God's dominion—a beginning, middle and end.

What kind of growth happens in this pilgrimage? In Ephesians we read that we,
the body of Christ, grow into Christ. "We grow up in every way into him who is the
head, into Christ, from whom the whole body, joined and knit together by every
ligament with which it is equipped, as each part is working properly, promotes the
body's growth in building itself up in love" (Eph 4:15-16).

We are born and baptized into this body, and our understanding, our perception of
life as Christ's faithful disciples, is nurtured and shaped, deepened and widened as we
mature in our appreciation and expanding gratitude for the tender mercies of God. For
it is by, in and through grace, which is not of human construction but is God's unexpected gift to us for our salvation, that we grow to maturity in Christ's body. The writer
of Ephesians is clear that we *all* "come to the unity of the faith and of the knowledge of
the Son of God, to maturity, to the measure of the full stature of Christ" (Eph 4:13).

There are chronologically and spiritually older and younger members of Christ's
body. But do young children on this pilgrimage understand or know much about
the pilgrimage? And what of those who are older, who desire to know more about
the journey? The response depends on the Christian community in which we live,
and on which issues are germane to the body of Christ at any one time. Jerome

---

[62]Chinua Achebe, *Things Fall Apart* (New York: Doubleday, 1994), p. 209.
[63]This compartmentalization is one of the critical problems with the monumental work of
psychiatrist Robert Coles. It is inevitable that a person's "spiritual life" will influence, shape
and determine his or her "moral life" and "political life," depending on how spiritual, moral
and political life are defined.

Bruner offers insight for resolving this dilemma of age appropriateness and teaching Christian life in a congregation or parish:

> "Any subject can be taught to any child at any age in some form that is honest." Another way of saying the same thing might be to say "Readiness is not only born but made." The general proposition rests on the still deeper truth that any domain of knowledge can be constructed at varying levels of abstractness or complexity. That is to say, domains of knowledge are *made* not *found:* they can be constructed simply or complexly, abstractly or concretely.[64]

Bruner is correct in asserting that a context can make any subject knowable to any child, depending on how the subject is presented or taught. For Christians, Jesus Christ, who is with us on pilgrimage, can be taught to any child or adult in a form that is honest and trustworthy. If we take Paul seriously, there are some people of the flesh who are like infants in Christ. They need milk, not solid food (1 Cor 3:1-2). And there are those who are ready for more complex, abstract food regarding the pilgrimage in which we find ourselves as Christians. Yet it is not just us mortals in this context of church who make growth or knowledge of God possible. In our context Christians acknowledge that we teach and grow in the body of Christ, in which both the people with whom we are in relationship and the Holy Spirit matter in our teaching. On the pilgrimage the young initiate is taught by the elders the stories and traditions of God's people. And in teaching the elders are reminded of and remember the stories and traditions as well. It is not only we who teach, but God's Spirit in us who teaches as well. Writes John Calvin:

> We see how God, who could in a moment perfect his own, nevertheless desires them to grow up into manhood solely under the education of the Church. . . . We see that all are brought under the same regulation, that with a gentle and teachable spirit they may allow themselves to be governed by teachers appointed to this function. Isaiah had long before distinguished Christ's Kingdom by this mark: "My spirit which is upon you, and my words which I have put in your mouth, shall never depart out of your mouth, or out of the mouth of your children, or . . . of your children's children" (Is 59:21).[65]

This kind of learning, and growing in such knowledge, occurs in the context of Christian friendship. A godly miracle that makes this pilgrimage not only a possibility, but a desire of our mind, body and spirit, are the friendships that prepare for God's kingdom. Gilbert Meilander states it well: "Life is a journey, a pilgrimage toward that community in which friends love one another in God. . . . Along the way, friendship is a school, training us in the meaning and enactment of love."[66]

---

[64]Jerome Bruner, *The Culture of Education* (Cambridge, Mass.: Harvard University Press, 1996), p. 119.

[65]Calvin *Institutes* 4.1.5.

[66]Gilbert Meilander, *Friendship: A Study in Theological Ethics* (Notre Dame, Ind.: University of Notre Dame Press, 1981), p. 66, in Paul Waddell, *Friendship and the Moral Life* (Notre Dame, Ind.: University of Notre Dame Press, 1989), p. 101.

4

SELF-CONCEPT

In Defense of the Word Soul

Jeffrey H. Boyd

I N BOOK 14 OF *THE CITY OF GOD,* AUGUSTINE DISTINGUISHES BETWEEN TWO CITIES on the basis of what they love. The city of God loves God above all else. The city of this earth loves itself above all else. The city of God arranges the priorities of life around the need to worship, pray, confess and enter into dialogue with God so as to seek God's guidance in all matters. The earthly city prefers to do whatever pleases itself, for it takes its own wishes and desires as the highest priority. In Augustine's time the earthly city was pagan Rome and the city of God was the church. In this chapter I will consider the earthly city to be secular American culture, especially the secular mental health movement. A great canyon divides Christian psychotherapy from secular psychotherapy because they belong to different cities. My focus is not on Christian psychotherapy, but on secular psychotherapy in relationship to theology. This relationship is different from what you might expect.

Whereas other chapters in this volume focus on psychotherapy, this chapter does not. My primary focus is on the self-concept or self-image of that silent majority of Americans who have never been in psychotherapy. Who does the average Joe or Josephine Schmoe think he or she is? How do they understand their lives? I will claim that Joe and Josephine usually think of themselves along secular lines. I live in both the city of God and the earthly city, for I am a man with two professional identities. On the one hand I am an ordained clergyman who has published three books and a dozen theological research articles in the arena of theological anthropology.[1] As such I find myself surrounded by citizens of the city of God.

---

[1]Jeffrey H. Boyd, *Christians Living with Chronic Illness* (Grand Rapids, Mich.: Baker, in press); "Biblical Psychology: A Creative Way to Apply the Whole Bible to Understanding

Were I to poll the readers of this chapter concerning the highest priorities in life, they would immediately say: "To love the Lord with all my heart, mind and strength; and to love my neighbor as myself."

I am also a psychiatrist. I was trained at Yale University School of Medicine, have been on the faculty of the National Institutes of Health and have published in the *New England Journal of Medicine*, and I currently serve as chairman of psychiatry and chairman of ethics at Waterbury Hospital, a Yale teaching hospital—that is, a secular hospital. When I am wearing my psychiatrist hat, I find myself living mostly among citizens of the earthly city. My daily work places me in a setting that is dramatically different from the counseling department of an evangelical seminary. You could say that I am courageous or you could say that I am a fool for choosing to work in such an inhospitable and Arctic environment.

Were I to stand before an audience of secular psychotherapists and ask them about the highest priorities in life, what would they answer? First, they would hesitate because many of them have never thought about ultimate priorities. But after hesitating many would come to the traditional answer of secular psychotherapists: "To fulfill my potential as an individual, to listen to and pursue my deepest desires, to nourish my self so that I blossom to the maximum extent, to become autonomous and self-determined, to become fully individuated, to become my own man (or woman)." Augustine himself could not state more clearly the goals of the city of this earth.

The secular mental health movement tends to place the self at the center as the highest value in life. Heinz Kohut, Carl Rogers, Abraham Maslow and Rollo May

Human Psychology," *Trinity Journal* 21 (2000): 3-16; "The 'Soul' of the Psalms Compared to the 'Self' of Kohut," *Journal of Psychology and Christianity* 19 (2000): 219-31; "What DNA Tells Us About the Human Soul," *Calvin Theological Journal* 33 (April 1998): 142-59; "A History of the Concept of the Soul During the Twentieth Century," *Journal of Psychology and Theology* 26 (spring 1998): 110-22. "Two Orientations of the Self," *Journal of Psychology and Theology* 26 (spring 1998): 66-82; "One's Self-Concept and Biblical Theology," *Journal of the Evangelical Theological Society* 40 (June 1997): 207-27; *Reclaiming the Soul: The Search for Meaning in a Self-Centered Culture* (Cleveland, Ohio: Pilgrim, 1996); "An Insider's Efforts to Blow Up Psychiatry," *Trinity Journal* 17 (fall 1996): 223-39; "Book Review: Kenneth J. Collins, *Soul Care: Deliverance and Renewal Through the Christian Life*," *Calvin Theological Journal* 31 (1996): 272-75; "Book Review: Keith Ward, *Defending the Soul*," *Calvin Theological Journal* 31 (1996): 213-16; "Apocalypse from Nuclear War Compared with the Expected Apocalypse of October 22, 1844," *Henceforth* 23 (spring 1996): 9-33; "The Biblical Soul as Seen Through Episcopal Eyes," *Plumbline* (winter 1996): 24-27; "The Soul as Seen Through Evangelical Eyes, Part I: Mental Health Professionals and the Soul," *Journal of Psychology and Theology* 23 (fall 1995): 151-60; "The Soul as Seen Through Evangelical Eyes, Part II: On Use of the Term *Soul*," *Journal of Psychology and Theology* 23 (fall 1995): 161-70; "Losing Soul: How and Why Theologians Created the Mental Health Movement," *Calvin Theological Journal* 30 (1995): 472-92; *Affirming the Soul: Remarkable Conversations Between Mental Health Professionals and an Ordained Minister* (Cheshire, Conn.: Soul Research Institute, 1994); *Soul Psychology: How to Understand Your Soul in Light of the Mental Health Movement* (Cheshire, Conn.: Soul Research Institute, 1994).

speak explicitly of the self as the focus of all therapy and the center of value. What is this word *self?* I use the word here to refer either to the whole person or to the subjective and inner person. It is embedded in the words *myself* and *yourself.* Heinz Kohut has written eloquently about the fragmentation and disintegration of the self, and the need to find ways to help clients in psychotherapy seek cohesiveness and unity of the self.[2] Implied by the word *self* are a person's self-esteem and self-concept. The word *self* is, in summary, the secular word that corresponds most precisely to the biblical word *soul.* Indeed, Bible translators often use the two words interchangeably, as synonyms.

Both *soul* and *self* are rich words, and they sometimes refer to the whole person, body and all, but for our purposes we will define both words as referring to the inner or subjective person, including both the conscious and the unconscious mind. Both words refer to that aspect of a human that immediately survives death and goes to be with Jesus in the intermediate state until the body is resurrected, and both words have a vast semantic overlap with the biblical words *heart* and *spirit.* The word *soul* differs from the word *self* in that *soul* is a theological word; therefore, the soul could never be mistaken as the highest value on earth.

My psychiatric work in the secular world places me squarely among citizens of the earthly city who promote the self as the idol to which they devote themselves above all else. According to Augustine this precisely is the decisive issue. The earthly city is populated by those who place the self above all else; the heavenly city is populated by those who consider God more important than the self. That's why the word *obedience* is so important in theology and so unimportant in secular psychology, because obedience means subjecting oneself to a higher power. Obedience means humility. The only obedience taught by the secular mental health movement is that of listening to one's own needs and aspirations.

Some readers, especially psychotherapists, object that my argument (and that of Augustine) is too simplistic because not everyone in the earthly city is self-centered. Many citizens of this earth are altruistic, generous and more ethical than some of us Christians. Furthermore, a woman who is addicted to her drug-addicted boyfriend takes her lover and not herself as the idol. Therefore, it is argued, the earthly city cannot be defined by the taking of the self as the idol. There is not space to address that objection here, but I have addressed it elsewhere.[3]

The two cities can be distinguished from one another in terms of their views of self-denial and self-sacrifice. The city of God emphasizes the need for self-sacrifice at times, in order to make it clear that we serve God and not ourselves. Our cruci-

---

[2]Heinz Kohut, *How Does Analysis Cure?* (Chicago: University of Chicago Press, 1984); *The Restoration of the Self* (Madison, Conn.: International Universities Press, 1990); *Self Psychology and the Humanities*, ed. Charles B. Strozier (New York: W. W. Norton, 1985); Ernest S. Wolf, *Treating the Self: Elements of Clinical Self Psychology* (New York: Guilford, 1988).
[3]Boyd, "Two Orientations."

fied Lord is an example. The secular psychotherapy city has a very different view of
self-sacrifice. It views self-sacrifice as dangerous because it threatens to belittle or
destroy the most important thing on earth, the self. Paradoxically, it speaks in favor
of a limited amount of self-denial and altruism, provided that sacrificing for others
makes you feel good about yourself. In other words, as long as self-sacrifice
enhances your self-esteem, secular psychotherapists are in favor of it. But if you
would become less of a person or would be threatened with death, they would
oppose self-sacrifice because the self is the idol and destruction of that idol never
makes sense.

The secular mental health movement has paradoxically contributed to the culture of narcissism.[4] I say "paradoxically" because narcissistic personality disorder is
defined in psychiatry as an illness that requires psychiatric treatment. The therapeutic culture of narcissism is a soil rich in nutrients for the growth of postmodern
deconstructionism.

I want to make a clear distinction between the God-centered city of God and the
self-centered city of this earth in terms of what they love most. In this chapter I
consider the secular mental health movement as equivalent to the Republican
Guards, the elite troops of the earthly city. We must remember that 94 percent of
American people believe in God, but only 43 percent of American psychiatrists and
psychologists do.[5]

When theologians think of psychologists, they think of their friends over in the
counseling department. That is a serious error. Better to think of a psychologist
named Albert Ellis, who writes:

> Devout, orthodox, or dogmatic religion (or what might be called religiosity) is sig-
> nificantly correlated with emotional disturbance. . . . The devoutly religious person
> tends to be inflexible, closed, intolerant, and unchanging. Religiosity, therefore, is
> in many respects equivalent to irrational thinking and emotional disturbance. . . .
> The elegant therapeutic solution to emotional problems is to be quite unreligious.
> . . . The less religious they [patients] are, the more emotionally healthy they will
> be.[6]

[4]Christopher Lasch, *The Culture of Narcissism: American Life in an Age of Diminishing Expectations* (New York: Norton, 1979).
[5]*American Psychiatric Association Task Force Report 10: Psychiatrists' Viewpoints on Religion and Their Services to Religious Institutions and the Ministry* (Washington, D.C.: American Psychiatric Association, 1975); Claude Ragan, H. Newton Malony and Benjamin Bert-Hallahmi, "Psychologists and Religion: Professional Factors and Personal Belief," *Review of Religious Research* 21 (spring 1980): 208-17, table 2 on page 212 shows that 17 percent of psychologists are "orthodox" in ideology and another 26 percent somewhat orthodox. At the bottom of the page, the text adds together these two percentages and arrives at 43 percent who believe in God. The article also shows that psychologists are also much less religious than academics in general.
[6]Albert Ellis, "Psychotherapy and Atheistic Values: A Response to A. Bergin's 'Psychotherapy and Religious Values,'" *Journal of Consulting and Clinical Psychology* 48 (1980): 635-39.

The Relationship Between the Two Cities

Augustine says that neither the city of God nor the earthly city can completely win its competition with the other city until the day of judgment. But in our day the city of this earth is surprisingly successful in setting the agenda for popular American culture. For example, during the Wheaton conference on the intersection of psychology and theology we repeatedly heard that America has a therapeutic culture. If theologians were setting the agenda and determining which vocabulary would be used, we might hear of a Christian culture and a sinful culture. But theologians are no longer in the driver's seat in America. Psychiatrists like me are in the driver's seat. In the paper I presented at the Wheaton conference I cited various statistics to demonstrate that the cultural trend in secular America is favorable to a secular mental health self-concept, not to a theological self-concept for the masses of America. But here it is not necessary to cite such statistical data.

When I gave this paper at the Wheaton conference, I was astounded at the reaction of the audience. They were more certain than I was that the Christian church has totally lost the war for the self-concept of ordinary Americans. We live in a therapeutic age. Theologian Rodney Clapp told me of evangelical experts who have advised preachers to avoid theological language and to use only secular psychology language in their sermons. The reason is that lay people experience psychological language as providing a practical, down-to-earth description of everyday reality, while they experience theological language as abstract and difficult to understand.

Everywhere I went at the Wheaton conference, I heard that the mental health vocabulary is the framework for theological discourse instead of vice versa. But if we use this vocabulary, we will lose every debate with those in the mental health movement. As David Powlison said to me, "Scripture has to lead."

In 1966 Philip Rieff wrote *The Triumph of the Therapeutic: Uses of Faith After Freud.* His thesis is that Christianity is dying as a system for organizing society and is being replaced by Freudian psychoanalysis, which offers individualism and makes no attempt to organize individuals into any common purpose. "Religious man was born to be saved; psychological man is born to be pleased," Rieff says.[7] Psychological soil has promoted the growth of postmodernism.

How to Fix the Problem

The good guys lost the war for the self-concept of rank-and-file Americans, but we might take some comfort in Augustine's statement that neither city will totally triumph over the other until the end of time. However, you may be surprised to learn

---

[7]Philip Rieff, *The Triumph of the Therapeutic: Uses of Faith After Freud* (1966; reprint, Chicago: University of Chicago Press, 1987), p. 25.

the extent to which our theological generals and admirals inadvertently lost this war. I do not make this argument in order to cast aspersions; rather, the key to winning the next war is to understand how we lost the previous war. By changing our assumptions we can avoid making the same blunders again.

Every general in today's U.S. military has studied why America lost the war in Vietnam. That study is the intellectual training ground for all our military strategists. How could it have happened? Why did some peasants in a Third World country who have little technology defeat the overwhelming firepower and technical superiority of the U.S. armed forces? By studying Vietnam our generals learned to correct those mistakes, and they won the Persian Gulf War.

Similarly, the generals in God's army need to start by studying why we lost the war against the secular mental health movement. It is not sufficient to say, "The secular psychologists won the hearts and minds of most Americans because their message appealed to human depravity." Depravity has been around ever since the Fall, yet rarely before has the city of God been so eclipsed by the city of this earth. We did not lose the war because our enemies were more powerful than God. We did not lose it because God abandoned us. We lost it because we abandoned one of the central teachings of the Bible: the doctrine of the soul.

If Augustine were alive today, the first thing he would say about contemporary theology is, "Where is the doctrine of the soul?" He would say that it is impossible to have a robust and healthy theology in the absence of a doctrine of the soul. If you told Augustine that the Bible speaks only of the Hebrew concept of the "whole person," he would scratch his head and wonder if you were thinking clearly. "What happens when you die and are no longer a whole person?" he would ask.

Starting with the 1926 publication of Johannes Pedersen's book *Israel*, there was an anti-soul campaign in biblical studies.[8] Pedersen writes that the Old Testament "soul" *(nephesh)* is the whole person, so that the body is part of the soul. Many leading Bible scholars and theologians, both conservative and liberal, joined the intellectual campaign against the soul, as I have documented elsewhere.[9] In his book *Nature and Destiny of Man* Reinhold Niebuhr blames the soul for most of the problems that exist in the world and urged that we get rid of it.[10]

A broad consensus emerged among biblical and theological scholars that soul-body dualism is a Platonic, Hellenistic idea that is not found anywhere in the

---

[8]Johannes Pedersen, *Israel: Its Life and Culture* (London: Oxford University Press, 1926).

[9]For a more extensive history of the theological discrediting of the soul and an explanation of the logical flaws in that position see Boyd, "History of the Concept of the Soul."

[10]Reinhold Niebuhr, *The Nature and Destiny of Man* (New York: Charles Scribner's, 1949), 1:5-13.

Bible.[11] The Bible, from cover to cover, promotes what they call the "Hebrew concept of the whole person." G. C. Berkouwer writes that the biblical view is always
holistic, that in the Bible the soul is never ascribed any special religious significance.[12] Werner Jaeger writes that soul-body dualism is a bizarre idea that has been
read into the Bible by misguided church fathers such as Augustine.[13] Rudolf Bultmann writes that Paul uses the word *sōma* (body) to refer to the whole person, the
self, so that there is not a soul and body, but rather the body is the whole thing.[14]
This interpretation of Pauline anthropology has been a theme in much subsequent
Pauline scholarship.[15]

In the middle decades of the twentieth century, Bible professors in both conservative and liberal Protestant seminaries began to teach two concepts: "The soul of
you is the whole of you," and "you don't have a soul, you are a soul." In other
words, whether you approach the person from the aspect of the soul or of the
body, you will discover that the Bible always implies a concept of the whole person, indivisible. Theologians forgot about death, when the allegedly indivisible person divides into two parts: the corpse and that which is not the corpse. In other
words, they failed to notice that the doctrine of the whole person negates the Christian hope at the graveside for immediate survival prior to the bodily resurrection.

In 1958 Oscar Cullmann published his infamous book *Immortality of the Soul or
Resurrection of the Dead?* Cullmann claims that the immortality of the soul is never
mentioned in the New Testament.[16] Rather, Scripture assumes the Hebrew concept of

[11]Oscar Cullmann, "Immortality or Resurrection?" *Christianity Today*, July 21, 1958, p. 6; O. W.
Heick, "If a Man Die, Shall He Live Again?" *Lutheran Quarterly* 17 (1965): 99-110; P. G.
Lindhardt, "Eternal Life," *Chicago Studies* 48 (1965): 198-210; H. V. White, "Immortality and
Resurrection in Recent Theology," *Encounter* 22 (1961): 52-58; R. W. Brockway, "Immortality
of the Soul: An Evangelical Heresy," *Religious Humanism* 13 (1979): 14-18; M. Bailey,
"Biblical Man and Some Formulae of Christian Teaching," *Irish Theological Quarterly* 27
(1960): 173-200; J. K. Brandyberry, "Important Forgotten History: The Roots of Opposition to
Resurrection Truth among Today's Evangelical Leaders," *Resurrection* 94-95 (1991): 6-7;
Theological Commission, "Some Current Questions in Eschatology," *Irish Theological
Quarterly* 58 (1992): 209-43; B. L. Bateson, "The Resurrection of the Dead: 1 Corinthians
15:25," *Resurrection* 93 (1990): 5-6, 8; R. O. Zorn, "II Corinthians 5:1-10: Individual
Eschatology or Corporate Solidarity, Which?" *Reformed Theological Review* 48 (1989): 93-104;
R. S. Weathers, "Dualism or Holism? A Look at Biblical Anthropology, Ethics, and Human
Health," *Journal of the American Scientific Affiliation* 35 (1983): 80-83.
[12]G. C. Berkouwer, *Man: The Image of God* (Grand Rapids, Mich.: Eerdmans, 1962), pp. 201-3.
[13]Werner Jaeger, "The Greek Ideas of Immortality," *Harvard Theological Review* 52 (1959): 135-
47.
[14]Rudolf Bultmann, *Theology of the New Testament* (London: SCM Press, 1965), 1:191-209.
[15]A. C. Purdy, "Paul the Apostle," in *Interpreter's Dictionary of the Bible*, ed. Charles A. Buttrick
et al. (Nashville: Abingdon, 1981), 3:681-704; E. Earle Ellis, "*Sōma* in First Corinthians,"
Interpretation 44 (1990): 132-44; J. A. T. Robinson, *The Body: A Study in Pauline Theology*
(Chicago: Regnery, 1952).
[16]Oscar Cullmann, *Immortality of the Soul or Resurrection of the Dead?* (New York: Macmillan,
1958).

the whole person and emphasizes the reality of death of the whole person. The Christian hope is resurrection of the whole person from the grave, so we are always embodied. But there is a contradiction at the center of Cullmann's book. He implies that the New Testament expects 100 percent death followed by 100 percent resurrection and that it offers no evidence of an immortal soul providing a bridge between who we are today and who we will be in the resurrection state.[17] But in a footnote Cullmann also endorses the concept of an intermediate state of disembodiment.[18]

Naturally this anti-soul groundswell has affected Bible translation. As Timothy Phillips, an editor of this volume, wrote to me, "Those in biblical and theological circles are just as molded and shaped by the current Zeitgeist as any other person." Translators have claimed that most verses that use the Hebrew word *nephesh* and the Greek word *psyche* are not referring to the soul at all.[19] They have evoked the concept of semantic elasticity so as to emphasize the enormous semantic range of English meanings of those words. Scholars have written articles about how those words refer not to "soul" but to "throat" or "life."[20] Translators have turned the word *soul* into a personal pronoun so that the verse that formerly said, "*My soul* abhors the wicked," now says "*I* abhor the wicked." Krister Stendahl—a leading New Testament scholar (and my teacher)—says, "The word *soul* was a prominent part of the Bible throughout history until suddenly in the twentieth century when the word disappeared from the Bible almost entirely."[21] One leading NIV translator told me, "We think it is better, whenever possible, to use a word other than *soul* to translate *nephesh* and *psyche* into English."[22] To illustrate the anti-soul bias of Bible translators, I offer a comparison between the King James Version and the New International Version translations of four verses.

■ "For he satisfieth the longing *soul*, and filleth the hungry *soul* with goodness" (Ps

[17]Harry A. Wolfson, "Immortality and Resurrection in the Philosophy of the Church Fathers," in *Immortality and Resurrection*, ed. Krister Stendahl (New York: Macmillan, 1965), p. 54.

[18]Cullmann writes, "The lack of New Testament speculation on this does not give us the right simply to suppress the 'interim condition' as such. I do not understand why Protestant theologians (including Barth) are so afraid of the New Testament position when the New Testament teaches only this much about the 'interim condition': (1) that it exists, (2) that it already signifies union with Christ." See Cullmann, "Immortality of the Soul or Resurrection of the Dead?" in *Immortality and Resurrection*, ed. Krister Stendahl (New York: Macmillan, 1965), p. 40 n. 34. But if Cullmann endorses an intermediate state, why did he present death as such a major catastrophe? Socrates's death is not so dramatically opposed to Jesus' death if there is an intermediate state.

[19]Heber F. Peackock, "Translating the Word for 'Soul' in the Old Testament," *Bible Translator* 27 (1976): 216-19.

[20]Hans Walter Wolff, *Anthropology of the Old Testament* (Philadelphia: Fortress, 1974), pp. 10-25.

[21]Boyd, *Affirming the Soul*.

[22]Boyd, *Soul Psychology*, p. 5.

107:9 KJV). "For he satisfies the thirsty and fills the hungry with good things" (NIV).
Nepeš is not translated in the NIV, although it is present in the NIV version of the
Hebrew text.

■ "Destroy all them that afflict my *soul*" (Ps 143:12 KJV). "Destroy all my foes"
(NIV). What happened to *nepeš*? A clever English translation avoids the Hebrew
word.

■ Paul calls "God for a record upon my *soul*" in the KJV translation of 2 Cor 1:23.
But in the NIV translation Paul calls "God as my witness." *Psychē* is not translated
into any English word. The translators skipped it.

■ We are "of them that believe to the saving of the soul," according to the KJV (Heb
10:39). But in the NIV translation we are among "those who believe and are saved."
The translators of the NIV did not choose to include the Greek word *psychē,* which
is present in the Greek original.

After I delivered the talk on which this chapter is based at the Wheaton Theology Conference, one of the NIV Bible translators came to me and said, "It is true that
we took the word 'soul' out of the Bible. For example, we often translated *nepeš*
into the English word 'person.' But there was no conscious policy that we should
systematically bias our translation in that way. It just happened without anyone
thinking about it." That's what Dr. Phillips means by Zeitgeist.

If you think that the soul is present in theology today, then please explain to me
why Professor Leander Keck, president of the Society of Biblical Literature, said, "I
kind of like *offbeat* ideas such as Dr. Boyd's idea that we should bring the soul
back into biblical studies!"[23] Assigning the soul to Siberia so that no one thinks
about it is not a policy that all Bible scholars agree with. However, the primary situation in theology today is that only the older generation of professors remembers
that the soul was exiled forty years ago. The 1997 Wheaton Theology Conference
was the first scholarly discussion of the Christian concept of the soul in forty years.
It is a delight to welcome the soul back from its sojourn in the wilderness.

If we are going to get serious about understanding the theology of the secular
mental health movement, then we must begin to use the word *soul* again. What
other theological word is available to explain what secular psychotherapists treat?
They claim they don't treat the spirit. They do treat what the Bible would call the
heart, but that word has a different meaning in the Bible than it does in secular
American culture today. Psychotherapists wouldn't understand if we told them they
are actually cardiologists. You could claim they treat the *nous,* which is true, but
that word is rarely used in the Bible, and it has zero recognition in popular American culture. There is one and only one fitting word that all Americans know. It is
the traditional word to refer to the self-concept of a lay person, namely, *soul.*

We need a word around which to rally. Without this single word—a simple

[23]Boyd, *Reclaiming the Soul,* p. 72.

word that ordinary lay people understand—the average American will never under-stand why the self is intrinsically theological. I propose that we raise the flag *soul* to provide a rallying point. During Civil War battles there was often mass confusion on the battlefield. Soldiers falling dead. Bullets and bayonets everywhere. Chaos. May-hem. Amidst the confusion the flag was the only organizing point on the battlefield. It allowed a dizzy soldier to get his bearings, to know where he was supposed to be. It was called the *standard*. Without a flag, a regiment would be overwhelmed with bewilderment. Therefore, when the standard-bearer fell in battle, the most urgent task was to drop your rifle and raise the standard, for the honor of God depended on it.

We need a flag. Now we lack a flag and our troops are in disarray, some of them going this way and some of them that way. The most urgent task inside Christian counseling today is considered to be the battle against Jay Adams and the biblical counselors. That misconception alone shows how disastrously our troops lack orga-nization. Why should Christian soldiers attack Christian soldiers? The enemy is upon us; they are ruthless and cruel. Should we not rather fight the enemy? Let *soul* be our flag. Then the army of God will begin to fight effectively.

What Does Scripture Say?

One of the senior leaders of the Society of Biblical Literature criticized me in March 1997, arguing that my ideas about soul-body dualism were naive, that they were "coming out of left field." He argued that the word *sōma* in Paul's letters always refers to the outward form of the *psychē,* not to the physical body that becomes a corpse. For example, Paul speaks of having a "spiritual body" after death (1 Cor 15:42-44 NIV). This fellow criticized me because he erroneously thought that I had not read the works of Pauline scholars such as Rudolf Bultmann and H. Wheeler Robinson.[24] Such scholarship points to *sōma* always in reference to the whole per-son and says Paul never allows the whole person to be subdivided body versus soul.

Did Paul believe that he would die and leave a cadaver behind, or did Paul believe that he would take his *sōma* with him after he departed? I argue that Paul's opinion on the subject changed as he grew older. In 1 Corinthians we see that he expected the parousia before he died, and he expected to be raptured (1 Thess 4:15-17). Therefore it never occurred to him that he would leave a cadaver behind. In his later writings, however, Paul expected to die before the *eschaton*, and there-fore he spoke of leaving his corpse on earth after he departed. In 2 Corinthians 5:8, Paul says he would "prefer rather to be absent from the body *(sōma)* and to be at home with the Lord" (NASB). Again in Philippians 1:23, he says he desires "to depart

---

[24]H. Wheeler Robinson, *The Christian Doctrine of Man,* 3rd ed. (Edinburgh: T & T Clark, 1958); and Bultmann, *Theology of the New Testament.*

and be with Christ" (NASB). The context makes it clear that he is referring to depart-ing from the flesh (vv. 22-24).[25] From this I conclude that Paul also believed in the existence of cadavers, which implies that he was a soul-body dualist. So he did not believe in the existence of the whole person after death and prior to resurrection. He was a dualist because he was a realist about the fate of the fleshly *sōma*. Paul distinguishes between two different bodies. The fleshly *sōma* of 2 Corinthians 5:8 is not identical to the spiritual *sōma* of 1 Corinthians 15:42-44.

When I delivered the talk on which this chapter is based at the Wheaton confer-ence, one Bible scholar from the Moody Bible Institute stood up and challenged me in the usual way that Bible scholars challenge me. He said that I was ignoring the vast literature on the holistic meaning of the Hebrew word *bāsār* and the Greek word *sōma*. Both words mean "body," but there is quite a bit of scholarly literature that argues to the effect that the whole person is a *bāsār* or a *sōma*. For example, this Bible scholar said, there is a physical quality to the dead spirits in *Sheol* in the Old Testament. In the New Testament there is a physical quality to the soul of Laz-arus lying on the bosom of Abraham (Lk 16:19-31), and there is a physical quality to the rich man burning in the fires and wanting a drop of water for his tongue. He has a tongue, which is a physical thing. Therefore, according to this challenger my argument has no scriptural basis because we humans are always whole persons, even after death, for we are physical beings even then.

I don't deny that physical metaphors are used to describe the intermediate state. To tell you the truth, I have a hard time imagining life without my body, and the more I think about what that would be like, the less I understand. I take comfort in the thought that if I were naked, if I were without this earthly tent (2 Cor 5:1-3), at least I would be with Christ.

Consider the story of Lazarus and Dives (Lk 16:19-21). Both men die and go immediately to heaven and hell, even while the rich man's five brothers are still alive. This means that the general resurrection has not yet occurred. If the five brothers dug up the grave of the rich man, they would have found his corpse (Lk 16:22). Therefore there is soul-body dualism because the corpse in the graveyard is different from the soul burning in the flames of hell. To say that there is a "physical quality to the soul after death" proves nothing.

The church fathers are helpful on this subject. In his book on the soul Tertullian cites the Lazarus and Dives story.[26] He notes that the rich man in the fire has a tongue that can be seen by Lazarus, who is lying on the bosom of Abraham. From this Tertullian concludes that there is a visible and physical quality to the soul, that "the soul has a body." He says there are two bodies: the fleshly body is identical to the soul's body during this life, but at death they separate. Something that is trans-

[25]C. J. De Vogel, "Reflections on Philippians 1:23-24," *Novum Testamentum* 19 (1977): 262-74.
[26]Tertullian *De Anima*, ed. J. H. Waszink (Amsterdam: J. M. Meulenhoff, 1947).

lucent and that is the shape of the human body departs from the physical corpse, for the soul has a body that is made of air and light. It is just like Hollywood's image of what happens when the soul departs at death: the soul has a kind of luminous, visible, ethereal body of its own. But Tertullian declares clearly that he is a soul-body dualist. The dead corpse that is left behind provides the proof. During the intermediate state there are two bodies ("corporeal body" and "body of the soul") implying dualism. Bible scholars have distorted the meaning of the word *dualism* as if the term always meant that one part is despised. The term simply means "dichotomy" or "two," according to the *American Heritage Dictionary*.

Would any Bible scholar like to claim that the writers of the Bible did not expect humans to leave a cadaver behind when they departed from this earth? Why is there so much talk about corpses and bones in the Bible? I argue that both Old and New Testament writers knew that people leave a dead body behind. Both Peter and Paul speak of departing from this earthly dwelling, meaning their body (2 Pet 1:13-15; 2 Cor 5:1-3). That makes both of them dualists, for there are two parts: the earthly dwelling and the "I" who will depart from that dwelling.

It is not scholarly for Bible scholars to redefine the word *dualism* as something that is antibiblical and then to argue that the Bible is not dualistic. That is circular reasoning. If you are going to engage the ancient theologians in argument about soul-body dualism then you have to accept the same definition of *dualism* that they used: that there are two parts. In a few places in his writings Augustine follows Plato and Plotinus in disparaging the body. But if we ferret out the central meaning of the phrase *soul-body dualism* in Augustine's writings, we find that it refers to the moment of death, after which the body is actually inferior to the soul because it disintegrates and rots. If twentieth century theologians had been more careful with their definition of the word *dualism* then there would be no debate about soul-body dualism, and the word *soul* would not have been dropped from the Bible. (Readers with a taste for philosophical theology may want to see a more extensive discussion of monism versus soul-body dualism; they should turn to my article "One's Self Concept and Biblical Theology.")[27]

Most theologians have never pondered whether their Christian doctrine of the whole person is similar to or different from the secular psychotherapy concept of the whole person. Nor have they ever asked themselves how their idea that the body is the whole person differs from the idea promoted in the Nike sneaker commercials that the body is the whole person. This failure of theologians to ponder the most obvious questions leaves me suspicious that they might have taken a twentieth century secular idea and read it into the Bible (eisegesis), without thinking about it. Here's what I want to know: did the Nike Corporation covertly pay biblical theologians a lot of money under the table to get them to promote a con-

---

[27]Boyd, "One's Self Concept and Biblical Theology."

cept of a self that is limited to life on this earth as a prelude to the Nike advertising campaign? I ask this preposterous question to provoke thought.

But there is a more important issue that biblical theologians have not asked about. To lay people does this alleged Hebrew concept of the whole person sound as if it were so similar to the secular view of human nature that they misunderstand it as being an endorsement of the secular mental health movement?

Some theologians have argued with me that if we focus on the soul then God tends to get pushed to the sidelines. "The God-human relationship is what is central," they say. I agree that the God-human relationship is central. But as far as who has been pushed to the theological sidelines in today's theology, it is humans. I claim that theology does not work if, within the framework of the God-human relationship, humans have a secular self-concept.

The battle to which I want to draw your attention is the battle for the self-concept of that great majority of Americans who never have been and never will be in psychotherapy. The problem, in a nutshell, is that American culture, not theology, is defining the way in which we talk. Our day is the first and only time in the history of the earth when the dominant viewpoint is that human nature is entirely secular. Theologians have lost the vocabulary to say otherwise.

There is one and only one word that can turn the tide. If we start talking about the soul as a centerpiece of biblical theology, all of a sudden we will be talking to Americans about something that they care about deeply: themselves. As long as the American people have a secular self-concept they care about keeping their jobs, paying for health care, saving for retirement, and enjoying the good life. But if they began to think of themselves as souls, suddenly they will be confronted with a future after death when they will have to face a Judge. If you think of yourself as a soul instead of a self then you might ask yourself, "Why would Jesus let me into Heaven?" A good question! That, in a nutshell, is the central question that defined the Protestant Reformation.

Preachers can talk until they are blue in the face about justification by faith alone rather than by works. Few Americans will understand because they have a secular self-concept and they are worried about justification in their own eyes, not justification in God's eyes. Secular psychologists ask their clients a thousand times a day, "How do you feel about that?" They never ask, "How do you think God feels about that?" They focus on how their clients evaluate their own lives, not on how God evaluates them. But if Americans thought of themselves as souls, they would need to wrestle with justification in God's eyes. The preacher who is tempted to deliver another sermon on works versus faith might consider shifting gears to a sermon titled "Who is the judge? You or God?"

A Theological Vacuum

Stanton L. Jones, the provost of Wheaton College, says that theologians have not sufficiently developed a theology of the soul. It is a disaster, he said during the panel discussion at the end of the Wheaton Theology Conference, for a pastor to refer a Christian lay person to a secular psychologist when the lay person wants to find a deeper understanding of his or her life—or soul. Jones said, "We need more engagement of theologians and biblical scholars, and not just negative engagement. We don't need to have them saying to psychotherapists, 'Your work is shallow and lacks quality.' We need biblical theologians to engage with psychology in a constructive way."

I recently surveyed members of the Evangelical Theological Society in New England about the soul and about their concept of human nature. Most of them told me that there is not a solid concept of human nature coming out of biblical theology today. My own reading has led me to believe that theologians have resigned from the task of writing about theological anthropology (what Franz Delitzsch calls "biblical psychology").[28] It is as if theologians have said, "We'll leave that subject to the counseling department." Have you ever gone to a bookstore to try to buy a recent book on theological anthropology? There are none in print. The secular mental health movement publishes a thousand books per year promoting a totally secular view of human nature, while theologians publish fewer than one book every ten years on theological anthropology.

James Barr, a leading Old Testament scholar, says, "In general biblical scholars have not chosen to go in a psychological direction in their work. And some day there is going to be a terrible price that will have to be paid for that failure."[29]

At the conference Ellen T. Charry, a theologian from Princeton, told me, "Jeff, it isn't just the word *soul* that is missing from Christianity. It is the entire theological underpinnings for understanding the person."

Conclusion

The city of God will not prevail against the city of this earth until the Day of Judgment. We could choose to be lazy and say that the battle is in God's hands. But I think we have a responsibility—just as American generals have a responsibility—to learn from our mistakes. Just as it is remarkable that North Vietnam used some uneducated peasants to defeat the American military, it is remarkable that secular psychologists and psychiatrists with zero theological sophistication triumphed over Christian theology. Today theology is considered irrelevant to the American people, but secular psychology is a required subject on every campus; there are psychological counselors in most American high schools, and psychobabble fills the mass media.

---

[28]Franz Delitzsch, *A System of Biblical Psychology*, trans. Robert E. Wallis (Edinburgh: T & T Clark, 1867).
[29]From a private communication I had with James Barr in 1994.

Military strategists discovered that the Vietnamese were skillful at exploiting American weaknesses and minimizing American strengths. For example, American generals during the Vietnam War ignored the effect that TV news coverage of wounded American soldiers had on the American public, but they paid careful attention to it during the Persian Gulf War.

The city of God lost the war against the secular mental health movement because instead of fighting against the secular enemy our generals turned against and attacked the self-concept of Christian lay people. Our own troops are not the enemy! To this day if you tell Christian lay people, "The good news is that there is no soul-body dualism; rather, you are a whole person," they will immediately wonder whether they should expect to be totally annihilated when they die. Sometimes lay people are more logical than theologians. We live in an Alice-in-Wonderland world where psychiatrists treat the soul but usually avoid God while theologians preach God but usually avoid the soul.

With all of these perplexities our theological anthropology is in disarray. Theologians and Christian lay people are no longer able to talk with one another about human nature. Many dozens of Bible scholars have advised me, "Don't talk to lay people about the soul. They don't understand about that." There are many indications that anthropology is the weak point of evangelical theology today. Therefore, theologians and pastors dwell on the area in which we are strong, namely, talking about God. Just as Ho Chi Minh and the Vietcong were able to exploit the areas where the American military was weak, so also secular psychologists have been able to exploit the areas where theologians are weak. In order to win the war against evangelical Christianity, the secular mental health movement claims that it has nothing to say about God or theology. Thus it has immobilized our strength.

Secular psychotherapists want to talk only about helping suffering people within a totally secular framework. They are leading with the suit of cards in which theologians are short. In previous centuries, when Christianity had a doctrine of the soul, we had a trump card in theological anthropology. In those days we would have been able to trump anyone who wanted to treat humans from a completely secular viewpoint. But we no longer have that trump card.

The so-called Hebrew concept of the whole person, which has been promoted as the biblical doctrine that is supposed to replace the discredited soul, does not do the job. There are about a dozen reasons that the whole-person doctrine fails, but here I will mention only three. First, the whole-person doctrine sounds like (and probably is) a present-day secular view of human nature, and therefore it is incapable of providing an alternative to the present-day secular view of human nature. Second, it is incapable of explaining what happens during the intermediate state of disembodiment between death and resurrection, and therefore it fails to answer the question that lay people care about passionately: "What happens at the moment of death?"

Third, if biblical theologians were sincere in promoting the so-called biblical concept of the whole person, then we would expect to find dozens of scholarly books and articles comparing and contrasting this view with the view of the whole person coming from the secular mental health movement and secular American culture. These books and articles do not exist.

If you wanted the American lay public, which has a seventh-grade reading level on average, to learn one word that would mean to them that their self-concept should be theological instead of secular, which word would you choose?

About once a month I am asked to speak about the soul on a television or radio talk show or at a church. Lay people respond with amazement. They have an "Aha!" response when they realize that they have been entertaining two contradictory self-concepts inside their minds. It is inspiring, they say, to hear that they should think of themselves as souls answerable to God, not just as selves answerable to themselves. This is the real work of integration at the grassroots level. Among the rank and file members of the body of Christ the word *integration* means asking, "Who do you love the most, yourself or God?"

5

THEOLOGY AFTER PSYCHOLOGY

Ellen T. Charry

F *I. Introduction*

ROM A THEOLOGICAL PERSPECTIVE, TO SPEAK OF THE INTERSECTION OF PSY-
chology and theology is imprecise and misleading. It casts psychology and theology as opposites rather than as different perspectives on the same topic: the
understanding of human personhood. Christianity has a distinctive take on these
issues because it cannot consider persons except as creatures of God. It is more
precise, therefore, to consider the relationship between secular psychology and
theological psychology, often referred to as theological anthropology.

A. The argument of this paper is twofold. On one hand, within some churches secular psychology has overwhelmed the care of souls so that theological psychology
has lost its voice. On the other hand, Christian doctrine has failed to incorporate
important insights from secular psychology with the result that pastoral practitioners have turned away from doctrine and toward secular psychology for help in
pastoral matters.

B. Role of + the pastoral arts
It is both impossible and unwise to expunge modern psychology from the pastoral arts. Indeed, pastors should become far more aware of mental health issues
than they often are. But that is different from suggesting that the pastoral arts are to
take secular psychology rather than Christian theology as their point of departure. It
may be possible to identify a distinctly Christian psychology and to translate some
insights of secular psychology into theological categories in order to put a theological foundation under the pastoral arts. This reclaiming and recalibrating could
revive the church's own call to care for souls in a genuinely theological manner that
attends both to modern psychology and to the Christian's grounding in God.

My procedure will be first to sketch the development of the modern self within
which modern psychology takes shape. Then I will identify the task of modern psychology within that framework and touch briefly on the importation of this outlook
into the churches. In the second part of this chapter I will discuss the Christian psychology developed by St. Augustine, identifying points of contact and tension

between these two outlooks. In conclusion, I will suggest a reconstruction of the care of souls as a way of thinking about theology after psychology.

The Secular Self and Modern Psychology

With the end of the millennium, we may justly call the twentieth century the psychological century. In the postindustrial West, psychology and capitalism set the terms for understanding human nature and human aspirations. In mid-twentieth century, post-Freudian psychology, which focuses on healthy psychological development, established itself in the universities. In popularized forms it spread to schools, the family, the workplace and churches. Today people use psychological measurements to divine whom they should marry, what field of endeavor they should pursue, even which church best suits their temperament. Four-year-olds and applicants to seminary must pass batteries of psychological tests before they are admitted to elite nursery schools or to ministerial candidacy. Therapy is often the first resort for the repair of marriages, families and ailing careers among the professional managerial class. Judges mandate counseling for people who are exhibiting antisocial behavior. It is widely supposed that persons who have difficulty in any area of their lives have psychological problems stemming from their family of origin. I have a cartoon of one person seated in the middle of a large, nearly empty auditorium. The caption reads, "The National Association of Children of Functional Families."

Much of American culture and business now thinks in psychological terms. Advertising is largely the art of manipulating desire rather than the promotion of products on their merits. Social problems too are viewed in psychological terms. Poverty among African Americans, for example, is widely viewed as being caused by either low self-esteem resulting from racism or passivity resulting from economic dependency. Both positions see the problem in essentially secular psychological terms.

The autonomous secular self, a product of Enlightenment philosophy and popularized post-Freudian psychology, whose motto might be "to thine own self be true," draws its identity from the ability to think independently and from the modern mandate to "be oneself." One's identity is crafted from the narrative of one's life and from one's own interests. It stands in tension with the Christian view that persons come from God, return to God, find their desires properly satisfied in God and are therefore to glorify God in thanksgiving.

The modern self developed simultaneously with deism and modern atheism. It evolved gradually through philosophy and literature beginning in the seventeenth century with René Descartes's *Meditations* (1641). It was shaped by John Locke's *Essay Concerning Human Understanding* (1689), Daniel Defoe's *Robinson Crusoe* (1719), David Hume's *Enquiry Concerning Human Understanding* (1748) and Jean-Jacques Rousseau's *Discourse on the Sciences and the Arts* (1750) and *Dis-*

l the Origins of Inequality (1755). It was further shaped by romanticism in *'s Emile* (1762), Goethe's *Sorrows of Young Werther* (1774) and Gustave Flaubert's *Madame Bovary* (1857). Individualism was boosted by John Stuart Mill's *On Liberty* (1859), the writings of Friedrich Nietzsche, James Joyce's *Portrait of the Artist as a Young Man* (1916), and the work of Virginia Woolf, to name but a few literary figures and their works.

Freud framed the question of healthy development in psychosexual terms. Later, post-Freudian psychologists, many of them fleeing from or sensitive to Nazism, drank deeply from the atheological wells of philosophy and literature, especially picking up the modern emphasis on emancipation from external constraint and social custom. Individuation became a central theme of childhood and adolescent development theory. The post-Freudians, including Rollo May, Karen Horney, Erich Fromm, H. S. Sullivan, Heinz Kohut, Margaret Mahler, and especially Carl Rogers, Abraham Maslow, and Erik Erikson, provided the direct link between the modern self and the psychologization of the pastoral arts and of certain interpretations of Christian doctrine.[1]

One rubric for understanding both modern secular psychology and Christian psychology is to see them as variants of ancient faculty psychology, especially that of Plato, Aristotle and the Stoics, who saw the soul as tripartite, with each aspect having special responsibilities for conducting the person's life. In *The Republic* Plato says that the soul has three capacities or aspects: impulse, or desire (the impulsive side); cognition, or mind (the capacity to reason, the highest capacity); and spirit, or energy (a mediating capacity that is capable of curbing desire and putting reason into action). Freud's tripartite structure of the self—id, ego and super-ego—seems to resemble this ancient view.

In the *De Anima* Aristotle bent Plato's schema to biology, finding in sense perception, nutrition and respiration the sources of the appetites or feelings that account for behavior. The Stoics, following Plato, explained mental disturbances as errors of perception or cognition arising from the impulses and overcome by the correct use of reason and the will. Ancient psychology provided the background for both Christian and modern psychology.

We shall follow the trajectory of Christian psychology in due course. Here it is worth noting that modern secular psychology develops ancient tripartite faculty psychology. Human functioning is understood as an interplay among affection (the expression of emotion), cognition (the process of reasoning by which one reaches conclusions about the world and the self) and behavior. Emotions and behavior are labile and easily unbalanced, leading to dysfunction, which is no longer labeled as sin but as illness, or in the case of some inappropriate behavior, as criminal. Secular

---

[1] E. Brooks Holifield, *A History of Pastoral Care in America: From Salvation to Self-Realization* (Nashville: Abingdon, 1983).

psychology eliminated God and sin from the modern analysis of hur
ing, seeing dysfunction as rooted in unconscious events in the recent or distant ,
rather than in a turning from God or a fall from grace.

Persons who come for counseling are usually impaired in one or more of the
three basic faculties. The assumption is that all three areas are interconnected so
that making a change in one will affect each of the other two. The psychotherapeutic approaches that are popular today attack the individual's problem at one of
these points. Behavior therapy works directly with impaired behavior; cognitive
therapy deals with faulty reasoning processes and the way that they are played out
in the person's life; and insight-oriented psychotherapies are designed to bring out
and examine emotions and their roots. The choice of therapy, at least ideally, is
made according to which area of the individual's functioning is most amenable to
change, and which approach best fits the person's temperament. Many therapists
are skilled in two or three of the techniques and use them at appropriate points in
their work with an individual who is seeking help.

Underneath their different techniques, these therapeutic orientations have three
things in common. Each has a narrative of origin to explain the genesis of the problem, each requires strong motivation for change, and each holds up a concept of
the ideal person and aims therapy toward helping the client to develop in the direction of that ideal.

The narratives of origin of the three schools differ somewhat from each other,
but the bottom line is the same: the sufferer is experiencing patterns of thought,
behavior, or feelings that were laid down in the past in a manner that was outside
of the individual's conscious awareness. For the insight-oriented therapist the problematic pattern developed as the result of conflicted affections and psychological
defensive operations called forth by affective stress. The behavior therapist sees the
problem in terms of conditioning: certain behaviors, though maladaptive, have
been rewarded and solidified. To the cognitive therapist faulty assumptions about
self and others have led the person to create self-fulfilling situations in which the
individual becomes convinced of the rightness of those incorrect assumptions. All
three therapeutic schools posit the existence of events in the unconscious realm,
outside of conscious awareness or understanding, but, interestingly, that that
unconscious realm lies completely within the human person.

Normal development is understood to entail the individuation of the young person from the family of origin. Past events, often having to do with family structure
and patterns of relationship in childhood, are harbored in the unconscious and
cause dysfunction. Thus mothers and, more recently, fathers are seen to be complicit in their children's psychological problems. One goal of therapy may be to rid
oneself of the internalized authority of the parents, which is seen as debilitating.

More recently, as medications have proven effective for treating mental illness
and some personality disorders, the phenomenon of mother blame—as in the myth

of the schizophrenegenic mother—have receded. Therapists now recognize that constitutional personality disorders and biochemical imbalances can give rise to maladaptive behavior; this is a move back to Aristotle's biological outlook.

From the perspective of the history of ideas, the political goal of emancipation from the power of the church and the king, which is at the core of democracy, was transferred first to the culture and eventually to the family. Jean Jacques Rousseau, and later John Stuart Mill, pointed to conventional society's dysfunctional effects on the flourishing of individuals. More recently, under the influence of Marxist and post-Marxist thought, the narrative of repression has interpreted social problems in such a way that society in general is held responsible for individual dysfunction. Secular psychology identifies maladaptive or pathological family relationships as the locus of psychological dysfunction. The cumulative effect of seeking factors outside the self to account for dysfunction has been to minimize individual accountability and to undermine the Christian doctrine of sin on which regeneration and reconciliation with God rest. Consequently, psychotherapy has not retained an ethical scope to its mandate; rather, it often focuses on supporting the self-development and goals set by the patient or client.

After three hundred years of unchallenged supremacy in the West, the modern self is now under criticism from many quarters. Perhaps the most popular articulation of that criticism is Robert Bellah's *Habits of the Heart.*[2] Social scientists, philosophers, journalists, educators and social critics are creating a considerable literature in this vein.[3] In various ways they all criticize the modern self, and fear for the cohesiveness of the society from unbridled freedom and individualism. As a nation we have lost the republican and civic virtues of public spiritedness and the classic virtue of self-restraint. The centrist communitarian movement and the politicization of evangelical Christianity from the right are two responses to these concerns. Rarely, however, are these problems framed in theological terms.

The Psychologization of the Liberal Churches

Liberal churches were psychologized with the creation of the field of pastoral counseling, and soon theological education followed by providing clinical pastoral education. In his excellent history of the subject, Brooks Holifield calls the therapeuticization of the churches a transition "from salvation to self-realization"

---

[2]Robert N. Bellah et al., *Habits of the Heart: Individualism and Commitment in American Life* (Berkeley: University of California Press, 1985).

[3]Allan Bloom, *Closing of the American Mind* (New York: Simon & Schuster, 1987); Jean Bethke Elshtain, *Democracy on Trial* (New York: Basic Books, 1995); Os Guinness, *The American Hour: A Time of Reckoning and the Once and Future Role of Faith* (New York: Macmillan, 1993); Alasdair MacIntyre, *After Virtue: A Study in Moral Theory,* 2nd ed. (Notre Dame, Ind.: University of Notre Dame Press, 1984); Charles Taylor, *Sources of the Self: The Making of the Modern Identity* (Cambridge, Mass.: Harvard University Press, 1989).

under the influence of post-Freudian psychologists. Churches today aim to be a
therapeutic force in people's lives by offering various kinds of counseling services.
These churches act as a general psychological life-support system, in much the
same way that the medieval church's sacramental system paved the way to eternal
life.

Christians have learned much of value from secular psychology, which currently
has a feminist accent. Through the popularization of personality inventories they
have come to recognize temperamental differences among persons and have
learned to be less judgmental of those differences. Serious mental illnesses affect
about 5 percent of the general population. The differentiation of those illnesses
from demon possession has enabled the church to minister more compassionately
to persons it had hitherto viewed as justly suffering God's wrath. A helpful effect of
the rising awareness of psychological issues, then, has been to distinguish illness
from sin.

Feminists have pointed out the helpful psychological insight that some people
sin not through pride but through selflessness, self-hatred, or pathological other-
centeredness and neurotic dependency. These traits appear in certain psychiatri-
cally defined personality disorders and may be treatable with psychotherapy and
medication. In some cases such traits may be reinforced by themes in the Christian
tradition itself.[4] The tradition has attended to those who suffer from self-centered-
ness, but timid souls need to grow in the opposite direction. This realization has
serious implications for soteriology as well as for the practical arts of preaching,
pastoral care and worship.

Not all the learning from psychology is unambiguously positive, however. As
helpful as secular psychology has been, it has also unseated Christian psychology
and, by extension, the teachings on salvation and the Christian life. As secular psychology came to dominate the intellectual landscape, Christian psychology,
grounded in the comprehension of a person's standing before God, appeared to
lack therapeutic value. And as an emphasis on divine judgment came increasingly
to be considered countertherapeutic and unconditional support and encouragement came to be viewed as therapeutic, the idea that behavioral problems are spiritual problems requiring confession, repentance and absolution receded from view.

The possibility that psychological understandings of salvation might overwhelm
rather than assist theology was first pointed out in 1966 by Philip Rieff when he
proclaimed in his stunning treatise "the triumph of the therapeutic."[5] He identifies

[4]Judith Plaskow, *Sex, Sin and Grace: Women's Experience and the Theologies of Reinhold
Niebuhr and Paul Tillich* (New York: University Press of America, 1980); Valerie Saving, "The
Human Situation: A Feminine View," in *Womanspirit Rising: A Feminist Reader in Religion,*
ed. Carol P. Christ and Judith Plaskow (New York: Harper & Row, 1979).
[5]Philip Rieff, *The Triumph of the Therapeutic: Uses of Faith After Freud* (New York: Harper &
Row, 1966).

the countercultural ethos of the 1960s, which derived from emancipation themes, as a threat to an ordered society. It is a hermeneutic that derives from Rousseau. Rieff's warning, echoed by Brooks Holifield, that psychology cannot be meshed with theology without doing violence to the latter, has gone largely unheeded.

Popular sentiment that meshes autonomy, individuality and emancipation but fails to speak of God's judgment and the moral reform of the self is in tension with St. Paul's understanding of the Christian self, a self that is based on transformation in righteousness by conformity to Christ. If the pastoral arts adopt this atheological popular sensibility, they lose their theological grounding and are unable properly to attend to the care of souls. They cannot properly undertake theological formation and direction. Recalling that the church's pastoral responsibility is the care of souls sets the terms of the intersection of theology and psychology on Christian ground.

Pastoral counseling, now perhaps viewed apart from spiritual direction, was created to bring modern psychology into church life. It is usually undertaken in moments of crisis or vulnerability in a person's life and at the behest of the distressed individual. Because it has become associated with crisis, often grief and failure in their various forms, pastoral counselors are vulnerable to offering God's comfort and strength at the expense of God's judgment and guidance for transformation.

The ease with which secular psychology has co-opted theology in liberal churches reveals not only the power of modern narratives, but also a threefold failure of theology. First, under the influence of the Enlightenment, Protestant scholasticism embraced elements of Enlightenment rationalism that obscured the pastoral function of doctrine, an obscurity from which that function has never fully emerged. Second, Protestant scholasticism proclaimed a one-size-fits-all view of human temperament that is no longer credible. And third, as an atheological outlook came to prevail, both salvation as life with God and damnation after this life became unintelligible, leaving a lacuna into which salvation as self-realization readily moved.

Secular psychology points out that both itself and Christian psychology are concerned with self-knowledge and behavior. Both aim to be therapeutic and supportive. There can be little doubt, however, that Christian and secular psychology are in tension at several basic points.

In sum, modern literature and philosophy undergird a secular vision of psychological well-being that stands in the place of the theological identity of the ransomed sinner. Pastoral counselors must be theologically astute when employing secular psychology in a pastoral setting. The church's responsibility is to provide the body of Christ with spiritual guidance and a strong and vibrant theological identity. As Holifield warns, "the temptation to allow psychological language to overwhelm or define the religious tradition has often been irresistible. . . . To say that Jesus was a 'good psychologist' or that therapeutic acceptance and Christian love are the same, is to render trivial both psychology and a religious traditi⟨

The Christian Self

Although the church fathers inherited ancient Greek psychology, they developed
their own framework for understanding the self, bringing the soul under divine
guidance. When reason and the emotions are oriented toward God, behavior is
properly directed. When these faculties are misdirected, unseemly behavior results.
The task of Christian therapy (the care of souls) is to help the individual to identify
the proper godly orientation for desire in order to regain control of the emotions
and behavior. Augustine realized that emotions and behavior are not readily vulnerable to the dictates of reason. He postulated that only divine grace, not any rational
capacity within the individual, can provide the support needed for change. Yet
despite his focus on grace, Augustine contributed to the development of modern
psychology, bequeathing to the West an introspective focus in which self-examination becomes key to self-understanding. The monastic tradition, however, relied on
spiritual disciplines to help the penitent refocus on God in order to retrain the emotions and behavior.

This does not mean that Augustine failed to appreciate the importance of the
material realm of existence. Indeed, he was a poor ascetic who bemoaned his overeating. In both his *Confessions* and the *De Trinitate* he pointed to the spiritual
sphere of human existence where happiness is more secure because it comes from
knowing and enjoying God; thus it transcends the vicissitudes of daily life. What he
failed to do, however, was to demonstrate adequately that the material world is the
appropriate theater for the spiritual life. This failure has left lingering doubt about
whether Christianity fully overcame the Manichean dualism that Augustine claimed
to have abandoned in favor of catholic Christianity.

Be that as it may, to the extent that secular psychology finds the material sphere
adequate and does not recognize happiness in God as the source and goal of
human happiness and well-being, it cannot see, let alone understand, Augustine's
vision of the happiness, self-esteem and personal security that come from attending
to God. Secular psychology is thus unable to communicate with a theological psychology which claims that turning from God is a cause of genuine unhappiness or
that turning toward God can provide a foundation for the self which can withstand
at least some of the vagaries of human life or provide a therapeutic base from
which to confront them. Secular psychology can suggest a different job, spouse or
climate, or the development of new behavioral skills and sensibilities to enhance a
client's personal efficiency, but generally psychology has been deaf to the spiritual
foundation of the self.

Even if some therapists are beginning to recognize that some clients bring spiri-

[6]Holifield, *History of Pastoral Care*, p. 355.

tual resources with them that can be called on in the therapeutic process, it still sees these as additional resources of support for a basically secular self. Psychology's secular foundation prevents it from seeing knowledge of God and Christian practices broadly as a foundation of psychological well-being. When used as an instrument of pastoral care, therefore, secular psychology lacks the very thing that pastoral care requires: a theological foundation.

One way of describing the difference between secular and Christian psychology is to suggest that secular psychology works with the self while Christian psychology is concerned with the soul. Care of the soul attends to spiritual malfunction. It grows out of the sacrament of penance, which was an expression of self-dissatisfaction and despair in the ancient church, and it offers the hope of repair of what is amiss. The church's tradition of spiritual guidance aims at the reform of the soul. During the Middle Ages, confession of sin, repentance, corporate worship, participation in the sacraments and works of charity properly undertaken aimed at reform of the soul (even though penitential practices became deformed at that time). Protestantism offered hope that one could rest in God's love by clinging to the hope of divine mercy shown forth in the cross of Christ. But neither penance alone nor faith alone is finally strong enough to effect the transformation of the self desired by Augustinian psychology because these later forms aimed primarily at the reduction of guilt rather than at the renovation of the soul.

Recalibrating Augustinian Psychology

I have argued that Christian psychology and secular psychology part company over the relevance of God. Christian psychology claims that we are made in the divine image but fallen from that basic identity, that on our own we are lost and confused. Our true identity is reclaimed for us by God in Christ so that we may return to our proper self. This is the healing of the soul. Secular psychology grounds the self in itself. The self is autonomous; it does not need God either to understand itself or to chart a path to true happiness and emotional and behavioral stability. And because the secular self has the upper hand in the dominant culture it is necessary to sketch out its Christian counterpart.

Augustine definitively shaped for the West an understanding of the Christian soul that finds its origin and destiny in God. While Augustine is infamous for having viewed original sin as a symbolic sexually transmitted disease and for denying that we can do anything good on our own, his theological psychology is more complex than these views suggest. With himself as the key witness for the prosecution, Augustine articulated a psychological dynamic of struggle in which the baptized believer is in an approach-avoidance conflict with the wisdom and goodness of God. In his *Confessions* and in the treatise on the Christian life in the *De Trinitate*, Augustine described the slow and bumbling search for God and self as a single undertaking. For it is only in grasping the triunity of God and groping toward the identity of having been created in the divine image that one comes to one's proper identity and dignity.

Augustine not only was the first one to articulate a Christian psychology, but he also deftly argued for understanding the self on the basis of the triunity of God and for grasping the triunity of God as analogous to the faculties of human consciousness. Unless one knows God—Father, Son and Holy Spirit—and oneself as echoing the Trinity, one has at best only partial self-knowledge, only surface contentment in life. "Our hearts are restless until they rest in you," Augustine writes at the beginning of the *Confessions*.[7]

In the *Confessions* Augustine began his reflection on human nature by observing children and reflecting on his own childhood. Unlike Rousseau, who had a romanticized view of children's natural goodness, Augustine saw infants as querulous, demanding and self-centered.[8] He saw his own struggles to curb overeating, addiction to sex and craving for fame as evidence that demandingness is not limited to childhood, but mutates into different forms in adult life.

In the classical view sin is pride. It is the urge toward self-gratification, self-aggrandizement and control of others. Augustine viewed excessive gratification of bodily desires, along with the urge, common in adolescence, to engage in random violence and destruction of property (an urge that he experienced when he robbed a pear tree as a member of a group of adolescent boys) as the result of turning from God to self-gratification. He reasoned that resistance to God is so strong in human beings that it had to be forcibly overcome by the dramatic events of the incarnation, cross, resurrection and ascension. These display the deep goodness and generosity of God that call us to recenter ourselves in him.

Augustine realized that recentering ourselves in God is a slow and arduous process. He explains it in the second half of his treatise on the Trinity. Christian therapy is emancipation from the distortions of the self to which all persons are liable. It begins with realizing that the source of one's proper dignity and nobility is God and no one or nothing else. Dignity and nobility are found in coming to understand God and in coming to see oneself as an echo of the Trinity. Augustinian freedom is freedom from maladaptive behaviors that arise from false or distorted desire. Augustinian conversion is the rebuilding of the soul by turning and clinging to the being of God.

Dysfunctional behavior can take both the forms that Augustine recognized and forms that he did not write about. Self-hatred and undue dependency arising from the lack of a proper understanding of one's dignity in God is just as appropriate to Christian psychology as is the more usual distortion of the soul recently dubbed selfism.[9] Both those who press themselves forward and those who are overly

---

[7]Augustine *Confessions* 1.1.1.
[8]Ibid., 1.6.9—1.12.19.
[9]Paul C. Vitz, *Psychology as Religion: The Cult of Self-Worship*, 2nd ed. (Grand Rapids, Mich.: Eerdmans, 1997).

dependent on the acceptance and nurture of others fail to rejoice in their dignity in God and may equally mutilate and abuse themselves and others. Both those who swagger and those who cringe resist the true source of their goodness and nobility, God. They cling instead to sources of immediate gratification that feed narcissistic desire or neurotic insecurity.

Augustine and the Western tradition following him used but one personality type as their model. The West generalized the sin of selfism and commended its opposite, humility, as its cure. Teachings on the Christian life failed to grasp that humility to the point of self-hatred contradicts the dignity that the self possesses by virtue of its homology with God. This feminist correction of Christian psychology and other corrections that secular psychology may identify must now be translated into theological categories and applied appropriately by the pastoral arts. And even if medication is able to provide a floor under those people who have fragile or overly robust personalities, a theological floor is also needed because it provides a firmer foundation than the self alone can ever provide. Augustine, holding tightly to the biblical insistence that we are made in the image of God, took the Trinity as the standard for the quest for a noble soul, for the soul as God created it to be, that finds its dignity in the goodness of the Trinity itself.

Before Augustine, Plato too had sought to understand and cultivate personal nobility. He attributed Sparta's defeat of the Athenian navy in the Peloponnesian War to the moral and spiritual decline of Athens. He held the Homeric gods partially responsible for morally malforming Athenian leadership, and he sought to cultivate moral excellence in Athens's citizens by stimulating in them a desire for justice, courage, self-control and friendship modeled by his teacher, Socrates. Plato and Aristotle thought that human excellence could be achieved through reasoned insight and practical experience. Once the city's leaders understood that moral excellence was the foundation of a well-ordered polis, they would seek this reasonable way through the philosophical friendships they nurtured among themselves and through the creation of the rule of law in a carefully structured republic ruled by wise leaders.

Watching the decline of Roman civilization, Augustine saw that wise leadership was not so easily achieved because we are not as rational as Plato thought we are. Following St. Paul he saw that we are readily lured away from the right and reasonable thing to do by the temptations of self-gratification, and he used himself as the prime example. Augustine broke with Christian Platonism when he concluded that to know the good is one thing, but to do it is another thing entirely. Augustine, perhaps picking up on Paul's short complaint about his weakness in Romans 7, was the first to offer sustained reflection on the dynamics of sin as a universal feature of human existence. He concluded that sin, as symbolized in the Garden of Eden story, results from a desire for misguided self-fulfillment fostered by a weak will.

Augustine, of course, had a resource for thinking about human psychology to which Plato had no access: the God of Israel made known in Jesus Christ, who created us from the dust to which we shall return. We are constituted not only by this relationship, but also by our creation in the Trinitarian image. Augustine framed the central issue of the personality as a spiritual struggle, a struggle to claim our proper identity in the image that alone can provide the nobility and excellence God intends for us. But because this struggle is impossible to win, we must rely on God's grace completely.

Augustine has been interpreted as suggesting that desire, or concupiscence, is wrong. That is not a complete interpretation. Augustine's view is that desire is easily deformed. He saw that we are caught between our worst self, which brings false happiness, and our best self, which brings true happiness yet lies dormant under our futile attempts to follow our own lights. The struggle for goodness and happiness is a spiritual one that will finally be resolved not through any short-term pleasure but only in a life pleasing to God, to whom we are indissolubly tethered and whose grace alone makes that life possible.

Augustine's point is not Luther's, that understanding the mercy as opposed to the wrath of God provides us the support and encouragement we need in order to remain calm and secure. Rather, Augustine's psychology is about two kinds of happiness. As long as one is content with material happiness alone one can never know true peace because material peace is evanescent; financial security and all jobs and relationships are shaky. Only when the soul rests in God as the ground of jobs, relationships and financial dealings is it possible for one to participate in the goodness of God and to thereby glimpse spiritual peace and live into one's true identity. The key to being able to handle the stresses of daily life with dignity and honor is knowing that one truly participates in the drama of redemption and the divine life by virtue of being an echo of the Trinity, and by faith and baptism into the death and resurrection of Christ through the Holy Spirit. These realities provide a secure foundation for daily living to which secular psychology has no access.

Christian psychology as framed by Augustine provides a theological identity on which a broad contemporary theological psychology might be built. Augustine has a place for what modern psychology recognizes as defense mechanisms, neurotic behavior and maladaptive character traits. He sees these, however, as stemming not from one's personal narrative but from the resistance to God that envelops everyone. He does recognize that some temperamental differences are constitutional: his mother was tempted by drink; he was tempted by fame. We are born with or develop certain personality issues, but this did not dissuade Augustine from seeing the spiritual dimension of such problems. What Augustine did not provide that the church today needs is a link between his moral psychology and his ecclesiology that would strengthen and deepen the individual's Trinitarian and, according to a more Pauline view, christological identity.

Pastoral nurture of the individual's theological identity is provided by other

Christian doctrines and practices, especially the doctrines of the church and of the communion of saints, the sacraments, and pastoral practices like anointing and penance. Recent developments in ecclesiology that focus on the laity together with the clergy as the body of Christ, convey the theological identity of the faithful and dignify their ministries. The liturgical renewal movement, which understands the Holy Spirit to be the agent of baptism, grafts the recipient of baptism into the divine life and further lifts the believer above a self-constructed identity. Similarly, sharing in the Eucharistic fellowship with the body of Christ is one way in which the individual is made one with Christ, the head of the church.

Anointing, unlike the washing with water, is a strengthening rite that may be repeated occasionally. While the medieval church used it only for the dying, today it is used for more extensive forms of healing. Penance, or reconciliation, which was lost to Protestantism in the Reformation and is now lost to Catholicism as well, could provide a powerful tool for the care of souls if reconstructed in a healthy way. Penance may be especially effective if used together with anointing and set in an appropriate liturgy. And finally, the reclamation of the communion of saints gives believers access to Christian friends, surrounding them with a great support network of those who, like themselves, struggle to live a godly life.

These doctrines and practices can nourish and strengthen the soul, which takes its identity from the being and work of God, in whose wisdom, goodness and sanctity it is created and into whose work in Christ it is baptized. This foundation for a healthy Christian self can support both the tough and the tenderhearted in ways that they need. For amendment of life in either direction both sorts of persons need the theological self-esteem that only God can provide. The Christian self is in a stronger position to cultivate healthy interpersonal relationships than is the secular self, for the Christian does not depend on interpersonal relationships for identity or security. God both constrains manipulative self-interest and provides a psychological security that challenges both self-hatred and neurotic dependence on others. When one lacks a healthy theological identity, the shallow self-esteem that secular culture claims and the relationships and projects that are built on it are liable to the distortions of desire that cause one to manipulate and abuse objects of desire in ingenious ways. Orientation to one's theological identity places all relationships and desires within the context of the glory of God.

Reconstructing the Care of Souls

A balanced Christian psychology would address the needs of both people who have prideful temperament and people who have constricted temperaments—and perhaps others as well. Prideful and constricted temperaments are opposites, but in many ways the common failing of people with these temperaments is that they lack a strong and healthy theological identity to which they can turn for judgment on their various weaknesses. That theological identity, we now see, must be broad enough to encompass various personality types.

It is here that spiritual direction complements secular psychotherapy and medication when indicated. If sin and repentance are envisioned apart from the personality issues and mental illnesses that affect personal performance and relationships with others, or if personality issues are envisioned apart from sin and repentance, the nexus of God, self, sin and relationships that distinguishes the Christian life from other ways of life may be missed. From a Christian point of view, medication and secular psychotherapy are necessary in some cases. Even though this is not the church's area of expertise, familiarity with mental health issues, various personality disorders and temperamental variation are essential to thoughtful pastoral care. The medieval church had none of this knowledge. Today, however, modern insights about personality must nuance a one-size-fits-all psychology.

At the same time, character defects such as jealousy, arrogance, anger, vengefulness, power seeking, self-aggrandizement, spitefulness and verbosity on the one hand, and timidity, passivity and self-hatred on the other hand, even if they are constitutional or have roots in family dynamics, all call for theological correction. Temperamental differences affect not only our personality, but also how we deal with moral concerns: how we treat other persons and our bodies, how we handle money (much to the fore in today's culture) and so on. These cannot properly be left out of the church's purview. The ability to call on one's theological identity as the dignified foundation to which the sinner is responsible provides a psychological cushion against undue embarrassment and guilt. It is a model to pursue.

The Christian view is that until one knows oneself in the reflected light of God and sees one's behavior in light of one's true theological identity, secular counseling—even if it is dressed in biblical language—will not provide the guidance needed for true flourishing as Christian faith understands it. Even granting that the church has had a lopsided view of sin as selfism only—a view that needs to become more nuanced with some help from secular psychology and feminism—persons who are victims of Christian myopia or Christian malpractice are still in need of God's help—sometimes in the form of judgment—and the church's proper guidance. This may require reeducating Christian ministers as well as laypeople and giving them new language to grasp the complexity of both human personality and behavior. They need theological training to provide theological guidance, and perhaps they also need to be encouraged to "speak Christian" again.

Persons who are victims of major mental illnesses, birth defects, troubling personality or character disorders, physical illnesses or handicaps, domestic abuse, racism or other forms of social or economic violence, random violence and so forth may suffer secondary spiritual damage from their suffering. To the extent that the church has not understood suffering well and has failed to stand against social ills it is complicit in that damage. The church must do more than encourage such persons. The damage done by such suffering may give rise to patterns of thought and

...at are self-destructive or damaging to others. It is relatively easy to call
... to account, but the church is also called to correct and thereby heal
those who sin, especially when dysfunctional defense mechanisms or maladaptive
behavior resulting from their particular sufferings become a way of life. Spiritual
guidance is needed both by those whose sins fit the more traditional model of the
tough-hearted and by those whose circumstances and personality dynamics are
more complex and tattered.

We turn to St. Augustine as a beginning point for addressing the weaknesses in
secular psychology because he interpreted the human person as having a theological self, a soul that needs to be in the ascendancy in order for persons to flourish
spiritually. The self that feigns autonomy is self-deluded. Paradoxically, human freedom requires recognition of dependency and admission of one's need for help
from God. Those who are sure that they can direct themselves aright and would
deny themselves divine aid and guidance, regardless of whether they need to
become more self-assured or more humble, are simply wrong in the Christian view.
Perhaps in our free-market environment Augustine might even see such persons as
dangerous, for they are guided by no identity beyond themselves that links them to
God and other people; there is nothing to check the penchant for pursuing self-
interest.

Christian psychology properly grounds freedom, pleasure and happiness in
God, restoring a link that modernity severed. A Christian vision of spiritual health
presses beyond skills that actualize one's desires or enable one to carry off one's
relationships with aplomb. Christian spiritual health is based not in the skills one
cultivates but in the deeper theological foundation from which they are cultivated.
God has put a floor under and a ceiling over human striving. Secular psychology is
not sympathetic to this room that God has constructed because modern thought
resists theological constraints. On secular psychology's terms it is possible to construe oneself adequately without reference to God.

Theology After Psychology

The argument for reclaiming and recalibrating Christian psychology and traditional
practices and enriching them with modern psychology and feminist insights suggests that theology has failed to assert the theological foundation of the self, leaving
pastoral practitioners without doctrinal resources to meet the spiritual needs of the
faithful. Practitioners have therefore sometimes applied secular psychological categories indiscriminately, paying insufficient attention to the doctrinal resources of
the Christian tradition that could be used for spiritual and pastoral care. Reclaiming
a pastoral theological psychology for the age in which we live is rightly the job of
the church's theologians. The absence of a theological psychology leaves a great
and ever-widening gap between theology and the practice of pastoral ministry. We
theologians have failed the church.

Reconstructed theological psychology and pastoral practices should be grounded in the biblical and theological heritage. Augustine grounds the Christian self in the triune identity of God. But the Christian self can also be grounded in the covenant of grace that was established at creation by the incarnate word of God, by whom humanity is raised to the dignity of God, or in the cross of Christ that remits sin and has made friends out of enemies (Eph 2). Despite their variety these themes all point to an identity that is given to, not created by, believers. The self that is based on the work of God in Christ is a genuinely Christian self.

Regardless of whether one is sympathetic to Augustine's trinitarian orientation to psychology, Augustine did make clear the connection between the doctrine of God and the healing of the soul. Others who have developed the doctrines of the person of Christ and the work of Christ and of the Holy Spirit have not always made this connection as plain. So pastors have understandably turned from doctrine to other sources of help. This need not remain the case, however. Christian doctrines can provide the foundation for the Christian self. They offer an alternative both to a haphazardly formed self that is vulnerable to the manipulations of the marketplace and to the Rousseauean view that the self is naturally whole and complete, needing only the proper growing conditions in order to flower. The latter view has led to tireless attempts to manipulate the environment so that delicate personalities might flourish. For its own reasons, then, psychology has been as inept in attending to the formation of human persons as have the more rigid forms of theological psychology.

Secular psychology has been helpful in revealing the complexity of the self and its functioning. Genetic factors, family dynamics, socioeconomic circumstances, educational background and even chance weave intricate patterns that form each individual personality like a snowflake. Secular psychotherapy has been far more sensitive to the texture of the personality and temperament than has its Christian counterpart. Modern sensibilities are of interest to doctrinal theologians, however, only to the extent that they enable theologians to offer pastoral practitioners deeper, genuinely theological insight into the self. For it is theology's responsibility to provide a salutary theological frame of reference that can strengthen, correct and empower the Christian for discipleship. This, perhaps, is finally what divides pastoral theology from secular psychology. We theologians have abandoned the practitioners, and we should be ashamed. Perhaps it is not too late to begin repairing the damage.

6

OUTLINE OF PAULINE PSYCHOTHERAPY

Robert C. Roberts

P SYCHOLOGISTS WHO ARE CHRISTIANS OFTEN SPEAK OF INTEGRATING PSYCHOLOGY with Christian thought and practice.[1] The "psychology" in question is the professional psychology of the twentieth century, the sort of thing that is taught and practiced in university psychology departments, written about in journals of the American Psychological Association and practiced in psychotherapy clinics. Psychology in this sense is a secular or extrachurchly enterprise, and that is why Christians speak of integration: psychology is something outside the church and Christian tradition that needs to be brought in, and it is in some respects sufficiently at odds with the practices and thought of the church to require a concerted activity of adaptation to our purposes.

Integration and Christian Psychology

At its best, integration is the careful adaptation, for Christian purposes, of concepts and practices from secular psychologies. The main Christian purpose in question is that of changing people so that they lead better lives. The careful adaptation of the secular material is designed to guarantee, as far as possible, that these personal changes will conform to Christian standards of personality development, and not subvert such development. At worst, integration is the adaptation of Christian concepts and practices to the purposes of one non-Christian therapy or another, so that the resultant therapy's goals and standards of personality development are really derived from a system alien to our tradition. In this case, integration is like a destructive infection in the life of the church that perverts our understanding of

---

[1]This chapter stems from studies conducted from 1992 to 1995 when I was supported by a generous grant from the Pew Charitable Trusts for research in Christian psychology.

ourselves, weakens our devotion to Christ, and replaces the kingdom of God in the hearts of his people with such aims as individuation, self-esteem, feeling good, congruence and satisfaction with life. The reality of this infection may be covered up by the use of Christian vocabulary in the practice of the psychology.

Christian psychologists often speak of integration, and they often practice it well. Less frequently attempted is a discipline that I call Christian psychology. Christian psychology starts with ideas and practices already established by centuries of Christian tradition, and it develops psychological concepts and practices from these with a minimum of reference to or influence from the psychologies of the twentieth century.

Whether or not one thinks that integration is a good thing, a Christian must think that Christian psychology is a good thing to do. If we are to do integration responsibly, we must be as articulate as possible about the psychological resources already present in Christianity. Those concepts and practices supply the standards by which we will decide what to adapt from secular psychology and how to adapt it. The discipline I am calling Christian psychology is the conceptual and clinical exploration of our tradition for its psychological resources. It is properly called psychology because it is a set of concepts by which the nature and well-being of the psyche are understood, by which healthy and unhealthy traits, behaviors, desires and emotions are identified and to some extent explained. It is a set of practices for making the transition from unhealthy to healthy traits, behaviors, desires and emotions. That is essentially what a psychology (and its allied psychotherapy) is. Psychology in this sense has been practiced by the church from the beginning. Of course some people will want to reserve the name *psychology* for an activity that employs the empirical and statistical methods characteristic of much academic psychology in the twentieth century, but historically this ideologically driven definition of psychology is too narrow.

Even if one thinks that integration is a fundamentally misguided enterprise, that by definition there is no such thing as doing it well, one must still think that Christian psychology is a good thing. Christians have never done well without psychology in the past, and we have no reason to think that we can do so today. Furthermore, we live in a society with a tremendous hunger for psychological knowledge and the help that can be had from it. It would be irresponsible for Christians, who have such a wonderful psychological heritage, not to offer our wisdom and help here, instead leaving psychology to be practiced in modes and with presuppositions that are often antithetical to Christian spirituality. But before we can offer Christian psychological wisdom to our culture, we must acquire it ourselves. We need to become practiced in the psychological help that the Christian tradition contains and to become articulate in voicing its insights and prescribing its interventions.

Two important theologians of the twentieth century might object to my claim that every Christian must approve of Christian psychology. According to Rudolf Bultmann's reading of Paul's anthropology, the human well-being that occurs in faithful response to the proclamation of Christ is not a psychological change at all; it is not, for example, a change of character or personality, of behavioral patterns or patterns of emotional response. Rather, faith is a change that transcends everything of that sort—everything psychological. It should be evident from what follows that I think Bultmann profoundly misreads Paul. Bultmann's position owes far more to Martin Heidegger, Bultmann's existentialist mentor, than to Paul.

The other demurral is inspired by Karl Barth, though it is not clear that Barth himself would endorse it. This Barthian objection is an analogical application of the Chalcedonian formula for Christ's two natures, "without separation or division, without confusion or change." The stress here is on "no confusion or change." Just as in Christ neither the divine nor the human nature changes the other, so psychology is to remain fully psychology, without any influence from theology, and vice versa. Thus Christian psychology is a confusion; it is like saying that in being divine and human, Christ is a little bit divine and a little bit human, in a mixed-up sort of way. A Barthian who opposes Christian psychology for this reason may, however, agree to use psychology side by side with theology.

This "Barthian" proposal overlooks two crucial facts. First, the psychologies of the twentieth century, like those of every age, are in fact theologies or quasi-theologies. Thus in some respects they stand in direct competition with Christian thought about humanity and God. We cannot give twentieth-century psychologies the kind of autonomy that the "Barthians" propose, because in their autonomous state they will undermine the goals of Christian personality in any number of ways, depending on which psychology is given autonomous sway.[2]

Second, the "Barthian" proposal overlooks the fact that the Christian theology of human persons (as exemplified, for example, in the thought of the apostle Paul) is also psychology. The Barthian objection trades on the modern disciplinary division between psychology and theology, on the notion of levels of discourse (the languages of psychology and theology), and on the supposition that the disciplinary divisions and levels of discourse somehow correspond to the two natures of Christ. A central question that the Barthian approach needs to answer is what reason we have for supposing that the intellectual discipline of theology is enough like Christ's divine nature, and that the discipline of psychology is enough like Christ's human nature, that we can apply the christological principle "without separation or division, without confusion or change" to the relationship of psychology to theology. The two sets of

---

[2]See my *Taking the Word to Heart: Self and Other in an Age of Therapies* (Grand Rapids, Mich.: Eerdmans, 1993), chaps. 2-7, for illustrations.

related entities appear, prior to such argument, to be very different kinds of things.[3]

In case you are wondering where I stand on integration, I am for it. I think much is to be gained from interacting with non-Christian psychologies, even the most virulently anti-Christian ones, such as Freud's. Indeed, by attempting to do integration we can sometimes learn things about Christian psychology that we would not have learned by simply consulting the Christian tradition. But while integration is a fascinating and potentially fruitful enterprise, Christian psychology is the more basic task for the Christian psychologist, and it is a pity that so little of it is done. Much of the ineptitude we see in the practice of integration can be traced to our failure to plumb the psychological depths of Christianity.

In this paper I construct a picture of a psychotherapy that trades on a cluster of leading ideas in Paul's letters. I focus especially on believer agency in the process of personal growth and in the correction of personal dysfunction. I will be asking how the Pauline therapist can facilitate such self-transforming action on the part of the believer. But to get to that point it will be necessary to study a couple of other, related ideas: Paul's notion of what Christ has done for us in his incarnation, death and resurrection; and Paul's notion of human dysfunction.

Paul's Notion of the Two Personalities

In Paul's view, leading a good life is a matter of accessing and actualizing a personality (a set of traits that are expressed in behaviors and emotions) that has been created for and in believers by virtue of the incarnation, death and resurrection of Jesus Christ. "For we are His workmanship, created in Christ Jesus for good works, which God prepared beforehand, that we should walk in them" (Eph 2:10 NASB). This personality, which exists in believers whether or not they manifest it in behavior and attitude, is called the *kainos anthrōpos* (new humanity, Eph 2:15; 4:24) or the *neos anthrōpos* (new self, Col 3:10) or the *esō anthrōpos* (inner self, Rom 7:22; Eph 3:16).[4]

The believer's new personality is characterized by a set of virtues: hope (Rom 5:5; 15:13), love (Rom 5:5; 1 Cor 13; Gal 5:22; Eph 4:2, 15; Col 3:14), rejoicing in God (Rom 5:11; 15:13; Gal 5:22), peace (Gal 5:22; Eph 4:3; Col 3:15), patience (1 Cor 13:4; Col 1:11; 3:12), kindness (1 Cor 13:4; Gal 5:22; Eph 4:32; Col 3:12), faithfulness (Gal 5:22), gentleness (Gal 5:23; Eph 4:2; Col 3:12), self-control (Gal 5:23)

---

[3]On Rudolf Bultmann's view see his *The Old and New Man*, trans. Keith R. Crim (Richmond, Va.: John Knox Press, 1967), and my *Rudolf Bultmann's Theology: A Critical Interpretation* (Grand Rapids, Mich.: Eerdmans, 1976). On the Barthian approach see Deborah van Deusen Hunsinger, *Theology and Pastoral Counseling: A New Interdisciplinary Approach* (Grand Rapids, Mich.: Eerdmans, 1995). On the claims that psychologies are theologies (actually, I call them spiritualities) and that the Christian tradition has its own psychology see Roberts, *Taking the Word to Heart*.

[4]See also 2 Cor 5:17, where Paul uses *kainē ktisis* ("new creation") in what is surely the same sense. In Eph 2:15 Paul says that Christ has created "one new humanity *(kainos anthrōpos)* in place of the two [Jew and gentile]."

and humility (Eph 4:2; Col 3:12). The new self is truthful (Eph 4:15), compassionate (Eph 4:32; Col 3:12), forgiving (Eph 4:32; Col 3:13), forbearing (Col 3:13) and thankful (Col 3:15, 16). These are some of the characteristics of the new self that God has placed in believers (or that God has placed believers in) through the incarnation, death and resurrection of Jesus of Nazareth. It is a personality that is flourishing and promotes the flourishing of persons who are in close relationship with it—flourishing by Judeo-Christian standards.

The new self stands in contrast and opposition to a dysfunctional personality that Paul names *sarx* (the flesh; Rom 7:5, 18; 8:9; 13:14; Gal 5:16-17, 19, 24), *sōma tēs hamartias* (body of sin; Rom 6:6), *sōma tēs sarkos* (body of flesh; Col 2:11), *palaios anthrōpos* (old self; Rom 6:6; Eph 4:22; Col 3:9), or just *sōma* (body; Rom 8:13). This self, Paul tells us, died with Jesus Christ on the cross (Rom 6:6) and was buried with Christ by baptism (Rom 6:4).

The old self too is characterized by a set of concerns, desires, behaviors and patterns of thought and emotion: greed (Rom 1:29; Eph 5:3, 5; Col 3:5), malice (Rom 1:29; Col 3:8), envy (Rom 1:29; Gal 5:21, 26), murder (Rom 1:29), strife (Rom 1:29; 2 Cor 12:20; Gal 5:20), deceit (Rom 1:29), gossip (Rom 1:29; 2 Cor 12:20), slander (Rom 1:30; 2 Cor 12:20), enmity to God, insolence, arrogance, and pretentiousness or pride (Rom 1:30). The old self is an inventor of evil, disobedient to parents (Rom 1:30), foolish, faithless, unloving and unmerciful (Rom 1:31). Its vices are jealousy (2 Cor 12:20; Gal 5:20); anger (2 Cor 12:20; Gal 5:20; Eph 4:31; Col 3:8); selfishness (2 Cor 12:20; Gal 5:20; Phil 2:3); conceit (2 Cor 12:20); impurity (2 Cor 12:21; Gal 5:19; Eph 5:3, 5); sexual immorality (2 Cor 12:21; Gal 5:19; Eph 5:3, 5; Col 3:5); sensuality (2 Cor 12:21; Gal 5:19); idolatry (Gal 5:20; Eph 5:5; Col 3:5); sorcery, enmity, division or dissension (Gal 5:20); party spirit (Gal 5:19); drunkenness; carousing (Gal 5:21); conceit (Gal 5:26; Phil 2:3); provoking one another (Gal 5:26); bitterness (Eph 4:31); anger (Eph 4:31; Col 3:8); clamor (Eph 4:31); slander (Eph 4:31; Col 3:8); indecent, foolish and dirty talk (Eph 5:4); passion (Col 3:5); evil desire (Col 3:5); shameful talk (Col 3:8) and lying to one another (Col 3:9).

Paul's message to the believers on whom he is practicing his special brand of psychotherapy is that the personality expressed in these behaviors and emotions—the *palaios anthrōpos,* or old self—is dead, having been put to death with Christ on the cross. But it is evident, in the passages in which Paul writes of the old self, that while it is dead, it is not gone. Though believers are in possession of the new self, they very often fail to manifest it in actual emotion and action. The standard Christian life is a battle for the supremacy of the new self over the old. The words in which Paul describes this battle strongly suggest that the people whose healing is in question are active participants in the process by which the new self comes to dominate and replace the old. Paul's writings also suggest, indirectly, that as a therapist he is a participant in this process as a coworker with the Holy Spirit. He facilitates the actions that his readers must take if they are to manifest the new creation that God has made after his likeness in true righteousness and holiness through Christ's work.

In the next section I turn to Paul's concept of self-transformative action. Then I will discuss ways in which present-day Pauline therapists might help those under their care to perform such action.

Paul's Notion of Self-Transformative Action

The core of the concept of Pauline therapeutic action is formed around a dozen or so verbs that the apostle uses to describe the believer's participation in actualizing the new personality that God in Christ has created and in taking leave of the old personality. These verbs should interest the Christian psychologist who is investigating Pauline therapy because they embody the way in which therapeutic change is made from the human point of view. I divide Paul's words into groups that form families of concepts.

Yield or present, let rule, let dwell. "We know that our old self was crucified with [Christ] so that the sinful body might be destroyed, and we might no longer be enslaved to sin. . . . We were buried therefore with him by baptism into death, so that as Christ was raised from the dead by the glory of the Father, so we too might walk *(peripatēsōmen)* in newness of life" (Rom 6:6, 4 RSV). But it is clear that Christ's identification with us, even combined with our belief in him and our baptism into his body, does not guarantee that we walk in newness of life, for Paul continues, "Do not present *(paristanete)* your members to sin as instruments of wickedness, but present *(parastēsate)* yourselves to God as those who have been brought from death to life, and present your members to God as instruments of righteousness" (Rom 6:13, NRSV). Paul says that Christians are free, in the action of *paristanein*, to choose between two masters. In either case they are slaves.

Paristēmi here seems to mean "put [oneself] at the disposal of," and so would stand in contrast to "withhold [oneself] from." If this is so, then when a Christian lives in sin (anger, envy, conceit, sexual immorality, greed and so on), we should perhaps think of him as exercising a kind of perverse self-control, a refusing to yield himself to God and to do what comes naturally to one who has died to sin. The usual way to think about backsliding is that it is the path of least resistance: sin is natural, righteousness unnatural; sin occurs when we go with the flow, but righteousness is upstream swimming. But in Paul's view the natural action for someone who is in Christ is to yield one's members to Christ, to go with *that* flow, to follow that nature, to presuppose the virtues in which we have been re-created. Such a reframing of the usual way of thinking about backsliding is more faithful to the Christian affirmation that we have died to sin. This reversal may come as a shock to the believer, but if the therapist can somehow facilitate thinking in these terms, the result may be liberating and therapeutic.

The relation to a master that is implied by *paristēmi* suggests that the new self is constituted of a relationship—of obedience, worship, thanksgiving and so on.[5] The effort to live the new and healthy life is reframed as yielding oneself to what one already is in Christ. Going along with this reframing would be a practice of prayer, worship and receiving of the Eucharist in such a way that the believer becomes increasingly conscious of being in a living relationship with Christ. *Paristēmi* is a thin action: it is less an action than it is a matter of going with a flow and letting oneself go. It is relaxation into conformity with a preexisting disposition. But it is decidedly not an indiscriminate going with the flow because there are two flows here, and the unwanted flow may well be dispositionally stronger than the desired flow. A chief task of the Pauline therapist is to reverse this situation, so that the believer's sense of self is that the natural thing is to yield to righteousness.

The Pauline therapist will help clients by sensitizing them to godly inclinations and to symptoms of the new self so that they can go with the new self's flow. Think of the praise of his readers' faith and other virtues with which Paul opens his letters to the Romans, Corinthians (1 Cor), Ephesians, Philippians, Colossians, Thessalonians, and Timothy (2 Tim) and Philemon. By contrast, the Pauline therapist will help the client see bad actions and emotions not as current traits of character, but as survivals of a character that is essentially dead. Part of this sensitizing involves the Pauline framework itself. Clients must be taught to see themselves (to diagnose themselves, as it were) in terms of the new self and the old; this is the "knowledge" of which Paul speaks from time to time (Col 1:9, 10; 3:10; Phil 1:9; Eph 1:17-18).

I have read *paristēmi* as a thin verb that directs believers to yield to certain tendencies in themselves. Believers should let themselves be carried in a certain direction rather than, or at least as much as, they should do anything positive. The same can be said with even greater emphasis about *brabeuetō* ("let rule") and *enoikeitō* ("let dwell"). Because these imperatives are in the third person ("let the peace of Christ rule in your hearts" [Col 3:15 RSV] and "let the word of Christ dwell in you richly" [Col 3:16 RSV]), one might think they are not being used as verbs of agency at all, but are merely expressions of Paul's wishes or prayers for the Colossians. But the context is exhortation, and verbs in verses 12 and 17 are in the second person plural imperative, indicating that the *let* in the RSV, with its suggestion of thin agency, captures the thought.

The peace of Christ, which we may take to be the dispositions, motives and actions characteristic of the new order that Christ has established in his incarnation, death and resurrection, is to be allowed to rule and order the self and the community. This peace is already established; it is already in some sense a characteristic of the Christian self and community. Because of Christ's identification with us these

---

[5]Sin and wickedness are of course not a person with whom one can have a relationship, and so the analogy of the two selves is incomplete. *Slave (doulos)* is figurative for the old self in a way that it is not for the new. But see the personification of sin in Rom 7:20.

qualities tend naturally to be manifested among us. They are indeed the real qualities of the self and community. Sadly, however, the actual rule of Christ's peace is often mitigated and subverted, so we need to perform the action of *letting* it rule.

How do we let Christ's peace rule? By reminding ourselves that it has already been established for us, that we are already in it and it in us. Then we must be skilled at identifying Christ's peace and sensitive to its working, and we must lean into it. Perhaps letting Christ's peace rule is a little like riding a sled. The energy and direction of the sled are set by its position on the hill, but the rider can contribute significantly to the sled's direction by leaning a little to the right or left. Because the leaning metaphor may help to frame the action for the subject of therapy, it may be therapeutic in itself. But how does one lean into the peace of Christ? I will offer some suggestions in the next section of this paper.

In the next verse Paul says, "Let the word of Christ dwell among you richly, in all wisdom teaching and admonishing yourselves in psalms, hymns and spiritual songs, in gratitude singing in your hearts to God" (Col 3:16, my translation). The new life in Christ is mediated by preaching and instruction about what Christ has done and about the consequences of this for our nature and our efforts. This fabric of discourse dwells among us richly when it is so clearly and sufficiently articulated that it speaks to our hearts, making us grateful and shaping our actions and interactions. Like the new self that has been established through Christ's re-creating work, this word *(logos)* is available to be accessed; it is abroad in the world and we can yield to it for sanctification. Our action is not to create the word, but to explore its riches and to feed our psyches on it. Effective Pauline psychotherapists will be able to articulate this word, speaking sensitively to the particular needs and concerns of the individuals and groups with whom they work. The therapist will be a chief locus of the word's dwelling in the midst of those who seek psychological growth.

Walk. Though the literal translation of *peripateō* is "walk," *peripateō* is a generic word, which the RSV translates variously as "behave," "lead a life," "practice," "act" and "conduct oneself." "We were buried therefore with him by baptism into death, so that as Christ was raised from the dead by the glory of the Father, we too might walk *(peripatēsōmen)* in newness of life" (Rom 6:4 RSV). "For we are his workmanship, created in Christ Jesus for good works, which God prepared beforehand, that we should walk *(peripatēsōmen)* in them" (Eph 2:10 RSV). "But I say, walk by the Spirit *(pneumati peripateite),* and do not gratify the desires of the flesh" (Gal 5:16 RSV). "Once you were darkness, but now you are light in the Lord; walk as children of light (Eph 5:8 RSV). "As therefore you received Christ Jesus the Lord, so live in him *(en autō peripateite)*" (Col 2:6 RSV).

Of the Pauline terms for self-transformative agency that we will look at, this one is the most behavioral. It suggests that one way to get into the new self and out of the old is just to start performing the kind of actions, or emitting the kind of behaviors, that are characteristic of the new self. This may sound therapeutically simplistic, and it may not always be the best approach, but clearly there are times in the lives of troubled people when they *can* behave better if they are challenged to do so, are willing to do so and are given a little guidance in how to do so. It seems to be common wisdom that changed behavior sometimes leads to changed perceptions, changed patterns of thinking and changed desires and emotions. Significant and deep-going changes in life and personality may be precipitated in this way. Pauline therapy will differ from straight behavior therapy because believers will undertake a new behavior under the encouraging and guiding thought that in the work of Christ they have been re-created for this kind of behavior, "which God prepared beforehand." The new behavior does not stand in isolation, nor is it sought merely for the private well-being of the therapeutic client. Rather, the new behavior is part of a complete personality with a full complement of healthy traits that has its telos in God's will and in the well-being of a larger community. Furthermore, the dysfunctional believer is somehow already fully functional, and so understands action as a matter of accessing preexistent new personality by "walking" in it.

Put on, take off, put away. "Put off *(apothesthai)* your old nature which belongs to your former manner of life and is corrupt through deceitful lusts, and be renewed in the spirit of your minds, and put on *(endysasthai)* the new nature, created after the likeness of God in true righteousness and holiness" (Eph 4:22-24 RSV). *Endysasthai* and *apothesthai* strongly suggest the donning and doffing of garments. The old *anthrōpos* is like an outfit of clothing that, with the birth of the new *anthrōpos,* becomes disposable: the old shoes, leggings, shirt, hat and so on, can be taken off, and the new ones put on. This is clearly something that the person or persons in question *do,* and the Pauline psychotherapist will want to know how this action is performed.

In the Colossians passage that corresponds to Ephesians 4:22-24, it becomes very clear that the items that are doffed are the vices, those traits of human psychological dysfunction that Paul lists at various places in his letters, and that the items that are donned are the Christian virtues: "Put on then, as God's chosen ones, holy and beloved, compassion, kindness, lowliness, meekness, and patience, forbearing one another and, if one has a complaint against another, forgiving each other. . . . And above all these put on love, which binds everything together in perfect harmony" (Col 3:12-14 RSV).

The clothing metaphor, along with Paul's talk about God's *having created* the new *anthrōpos,* suggests that Pauline therapeutic action is best thought of not as aspiring after an ideal, but as exploiting a perfection already present. In this respect Pauline therapeutic agency is more like a Rogerian sloughing off conditions of worth and letting his organismic valuing process speak, or like the process of getting in touch with one's inner child, than it is like the Stoic or existentialist strategy of taking control of one's own life and making oneself into something. The difference is that the new *anthrōpos* is not a natural or generic feature of the human psyche, but a result of God's special creative and saving work through the life, death and resurrection of Jesus Christ.

Kill. Another verb of self-transformative action—"put to death" *(nekroō, thanatoō)*—connects with the pervasive theme of Pauline soteriology that the believer has died *(apothnēskein)* with Christ. "We know that our old self was crucified with him so that the sinful body might be destroyed, and we might no longer be enslaved to sin" (Rom 6:6 RSV; see also vv. 2-5). "I have been crucified with Christ; it is no longer I who live, but Christ who lives in me" (Gal 2:20 RSV). "You were buried with him in baptism, in which you were also raised with him through faith in the working of God, who raised him from the dead" (Col 2:12 RSV). "You have died, and your life is hid with Christ in God" (Col 3:3 RSV).

The logic here is that the old self with its nasty traits, bad actions and corrupt desires and emotions is actually dead because on the cross Christ took it down with him into the grave. Yet the inertia of the old self's motions, the old self's stench and its wayward spirit constitute a pressing legacy, as if the old self were still alive. The ghost of this dead self haunts the believer, so that we may sometimes feel that our actual present life is a "body of death" (Rom 7:24). So the Christian life is characterized by ongoing defensive suicidal action against these bad personality remnants. "If by the Spirit you put to death *(thanatoute)* the deeds of the body, you will live" (Rom 8:13 RSV). "Put to death *(nekrōsate)* therefore what is earthly in you: immorality, impurity, passion, evil desire, and covetousness, which is idolatry" (Col 3:5 RSV). The thinness of Pauline therapeutic action is implied in "to kill" as it is in other words: the believer does not kill his bad personality outright, but pushes back into the grave what is already there but is leaking out.

Consider, set the mind on, give thanks, rejoice. Paul also commends explicitly mental action that exploits the new situation in Jesus Christ for the purposes of psychic health. In connection with the theme of the death of the old self he says, "So you also must consider *(logizesthe)* yourselves dead to sin and alive to God in Christ Jesus" (Rom 6:11 RSV). It seems that we make good on the new *anthrōpos* in Christ and take our leave from the old *anthrōpos* in part by practicing a self-interpretation in which we construe ourselves in terms of what Christ has made of us in what he has done for us.

By actively considering ourselves dead to sin and alive to God in Christ we bring it about that we are actually more dead to sin and more alive to God in Christ. Paul uses *phroneō* and *phronēma* to a similar purpose: "Those who live according to the flesh set their minds *(phronousin)* on the things of the flesh, but those who live according to the Spirit set their minds on the things of the Spirit. To set the mind on *(phronēma)* the flesh is death, but to set the mind on the Spirit is life and peace" (Rom 8:5-6 RSV). The things of the flesh and the things of the Spirit include more than the old *anthrōpos* and the new, although these are certainly a thing of the flesh and a thing of the Spirit. Paul seems to be recommending attention to and reflection on holy things—whether they be one's new self, or episodes in the ministry of Jesus Christ, or the grace of God as manifested in the atonement of Christ, or some especially Christlike action of a fellow member of one's church, or edifying sayings of wise Christians or the character of conspicuous saints (see also Phil 2:1-2). Such attention and reflection are important actions of Pauline psychotherapy and may be clues to the content of other psychotherapeutic actions, such as presenting your members to God, putting on the new self, and putting to death the old self.

Connected with the mental therapeutic actions of *logizesthai* and *phronein*, it seems to me, are Paul's commands to give thanks *(eucharistein)* and rejoice *(chairein)*. "Finally, my brethren, rejoice in the Lord" (Phil 3:1 RSV); "Rejoice in the Lord always; again I will say, Rejoice" (Phil 4:4 RSV; see also 1 Thess 5:16 and 1 Cor 13:6: "[love] does not rejoice at wrong, but rejoices in the right" [RSV]). Paul says that we should be "always and for everything giving thanks in the name of our Lord Jesus Christ to God the Father" (Eph 5:20 RSV). "And whatever you do, in word or deed, do everything in the name of the Lord Jesus, giving thanks to God the Father through him" (Col 3:17 RSV). "Give thanks in all circumstances" (1 Thess 5:18 RSV).

The connection between *phronein* and these emotions is that sincere thanks-giving (which includes feeling grateful) and rejoicing require giving attention to, or setting one's mind on, whatever one gives thanks for or rejoices in. But these emotions involve exactly the kind of attention in which the goodness of their objects is personally appreciated. They are the perceptual states in which the eyes of the heart see the glory of the saints' inheritance and the greatness of the power of God (Eph 1:18-19).

Only the new *anthrōpos* rejoices in the Lord and gives thanks for all that God has done in Jesus Christ. So to the extent that believers have set their minds on the things of the Spirit in such a way as actually to rejoice in them and be grateful for them, those believers have in fact accessed the new self and yielded their members, in this small way, to righteousness.

How Pauline Psychotherapy Is Done

We have explored Paul's notion of the two personalities—the old, sinful self and the new self that has been created in the incarnation, death and resurrection of Jesus Christ. We have noted the traits, emotions and actions that belong to each of these personalities; we have a sketch of each personality by which to recognize it. And we have examined some of the verbs that denote actions by which a person or community can promote the manifestation of the new personality and mitigate that of the old. These are perhaps the three main parameters of a Pauline psychother-apy. They correspond to three aspects of therapy that we can call assessing the believer, clarifying the gospel and teaching agency. They should not be regarded as stages of therapy to follow in chronological order; they are interconnected aspects that will be deployed, redeployed and combined as needed in the course of therapy.[6]

Assessing the believer. In developing a Pauline psychotherapy our goal is to understand human psychological dysfunction using primarily Paul's categories of good and bad functioning. (Notice that *functioning* here is to be understood holistically and not as meaning "behavior" in a thin sense. The traits of the new and old selves are not merely behavioral but more fundamentally passional and emotional. They are also relational—ways of relating to neighbor and to God.) Pauline psychology must clarify and extend Paul's framework of personality evaluation both informally as individual therapists gain skill with this conceptual framework by applying it in the clinical setting, and formally in systematic discursive psychology, of which the present essay is representative. The Pauline categories must be connected conceptually and practically to the problems with which people come to therapy. The therapist will help the client see these connections, laying the foundation for undertaking therapeutic actions.

A believer who comes for therapy has presumably been moved to come by some problem in living. Perhaps the person is anxious and depressed or unable to get along with family members or coworkers. Maybe the person's children are out of control or the person has an addiction to alcohol, pornography, sex or shopping. Or the person has trouble making friends or cannot get motivated to succeed in school work. Maybe the person has a phobia of public speaking or is paralyzed by feelings of guilt because of something that happened in the past. Perhaps the person is subject to uncontrolled fits of anger and even physically or emotionally abuses family members during these fits. Or perhaps the person is just in a rut of negative thinking (Jana Pressley). All of these dispositions would seem to be causally connected with the personality profile of what Paul calls the old self. We must be open to the possibility that not every trait or behavior or emotion characteristic of the old self is found in Paul's lists. The lists may be representative samples from which the wise Christian in another age or culture will take clues about the old self as it appears in the later cultural context. It will be part of Pauline psychotherapy, as I am conceiving it, to construct a profile of the old self that will enable therapists to recognize—and to help their clients recognize—its traits.

Paul's lists do not present the markers of the old self systematically. But the

---

[6]In the fall semester of 1997 I asked students of clinical psychology in the Wheaton College Graduate School to read an earlier draft of this chapter, to raise objections to the conception of a Pauline psychotherapy and to suggest supplements and improvements to the practical suggestions that I make under the three headings below. They made an abundance of worthwhile suggestions, and the names in parentheses in this portion of the paper indicate the contributors of those ideas.

Pauline therapist will want to understand the inner connections of the traits Paul lists, the lines of causation and support among them and their connections to other traits, emotions and behavior patterns that the therapist may wish to help clients modify. Some of the traits that Paul mentions are consequences of or ingredients in other traits that he mentions. For example, malice may be a consequence of both envy and anger, and a motive for both murder and slander. If so, then envy and anger would be more basic structures of the old self than the other dispositions. This proposal accords with a persistent strand of Christian psychology, which gives diagnostic centrality to anger and envy as two of the seven deadly—destructive, unhealthy—sins. Another trait of the old self that Paul stresses is greed; he reflects Jesus' concern with inordinate attachment to possessions. Greed seems to be a disposition with many potentially deep and devastating pathological consequences, including deceit, envy, slander, strife and other conditions that Paul does not mention, such as marital breakdown, out-of-control children, depression, anxiety, friendlessness and self-hatred. A major task of Pauline psychology will be to explore and come to understand the logic and inner dynamics of the old self. This will provide a basis for the therapeutic process of taking off the old self and putting it to death. Some help in this project may be available in the older discussions of the seven deadly sins.

A general analysis of the inner dynamics of the old self, as important as it is to Pauline therapy, will need to be sensitively adapted to the condition of the individual client. Greed, for example, may not play the same role in each person's old self. In one person greed may stem from envy, while in another envy may stem from greed. Malice will have different sources and roots in different individuals. Being unmerciful can arise from selfishness or arrogance or both, or perhaps even from sensuality. So the aspect of therapy that I am calling assessment of the believer will be an individualized application of the therapist's Pauline wisdom about the flesh; assessment may be quite demanding of the therapist's diagnostic skill.

The therapist and the client will explore the client's old self conversationally. The therapist will listen as the client gives voice to a problem, and the therapist will gradually and tentatively construct a Pauline interpretation and explanation of the client's presenting problem. The therapist will bear in mind that the client's account will probably be skewed by the delusive old self (see Eph 4:22). The therapist may seek information about the client's behavioral, emotional and cognitive patterns from other sources as well: through observing the client's reactions in the interview, through consulting with some of the client's family members or fellow church members if the therapist can secure the client's permission for this, and through insight given by the Holy Spirit during prayer (Stephanie Gillis).

The traits that the Pauline therapist is trying to help make manifest in the client are all forms of relationship to God, even when they are forms of relationship with the neighbor. Christian hope is hope for God's kingdom, joy is joy in the Lord, gratitude is gratitude to God; but also patience is based in trusting God, and forbearance and peace are imitations of God's forbearance and peace. Conversely, the traits of the old self are forms of bad relationship to God: disobedience, distrust or disregard of God, idolatry or setting oneself in the place of God and so on.

Deep distortion in a person's concept of God can be an important aspect of the old self and a big hindrance to putting on the new self. The Pauline psychotherapist will therefore want to explore the client's concept of God, especially if the therapist suspects that the client's concept of God is significantly distorted (Brian Richardson, Nori Menendez, Jody McCain). The therapist might ask clients to describe God, and to describe themselves as they believe God sees them. The therapist might ask the believer to write a letter to God and a letter from God to the client, then to discuss the letters with the therapist. Some clients' self-exploration may be better facilitated by asking them to draw pictures or sing songs about their relationship with God (Jody McCain). The aspect of therapy that I call clarifying the gospel will include efforts to correct any distortions that the therapist discerns in the believer's concept of God.

As Pauline psychotherapy becomes better grounded conceptually we can imagine the development of a testing instrument that might be called the Pauline Self-Dynamics Inventory (PSDI). The PSDI would produce a profile of the new and old selves in a client. It would provide information about the interaction between the selves and between each self and other factors such as communal environment, drug or alcohol use and so on (Javier Sierra, Sean Youngstedt).

The therapist will teach the client to think in Pauline categories about the old self, so the client will understand better the sources of pathology and be better able to take off the old self and put on the new one. But the teaching should mostly have an indirect dimension, in which the client, under the refining guidance of the therapist, is encouraged to formulate insights about the old self. The therapist might alienate the client and arrest therapy prematurely by speaking too directly of the client's corrupt traits, especially if the client has not yet begun to acknowledge that problems originate from those traits. The therapist will need to lead the believer gently, with skill and sensitivity, into the more characteristically Pauline self-assessment (Michael Smalley, Sean Youngstedt, Kevin Novotny).

Once a client begins to feel reasonably comfortable acknowledging traits of the old self, the client can be asked to bring to mind specific relationships and incidents in which the old self prevailed and to identify the nasty consequences. Then the client is encouraged to explain what at first might seem too obvious for comment: how the behaviors, thoughts and emotions of the old self lead to the consequences that are so troubling (Linda Lake). Other devices may also be useful for deepening a client's understanding of the old self as a source of personal problems. The client might be asked to role-play the actions of the old self in a particular hypothetical situation, and the therapist would then role-play the actions of the client's new self in the same situation. They could then discuss their impulses, thoughts and emotions in the two versions of the scenario. The therapist and the client could then reverse roles and discuss the outcome (John Laskowski).

When assessing the believer the Pauline therapist must be careful not to fall into using a modern, hyperindividualistic, hyperresponsible concept of sin. It would be quite un-Pauline to think that the old self as manifested in an individual's behavior and emotions is completely a result of *that* individual's fully responsible sinful *actions*. In Paul's conception, sin is as much like a burden or a disease or a pervasive condition of the human race as it is a class of responsible actions of individuals (see Rom 7). Sin is to some extent an inheritance (Rom 5:12). Even the natural creation is in "bondage to decay" (Rom 8:21 RSV).

The old and new *anthrōpos* are not merely individual entities—your new and old *anthrōpos* and my old and new *anthrōpos,* and so on. The old *anthrōpos* does not belong just to this individual and that individual but to humanity. Similarly, the new *anthrōpos* is a new humanity as well as the new self of each individual believer. Consequently, it seems consistent with Pauline thinking not to limit our diagnosis of individuals to the actions and traits of those individuals. We can also look to the larger context of their social world, their family and society for explanations of dysfunction. If we locate the origin of an individual's anxiety and depression in the greedy character of the old self, we may also locate its origin in the acquisitive spirit of the individual's society or ethnic group or in the spirit and interaction patterns of the individual's family of origin (Carol Josefson, Aaron Bell, Stephanie Gillis). The Pauline therapist will help the believer to understand the old self in this larger sociohistorical context, but without undermining the believer's legitimate sense of responsibility for the thoughts, actions, desires and emotions of the old self.

Most Pauline diagnosis will be driven by the notion of the new self. Paul tends to list the traits of the two selves in close proximity to one another, showing their stark contrast. Thus we will try to understand why a person is functioning poorly by keeping in mind that this person has been re-created for love and patience, for bearing neighbors' burdens and rejoicing in God, for giving thanks in all circumstances and being eager to forgive neighbors' sins.[7]

The Pauline psychotherapist will want to make judicious use of modern knowledge about emotional and behavioral dysfunctions that have a distinctly physiological origin, such as some forms of depression, anxiety disorders and schizophrenia (Carol Josefson). This is a compromise of our basic project of deriving a psycho-

---

[7]See Cornelius Plantinga Jr., *Not the Way It's Supposed to Be: A Breviary of Sin* (Grand Rapids, Mich.: Eerdmans, 1996). Plantinga expounds the concept of sin with close attention to the concept of shalom, the contrary of sin.

therapy from the writings of Paul; it is a case of integration. But the Pauline therapist may want to combine drug therapy with elements of Pauline therapy where
this is clearly warranted. Of course the Pauline therapist will see even genetic and
physiological causes of dysfunction as ultimately attributable to the sin under which
the whole creation groans.

Some dysfunctions may be partly attributable to skill deficits. For example, some
aspects of incivility seem to be as much a matter of ineptitude as of sin, as when a
person poisons relationships with others by being too blunt or has not learned the
self-management skills required for effective anger control (Jennifer Messer). When
doing assessment the Pauline therapist will want to keep in mind the distinction
between the hard-core traits of the flesh and these less "spiritual" defects. In these
cases the teaching of therapeutic agency will include training in the skills that are
lacking. Still, skill deficits are deeply intertwined with the hard-core traits of the old
self. Seldom is incivility or inordinate anger simply a lack of skills.

In this outline of Pauline therapy I have made the concepts of the old self and
the new self central to assessment and therapy because they seem to be both central to and distinctive of Paul's psychology. The idea is that psychological dysfunction corresponds to a failure to put on one's new self as created in Jesus Christ. The
central explanatory strategy addresses the believer's character rather than the
believer's circumstances. But if we define psychological dysfunction broadly
enough to include all debilitating emotional suffering, it seems clear that circumstances are often major contributors to that dysfunction.

A child dies and neither the father nor the mother seems able to resume a normal life. At age fifty-five a man is laid off in a wide sweep of corporate downsizing
and lacks the motivation or confidence to look for another job. A wife, angry and
depressed, comes to therapy because her Christian husband is having an affair and
refuses to give it up, even when confronted by the church elders. A young woman
has suicidal thoughts seemingly because her father has sexually abused her (Jody
McCain). In such cases assessment in terms of the old and new self does not seem
most to the point (though it will not be completely irrelevant). The dysfunction can
probably be explained in large part by the impingement of a twisted world on a
creature designed for shalom. In some parts of his letters Paul writes also of God's
comfort, hope and providential love to those who are suffering at the hands of others, and he models that comfort and hope in the midst of his own troubles (see
2 Cor 1:3-7; Rom 8:18-39). In some cases these passages seem the most immediately relevant to the Pauline therapeutic process.

Clarifying the gospel. Central to Pauline psychotherapy will be teaching clients
that they have been re-created in Jesus Christ, that they already have a personality
that is perfectly healthy and proper before God, insofar as they are in Christ. I have
said that the therapist should understand the inner dynamics of the old self; just as
important is the therapist's understanding of the new personality. It is not enough

just to reiterate to believing clients that they have been made new in Jesus Christ. An important part of therapy is communicating the characteristics of this new personality and conveying a practical understanding of how its various emotions, cognitions and behaviors interact: how forbearance of neighbor flows from and reinforces love of neighbor, how love of neighbor and thankfulness to God both derive from and reinforce love of God, and how love of neighbor and God lead to joy and peace and discernment. And while the therapist guides believing clients in deepening this understanding, it is important for the clients to formulate the understanding themselves much of the time, and as much as possible to do so in the context of their own lived experience.

It might be useful for clients to be led through some exercises of imagination in which they get in touch with their new selves in Christ. After identifying some paradigmatic scenarios in which the believer's old self is persistently manifest, the therapist might help the client imagine how the new self in Jesus Christ would think, behave and feel in the same scenarios. The therapist might encourage clients to imagine themselves behaving as Jesus would in the troublesome scenarios of life. A similar exercise might involve reading about saints like Mother Theresa, Billy Graham, Dietrich Bonhoeffer, Saint Francis of Assisi or an exemplary member of the client's own congregation—people in whom the new self is particularly manifest. Clients would read about these people and imagine themselves behaving and thinking and feeling in similar ways,[8] always keeping in mind that in Christ they already have, in their unique way, the traits that they see in these developed Christians, and that the traits of the old self that distress them (or perhaps do not distress them enough) are gone from them, the old self having died with Christ.

The believer might write a description of her true self, remembering that to the extent that it describes her correctly it is a portrait of how she already exists in Jesus Christ. This is the life in which she is trying to walk, the personality she is trying to give scope to, to manifest, to put on. Then the therapist and the client discuss the description that the believer has written, and the therapist gently leads the believer to formulate ways in which the sketch might be made more true to life, that is, more true to the new life that is hers in Christ. A variant of this might be to ask a Christian who is close to the believer—a friend, a family member or a member of her fellowship group—to write a vision statement of her potential in Jesus Christ and to share it with the believer and the therapist (Kimberly Gaines).

Setting one's mind on one's new self facilitates the identification of ways in which the new self is already manifest in one's behavior, thoughts and emotions. Seeing and appreciating the fruit of the Spirit in oneself is encouraging. It facilitates acts of thanksgiving and the thin self-forming action of yielding one's members to righteousness.

---

[8]When we engage in exercises of imagination like these, we are surely setting our mind on the things of the Spirit.

In impressing on clients that they already have a new self in Christ, the therapist causes them to see increasingly vividly the discrepancy between the new self and the self that they are manifesting much of the time. The risk is that clients will be burdened with guilt and become discouraged—which is just the opposite of the intended effect (Kristee Jackson). Paul feels this discrepancy acutely (see Rom 7:13-25) and feels severely burdened with the old self, yet he does not feel guilty or become discouraged. Instead, he appeals resolutely to the claim that his real self is not the one that is manifested in dispositions of the flesh but is the new one that has been re-created in Christ. Thus Paul says of his sinful action, "It is no longer I that do it, but sin that dwells within me" (Rom 7:17). A significant part of the clarification of the gospel in Pauline therapy will be to impress the client with this way of thinking about dysfunctional traits. When we think like this, we experience pessimism about the likelihood of ever completely putting off the old self in this life. As Paul says, "I find it to be a *law* that when I want to do right, evil lies close at hand" (Rom 7:21 RSV, italics added). If clients begin to feel discouraged or inordinately guilty, it will be therapeutic to remind them of Paul's experience: "This is just the way things go in human life," the therapist might say, "you are really pretty normal" (Christy Adams, Timothy Shields). The therapist might also acknowledge his or her own struggles with the old self, while modeling the love and patience and compassion that are characteristic of the new self (Kristee Jackson).

In the disowning of the old self lurks a danger—the danger of complacency or of dissociating from one's dysfunction in a dishonest, un-Pauline way. It is part of Paul's gospel that we can and should dissociate from our old self: insofar as we are in Christ, our old self is not our real self. When Paul dissociates from his sinful self, he is not at all unconscious of that sinful self or dishonest about its existence. On the contrary, he is intensely aware of his sinful self, of the evil of it, and of the burden that it constitutes. But he also has the freeing and therapeutic sense that that burden is not, in the last analysis, a part or corruption of *himself*. This is the rather complex vision that the Pauline therapist will endeavor to communicate to the client.

Each individual is given a different new self in Jesus Christ. All new selves resemble one another in broad ways—they are all loving and patient and humble, for example—but there are many different ways to have these traits, and each individual is unique in the actual character of his or her new self (Rom 12:4-8; 1 Cor 12:4-31). The client should be encouraged to imagine a realistic new self rather than a highly idealized one, and also to realize that any conception of the new self will always be only an approximation because the new self is hidden with Christ in God and is actually more glorious than anything that can be imagined. At first the client will probably be inept at imagining the new self and will have all kinds of misconceptions about it that the therapist will gently correct in his Christian wisdom.

Some modern psychotherapies may lead believers to think that to the extent that they put on the new self in Christ, they will have no more negative experiences, no more disappointments, no more sadness, no more anger—that they will simply feel good. It is true that the new self is full of joy and hope, but it is also true that the new self is subject to griefs and frustrations to which the old self was insensitive. It is, after all, Paul's new self that says "I have great sorrow and unceasing anguish in my heart" (Rom 9:2 RSV) about the failure of many of his people to accept Jesus' messiahship, and it is his new self that speaks of a godly grief (2 Cor 7:9). Our Lord himself was subject to intense sadness (Lk 19:41; Jn 11:35; Mt 26:37-38). It will sometimes be therapeutic to remind a client that her painful emotions are not necessarily manifestations of her old self (Jo Ann Thomas).

The character and demeanor of the therapist is immeasurably important in the clarification of the gospel. As a pastor Paul was both tenderhearted and uncompromising in his insistence on godliness. When clarifying the gospel for the client, the therapist naturally becomes the human being most immediately symbolic of the gospel message. By attentively listening to the believer's problems, the therapist demonstrates palpably for the believer something of the grace by which God accepts us while we are still sinners. With a gently probing insistence on truthfulness and a seriousness about sin, the therapist demonstrates God's uncompromising character in a small and distant way. If the therapist is an image of God for the client, the clarification of the gospel will increase in power; if the therapist is not, the therapy will be weakened. If the therapist demonstrates the traits of the new self in Christ, the client will receive further nonverbal guidance and will be encouraged (Javier Sierra, Carol Josefson, Stephanie Gillis, Nori Menendez, Kevin Novotny, Leslie Bissell, Nancy Duarte-Gómez, David Thornsen).

When he speaks of the old and the new self, Paul does not lose sight of what we might call the commonsense unity of the self. The old self and the new self are not two different people. Paul is the one who was the old self (who had those traits) and is the very same one who has now been remade (who has been given a new set of traits) in Christ. While we were still sinners, Christ died for us as people in this ordinary sense, not for old selves or new selves (Rom 5:8). It is people who "children of God through faith" (Gal 3:26). It is people who, because of Christ, are no longer under condemnation (Rom 8:1). A practitioner of Pauline psychotherapy will not forget that the client is a person whom God loves in Jesus Christ, and will not neglect to communicate this to the client during therapy. The therapist will proclaim, "This is the gospel: that God so loved you that he gave his Son for you" (Jody McCain). Paul puts a special twist on the gospel: The central substance of God's love for us is that through salvation God has given us a new self in Christ.

Teaching therapeutic agency. The first two aspects of Pauline psychotherapy are clear. The therapist assesses the active personality of the believer, determining just which traits of the old self are most in evidence and most central, then helps the believer to understand the causal and motivational dynamics of this old self. At the same time the therapist proclaims the gospel to the believer, trying to convey vividly to him that his old self is not his real personality, which has been crucified with Christ, and that the believer already has a new self with traits that are quite opposite the ones that underlie his present problems. In interviewing the believer the therapist tries to help him identify ways in which he is already manifesting the new self that God has created in Christ. The therapist explains to the believer that therapeutic progress is achieved by yielding one's members to righteousness, by putting on the new self and by taking off or putting to death the old. The third aspect of Pauline therapy consists in helping the believer to perform the actions of yielding, putting on, taking off, putting to death and walking in the Spirit.

In this chapter I can only sketch what should be explored in much greater detail both in reflection and in clinical experience. The Christian church is full of resources for putting on the new self even though the church has not always fully exploited the two-self way of thinking about the therapeutic process. We can take off the old self and put on the new through fellowship, confession and prayer and meditation, by reading Scripture and other edifying literature, celebrating the Lord's Supper, reframing sufferings and doing good works.

It is significant that Paul writes his exhortations to the new life in the second person plural, presupposing congregational life. Although I have mostly been discussing a dyadic therapist-believer relationship, this relationship is only adjunctive to the primary locus of therapeutic action, the congregation. The therapist will form a relationship with the sufferer, and together they will be part of the body of Christ, but the therapist will aim to facilitate the believer's incorporation into the larger church, where most of the healing will be expected to take place. Let us now briefly consider some of the traditional Christian therapeutic activities and discover how the Pauline therapist will facilitate the believer's use of them.

■ Prayer. A central function of prayer is the pursuit of intimate fellowship with God, the achievement of a vivid sense of God's presence and goodness and ownership of oneself. The Pauline therapist will be particularly concerned that believers sense strongly the presence of Jesus Christ and their connection with him. They should sense that they belong to him, that they are in him and that he is in them. In his character and in his identification with humanity, Christ is the basis for the new self with which we have been endowed. The therapist may pray with the client during the therapy session and may assign the client to pray a certain number of times each day, or perhaps to pray whenever the behavior of the old self becomes especially dominant. The therapist might assign a particular prayer that can be used in this routine. For example:

Jesus Christ, gracious Lord, you died on the cross for my sake, and in your death my old corrupt self, with its *[here the client names some of the client's own troublesome traits]*, died also. You were raised, O Lord, to the right hand of the Father, in perfect righteousness, holiness and well-being, and in your resurrection I am given a new self, with *[here the client names some traits of the new self that are opposite to the troublesome traits of the client's old self]*, which I grasp by faith. Give me the power of your Holy Spirit, O Lord, that I may put on this new self that you have provided for me and take off the old. Grant, O Lord, that my new life in you may be manifested in what I do, think and feel. Amen.

The therapist may also assign the client to pray passages of Scripture, such as the first eighteen verses of Psalm 139 or the first twelve verses of Psalm 51. Verses may be selected that address special personal needs. For example, if therapist and client have determined that the client needs to work especially at putting on humility, the therapist may assign the client to pray a suitable adaptation of Philippians 2:1-11. As the client progresses, the therapist may assign the client to search for other Scripture passages that can be used in prayer. Hymns and choruses may also be used (Laura Edwards, Aaron Bell, Jennifer Messer, Becky Crisafulli). Pauline psychotherapy assumes that healing is effected not just by human manipulations and devices, even though these might make central use of the means of grace, but by the work of the Holy Spirit of God. Prayer, at its best, is an opening of the self to God's guidance and power in healing. It is a way of giving God the reins of the process (Kimberly Gaines).

Christian history is full of people who had a strong sense of fellowship with the Lord but exhibited behavior and attitudes that were quite contrary to the personality of Jesus. Think of Oliver Cromwell and his slaughter of the Irish, or the attitude of Christian racists, or family abusers. Deception in prayer is a live possibility. Therefore, it is very important that people learn the prayer of fellowship with Christ in the context of a careful study of the actual personality of Jesus, which includes the traits of the new self. Such prayer fosters a sense of fellowship and intimate association with Christ that will be an important basis for the Christian's yielding his or her members to righteousness, for putting to death the old self, and for clothing oneself in the new.

■ Suffering. Paul affirms that our sufferings can be turned to God's purposes in transforming us: "Suffering produces endurance, and endurance produces character, and character produces hope, and hope does not disappoint us, because God's love has been poured into our hearts through the Holy Spirit which has been given to us" (Rom 5:3-5 RSV). The problems of clients who come for therapy are sometimes traceable less to their corrupt traits and more to their sufferings at the hands of others. In these cases clients need to be shown God's love and led out of their bondage to those sufferings. In the Pauline framework liberation from suffering may consist, in part, in learning about the significance of suffering for Christians. This learning does not remove suffering so much as reframe it so that it can be accepted. The client can see suffering not as pure catastrophe, but as an occasion for growth.[9] Indeed, suffering can aid the client in putting on the new self with its traits of endurance and hope.

The therapist might help the client to see how suffering can be used for the benefit of others. For example, a man who is disabled may come to see that his disability can give him insight into others with disabilities and might cause them to listen to what he has to say. Or he might see that his limitation enhances his appreciation for the powers that he does have, and so makes him more grateful than he might otherwise be. If his disability was caused by another person, he might feel a special identification with Christ, who suffered at the hands of others. The therapist will tailor her approach to individual sufferers, encouraging the believer to construe his suffering in such a way that his love of God and neighbor increases, reflecting all the virtues of the new self (Linda Lake, Elizabeth Hayen).

■ Fellowship. In at least one manifestation the new self is the spirit of the Christian community when that community is expressing its devotion to Christ and its members are bonding to one another in Christ's love (Eph 4:1-16). Small fellowship groups that meet for study, prayer and mutual support and encouragement can thus be an important resource for putting on the new self and putting off the old. More mature members of the group may supply a model of the new self that helps the client to distinguish between the new and old self in the client's own behavior and attitudes, and to encourage him or her that such a life is actually possible.

The Pauline therapist will surely want the believer to be a member of a fellowship group, and part of the therapy will consist in helping the client to understand what is going on in the group, how it is affecting her, and how she can make better use of the group in her efforts to yield to righteousness. The therapist may also encourage the believer to enter into a discipling or mentoring relationship with another Christian. With the believer's permission the therapist may occasionally touch base with her mentor to share information and impressions about the client's progress and to talk about how to help her (Christy Adams, Stephen Tate).

A client might also find fellowship in a Pauline therapy group for people with a particular pattern of dysfunction. For example, a group might be formed of men who have perpetrated domestic violence. Such men typically use intimidation with their wives and thus have a common need to put on gentleness. A man in this pattern tends to humiliate his wife—he puts her down, tries to make her feel badly about herself, calls her names, tries to make her think she's crazy and plays mind games with her. He needs to put on compassion. Such a man typically abuses his male privilege; he distorts the biblical concept of male headship by making all the

---

[9]See Walter Sundberg, "The Therapy of Adversity and Penitence," in *Limning the Psyche: Explorations in Christian Psychology*, ed. Robert C. Roberts and Mark R. Talbot (Grand Rapids, Mich.: Eerdmans, 1997).

decisions, treating his wife like a servant and acting like the king of the castle. He needs to put on humility, to count his wife better than himself (Phil 2:3) after the model of Christ, who "emptied himself, taking the form of a servant" (Phil 2:7 RSV).

A pair of Pauline therapists (preferably a male and a female) might teach a group of wife abusers about the Pauline understanding of marital relations. The therapists would use several strategies for helping the clients put on the new self, and the men would hold one another responsible for putting on new patterns of thought, feeling and action in relation to their wives. They would form a bond of fellowship and common purpose that would be a powerful encouragement to put on and keep on their new gentle, compassionate and humble selves in Christ (Ozella Warren, Sean Youngstedt).

■ Confession. Confession of sin involves recalling, articulating and acknowledging responsibility for one's sinful actions, thoughts and emotions, and rejecting or disowning those sins in an attitude called repentance. When one is contrite or penitent, one sees one's sin as ugly and unworthy, as alien. Thus, it is a kind of dissociation or putting away of the sinful episodes, and it contributes to the putting off of the sinful disposition. Confession is not the morally neutral self-exploration that is done in some psychotherapies, nor is it unburdening oneself in order to feel better. Confession is a disowning of a part of oneself by taking responsibility for its actions; it is feeling the horror of those actions in the presence of a merciful and forgiving God.[10]

Mark McMinn tells of a depressed client with whom he did cognitive therapy for a fairly long period of time. After the therapy had been terminated, he learned that the client had sexually abused his daughter. Mark reflected on the possibility that the client's depression was rooted, at least partially, in the memory of this sinful activity, and that the client would have been helped more if he had been encouraged to confess his sin. Mark was making a point about how important it is for the therapist to know when to be silent so that deeper and more hidden things can emerge.

■ Reading and meditation. The therapist can assign meditative reading of books that clearly expound and vividly illustrate the concept of the old and new self and their respective traits (envy-humility, greed-generosity, anger-forgiveness, deceit-truthfulness, selfishness-compassion and so on). Such reading will cultivate the believer's Christian mind and provide occasions for the therapist to elicit from the believer original suggestions about how the one kind of trait might be taken off and put to death, and the other kind might be put on and yielded to. The reading may also be done in the context of a small fellowship group. The client might use the *lectio divina*, a very old method of reading Scripture therapeutically (Brian Richard-

---

[10]For more discussion of contrition and its relation to confession, see my "The Logic and Lyric of Contrition" *Theology Today* 50 (1993): 193-207.

son). Diogenes Allen describes the exercise that helped him to overcome a tendency to inordinate anger: "Most simply, the *lectio divina* consists of four interlocking aspects: reading a passage of Scripture to yourself aloud; meditating or thinking about what you have read; praying about what rises up in your mind and heart in meditation; and then contemplation, which is simply resting silently in God for a time after you have prayed."[11]

In another exercise, the therapist may assign the client to read some chapters of Paul's writings (say, the book of Philippians) every day for a week and to write down each day something that the Holy Spirit illuminates, especially about the new self or old self (Laura Edwards). The importance of memory in Paul's thought (see, for example, 1 Cor 4:16-17; Eph 2:11-12; 1 Thess 1:2-3; 2 Tim 2:8) suggests the value of therapeutic memory exercises. Clients who arc struggling with anger might be asked to remember times when members of their family did not get angry with them despite being provoked; to remember three times when they were successful in controlling their anger; or to remember the adverse consequences that flowed from anger the last time they flew off the handle (Stephen Fairley).

■ Worship. In public worship we celebrate the Lord's Supper, read Scripture, hear the interpretation of God's Word, pray and sing hymns. Public worship provides a setting for the work of the Holy Spirit. It brings into prominence the impression that Christ has completed his work of creating the new self, that the new personality is there to be put on. Worship as it is practiced in most congregations includes exercises in some of the therapeutic actions of Pauline therapy, such as setting one's mind on the things of the Spirit and giving thanks and praise to God. These actions can include, or can at least facilitate, the yielding of oneself to righteousness; one can make decisions that express the softening of obstinacy to God's grace in Jesus Christ.

When the typical actions of worship fail to be therapeutic for certain believers it is because those believers are not really performing the acts of worship or are performing them with only a dim conception of their significance. Here the Pauline therapist can play a supportive role. The therapy sessions can interact with the experiences of worship, each making the other more effective in the process of self-transformation. The therapist can interpret the actions of worship so that clients better achieve self-transformation, and clients can gain experience in worship that will enable them to profit better from the therapist's guidance about self-transforming actions that they can perform outside of worship.

■ Works. One of the most important ways in which we put on the new self and take off the old is by "walking" in the good actions (Eph 2:10) that are characteristic

[11]Diogenes Allen, "Ascetic Theology and Psychology" in *Limning the Psyche: Explorations in Christian Psychology*, ed. Robert C. Roberts and Mark R. Talbot (Grand Rapids, Mich.: Eerdmans, 1997), p. 312.

of the personality that has been created in Christ. Accordingly, a Pauline therapist who discerns that a depressed client is suffering in large part from selfishness and greed might prescribe spending a series of Saturdays working at a Habitat for Humanity home-building site. There the client would literally present his arms and legs and shoulders and mind as a living sacrifice to God (Rom 2:2), with the result that he puts to death that "earthly member . . . greed, which is idolatry" (Col 3:5, my translation).

The therapist can help to shape the client's works by role-playing the actions of the new self with the client. Having identified some area of a client's life in which she especially needs to walk differently, say, in her interaction with her teenage son, the therapist may play the role of the son in a typical situation. The therapist will coach the client in the kind of behavioral responses that make manifest the new creature in Christ. At the next session the client will report on her success or failure, receive hints for improvement, and perhaps do more role-playing to fine-tune these works (Christy Adams, Stephen Tate). An especially important kind of work in Pauline therapy will be the seeking and giving of forgiveness. The therapist will play an important role, instructing the client in the nature and meaning of Christian forgiveness and providing coaching as the client goes about seeking and giving it (Stephanie Gillis).

We often encounter glimpses of the new self in a life that is not on the whole manifestly renewed. Thus, a husband who does not like his wife very well and is more given to irritating her than to honoring her may nevertheless occasionally see something precious in her. Even if such perceptions tend to coincide with gonadal rhythms, the Pauline therapist will see them as urgings of the new self. The therapist will try to sensitize the client to these healthy passions and train him to capitalize on them for the sake of the kingdom. "When you find yourself feeling tenderly toward her, make the most of it: go with the flow! How do you go with the flow? Give her a kiss. Say something nice to her. Do something nice for her. By doing such actions you yield your members to righteousness, and you will find that the new self, created in Christ Jesus for good actions, grows in dominance over the old."

Four Objections

As I have presented the idea of a Pauline psychotherapy to various audiences, four objections have repeatedly surfaced.

Pauline therapy has limited application. Pauline psychotherapy appears to have limited application because it does not seem to address problems whose origins are organic. That may be true, but I have proposed that the Pauline therapist make judicious use of modern medical knowledge about organic disorders. The Pauline therapist should be able to consult with a psychiatrist and to combine physical interventions with Pauline therapy where needed. In this regard Pauline therapy does not differ from any of today's psychotherapies.

Another form of the objection is that this therapy cannot be practiced in a secular setting where the use of prayer and references to God and Jesus Christ are taboo. But I suppose there are also plenty of clinics where Jungian analysis or rational emotive therapy would not be tolerated. If Pauline therapy cannot be practiced in intolerant secular clinics, then it will need to be practiced elsewhere—in churches or in Christian clinics or in tolerant secular clinics.

Some people seem to think that Pauline therapy is more limited than other therapies because it presupposes certain beliefs on the part of the client. Every psychotherapy is based on some set of contestable beliefs, and in many cases therapy cannot proceed unless the client accepts at least part of the belief system in question, or at least suspends disbelief about it in the initial stages of therapy.

A person who goes to a Jungian analyst will be asked to believe that dreams have deep psychological significance; a client who insists that dreams are nothing but meaningless vagrant epiphenomena of neural processing will not be able to accept the analyst's interpretations of his or her dreams, and thus will not be able to profit from what is distinctive about Jungian therapy. A person who goes for psychoanalysis will be asked to accept beliefs about the human unconscious and about defense mechanisms; a client who refuses to accept these beliefs will not profit fully from psychoanalysis. In the same way, a cognitive therapist will ask the client to accept certain beliefs about what is rational and irrational in the way of thought, emotion and behavior; if the client insists on adhering to different standards of rationality, the therapist may not be able to work with the client.

So in requiring the client to accept some beliefs about Jesus Christ and the new self that has been created in him, Pauline therapy is not so different from these secular psychotherapies. It is different in the particular beliefs that are required, but it is not different in presupposing some contestable beliefs. Christians who accept the prejudice against the Christian framework are saying, as it were, that it is correct for other psychotherapy models to presuppose certain contestable beliefs on the part of their clients, but Christian therapists must not presuppose Christian beliefs on the part of *their* clients. It is just as legitimate for a Christian therapist as for any other kind of therapist to say to a client without apology, "The kind of therapy that I practice presupposes some beliefs, and the therapy is not likely to help you very much if you do not accept those beliefs."

Does this mean that Pauline psychotherapy can be practiced only with Christian believers? Not necessarily. To suppose so is analogous to saying that psychoanalysis can be practiced only with previously strongly convinced Freudians. This is not how things actually go with clients. Often the client comes to a therapist seeking help and has only a vague conception of what the therapist believes about the psyche and about the nature of the universe. The client is inducted into the therapist's way of thinking about these things only in the course of therapy. It may not be necessary for the client to have strong convictions about the beliefs the therapist presupposes; it may be enough, at least at first, for the client to suspend disbelief about these things, to accept them for the sake of the therapeutic process. If the process is successful, the client's conviction about the therapeutic presuppositions may be deepened.

In a similar way, I wonder whether the Pauline therapist working with non-Christian clients, or with clients who are not very firmly convinced of Christian beliefs, might tell clients that they do not need to have full conviction about being given a new self in Jesus Christ, but that the therapy may work if they can just adopt this way of thinking about themselves for the purposes of therapy. If they find reality in this way of thinking, if the thinking makes sense to them and works in their lives, then perhaps their conviction will grow and they will become Christians. Obviously, this approach will not appeal to every client. It presupposes an openness about Christian beliefs and a willingness to participate in the life of the church. Still, Pauline psychotherapy does not seem to differ much from psychoanalysis, Jungian analysis, rational therapy and many other therapies in making presuppositions about clients' belief or willingness to believe.

Some of my students have strongly advocated the possibility of what we might call indirect Pauline therapy for people who are so repelled by the Christian beliefs that they will not even entertain them hypothetically. Perhaps privately the therapist can think of the client's problems as stemming from the sinful old self, and think of the goal of therapy as helping the client to put on something like the new self in Christ, yet without speaking in these terms to the client. Perhaps the therapist will speak, instead, in terms of rational thought and behavior, or of the client's self-acceptance, or of unconscious conflicts stemming from childhood traumas. Or perhaps the therapist will speak in no particular terms at all, but just listen empathetically while letting the client talk it out.

If the therapist is well down the path of putting on the new self in Jesus Christ, the client will sense something unusual and attractive about the person of the therapist. The client will find, in the relationship with the therapist, a healing whose source the client cannot fully acknowledge. Without saying so, the therapist will be gently guiding the client toward such virtues as gentleness, patience, self-control, humility, and compassion. If at the same time the client is well aware that the therapist is holding back some of the resources for healing, a time may come when the client will want to hear specifically about the gospel and the healing power of the Holy Spirit.

The traits of the new self in Christ are all elements of relationship with God as revealed in the teachings and work of Jesus. Thus, a person who is gentle, patient, self-controlled, humble and compassionate, but does not acknowledge God in Christ, does not have the Christian virtues but an analogue of them. By Christian standards, a person who has non-Christian forms of these positive traits is almost certainly functioning better than somebody who has their negative counterparts, but it is important that the Pauline therapist be very conscious that these virtues are only substitutes for the traits of a fully healthy person.[12]

Pauline therapy is a misreading of Paul. A second objection I often hear is that Pauline therapy treats the Bible like a psychology book, whereas the Bible is no such thing. Trying to read everything in Paul's writings as though it is a systematic psychology is bad exegesis. Some people clarify the objection by saying that the books of the Bible—or at least the writings of Paul—are about theology and not about psychology.

It is true that Paul has much to say about God, but the writings of Paul do not constitute a systematic theology any more than they constitute a systematic psychology. They are about God and they are about the human self, but they are not systematic in the ways that we expect modern theology and modern psychology to be. On the other hand, Paul's comments about God and about the human self can both be systematized: one can expound them as a complex and consistent view.

But granting that it is not a systematic exposition of any system of ideas, Paul's writings contain as much about human psychology—about what it takes to be a fully functioning specimen of humanity, about what the corrupt or unhealthy psyche is like and why it is as it is, and about what has been done and can be done to repair the damage—as it does about the nature and activities of God. These topics are interwoven, so that Pauline psychology is also a theology (and vice versa). And in each case, Paul leaves gaps that must be filled in by someone who has systematic pretensions. We will learn whether the exegesis is possible by seeing whether it can actually be done, and this paper (which leaves much Pauline psychology unformulated) shows, in a preliminary way, that it can be done.

Pauline therapy is narrow-minded. The third objection is that it is reactionary or perversely self-constricting to try to construct a psychotherapy with as little reference as possible to the psychologies of the twentieth century. What is the point of formulating such a psychology? If we distinguish the enterprise of Christian psychology from that of integration, as I do in the first section of this chapter, then the effort to formulate a Pauline therapy with minimal reference to twentieth-century psychologies is not reactionary or self-constricting. It is just a different activity from that of adapting twentieth-century psychologies for Christian use. It is an effort to see how far we can go without major importations from outside our tradition. We are not likely to push the psychological limits of our tradition if we do not try to formulate such a psychology.

Even if we decide that the very best psychology that we can formulate is an integrated one—and I think this may be true—we still have a very large stake in know-

---

[12]Steve Ater, Stephen Tate, Ozella Warren and Elizabeth Hayen especially deserve credit for stimulating the thoughts in this and the preceding two paragraphs.

ing what a nearly pure Christian psychology looks like. In the ideal case, Pauline psychology will be the one into which items from the secular psychologies are integrated. If we start with the secular models and add on a few Christian bells and whistles, or if we just leave out a few dimensions of the secular models that seem to conflict with Christian principles, our integration is likely to omit Christian distinctives like the concept of the new self and the activities of putting it on. When we start with secular models, we run a much greater risk of letting alien moral and spiritual traditions—for that is what the twentieth-century psychologies in their pure form are—drive the formation of Christians and the healing of our psyches. And we miss an opportunity to show people outside the church the power of our own psychology to make sense of their lives and to begin to set them right.

Pauline therapy is neither fish nor fowl. The fourth objection comes from people who are concerned about keeping professional and disciplinary boundaries clear, who want to make sure that what Christian psychologists are doing is really psychology. Isn't Pauline psychology just pastoral counseling by a fancier name?

The first part of my answer is that the disciplinary boundaries are already blurred by the secular psychologies. In *Taking the Word to Heart* I argue that such models as client-centered therapy (Carl Rogers), rational emotive therapy (Albert Ellis), assertiveness training, contextual therapy (a form of family therapy developed by Ivan Boszormenyi-Nagy), analytic psychotherapy (Carl Jung), and the psychoanalysis of Heinz Kohut are not spiritually neutral medical disciplines as they sometimes claim to be. In form they are spiritualities parallel to Christianity, though materially different from Christianity and from one another.

Psychotherapists in these traditions are teachers of various philosophies that attempt to instill in clients a particular self-understanding, sense of the meaning of life and set of virtues in which clients will find fulfillment. If this argument is right, then many of the secular therapies are already very much like pastoral counseling. But these psychologies also differ from the counseling that pastors have done since the church's inception. Therapists tend to charge a fee, and they are often more intensively diagnostic and more theoretically informed. They tend to have a fairly well-worked-out arsenal of intervention strategies. Psychotherapy tends to be more structured and formal than pastoral counseling tends to be. According to these loose criteria, it seems to me that Pauline psychotherapy as I have outlined it in this chapter is a form of psychotherapy rather than pastoral counseling.

Another version of the fourth objection trades on the distinction between the psychological and the spiritual, claiming that Pauline psychology is an impossible hybrid. Paul writes about spirituality and its problems, but psychotherapy is about people's psychological nature and problems. So the project proposed in this chapter is a mistake.

This objection is reminiscent of Rudolf Bultmann's reading of Paul, which I mentioned in the first section. But it is difficult to know what spiritual change would be if it was construed to be different from psychological change. Psychological change includes a change in behavior, thought and emotion—not a change in a particular thought, behavior or emotion, but a change in *disposition* toward these things. It is a difference in the *type* or *pattern* of one's behaviors, thoughts and emotions, something like a change of character.

Consider a husband who ceases to think about how to intimidate his wife. He stops behaving in intimidating ways and experiencing rage when she is not perfectly "obedient." He begins thinking in terms of her needs, treating her as a person with dignity, and experiencing joy when she thinks and behaves independently of him in the interest of their family life. This is a psychological change. It is the kind of change that psychotherapists try to effect in their clients. But it is also the kind of change that Paul encourages in his letters and attributes to the Holy Spirit and the work of Christ. Spiritual change does not occur in a different part of the soul from psychological change. It too is a dispositional change in thought, behavior and emotion.

Christians speak of the spiritual occurring where the Holy Spirit is especially at work, and they believe that the Holy Spirit is especially active where the saving work of Christ is being proclaimed. Spiritual change, then, is a *kind* of psychological change, namely psychological change brought about by the proclamation of the gospel and the work of the Holy Spirit in the life of the believer. It is psychological change in which a person's behaviors, thoughts and emotions are informed by God and reflect his ways. Spirituality is the kind of psychological change that Pauline psychotherapy aims to promote.

Conclusion

The basis of a rich therapeutic psychology is to be found in the letters of the apostle Paul. The main ideas of this psychology are these: First, Christian believers have two selves, a new one created in Christ, which is their real self, and an old remnant self that can nevertheless be very troublesome. Second, the new self is characterized by traits of health and well-being that are beneficial not only for the individual but also for the individual's community, while the old self is dysfunctional and destructive. Third, there are a number of actions by which the individual who is within a Christian community can access, actualize and encourage the growth of the new self, and stifle and abandon the old self.

This outline includes some fairly concrete suggestions that my students and I have devised for implementing Pauline psychotherapy in a clinical setting. The method needs to be developed both practically and theoretically. Central to its development will be its use by practitioners who are interested in sharpening it conceptually. Communication among interested practitioners and theoreticians would facilitate mutual enrichment and correction.

7

TO VENT OR NOT TO VENT?

What Contemporary Psychology Can Learn from Ascetic Theology About Anger

---

Dennis L. Okholm

For the nature of anger is such that when it is given room it languishes and perishes, but if openly exhibited, it burns more and more. (CASSIAN *CONFERENCES* 16.27; CF. PROV 29:11)

N OT LONG AGO WHILE MY WIFE WAS WAITING IN LINE AT THE GROCERY STORE to pay for her groceries, an older man in front of her yelled to a female employee at the next counter whom he thought should be bagging his groceries: "Hey, Stubby, get over here and start doing your job." My wife was stunned. The man's words were so startling that she was not sure she had assessed the situation correctly, so she asked (with a tinge of sarcasm, since she thought she probably had understood correctly), "Were you joking with her or were you talking to another human being that way?" He told her this was none of her business. She replied that it was not right to talk to someone that way. His response did not match his chronological age: he rattled off a list of insults you might hear on an elementary school playground. "I'd hate to be your husband and wake up to see your face every morning." (It is clear that he not only lacked emotional maturity, but also had poor esthetic judgment.) My wife answered these insults by calmly retorting "I feel sorry for you" and "That's very sad." [1]

---

[1]This article is part of a larger research project made possible through the support of the Pew Evangelical Scholars Program.

Should my wife have blown up in response to this man's anger? Is there any place for anger in the Christian's life? Without hesitation our contemporaries would say, "Of course." But what happens when we listen to some of those in our Christian family who lived 1,500 years ago? Were they on target in their recommendations of how to live the Christian life and remain healthy? Will we consider them naive or ill-informed because they were not "scientific"? What happens when we listen to premoderns who did not know they were doing theology and psychology at the same time?

Not too long ago *Christianity Today* ran an article assessing the status of the Christian counseling movement.[2] The item included a diagram of a tree that detailed some of the current branches of Christian psychology. Most of us would recognize the names on the tree. On the trunk were inscribed the names of Narramore, Tournier, and Menninger. Clearly the author was selective about whom to include on the parts of the tree that were above ground, and his choices are debatable. But below ground were the roots of Christian psychology. Here lay the pioneers, including Rogers, Jung, Freud, Maslow, Skinner and Satir. If the diagram is accurate, it is lamentable, for the roots surely determine the meat of the fruits, even if those fruits are polished on the outside with a Christian veneer to make them attractive to the consumer. Contemporary Christian psychology is a tree that might properly include grafts from Rogers, Freud and Skinner but its roots should be found elsewhere.

The fact is that except for a few lone contemporary voices, such as those of Benedict Groeschel, Thomas Oden and Solomon Schimmel, ancient and early medieval Christian sources have been virtually ignored in the area of practical theology by the church as a whole and even by contemporary Christian psychologists.[3] Even when ancient and medieval sources are taken into account, they are often filtered through modern paradigms that distort the teachings of the ancients.[4] My con-

---

[2]"Hurting Helpers," *Christianity Today*, September 16, 1996, pp. 76-80.
[3]See Benedict J. Groeschel, *Spiritual Passages: The Psychology of Spiritual Development* (New York: Crossroad, 1983); Thomas C. Oden, *The Care of Souls in the Classical Tradition* (Philadelphia: Fortress, 1984); Solomon Schimmel, *The Seven Deadly Sins: Jewish, Christian, and Classical Reflections on Human Nature* (New York: Free Press, 1992). Oden has documented and criticized recent clinical pastoral counseling's neglect of centuries of Christian wisdom having to do with counseling. See his *Care of Souls,* chap. 1. Schimmel, a Jewish psychologist, has a similar reaction toward psychotherapy in general, admonishing his colleagues to learn from classical, Jewish and Christian theologians and moralists: "Modern psychology's disdain for the teachings of the great moral traditions is an example of intellectual hubris" (*Seven Deadly Sins,* p. 5; see also chap. 1 of the same book.)
[4]For example, see Alan Jones, *Soul Making: The Desert Way of Spirituality* (San Francisco: HarperCollins, 1985). Jones purports to unpack the desert tradition and to demonstrate its relevance for today, but curiously the book has few references to the desert fathers and mothers; the book is more modern and psychoanalytic than rooted in the desert tradition. Even a glance at the index demonstrates this. As a result, Jones distorts and misrepresents the

tention is that ascetic theologians and monastics of the fourth through seventh centuries—particularly Evagrius Ponticus, John Cassian and Gregory the Great—provide the church with a psychology that is not only specifically Christian in its orientation, but is also relevant to modern people if it is taken seriously. Quite often the claims made about life issues by ascetic theologians, monastics and Aquinas[5] are borne out by the empirical observations of contemporary psychology. I will attempt to demonstrate this in a consideration of the problem of anger.

Deadly Sins

Anger was on Evagrius's original list of eight evil thoughts *(logismoi)* with which demons tempt us. In Cassian those eight evil thoughts become the eight principal faults, the universal human tendencies from which sins result.[6] Cassian stood as the link between the Eastern theologian Evagrius and Western Benedictine monasticism. Gregory, the first Benedictine monk to become a pope, modified Cassian's list, enumerating "seven principal vices." He placed pride in a category by itself as the root of all sins, he added envy, and he merged spiritual lethargy *(accidie)* with sadness *(tristitia)* into sloth. These became our present-day list of the seven deadly sins.[7]

Calling all of these sins deadly is not entirely accurate. As Aquinas makes clear in the *Summa,*[8] Gregory's seven are capital or chief or cardinal sins, but they are

---

spirituality of the desert monks. Compare, for example, Jones's comment about the perfection of the desert fathers with a paradigmatic quote from Cassian. Jones writes, "The perfection which he or she [the desert ascetic] seeks is of a very different order from that of worldly success." True enough. "It comes only as a gift and *never* as an achievement" (p. 41, italics mine). Cassian typifies the desert tradition that preceded him: "Consider therefore that you belong to the few and elect; and do not grow cold after the examples of the lukewarmness of many. . . . You should therefore realize that it is no light sin for one who has made profession of perfection to follow after what is imperfect. And to this state of perfection you may *attain* by the following steps and in the following way" (*Conferences* 5.38, in The Nicene and Post-Nicene Fathers, 2nd series, ed. Philip Schaff and Henry Wace, trans. Edgar C. S. Gibson [Grand Rapids, Mich.: Eerdmans, 1986], vol. 11, italics mine). If Jones is correct, it is difficult to understand how Cassian, who summarizes the desert tradition he inherited, could ever have been accused (rightly or wrongly) of being semi-Pelagian. Jones's book is still valuable. Despite his misrepresentations and sometimes careless use of words and categories, he has many good insights.

[5]While Aquinas is not an ascetic theologian, on this topic he draws heavily on the ascetic tradition.

[6]For the list of eight principal faults see John Cassian *The Twelve Books of the Institutes of the Coenobium* 5.1, in The Nicene and Post-Nicene Fathers, 2nd series, ed. Philip Schaff and Henry Wace, trans. Edgar C. S. Gibson (Grand Rapids, Mich.: Eerdmans, 1986), vol. 11. In *Conferences* 5.16 Cassian calls the faults sins.

[7]See Gregory *Morals on the Book of Job,* trans. J. Bliss (Oxford: John Henry Parker, 1850), vol. 3, comments on 39:25; Schimmel, *Seven Deadly Sins,* p. 25.

[8]Thomas Aquinas *Summa Theologica* 2a2ae, Q148, art. 2, trans. Fathers of the English Dominican Province (Westminster, Md.: Christian Classics, 1948).

not necessarily always mortal sins. Each of the seven is a cardinal sin in part because it is the parent of "daughter" sins. For instance, Gregory teaches that anger propagates an army of sins, including strifes, swelling of mind, insults, clamor, indignation, and blasphemies.[9] Whether a cardinal sin is mortal or venial depends on whether it is opposed to the love and grace of God. Aquinas implies that both anger and hatred involve wishing evil on another, but that anger should involve wishing evil according to the virtue of justice. Anger's devolution into hatred involves wishing evil without measure and for its own sake. Further, anger turned to hatred is long lasting; in fact, it arises from a disposition, a habit, by which a person considers the object of the hatred to be contrary and hurtful to him or her.[10] Obstinate racism is a good example of anger that has devolved into a deadly sin, both spiritually and physically.

The order in which the thinkers discuss these thoughts signifies that they viewed the eight as interconnected.[11] For example, Cassian groups the vices in pairs: the deadly thoughts form alliances against us.[12] Anger is often the bedfellow of envy, and it is frequently aroused by frustrated greed and lust. The connections observed between these vices and sins in everyday life is the genius of ascetic theologians like Evagrius, whom one translator calls "the anatomist of the passions of the psyche both in their manifestations in behavior and in their intrapsychic activity."[13] Evagrius calls us to carefully observe, describe and analyze the precise nature of our thoughts. This knowledge will work to our advantage as we work with or against the thoughts, or our memories of them. Some passages in the *Praktikos* contain insights that our contemporaries have only recently rediscovered and recorded in the psychoanalytic literature.[14]

Gregory follows in Evagrius's footsteps, and he sounds like one of us when he analyzes the connection between melancholy and avarice: "When the disturbed has

---

[9]Gregory *Morals on Job* 39.25.

[10]Aquinas *Summa Theologica* 1a2ae, Q46, art. 6.

[11]"But they are, each of them, so closely connected with each other, that they spring only the one from the other" (Gregory *Morals on Job* 39.25).

[12]Cassian *Conferences* 5.10.

[13]John Eudes Bamberger, introduction to Evagrius Ponticus, *Praktikos and Chapters on Prayer*, trans. J. E. Bamberger (Spencer, Mass.: Cistercian Publications, 1970), p. lxxxii. In the same vein, Solomon Schimmel writes: "The diatribes against traditional religion and morality that one encounters in psychological circles reflect a superficial understanding of sin, vice, and virtue and other concepts in the moral vocabulary of the past. The deadly sins are not arbitrary, irrational restrictions on human behavior, imposed by a remote deity indifferent to human needs. On the contrary, most sins or vices, and the seven deadly sins in particular, concern the core of what we are, of what we can become, and most important, of what we should aspire to be" *(Seven Deadly Sins,* p. 5).

[14]For example, see Evagrius *Praktikos,* pp. 43, 50. Oden gives specific examples of ways in which Gregory's *Pastoral Care* (trans. Henry Davis [New York: Newman Press, 1950]) anticipates modern psychotherapy. See Oden, *Care of Souls,* chap. 2.

lost the satisfaction of joy within, it seeks for sources of consolation without, and is more anxious to possess external goods, the more it has no joy in which to fall back with it."[15] These observed connections among thoughts become clear when we explore the features of anger.

Of the principal thoughts or deadly sins, anger is crucial. Evagrius says that "the most fierce passion is anger," and he mentions anger more than the other deadly sins.[16] If Schimmel's assessment is accurate when he says that as a therapist he spends more time helping clients with their anger than with any other emotion,[17] then we should not be surprised that the ascetics also identified anger as the predominate temptation of the monk, considering it more detrimental to sought-after tranquility than almost anything else.[18] Consequently, managing anger is crucial.

Anger Deconstructed

Evagrius defines anger as "a boiling and stirring up of wrath against one who has given injury or is thought to have done so."[19] This "boiling" constantly irritates the soul, especially when the injured is at prayer and the offender appears in a mental picture.

The ascetic theologians distinguish among various types of anger. They catalog them differently from one another, sometimes using different words, but they always describe certain distinct characteristics. Some anger rages within, while some breaks out in word or deed; some anger arises quickly and dissipates quickly, while some lasts for days.[20] The ascetic theologians also recognize that some outwardly directed anger is irrationally aimed at inanimate objects or animals; the former may be an easy target since they cannot talk back, and if our definition of anger means anything, in both cases the angry person thinks of the nonhuman objects of anger metaphorically as rational animate creatures. Finally, these early

---

[15]Gregory *Morals on Job* 39.25.

[16]Evagrius *Praktikos,* p. 11.

[17]Schimmel, *Seven Deadly Sins,* p. 83.

[18]For example, in *Conferences* 16.7 Cassian writes: "As then nothing should be put before love, so on the other hand nothing should be put below rage and anger . . . because we should reckon nothing more damaging than anger and vexation, and nothing more advantageous than love." He points us to Prov 10:12.

[19]Evagrius *Praktikos,* p. 11. Similarly, Aquinas defines anger as "the desire to hurt another for the purpose of just vengeance" in response to an injury received (*Summa Theologica* 1a2ae, Q47, art. 1; cf. Q46, art. 1.)

[20]Cassian, in *Conferences* 11.4, distinguishes among *thymos, orgē* and *menis.* Gregory catalogs four sorts of anger according to speed of onset and dissipation; anger that arises quickly and dies slowly is the worst, while anger that catches slowly and parts quickly is the best (Gregory *Morals on Job* 5.2). Aquinas lists three species of anger: the choleric *(akrocholoi),* the bitter *(pikros,* similar to Cassian's third) and the ill-tempered *(chalepoi,* similar to Gregory's worst). Interestingly, Carol Tavris describes a catalog similar to Gregory's in *Anger: The Misunderstood Emotion,* rev. ed. (New York: Simon & Schuster, 1989), p. 12.

psychologists knew that anger could also be directed inwardly, against oneself.[21]

The etiology of anger is often a factor of the connections among the eight *logismoi* or seven sins. Not only do they have in common the characteristic of misplaced desire (with which a psychodynamic theorist could have a field day), but they are also in a kind of causal relationship to one another.

The arrangement of the eight *logismoi* indicates that anger most often arises from avarice, its predecessor on the list. Desire for worldly attainments and material possessions often lies at the root of anger. When our desires to possess or control are thwarted (and such desires are usually assisted by envy, vainglory or pride), then we are enraged.[22] There is more to it than this, but in our culture we can quickly see the connection. The movie *Fargo* gives us a graphic example of a man whose life is so consumed with avarice that he lashes out in anger at his employer, his wife and even the thugs he has employed to do his dirty work; the greed-induced rage finally erupts into the point-blank murder of his father-in-law and the death of his wife and a host of others. Or consider the anger or smoldering resentment that we feel when a "less deserving" colleague receives kudos or a merit raise that we desire for ourselves. These connections led the ascetics to prescribe contempt for material possessions as a cure for anger.

Anger can easily lead to its successors as well: dejection (or melancholy) and sloth *(accidie).*[23] Once one's life is thrown into turmoil because one's avaricious goals are frustrated, anger often leads to confusion and melancholy, and even to giving up trying. Modern psychology recognizes that sometimes depression follows anger.[24]

---

[21]Aquinas *Summa Theologica* 1a2ae, Q46, art. 7.

[22]Gregory gives us the most explicit and precise exposition of these connections. In *Morals on Job* 39.25 he reverses the etiological direction so that envy gives rise to anger. But we should note that envy and avarice have some very similar qualities. For the connection between desire, avarice and anger, see Evagrius *Praktikos,* p. 99, where he quotes a monk: "I have this reason for putting aside pleasure—that I might cut off the pretext for growing angry. For I know that anger constantly fights for pleasures and clouds the mind with passions that drive away contemplative knowledge." Compare this to Evagrius *Chapters on Prayer,* p. 27: "Armed as you are against anger do not submit to any powerful desire. For it is these which provide fuel for anger." Several times Cassian warns that regard for material things is the first ground of discord leading to anger. For example, see *Conferences* 16.6, 9.

[23]See Gregory *Morals on Job* 39.25.

[24]See Tavris, *Anger,* p. 108: "When anger is unsuccessful in averting danger or removing obstacles, when it does not restore your sense of control over the environment, you may eventually begin to feel apathetic. According to the *hopelessness theory of depression,* the key cognitions in depression are that nothing good will ever happen ('It's all hopeless'), and that the person is helpless in changing this bleak future. Depressed people tend to believe that negative events have internal, stable and global causes ('It's my fault; it will always be my fault; and it will affect everything I do'). In such cases of depression, though, it is not quite right to say that anger has been 'turned inward.' More accurately, it has been extinguished." Tavris delineates several relationships (and nonrelationships) between anger and depression.

I recall my feeble attempts to learn the game of tennis when I was a boy. My father would take me to the courts and instruct me. Though I had no illusions of going on the circuit and winning at Wimbledon, I did want to be as good as some of my peers who seemed quite adept at the game. But the more I tried to "possess" the skills without patiently practicing the fundamentals, and the more the ball would slam into the net or sail over the fence, the angrier I got. The only thing I could do was to perform antics that would later be imitated by John McEnroe. I was good at throwing my racket down, stomping around the court, and yelling words permitted by my limited Fundamentalist vocabulary. Finally, I gave up in frustration. Anger had won the day and a kind of sloth *(accidie)* had set in.

Is It Okay to Be Angry?

Modern hearers might be surprised to learn that John Cassian told his fellow monks that the first remedy for anger is to make up their minds never to be angry: "The athlete of Christ who strives lawfully ought thoroughly to root out the feeling of wrath." Ephesians 4:31 commands us to accept no anger as "necessary or useful for us." And the goal in acquiring the virtue of patience consists, "not in being angry with a good reason, but in not being angry at all." [25]

Are there any legitimate expressions of anger? Cassian's interlocutor responds to Cassian: "There is nothing wrong in being angry with a brother who does evil because God is said to be angry with such people (Ps 6:1, 106:40)." Cassian bristles; he and Gregory often mention how easily we misuse Scripture to rationalize our behavior. [26] (Cassian expresses his objection to rationalization especially well in his treatise on avarice; he would not tolerate the way that Western Christians have rationalized their greed into a virtue.) True, Cassian observes in response to his interlocutor, some try to excuse "this most pernicious disease of the soul" by employing a "shocking way of interpreting Scripture," ascribing to God the taint of human passion. In this theological argument against the anthropomorphites, Cassian reminds us that Scripture speaks of God metaphorically, depicting him sleeping, standing, having parts of the human body and experiencing human passions. What we are to understand about God's anger is "that he is the judge and avenger of all the unjust things which are done in this world." Accordingly, we should dread his judgments and fear to do anything against his will. [27]

---

[25] Cassian *Institutes* 8.22; 8.5; 8:21.

[26] At one point Cassian employs what we consider higher critical tools to reprimand translators who had added "without a cause" to Mt 5:22 to justify anger for just causes. He argues that the phrase does not appear in X, B, Origen and the Vulgate. (Compare the KJV, which retains the phrase, with the NIV and NRSV, which only footnote it.) Insightfully, Cassian argues that "certainly nobody, however unreasonably he is disturbed, would say that he is angry without a cause" (ibid., 8.21).

[27] Ibid., 8.2-4.

Cassian also turns his attention to Ephesians 4:26: " 'In your anger do not sin': Do not let the sun go down while you are still angry." Because of the verse's context some people want to believe that we owe such forbearance only to unbelievers and blasphemers, who should rightly be endured, but not to brothers who should know better but have provoked anger with reproachful words. (Some people try to do the same sort of thing by twisting Matthew 5:22.)[28] This is another rationalization that Cassian does not permit.

Then is there no room for anger according to Cassian? In Ephesians 4:26 we are commanded to be angry in a wholesome fashion, which Cassian interprets as being angry with ourselves and with the evil thoughts that arise in us. In a bit of clever medieval exegesis he explains the verse this way: "Be ye angry with your faults and your tempers, lest, if you acquiesce in them, Christ, the sun of righteousness, may on account of your anger begin to go down on your darkened minds, and when He departs you may furnish a place for the devil in your hearts."[29] Cassian is consistent, even if he does strain credulity in this exegetical maneuver. Cassian is following the wisdom of Evagrius before him, who insisted that anger "is *given* to us so that we might fight against the demons and strive against every pleasure." In fact, Evagrius admonishes us not to fall immediately to prayer when we are tempted, but first to utter angry words against the one who afflicts us.[30]

Gregory, who inherited the wisdom of Evagrius and was reared on the writings of Cassian,[31] would not have shared Cassian's interpretation of Ephesians 4:26. This is obvious from his insistence that Psalm 4:4 is wrongly interpreted by those who say that we should be angry only at ourselves and not with others when they sin: "For if we are bidden to love our neighbors as ourselves, it follows that we should be as angry with their erring ways as with our own evil practices." To illustrate his point Gregory cites Eli, whose lukewarm response to the evil practices of those under his charge led to his demise. Eli should have been angry with them, and he might have been if he had distinguished between "the anger which hastiness of temper stirs" and "that which zeal gives its character to" and "is kept under the control of reason."[32] The whole thrust of Aquinas's treatment of anger follows Gregory's; it is born out of sorrow at being wronged and out of hope at the prospect of a just revenge.[33]

But even though Aquinas recommends the positive role of anger far more than

---

[28]See Cassian *Conferences* 16.17.

[29]Cassian *Institutes* 8.9.

[30]See Evagrius *Praktikos*, pp. 23, 42 (italics mine). Cf. Cassian *Institutes* 8.7, where he seems to echo Evagrius intentionally, insisting that the only case in which anger is "excellently implanted in us" and is useful is when we "are indignant and rage" against the "lustful emotions of the heart."

[31]*Rule of Benedict* 73.5.

[32]Gregory *Morals on Job* 5.2.

[33]See Aquinas *Summa Theologica* 1a1ae, Q46-48.

the earlier ascetics did, he echoes their assessment of anger's danger: "Of all the passions anger is the most manifest obstacle to the judgement of reason." Citing Gregory, Aquinas recognizes that with regard to its formal element, anger is satisfactory as an appetitive movement that begins in the reason. With regard to its material element, however, the passion of anger forestalls the perfect judgment of reason because its commotion cranks up the heat that urges instant action.[34] Evagrius does not even allow for the justification of anger that is directed outwardly in the name of justice. Even the anger that is given to us to fight temptation and the demons is easily redirected by the demons to worldly desires so that we end up fighting with others, and thus "blinded in mind and falling away from knowledge, our spirit should become a traitor to virtue."[35] Cassian, who thinks that *nothing* justifies anger, puts it bluntly: "It makes no difference whether gold plates, or lead, or what metal you please, are placed over our eyelids, the value of the metal makes no difference in our blindness."[36]

Why the Angry Do Not Have a Healthy Prayer Life

If we can understand the ascetics' concern about the effects of anger on the practice of discernment, then we will have arrived at the key reason that someone like Cassian proscribes anger altogether. To better understand we first need to consider the goal of the monk.

Ascetic theologians called the health of the soul *apatheia*.[37] Though early monastics were influenced by Stoic and Neo-Platonic philosophies, they adapted rather than adopted this Stoic concept.[38] *Apatheia* is not simply the leveling out of human

---

[34]Aquinas *Summa Theologica* 1a2ae, Q48, art. 3. According to Aquinas, reason needs certain sensitive powers to execute its acts, so it is hindered when the body is disturbed. Any hindrance in the body, such as drunkenness or drowsiness, hinders the judgment of reason. Anger above causes a bodily disturbance around the heart in such a way that it affects the outward members; hence, Aquinas's assessment of anger's debilitating effects. The physiological effects of anger are also recognized by the early ascetic theologians, and it is interesting to note that 1,500 years later physiology has become perhaps the most important area of research for studies about anger. For example, see Margaret A. Chesney and Ray H. Rosenman, eds., *Anger and Hostility in Cardiovascular and Behavioral Disorders* (Washington, D.C.: Hemisphere, 1985); and Aron Wolfe Siegman and Timothy W. Smith, eds., *Anger, Hostility, and the Heart* (Hillsdale, N.J.: Lawrence Erlbaum, 1994). Also, see Tavris, *Anger,* pp. 119-27. Though it is overestimated, a relationship between anger and coronary heart disease does exist.
[35]Evagrius *Praktikos,* p. 24.
[36]Cassian *Institutes* 8.6. Cf. chap. 21 and Cassian *Conferences* 16.6, 16.
[37]See Gerald G. May, *Addiction and Grace* (San Francisco: HarperSanFrancisco, 1988), p. 192 n. 1: *Apatheia* is not to be confused with *accidie,* which is closer to what *we* mean by "apathy"—a "dull, lethargic absence of caring and interest."
[38]See Bamberger's introduction to Evagrius's *Praktikos.* Bamberger suggests that in Evagrius the concept of *apatheia* is more biblical than Stoic. It is something like the fear of the Lord (see p. lxxxiiiff. and n. 233; also, cf. Cassian *Institutes* 4.43).

emotions or the extirpation of the passions.[39] Ascetics like Evagrius and Cassian borrowed from the Stoics, from Clement of Alexandria, and from Egyptian sources, such as Anthony, and put their own stamp on the concept.[40] For the ascetics *apatheia* is an abiding sense of peace and joy that comes from the full harmony of the passions, a habitual state developed through discipline *(ascesis),* which is why we call it a virtue. Through various exercises one learns to be in full possession of one's affective faculties so that disordered desires are held in check and rightly ordered and one can experience a state of deep calm, a "repose," as Cassian calls it.[41] According to Evagrius one of the marks of the presence of *apatheia* in one's life is one's ability to remain calm and peaceful even while remembering situations or events that tend to stimulate and disorder the passions.[42]

This harmonious integration of the emotional life always remains exposed to the attacks of demons, so emotional health, *apatheia* must be maintained with effort. Of course, this is to be expected: good health is never a given; one must work at it with care. This implies that *apatheia* can be had or lost by degrees. Furthermore, *apatheia* is subject to the limitations of each person's unique constitution. We must not overlook this when we consider the relationship between anger and physiology.[43]

Evagrius teaches that the offspring of *apatheia* is *agapē*. Maintaining the harmony of one's passions enables one fully to love others and God, because the acquisition of *apatheia* can stamp out anger, sulking, lust, resentment, envy and all other impediments to self-giving love. Without love *apatheia* alone is of little value. Evagrius reminds us that true prayer is not simply the absence of impure thoughts: "It is quite possible for a man to have none but the purest thoughts and yet be so distracted mulling over them that he remains the while far removed from God."[44] Gregory is quite specific. Discussing fasting, he illustrates in practical terms that acquiring *apatheia* cannot be divorced from *agapē:*

> In this matter we must consider how little the virtue of abstinence is regarded, unless it
> deserve commendation by reason of other virtues. . . . To sanctify a fast is to show

---

[39]There is some language that sounds like this; for example, see Evagrius *Praktikos,* p. 87. But because the goal is the passion of love, we must be careful how we understand this language. Refer to the previous two notes.

[40]See Bamberger, introduction to *Praktikos,* pp. lxxiiff.

[41]Cassian's favorite term for *apatheia* is "purity of heart" (see *Conferences* 1.4). *Apatheia* is a state of undistracted prayer.

[42]Evagrius *Praktikos,* pp. 34, 64-67, 69. See Tavris, *Anger,* chap. 3.

[43]*Apatheia* refers to the first half of spiritual development in ascetic theology, the active ascetic life, which begins in faith, diminishes the force of the passions "until they are destroyed" and results in charity. This leads to the second phase, the contemplative, which begins with the contemplation of nature, diminishes ignorance and results in theology. See Evagrius *Praktikos,* p. 84. The disciplines in ascetic theology have to do with the first step (namely, purgation) of the threefold assent that ends in union with God.

[44]Evagrius *Praktikos,* p. 55.

abstinence of the flesh to be worthy of God by other good things added to it [such as giving to the poor what one has abstained from]. . . . A man fasts not to God but to himself, if he does not give to the poor what he denies his belly for a time, but reserves it to be given to his belly later.[45]

It is *ascesis,* or discipline, that leads to *apatheia.* Evagrius puts it succinctly:

> *Agape* is the progeny of *apatheia. Apatheia* is the very flower of *ascesis. Ascesis* consists in keeping the commandments. The custodian of these commandments is the fear of God which is in turn the offspring of true faith. Now faith is an interior good, one which is to be found even in those who do not yet believe in God.[46]

Now we begin to see the import of Gregory's caution that despite the fact that we sometimes act out of a sense of justice, "anger joins it from the side . . . [and] wounds all the healthiness of our inward tranquility."[47] The anger that "darkens the soul" defiles the mind as much as do vivid images of sexual pleasure, so that the mind is otherwise preoccupied during prayer, pure prayer is not offered to God, and the demon of *accedie* falls on the person who is praying.[48] And not only is prayer affected, reason's ability to appropriately redress injustices is hindered in those cases in which Gregory and Aquinas have given us permission to be angry. As Aquinas observes, anger does not listen perfectly to reason in meting out vengeance. The irony is that even when our anger may be justifiable, "anger requires an act of reason, yet proves a hindrance to reason."[49] Let us examine these two related debilitating effects of anger.

First, being angry about injuries that are done to us interferes with our prayer and prevents us from drawing near to God. Evagrius asserts this repeatedly in his *Chapters on Prayer.*[50] If this is true, Cassian wonders, then how can we obey God's commands to pray without ceasing (1 Thess 5:17) and in all places (1 Tim 2:8; note Paul's reference to anger) while we retain bitterness or allow another to retain bitterness against us?[51] We certainly cannot obey Matthew 5:23-24 in such a case. Cassian believes that anger is dangerous and wrong. He asks how we can endure it in ourselves or in someone else if in either case we cannot pray. God does not allow the gifts of our prayers to be offered to him even if our brother or sister has some-

---

[45]Gregory *Pastoral Care* 3.19, trans. Henry Davis (New York: Newman Press, 1950).

[46]Evagrius *Praktikos,* p. 81.

[47]Gregory *Morals on Job* 1.5. Compare his comments on 41.11: "For this smoke deadens in truth the keenness of the heart, because with the cloud of its darkness it disturbs the serenity of inward peace. But God cannot be recognized, except by a tranquil heart." We are commended here to Ps 46:10.

[48]Evagrius *Praktikos,* p. 23.

[49]Aquinas *Summa Theologica* 1a2ae, Q46, art. 4; cf. art. 6.

[50]Evagrius *Chapters on Prayer,* pp. 12-13, 21-22, 24, 26-27, 53, 64, 137. For example: "The man who strives after true prayer must learn to master not only anger and his lust, but must free himself from every thought that is colored by passion" (p. 53).

[51]Cassian *Institutes* 8.6.

thing, no matter how trivial, against us, and this is so whether we think the other
has something against us rightly or wrongly. After all, Christ did not say, "If your
brother has a *true* ground for complaint."[52] The bottom line for Cassian is that we
simply should not pray when we are angry.[53]

My experience bears this out. Perhaps the psalmist's spiritual maturity was such
that his prayer life was not affected by anger, but for us who are still in our spiritual
infancy, it is nearly impossible to pray the imprecatory psalms while being conscious that we are a temple of the Holy Spirit. Once when I was in a choir at Blue
Cloud Abbey in South Dakota, an imprecatory psalm came up in the sequence. I
had a very strange experience reciting in a monotone the psalmist's desire that the
heads of his enemy's children would be dashed upon the rocks; it was all the more
strange because as I spoke the words, I heard them behind me and to my right and
left. After we were finished, one long-bearded monk, Brother Gene, approached
me. "Does it bother you to pray those psalms in choir?" he asked. I replied that it
did. "It does me, too," he answered. "So I just remember all the people in the world
today who are being treated unjustly and might feel that way, and I pray for them."
Gene had to dissociate himself from the anger expressed in the psalm in order to
continue praying.

Second, anger affects discernment or discretion and cuts us off from good counsel. Discernment is a crucial aspect of the monk's life under the *Rule of Benedict,*
particularly in the administration of monastic life. Cassian leaves no room for doubt
about the blindness to which anger can lead: "We can neither acquire right judgment and discretion, nor gain the insight which springs from an honest gaze, or
ripeness of counsel, nor can we be partakers of life, or retentive of righteousness,
or even have the capacity for spiritual and true light."[54] The list goes on. Apropos in
a culture that would find Cassian's remark extreme, he insists that we are cut off
from all good judgment even though we are thought to be the wisest, most prudent
and most knowledgeable.

Even the less strident Gregory zeroes in on the crucial loss of discernment
brought on by anger, linking it to a theological concern: "We must above all things
know, that as often as we restrain the turbulent motions of the mind under the virtue of mildness, we are essaying to return to the likeness of our Creator. For when
the peace of the mind is lashed with Anger, torn and rent, as it were, it is thrown
into confusion, so that it is not in harmony with itself, and loses the force of the
inward likeness."[55] Anger does away with wisdom, leaving us in ignorance about
what to do. And even if we could discern with good judgment what to do, Gregory

---

[52]Cassian *Conferences* 16.6, 16.
[53]Cassian *Institutes* 8.22.
[54]Ibid., 8.1.
[55]Gregory *Morals on Job* 5.1.

insists, the mind is still so confused that it cannot execute the action.[56]

So Gregory agrees with Cassian that anger, even born out of a love of virtue, obscures the sight of transcendent objects that can only be beheld in a state of tranquility (or, to use Cassian's favorite phrase, in a state of "purity of heart") because the mind is disquieted and agitated. But unlike Cassian, Gregory admits that a brief anger that is associated with a righteous cause can, after a while, enable a person to see more of the transcendent, as ointment applied to a diseased eye temporarily clouds vision before it restores sight.[57] The problem, as Gregory later admits, is that it is easy to confuse "furious anger" with a zeal for justice, so that one can end up sinning in the correction of sin by punishing a fault immoderately. Instead of applying correction, one oppresses. In correcting faults, anger should be the employee, not the employer of reason. Why then do some people overdo their expressions of anger? Here Gregory returns to the foundational reason for the ascetics' concern about anger's effects on discernment: in the end, one cannot see clearly because one's eyes are focused not on a single thing, but on many things (including, temporarily, the object of anger). Instead of being intent only on loving our Creator alone, one desires many things, and we are distracted with countless thoughts involving transitory cares.[58]

Neither Vent nor Suppress

Cassian nicely summarizes the concern of the ascetic theologians when he says, "Wrath that is nursed in the heart, although it may not injure men who stand by, yet excludes the splendor of the radiance of the Holy Ghost, equally with wrath that is openly manifested."[59] Whether they tolerate anger for justice's sake or not, the ascetics recommend neither venting anger nor suppressing it. The insight of this should not be lost on us moderns who have recommended first one and then the other as the appropriate way to manage anger, only for medical researchers and psychologists to now "discover" that neither venting nor suppressing anger is the way to physical, emotional and spiritual health.

Carol Tavris traces the legacy of Darwin (who taught that human anger is just another brand of animal rage) and of Freud (whose followers used a hydraulic model that demanded catharsis). Those theorists led us out of the belief that we can and must control anger, into the belief that we cannot control it, and now to the current conviction that we should not control it.[60] Tavris would agree with our early

---

[56] Aquinas says something similar when he observes that while anger can sometimes hinder reason from curbing the tongue, it can also go so far as to paralyze the tongue and bodily expression. See Aquinas *Summa Theologica* 1a2ae.Q48, art. 4.

[57] Gregory *Morals on Job* 5.2.

[58] Ibid., 36.18-21.

[59] Cassian *Institutes* 8.12.

[60] Tavris, *Anger*, chap. 2, especially p. 33.

Christian psychologists that judgment and choice are the hallmarks of human anger, but current popular thought, even among some clinical psychologists and psychiatrists, is that anger must be ventilated.[61]

But beginning in 1956 with studies by Feshbach, followed by Hokanson's very important research that was published in 1961, the aggression-frustration-catharsis theories were found to be unsubstantiated, even though the authors of some studies continue to argue in favor of those theories. A conclusive study published by Mallick and McCandless in 1966 demonstrated that while frustration leads to heightened aggressive feelings, subsequent aggressive behavior does not reduce the aggression, has no cathartic value, and, especially in the case of verbal aggressive retaliation, may actually increase aggression. Surprisingly, Mallick and McCandless also demonstrated that when cultural expectations were removed, there were no significant gender differences in behavioral aggression toward frustrators.[62]

Some might be amazed to learn that the early Christian psychologist Evagrius observed what these studies now demonstrate: "Both anger and hatred increase anger. But almsgiving and meekness diminish it even when it is present."[63] We will deal later with Evagrius's recommendation of a countermeasure for handling anger, but it is important to see that the ascetic theologians did not endorse venting (though the manufacture of foam bats may have made a lucrative cottage industry for the monastery). In fact, Gregory astutely understands our modern tendency to turn the ventilation of anger into a virtue. He writes: "Anger is also wont to exhort the conquered heart, as if with reason, when it says, The things that are done to thee cannot be borne patiently; nay, rather, patiently to endure them is a sin; because if thou dost not withstand them with great indignation, they are afterwards

---

[61]Ibid., p. 38, 45.

[62]See Shahbaz Khan Mallick and Boyd R. McCandless, "A Study of Catharsis of Aggression," in *Journal of Personality and Social Psychology* 4, no. 6 (1966): 591-96. They begin the article in this fashion: "Many of those interested, theoretically or practically, in personality theory, therapy, or general social psychology, for that matter, believe that aggressive acting-out behavior reduces aggression and hostility. Most theory of play therapy is still based on this hydraulic notion: the frustrated, angry, hostile child behaves aggressively, and this aggressive behavior reduces his level of hostility and aggression. Many parents and teachers accept the dictum that it is well to allow their children to blow off steam. Boxing, wrestling, and other intramural athletics are considered by some to provide catharsis for hostile aggression (Miller, Moyer, and Patrick, 1956). Freud spoke of Thanatos or a death instinct constantly working to return the organism 'to the quiescence of the inorganic world [Freud, 1959, p. 108].' Libido interacts with the death instinct, neutralizing its effect on the person, by directing it outward as destruction, mastery, and will to power, concepts which may be subsumed under the general term *catharsis*." Also, see the study reported by Tilmer Engebretson and Catherine Stoney in the *International Journal of Behavioral Medicine* (1996).

[63]Evagrius *Praktikos,* p. 20. Compare to Cassian *Conferences* 16.27: "We ought then to restrain every movement of anger and moderate it under the direction of discretion, that we may not by blind rage be hurried into that which is condemned by Solomon" (see Prov 29:11).

heaped upon thee without measure."[64] Indeed, on the highways we have turned patient endurance into, at worst, a vice and, at best, a naive response; afraid of being taken advantage of, we have made a virtue of demanding our own way.

The ascetic theologians did not condone the strategy of suppression either. Gregory writes about those whose anger is not displayed in an open frenzy through the hands and tongue, but in whom anger "inwardly burns the worse."[65] In graphic terms Cassian describes those who would not dare or are not able to show their anger openly: "They drive in, to their own detriment, the poison of anger, and secretly cherish it in their hearts, and silently feed on it in themselves; without shaking off by an effort of mind their sulky disposition but digesting it as the days go by, and somewhat mitigating it after awhile." Some of these can only completely satisfy their anger or sulkiness if they become unleashed completely, so they stew until the opportune moment, retaining their feelings in the hope of an optimal opportunity for revenge.[66]

Whether or not they eventually unleash it in revenge, those who suppress their anger can ruin relationships in the meantime with what Cassian and Gregory identify as feigned patience and spiteful silence.[67] These might do more damage to the object of anger and to the relationship than a quick venting of anger would. Gregory admits that the "rigorousness of silence" can be part of an interior discipline, like counting to ten. But sometimes, he observes, "the incensed mind forgoes the wanted converse," and the anger is transformed into hatred. The angry person finds "louder riot in its silence, and the flame of pent-up anger preys upon it the more grievously." This prohibits the anger from being removed from one's own mind and at the same time often feeds anger in the other party. Cassian says that people who suppress anger often imagine themselves to be patient. They mistake the suppression of outward expressions of anger for the fulfillment of God's commands, while God is interested in our resolution of the conflict no matter who initiated it.[68]

This kind of suppression deceitfully mocks the object of the would-be anger with its feigned patience (after the manner of Judas's deceitful kiss) and blasphemes God to whom prayers are offered. One blasphemes God, for example, when one pursues the sacrilege of a two-day fast that is incited by rage while sustaining oneself on a surfeit of anger, so that in reality one's sacrifices and prayers are offered to the devil (Deut 32:17). People might suppress anger in this way because they are abusing or misunderstanding Christ's command in to turn the other cheek (Mt 5:39). They might miss the intention of the passage: that we are to

---

[64]Gregory *Morals on Job* 39.25.
[65]Ibid., 5.1.
[66]Cassian *Institutes* 8.11-12.
[67]See Gregory *Morals on Job* 5.1; and Cassian *Conferences* 16.18, 20, 22, 27 for what follows.
[68]Cassian says that there is no difference between pushing a blind man down and neglecting to save him when it is in our power to do so (*Conferences* 16.18).

not only avoid retaliation and strife, but also mitigate the wrath of the striker rather than merely to walking away.[69] Certainly most people who are married can identify with Cassian's description of those who imagine that they are paragons of virtue when they respond to their partners in "sullen silence or scornful motions and gestures."[70] Gregory and Cassian are right when they observe that such suppression of outward expression only exacerbates the problem.

This description of the person who lacks the virtue of patience but exhibits outward restraint is something like Cassian's description of continence vis-à-vis chastity. The latter involves far more than mere abstinence from sex, just as getting a handle on anger is far more than mere suppression. But the difference between dealing with lust and dealing with anger is that while continence is commendable even in the absence of chastity, suppression of stored-up anger is not beneficial. Moderns wrongly think that suppressed sexual expression harms us, but suppressed, stored-up anger truly does harm us. Cassian points to a telltale sign that we have not acquired the virtue of patience, though we have suppressed anger rather than outwardly directing it at persons: "The feelings of passion still retained will spend themselves on dumb and paltry things, not allowing a continuous state of peacefulness or freedom from remaining faults."[71] Certainly this is borne out in modern-day observations that repressed anger sometimes manifests itself in other ways.

If the ascetic psychologists will permit us neither to vent our anger nor to suppress it in order to manage it, what is left? If anger is so detrimental to prayer and to the maintenance of discernment, both of which are necessary for our health, then how will we manage anger, or more in the spirit of the ascetics, how will we rid ourselves of it?

Curing Anger: Cultivating Patience and Humility in Community

The primary antidote for anger is to cultivate the virtue of patience, the virtue that is the opposite of the vice of anger. (Each of the deadly sins or principal faults has a corresponding virtue.) Humility is often mentioned alongside patience, and the two are fundamental qualities that underlie the healthy spiritual life, as Cassian and the later *Rule of Benedict* make clear. In the case of anger, patience allows the heart to be widened in order that anger may be diffused.

---

[69]Cassian insists that the inward tranquility of the stricken must match his or her outward gentleness because that is the only hope of reducing anger in both parties, "for it bears no fruit of righteousness to profit oneself by keeping calm and quiet if the other is spoiled in the process" (*Conferences* 16.22; cf. 28).

[70]Cassian *Conferences* 16.18.

[71]Cassian *Institutes* 8.18. Cassian says, somewhat humorously, that there might be *some* advantage to the fact that inanimate objects can not "talk back" and provoke worse fits of passion.

Gregory mentions another kind of silent response in place of anger, a restraint that is not counterproductive but is part of an interior discipline. Cassian seems to be referring to the same thing when he teaches that one who becomes even slightly disturbed by another person should keep his lips and the "depth of his breast" unmoved, to "keep himself in by entire silence." Cassian appeals to Psalm 39:1-2 and 77:4: "And he should not pay any heed to his present state, nor give vent to what his violent rage suggests and his exasperated mind expresses at the moment, but should dwell on the grace of past love or look forward in his mind to the renewal and restoration of peace, and contemplate it even in the very hour of rage, as if it were sure presently to return."[72]

This silence, then, is not the kind of unhealthy suppression that allows the subject to stew until the pressure can be retained no longer, nor is it the kind of silence that is likely to further offend the other party. This silence requires a disciplined memory and a robust hope in order to settle the quake that threatens to destabilize the subject's spiritual and emotional equilibrium. But this is only the beginning of what Cassian is after when he discusses the cultivation of patience.

Toward the end of his discussion of the topic of friendship, Cassian indicates how anger should be disciplined. He describes metaphorically what patience, long-suffering and courage accomplish. Again employing clever medieval hermeneutics, this time of Romans 12:19 (specifically the phrase "but leave room for God's wrath" [NIV]), he argues that our patient restraint "enlarges" the heart so that it has "safe recesses of counsel" to receive, diffuse and thereby do away with the "foul smoke of anger." Following the advice of Proverbs 12:16, Cassian prescribes covering up anger for the moment in order to destroy it forever:

> For the nature of anger is such that when it is given room it languishes and perishes, but if openly exhibited, it burns more and more. The hearts then should be enlarged and opened wide, lest they be confined in the narrow straits of cowardice, and be filled with the swelling surge of wrath, and so we become unable to receive what the prophet calls the "exceeding broad" commandment of God in our narrow heart.[73]

Suppressed anger might be likened to water passing through a narrow pipe with increased pressure, but anger that is diffused in an widened heart might be likened to water passing through an enlarged pipe with decreasing pressure and movement. Cassian is arguing that the pressure of anger waiting to be released dissipates when our hearts are widened, for instance, by our memories of God's forgiveness of and patience with us or by visions of future reconciliation.

In other words, the temporary restraint of our anger accompanied by intentionally focused mental exercises might mollify our anger toward another person. Certainly this is what some psychological prescriptions entail today, for example, the

---

[72]Cassian *Conferences* 16.26.
[73]Ibid., 16.27.

recommendation that the subject exercise an empathetic response in the moment of passion, whereby, so to speak, the heart is enlarged. In some psychological circles this technique is referred to as "cognitive reappraisal" or "reframing," in which one reinterprets an event. For example, I might say, "Oh, he did not intentionally cut me off in traffic to be mean to me or because he is a reckless driver or because he was preoccupied by using his car phone so he could be the sixth caller in a local radio-station contest. Perhaps he just received some tragic news and he is now in a hurry to attend to the situation." By delaying my angry response and avoiding my typical verbal venting ("What a jerk!"), I can enlarge my heart and further widen it as my mind works to realize how many times *I* have been the "jerk" on the highway and thus the object of other people's wrath or forgiveness. Indeed, Mallick and McCandless's study concludes just that: "Reasonable interpretation of a frustrator's behavior is strikingly effective in reducing both behavioral and verbal aggression toward him."[74] Discretion and discernment are once again called for.

My wife's attempt to first understand the intention of the angry man in the checkout line was an effort to reframe the event. Perhaps she could have paused longer to ask herself if there were other circumstances in this man's life that helped to explain his attitude toward the bagger. But at least her pause and attempt to reappraise the situation had the effect of reducing her subsequent verbal aggression. Besides that, my wife is just blessed with a lot more patience than I am.

This patience is not something that we can develop "in thirty days or our money back." Like the cultivation of all virtues in the monastic tradition, developing patience requires training over a long period of time in the company of like-minded individuals. Each of the eight principal sins has a specific cure. In the case of sloth, the ascetics taught, one must return to one's cell and attend to spiritual readings and prayer. In the case of lust one must run from the object of desire. But in the case of anger, according to Cassian, one should *not* leave those with whom one is angry, thinking that solitude and psalm singing will ameliorate the angry feelings. Though we might think we are softening bitter thoughts by seeking solitude, we are actually losing the opportunity to obey Christ's command (Mt 5:22-24) to demonstrate care and humility or to offer a "well-timed expression of regret."[75]

Cassian insisted that a monk must be trained in the *cœnobium* (the monastic community) before he ventured forth into the desert alone. Only those who are

> perfect and purified from all faults ought to seek the desert, and only when such people have thoroughly exterminated all their faults amid the assembly of the brethren, should they enter it not by way of cowardly flight, but for the purpose of divine con-

---

[74]Mallick and McCandless, "Study of Catharsis," pp. 591, 596. Cf. Tavris, *Anger,* p. 290.
[75]Cassian *Conferences* 16.15.

templation, and the desire of deeper insight into heavenly things, which can only be gained in solitude by those who are perfect. *For whatever faults we bring with us uncured into the desert, we shall find to remain concealed in us and not to be got rid of.*[76]

Solitude only intensifies uncorrected faults. When we are in solitude, we appear to ourselves to be patient and humble and loving, but we quickly revert to the untrained nature when we are interacting with others and the opportunity comes to display it. Qualities such as patience, humility and love can only be developed with practice in community. Cassian wisely observes that the shadow or pretense of patience that the untrained person displays out of respect or concern for publicity is lost altogether through sloth and carelessness.[77]

One of the important ingredients in the cultivation of patience and humility that the angry person will miss by retreating into solitude is the advice of elders and the "common consent" of like-minded people. What sounds good to two friends, even friends who are equipped with Scripture, may sound to the community like a case of poor judgment and misuse of Scripture. Special revelation certainly must be the norm and the source for a Christian psychology (as Robert Roberts demonstrates in his chapter of this book), but we also need advice and admonition from our traditions and our elders in order to understand and apply Scripture.

The advice of others is an important ingredient in monastic spirituality as it emphasizes obedience. Cassian warns us not to trust our own judgments more than the community's advice; if we accept his admonition, we will avoid self-deception and check Satan's attempts to confuse and obscure our thoughts (2 Cor 11:14). We must receive advice "in a humble and gentle heart" and submit our own ideas for consideration by those who are more experienced and have been approved as leaders. Cassian suggests that we operate under the rubric of Philippians 2:1-3, that we think more of the knowledge and holiness of our partners and believe that "the better part of true discretion [which, again, anger blinds us from seeing] is to be found in the judgment of another" rather than in our own judgment. Cassian insists that this rubric applies even to the most keen and learned because "no one however learned he may be, should persuade himself in his empty vanity that he cannot require conference with another."[78] Once again, we see the connection among the eight *logismoi* or seven deadly sins: avarice, sloth, vainglory and pride will do us in if we do not cultivate patience and humility in a community of like-minded friends. And anger precludes such

---

[76]Cassian *Institutes* 8.17, italics mine.

[77]This may explain, in part, why people are often surprised at the failings of public figures whom they have only known in the "solitude" of their conference-speaking or professional position.

[78]Cassian *Conferences* 16.10-12.

friendships, which is why the ascetics refer to it as the traitor of virtue.[79]

It should now be obvious why Cassian prescribes taking responsibility for our own anger rather than blaming others. Those who blame others for their anger place themselves in a position of solitude, either voluntarily or involuntarily. It is difficult to blame others for our anger and still seek them out for help in overcoming anger. We will not be improved by blaming others for our impatience and by seeking solitude so that no one will provoke us to anger. Cassian wisely says,

> The chief part then of our improvement and peace of mind must not be made to depend on another's will, which cannot possibly be subject to our authority, but it lies rather in our own control. And so the fact that we are not angry ought not to result from another's perfection but from our own virtue, which is acquired, not by somebody else's patience, but by our own long-suffering.[80]

Cassian compares people who lack virtue and blame others for their anger and other faults to people who are affected by a bodily malady but blame their cooks and attendants for the delicacy of their stomach and weak health: "They ascribe the grounds of their upset to those who are in good health, as they do not see that they are really due to the failure of their own health."[81]

What might help us, then, to accept responsibility for the management our anger? Cassian and Gregory offer some advice.

Practices, Preparation and a Precept

We can manage our anger by engaging in certain practices, such as negative exercises that ward off sins related to anger. Cassian recommends contempt for material or worldly possessions, which might help us to ward off the avarice that so often leads to anger.[82] A neighbor told me that his method of dealing with anger at motorists who "take his space" on the highway is to remind himself that none of the highway is really his space to begin with. By eliminating his avaricious attitude

---

[79]See ibid., 16.6 for Cassian's description of the ways in which sins such as avarice and pride can poison a friendship with anger and preclude the advantage the friendship affords to grow in virtue. Cassian begins the conference on friendship by distinguishing dissolvable friendships based on some expediency and indissolvable ones based on a mutual commitment to virtue. The treating of anger by cultivating patience in community is to take place in a community of indissolvable friendships. A modern-day parallel might be the church if Christians today understood better the role of the Christian community in the moral shaping of its members. I would like to be able to ask Cassian whether the same rules apply when we are not in a community of like-minded people who are seeking to reduce all of their desires to the love of God. Cassian does not say much about dissolvable relationships, but it would be helpful for us to know what he would think about the modern therapeutic relationship between counselor and client if he had had the opportunity to speak to that "friendship."

[80]Cassian *Institutes* 8.16.

[81]Cassian *Conferences* 16.3.

[82]Ibid., 16.6.

on the highway, Paul was able to cut off anger at the pass. Gregory recommends another negative exercise that fosters the humility we need to counter pride and vainglory: we should refuse to imagine ourselves to be wise and experienced people who prefer our own opinions to our neighbors'. Likewise, when we are tempted to be angry at the transgressions of others, we must recall our own transgressions.[83]

When our son lost his glasses in the lake one summer as the result of his lack of forethought, my anger didn't stand a chance when I remembered the two times during high school when my glasses ended up in muddy waters. When our son was an inexperienced driver and nicked another car as he maneuvered into a parking space, my anger didn't stand a chance when I remembered the time I backed my mother's little car into my father's Impala in the driveway.

Evagrius prescribes some positive exercises. They involve the ascetics' common ploy of countering vices with the opposite behavior. Evagrius observes, "Turbid anger is calmed by the singing of Psalms, by patience and almsgiving." Later, he echoes his almsgiving prescription by noting that "a gift snuffs out the fires of resentment."[84] Indeed, it is difficult to remain angry while joyfully giving a gift or singing a psalm of praise.

Gregory recommends a way to relax anger's hold on the mind. It involves a preemptive strike, and it requires preparation. One anticipates all the insults one might experience and keeps in mind at the same time the treatment of Jesus: "For he that forecasts impending ills in a spirit of earnest heedfulness, as it were, watching in ambush, awaits the assaults of his enemy. And he arrays himself in strength for the victory in the very point wherein he was expected to be caught in entire ignorance."[85]

To anticipate the assaults of anger one needs to gain some self-knowledge, monitor the patterns of past episodes, and plan a course of action that will keep anger from arising. This is precisely the first step in anger management recommended by psychologist Roy Novaco: the individual must "become an expert on his or her anger" in order to see patterns—people, situations, provocateurs. He suggests keeping a journal to track triggers, frequency, intensity, duration and modes of expression of one's anger.[86]

Finally, one must keep in mind a theological concept: eschatology. To cure anger, Cassian recommends, one should remember "what is undoubtedly generally decisive in regard to all faults; viz., that he should realize daily that he is to pass away from this world; as the realization of this not only permits no vexation to lin-

---

[83]Gregory *Morals on Job* 5.2, 36.18-21.
[84]Evagrius *Praktikos*, pp. 15, 26.
[85]Gregory *Morals on Job* 5.2.
[86]Cited in Tavris, *Anger*, p. 289.

ger in the heart, but also represses all the motions of lusts and sins of all kinds."[87] Cassian frequently reminds us of the eschatological perspective that must pervade our thinking about life, an emphasis that is glaringly absent from present-day practical theology and Christian psychology. Yet if we are to believe what Paul writes in 1 Corinthians 15:14, Christ's resurrection is the only thing in the Christian narrative that ultimately makes worthwhile the story into which we have been baptized.

Cassian reminds us that when God assesses our lives, neither our sexual purity nor our renunciation of possessions nor our fasts and vigils will mitigate God's judgment of our anger and hatred. In light of God's assessment of our works and the resurrection promise that our work is not in vain (1 Cor 15:58), perhaps some things are not worth God's wrath.[88] And Cassian adds a soteriological concern: theology must hold the reins on our anger because God wishes all to be saved, and anger does not accomplish the righteousness of God. As Carol Tavris puts it in a secular context, "The ultimate purpose of thinking twice about anger is to enhance the long-term benefit of the relationship, not the short-term relief of the individual."[89] In this light Cassian insists that we try to cure the anger others have against us because it is as harmful to us as our own self-destructive anger.

What About Abuse?

That leaves us with one vexing issue: What should we do about the extreme cases, particularly those involving abuse. We read in Cassian's conference on friendship that we are to preserve tranquility of heart no matter what evil transpires, and that not only should we keep ourselves from the anger that disturbs us, "but also, by submitting to their injuries, compel those, who are disturbed by their own fault, to become calm, when they have had their fill of blows; and so overcome their rage by our gentleness."[90] This sometimes works. When I was in high school, a boy named Rocky (his real name!) hit me in the left jaw, which still pops to this day. Later Rocky apologized in public because I had not retaliated.

But rage is not often overcome by gentleness in some cases, spousal abuse, for instance. Cassian is to be commended for trying to translate Romans 12:21 into our lives, and it ought to give the Anabaptist quadrant of our Christian sensibilities some hope. Cassian is correct when he says that "in general he plays a stronger part who subjects his own will to his brother's, than he who is found to be the more pertinacious in defending and clinging to his own decisions," because the latter must be pampered and petted. And only the strong can bear the weak and restore them to health (Gal 6:2).

---

[87]Cassian *Conferences* 16.6.
[88]Cassian *Institutes* 8.22.
[89]Tavris, *Anger*, p. 319.
[90]Cassian *Conferences* 16.22-24 for this and what follows.

But what if the weak one does not come around? Cassian says that when two people are not like-minded in their spiritual goals, there will come a time when the strong one will no longer bear the weak one.

> The miserable condition of the weak, encouraged by the tolerance of the perfect, and daily growing worse, is sure to give rise to reasons on account of which he himself ought no longer to be borne; or else with a shrewd suspicion that the patience of his neighbor shows up and sets off his own impatience at some time or other he chooses to make off rather than always to be borne by the magnanimity of the other.[91]

Perhaps Cassian would admit that the same rules do not apply when the friendship of like-minded individuals who seek virtue breaks down. This requires further reflection, and perhaps same-gender monastic communities are not the best source of wisdom here.

Nonetheless, I have tried to demonstrate in general that in the case of anger management modern secular psychology has not progressed beyond the insights of these ancient Christian psychologists, that moderns have in a few cases reversed their theories only to arrive at the conclusions reached by ascetic theologians 1,500 years ago, and that Christian psychology would do well not only to heed, but to begin with its own heritage, its own roots, in any attempt at integration.[92]

---

[91]Ibid., 16.26.

[92]See the similar conclusion of Simon Kemp and K. T. Strongman in "Anger Theory and Management: A Historical Analysis," *American Journal of Psychology* 108, no. 3 (1995): 397-417: "At the outset, it is interesting to note that despite the ubiquity of anger in everyday affairs and despite a proliferation of theory and empirical research on emotion in the last twenty years, psychologists do not, in general, have much to say about anger" (p. 405). "In recent years, there has been a large discrepancy between practice and theory in anger control; practice has been rife and theory has been sparse" (p. 411). "Perhaps it is not surprising that our knowledge of anger and its control has developed little in two millennia" (p. 414).

8

THE INTEGRATION OF PSYCHOANALYTIC PSYCHOLOGY & CONTEMPLATIVE THEOLOGY

Lessons from the History of Spiritual Direction

Michael W. Mangis

CHRISTIAN THINKING IN THE PSYCHOANALYTIC TRADITION DESERVES A SIGNIFI-
cant chapter in the history of the integration of psychology and theology. Although
the integration of psychoanalytic psychology with Christian theology has been a
marriage fraught with tension, the psychodynamic study of the depths of the
human mind has provided a rich literature and many fruitful insights for the Christian understanding of the depths of the soul. There truly is, however, nothing new
under the sun and, therefore, those attempting to integrate psychoanalysis with
Christian theology will find much of value in an examination of the history of the
care of the soul, a discipline that is much older than the relatively young profession
of psychology. In particular, the tradition of contemplative spirituality provides
many important lessons for the integration of psychodynamic theory with Christian
faith. The centuries-old contemplative tradition also provides alternative solutions
to the problems that have plagued the integration of psychoanalysis and theology.

Psychoanalysis and the Search for Moral Authority

Since the fundamentalist-modernist debates of the first half of the twentieth century
the church has often maintained an antagonistic stance in relation to psychoanalysis. This antagonism developed in opposition not so much to the method or basic
theory of psychoanalysis as to its presuppositional foundation, which Freud placed

squarely in the modernist worldview. For Freud, and for many decades of theorists who followed him, the modernist quest for objectivity in our understanding of the world was paramount. Human perceptions are distorted, they believed, by attachment to illusions. Perceptual illusions were constructed in our early lives as a way of dealing with the clash between our passionate and fearful internal world and the external world with its rules and dangers. Illusions about ourselves and the world allow us to make sense of what might otherwise be overwhelming, especially during infancy and childhood, when the illusions are first constructed. The goal of maturity, and particularly the goal of psychoanalysis, is to strip away illusions and to see both the inner and the outer world clearly.

The greatest antagonism from the church was mostly in response to the psychoanalytic assumption that the process of dis-illusionment must necessarily involve stripping away lingering myths about or beliefs in a reality outside of the natural and observable world. Maturity, to Freud and his followers, is completely incompatible with a religious worldview. Religion, in fact, is seen as the organized cultural protector of immature illusions without which the enlightened adult should learn to live.

In spite of the modernist assumptions of psychoanalysis, many people have seen the value of the psychoanalytic perspective for the understanding of Christian faith. Acknowledging that our perceptions of life, and even of the object of our faith, are distorted by safe illusions does not require the catastrophic conclusion that the faith distorted by illusion is itself illusion. Westphal, in fact, argues that Christians should welcome at least some of the humbling influence of the hermeneutic of suspicion. Christians' first task, he asserts, "as they face the likes of Marx, Nietzsche and Freud is not to refute or discredit them. It is to acknowledge that their critique is *all too true all too much of the time* and to seek to discover just where the shoe fits, not 'them' but ourselves."[1] Freud proposed that religion is an illusion we construct to defend ourselves from the fearful notion that there is no supernatural authority on which to base our faith. We must acknowledge, as Westphal suggests, that there is more truth in his proposition than we would like to admit. Much of organized religion, especially in the mind of individual believers, fulfills just that purpose.

On what then can we place our faith? Freud's replacement worldview, that of science, is now equally discredited. It is no small irony that Freud, who pledged allegiance to the modernist worldview, provided the most powerful tools with which the assumptions of modernism would be dismantled. Freud maintained that humans view their world through the distorting filter of illusions and schema con-

---

[1]Merold Westphal, *Suspicion and Faith: The Religious Uses of Modern Atheism* (Grand Rapids, Mich.: Eerdmans, 1993), p. 16.

structed out of the experiences of our early lives. With equal strength he asserted that once humans acknowledge this fact and set about the process of stripping away those illusions they can attain purity and objectivity of sight.

As modernism was evaluated using its own methods, however, this ultimate hope for objectivity was itself called into question. Even the psychoanalyst, the scientist of the mind, was found to be limited by the distortions of a value-laden perspective. Contemporary psychoanalytic theorists, for example, now readily discuss the therapist as participant-observer. The value-laden task of therapy is seen as an engagement in a relationship that is co-constructed by analyst and client. The methods of psychoanalysis were used to reveal the flaws in those methods themselves. Freud, the champion of modernism, helped to usher in the hermeneutic of suspicion that so characterizes the postmodern situation.[2]

Freud's psychoanalysis seeks to eliminate both religion's assertion that there is a supernatural source of authoritative truth and religion's primacy as the interpreter of truth. However, it offers no replacement for the authority of a supernatural measure for truth. Using psychoanalysis alone one could set out on the road away from foundationalism, but one would have no countering influence to keep one from the inevitable destination of relativism. Once humans, who are confined by the limitations of nature, are revealed to be incapable of objectively measuring truth, there can be no honest argument that an objective measure of truth exists unless we propose an observer who is not confined by the same limitations. It is at this point of conflict that contemplative theology has the most to offer the integration of psychology and theology.

The Lessons of Contemplative Theology

The field of psychoanalysis is rich with lessons for the Christian psychologist and theologian. In particular, in its search of the deceptions of the human heart, psychoanalysis provides wonderful insights for those who seek to purify their understanding of themselves and of God. In our infatuation with all that is new, however, we are tempted to assume that the pursuit of undistorted vision and the study of distortions of vision are the inventions of twentieth-century psychology. Given the dead end in which the psychoanalytic search can easily end—the slippery slope of relativism—we can indeed be thankful that they did not originate in modern psychology. Psychoanalysis provides a systematic method for exploring the deceptions of the unconscious mind, but within the Christian church there is a tradition that provides a more encompassing method for exploring the deceptions and corruption of the soul.

The contemplative tradition of Christian spirituality has been compared to psy-

---

[2]Paul Ricoeur, *Freud and Philosophy: An Essay on Interpretation,* trans. Denis Savage (New Haven, Conn.: Yale University Press, 1970).

choanalysis in both its search and its methods.[3] Unfortunately, there has been inordinate excitement within some spiritual traditions for the new insights, or at least
new terminology, that psychoanalysis offers to the study of Christian spirituality. At
the opposite extreme, those who reject psychoanalysis because of its nonfounda-
tionalist assumptions forget that foundationalism has not always been wedded with
Christian faith. Ancient and present-day writers within the desert or contemplative
tradition have always asserted with the Scriptures that the human heart is deceptive
and self-serving.

Left to its own the heart cannot be trusted ultimately to arrive at objective truth,
especially truth about its own illusions. When the human heart perceives itself
accurately it is usually through an encounter with God. Honest self-perception is
not something that can be mustered through human effort. As the author of *The
Cloud of Unknowing* proposes, "just as you cannot see or know that there is a dirty
mark on your actual face without the aid of a mirror, or somebody telling you, so
spiritually, it is impossible for a soul blinded by his frequent sins to see the dirty
mark in his conscience, without reading or hearing God's word."[4]

In the psychoanalytic worldview we find an implicit assumption that the human
heart is restless. Contemporary psychoanalytic theorists especially acknowledge
that the human quest is a quest for meaning. We long for satisfaction, usually conceived of in relational terms and sought through relationship; in other words, we
are driven by our desire for attachment. Therapy, as conceived within this contemporary psychoanalytic worldview, is the process of assisting people in their search
for meaningful attachments. Ultimately because our sense of satisfaction and completion is frustrated by a history of relationships that have not adequately met our
needs, healing comes in breaking unhealthy cycles of relating and in finding the
means to relate to others in much healthier ways. As long as the road leads to
greater satisfaction and flexibility in relating, the process is considered successful.
The therapist and client enter into relationship with the hope of developing,
together, a model of relating that the client can transfer into other areas of life.

In this thoroughly orthodox summary of psychoanalysis (which is not the only
way in which someone might describe the process) there is nothing that a Christian
would necessarily find objectionable. On the other hand, the process does not
necessitate that the path of satisfaction that the client and therapist travel together
will lead in a direction consistent with the guidelines outlined in God's word for
Christlike life and character. God's word is written on our hearts, and many of the
arguments about psychotherapy from a Christian perspective have centered on the

---

[3]Benedict J. Groeschel, *Spiritual Passages: The Psychology of Spiritual Development* (New York:
Crossroad, 1992); Alan Jones, *Soul Making: The Desert Way of Spirituality* (San Francisco:
HarperCollins, 1985).
[4]*The Cloud of Unknowing,* trans. Clifton Wolters (New York: Penguin, 1978), p. 102.

truth that the road to health heads generally in the direction of God's image within us and away from an end point that is not resonant with that image.

It is not the purpose of this chapter to delve too deeply into these arguments. However, the contemporary psychoanalytic acknowledgment that the analyst is a fully subjective participant-observer includes the enormously revealing confession that the journey of psychotherapy is a subjective journey. Psychotherapy has no objectively or authoritatively defined end point that transcends differing theoretical positions on the nature of psychological health. The direction in which the client moves is defined by the dynamics of the relationship that the therapist and client cocreate. The therapist and client each bring admittedly subjective and deceptive distortions of perspective.

Subjectivity and Therapeutic Change

This admission of subjectivity of the therapist in the dance of therapy carries profound importance for those who wish to think Christianly about psychology. The character of the therapist matters. Because the person whom the client is becoming is a cocreation of the therapist and client, the end product is partly defined by who the therapist is. In most cases this is a good thing. Most of the time therapy leads to healthier relationships, to a more honest sense of self, to greater tolerance of others, and to a greater capacity for attachment. In most cases clients end up a little more Christlike than when they started, whether they are Christian or not and whether or not they are any nearer to pursuing a deeper relationship with God.

It is a truism hardly worth mentioning that therapy in this sense can be an important part of God's process of drawing people to himself. What the postmodern hermeneutic of suspicion teaches us, however, is that the goodness that therapy generally achieves may have more to do with God's powerful drawing of creation toward himself than it does with any fundamental safety of the therapeutic method. Once we acknowledge that the character of the therapist is inextricably woven into the texture of therapy, we must acknowledge that therapy is just as capable of leading clients subtly away from Christlikeness as it is capable of leading them toward Christlikeness.

People who are in the faith traditions that emphasize the role of a spiritual director in one's spiritual life have been far more explicit about how important it is that the spiritual director be a person whose character has been powerfully shaped after the character of Christ. One of the desert mothers, Amma Syncletica, says regarding the necessity of thorough preparation on the part of the spiritual director, "For if someone who owns a ruined house receives guests there, he does them harm because of the dilapidation of his dwelling. It is the same in the case of someone who has not first built an interior dwelling; he causes loss to those who come. By words one may convert them to salvation, but by evil behaviour, one injures them."[5] Similarly, fourteenth-century Dominican Johannes Tauler emphasizes the dangers of spiritual leadership by those unequal to the task. "An unfaithful spiritual director is like a bad hunting dog. Instead of bringing the rabbit to its master, it devours the rabbit itself."[6]

Psychoanalysis provides no anchoring point of protection against the danger that a therapist's unhealthy and unregenerate self will intrude into the development of the client. The fundamental reason for the lack of such an anchoring point is that psychoanalytic theory, or any psychological theory, by itself has no authoritative measure within the natural order. It acknowledges that we are fundamentally broken, but it can provide only approximate models for reparation. Those models, therapists, are acknowledged to be subjective and flawed themselves.

Obviously many Christian critics of psychology have pointed out this fundamental deficiency. The argument is not new to most people who have done significant study of psychology from a Christian perspective. Often, however, the argument that psychoanalysis, or psychology in general, has no anchor in anything that provides moral authority is followed by the argument that psychology should be abandoned as an endeavor with which Christians should engage. Such catastrophizing, however, is unfounded. To argue that we need to acknowledge the validity of the hermeneutic of suspicion in the search for meaning does not carry a demand that we also deny the existence of any authoritative truth at all. It merely requires that we assert an observer and definer who is not limited by the fallen human perspective and thereby anchor ourselves so that we do not slide down the slope to relativism.

To prevent the slide toward moral relativism we need an anchoring point that has not been provided within psychoanalysis itself. Fortunately, the search for methods for purifying the individual's internal sight existed long before Freud introduced his own methods. Within the Christian tradition a parallel to psychoanalysis exists in the literature and centuries-old practice of spiritual direction, especially as found in the contemplative tradition.

Spiritual Direction and the Contemplative Quest

Spiritual direction is an ancient tradition that is primarily found within the liturgical churches (Eastern, Roman and Anglican) in which religious orders have been maintained. The tradition predated psychotherapy by many centuries. It was assumed that those called to religious orders required guidance and spiritual parenting in order to grow into the union with God that was their quest. In some traditions of spiritual direction the care of souls has been considered important for lay people as

[5]*The Sayings of the Desert Fathers,* trans. Benedicta Ward (Kalamazoo, Mich.: Cistercian Publications, 1975), p. 195.
[6]Johannes Tauler, quoted in *Writings on Spiritual Direction by Great Christian Masters,* ed. Jerome M. Neufekler and Mary C. Coelho (New York: Seabury, 1982), p. 112.

well, at least those who have been involved in lay leadership.

Many different streams of thought and practice have existed within the spiritual direction tradition. The broadly contemplative traditions have the most significance for the purposes of our discussion because of their similarities to the worldview of psychoanalysis. The broadly contemplative tradition includes the collected writings of the desert fathers and mothers and the traditions of Anglican, Eastern, Dominican, Benedictine, Ignatian and Carmelite spiritual formation. Though we can not do justice to these extremely varied traditions by lumping them together, viewing them together will ease our comparison. It is this broad heritage to which I will refer when I speak of spiritual direction in the contemplative tradition.

Like present-day psychoanalysts the contemplatives in these traditions sought purification of sight. They also believed that human nature was fundamentally characterized by a longing for completion and relational union. They believed that patterns of brokenness permeate our lives and that we require reorientation toward healthy patterns of relatedness. The spiritual director in the contemplative traditions, however, differs from the psychotherapist in profound ways. Both agree that humans are defined by their longings, but the spiritual director assumes that the ultimate source and proper end of that longing can be found only in God. We are created for union with God and, as Augustine asserted, our hearts are restless until they find their rest in God through Christ Jesus. The relationship between the spiritual director and the directee exists for one defining purpose: to draw the directee closer to God.

Even the process by which the directee increases in self-knowledge must be secondary to the primary purpose of drawing the directee to God. Self-knowledge is a step in the process of coming to know God, but only because it is required in the process of stripping away the illusions that keep us from that knowledge. Columba Stewart points to this emphasis in the contemplative writings of the desert fathers:

> It was the commitment to truth, to seeing things as they are, that disposes the monk for contemplation of God. The classic hierarchies of contemplation described by Evagrius and others moved from disciplined work on the self to contemplation of the created world, to contemplation of the spiritual world, to contemplation of God. The commitment to truth is initially expressed and realised in the ascetical labour of self-knowledge. To see things as they are, and to see God as God can be seen, without masks of fantasy, projections, pious wishes, depends in the first place upon stripping away the masks of fantasies and projections about ourselves. We find that the masks we place on our selves and the masks we see on the face of God are, in the end, the same, and are of our own making.[7]

The desert fathers and mothers taught that we need to know ourselves with radical self-honesty so that we can separate our wishes and illusions from the truth of who God is.

---

[7]Columba Stewart, "The Desert Fathers on Radical Self-Honesty," *Vox Benedictina* 8 (1991): 11.

In an exhortation to spiritual directors, John of the Cross points out the need to adapt guidance to the individuality of the directee:

> Let such guides of the soul as these take heed and remember . . . that they themselves are only instruments to lead souls in the way of perfection by the faith and the law of God, according to the spirituality that God is giving to each one. Let them not, therefore, merely aim at guiding these souls according to their own way and the manner suitable to themselves, but let them see if they know the way by which God is leading the soul, and, if they know it not, let them leave the soul in peace and not disturb it. [8]

Each soul must come to know itself. God's leading will, therefore, is entirely individual to that soul. In a certain sense, the reverse is true as well. Julian of Norwich taught that knowledge of God will lead to knowledge of self: "God is nearer to us than our own soul. . . . And therefore if we wish to know our soul, and have communing and dalliance therewith, we will need to seek into our Lord God in whom it is enclosed."[9]

One might do psychotherapy from the perspective that all of the client's relationships, including the relationship with God, will be transformed by the reformation of patterns of relating. Many Christian mental health professionals define integration this way—lumping the relationship with God in with all the other parts of a person's life that will be improved through therapy.

The spiritual director in the classical tradition, however, has only the transformation of the relationship with God in mind as the ultimate goal. The transformation of other relationships will result from that fundamental reorientation to God, not in addition to it. In the classical spiritual direction relationship, in fact, most of the content of the typical psychotherapy session would seem oddly out of place. Even the themes that might be found in both would lead in different directions. While the therapist wants to see the client relate to other people in less distorted and self-serving ways, the spiritual director in the classical literature wants to see the directee evidence a capacity for deeper and truer prayer. Prayer, as the primary means of our communication with God, should provide the greatest evidence of our transformation.

Psychotherapy and spiritual direction differ in significant ways. While both deal with matters of the soul and of ultimate meaning, only spiritual direction truly acknowledges this connection. Psychotherapy is not the benign activity that some have presumed. I would certainly not suggest, however, that psychotherapy ought to be abandoned and that spiritual direction ought to take its place. The rich literature in the integration of psychology and theology has sufficiently provided many reasons that that cannot and should not happen. The argument for abandoning psy-

---

[8]John of the Cross, *The Complete Works of Saint John of the Cross*, ed. E. Allison Peers, trans. P. Silverio De Santa Teresa (Westminster, Md.: Newman, 1945), 3:184-85.
[9]Julian of Norwich, *Revelation of Love*, trans. John Skinner (New York: Doubleday, 1996), p. 124.

chology because it can be antagonistic to faith is wholly unconvincing.

However, the belief that psychology is benign and requires no redemption on the part of the Christian mind is equally hollow. The common claim that psychology is merely a study of God's natural revelation like any other discipline is simply disingenuous. Psychotherapy is largely about the study of worldviews. When it is used to construct models for understanding the human search for meaning, as is the case with psychoanalysis, psychology crosses into the realms of theology and philosophy. Therapists have an influential role as cocreators of a new experience of the world, and in this role they enter the domain of pastors and spiritual directors.

Psychoanalysts and contemplative spiritual directors both seek self-knowledge in order to find a deeper experience of meaning by removing the distortions of their own impure motives. In their commitment to rooting out these distortions, however, the contemplatives do not speak of breaking the bondage to defensive illusion; rather, they speak of breaking the bondage to sin. By naming the brokenness sin the contemplatives place the discussion squarely into the realm of spirituality, giving the search for meaning eternal significance. When the brokenness is named sin rather than pathology, the goal becomes the working out of the directee's salvation, not the directee's personal preferences. Illusion and personal biases of perception are more than hindrances to happy relationships. They limit our capacity to hear God.

The similarities between modern psychoanalytic and classical contemplative language is often striking. In the fourteenth century Johannes Tauler exhorted, "some people cling to hidden attachments of which they are generally unaware. . . . These false and hidden motives could prevent them from entering God's presence. Such people may indeed have led exemplary lives and excelled in exercises of great piety, but that to which they cleave and cling lies so deeply buried that they are not even conscious of it."[10] The modern notion that such self-knowledge can be an end in itself, however, would be abhorrent to these writers. For example, Teresa of Ávila, the sixteenth-century founder of the Carmelite order, could see no adequate purpose for knowledge of self other than that it is a step toward knowledge of God. We should seek, she exhorted, "to understand how glad Our Lord is when we get to know ourselves and keep trying all the time to realize our poverty and wretchedness, and to reflect that we possess nothing that we have not been given."[11] What other than the longing for deeper union with God could adequately motivate one to the painful task of radical self-honesty?

Meaning in Pain
Both the psychoanalytic and the desert traditions seek deeper and more accurate

---

[10]Johannes Tauler, *Johannes Tauler: Sermons,* trans. Maria Shrady (New York: Paulist, 1985).
[11]Teresa of Ávila, *Interior Castle,* trans. E. Allison Peers (New York: Doubleday, 1961), p. 160.

self-awareness. Both also assume that that search will be a painful and difficult process. The process of healing and growth in these traditions is assumed to be found not in the removal of pain but in the making of meaning from pain. Again, however, the psychoanalytic and the contemplative traditions differ in their assumptions about what that meaning will be. In the psychoanalytic tradition self-awareness that strips away illusions is seen as an end in itself. The loss of illusions is painful and requires mourning, and in the end the psychoanalytic process typically results in the acceptance of the limitations of the self. The contemplative process, on the other hand, is expected to lead the directee to awareness of the one who transcends the self—God.

John of the Cross describes the Christian pilgrim undergoing the painful mourning of the sinfulness and inadequacy of the self. This mourning is essential to spiritual maturity, but to the observer it can appear morbid and even sick. John draws a parallel between the trials of Job and the pain of the soul mourning the loss of immature attachment to illusions. Further, just as Job's companions eventually attributed his pain to his own sinfulness, so the friends of a person who is in this spiritual state of mourning

> will proclaim that that state is due to mental illness or depression or temperament or some hidden personal evil, and that as a result God has abandoned the mourner. Others will say that regression is taking place because the mourner no longer experiences pleasure or consolation in the things of God as previously. Such talk only doubles the trial of the poor soul because the greatest suffering is caused by the knowledge of his or her personal miseries. That it is filled with evil and sin is as clear as day—and even clearer because God is the creator of this enlightenment in the night of contemplation.[12]

Far from viewing this pain as something to be removed, John believed that the soul is blessed to have matured to the point of being capable of enduring this period of weaning in the spiritual desert from dependency to illusions. Eighteenth-century Russian bishop Tikhon of Zadonsk prescribed contemplation on painful things as the perfect antidote to depression: "The thought of death, which may perhaps cross your mind, the thought of Christ's judgment, of eternal punishment and of eternal joy do away with depression. Prayerfully reflect on these things."[13] The way to health and spiritual maturity is never in a direction away from the truth. The psychoanalytic insight into the connection between depression and unresolved mourning is not new to the twentieth century. Facing reality has always been therapeutic.

Spiritual Safeguards
In the psychoanalytic worldview the road to healing is through a truer awareness of

---

[12]John of the Cross, *Ascent of Mount Carmel,* in *Writings on Spiritual Direction by Great Christian Masters,* ed. Jerome M. Neufelder and Mary C. Coelho (New York: Seabury, 1982), p. 111.

[13]Tikhon of Zadonsk, *Letters of St. Tikhon,* in *Writings on Spiritual Direction by Great Christian Masters,* ed. Jerome M. Neufelder and Mary C. Coelho (New York: Seabury, 1982), p. 144.

oneself. The individual is believed to be locked into patterns of relating and experiencing that replicate old unhealthy patterns and limit the capacity for intimately relating to others. The therapeutic experience is thought to bring those maladaptive cycles into the context of the therapist-client relationship. Rather than simply replicating past experiences, however, the therapist refuses to play the prescribed roles. The client's expectations of old patterns are not met; a new and emotionally corrective experience is provided. In longer-term therapy this cycle of highlighting and changing old patterns is repeated many times, and in the end the client begins to see with new eyes. The client is given the capacity to step back and look at the others with increased, though never complete, objectivity.

Again, there is nothing objectionable in this description of psychotherapy. All of us need more of such experiences in our lives. If the depth psychotherapies merely offered deeper glimpses into the self's illusions there would be cause only for great hope in the process. The self, however, is always glimpsed in part in the mirror of the therapist. The client comes to see him- or herself in part through the therapist's eyes. And psychoanalytic theory acknowledges that therapists have their own distortions and biases. Simply put, every set of eyes perceives the world through the grid or filter of the observer's own worldview. How the client comes to perceive him- or herself, therefore, is partly defined by the therapist's values and perceptual system.

In the tradition of spiritual direction the illusions and distortions of the director are not only assumed but are considered a very serious matter. This is a powerfully important element that differentiates the spiritual direction tradition from modern psychotherapy. Spiritual direction has always occurred in the context of a system of hierarchical authority. Historically, spiritual direction existed primarily in the context of religious orders. The early writings by spiritual directors were almost always produced by monks and nuns.

Spiritual direction was not a profession that one chose, as psychotherapy is today. It was a calling that chose the spiritual director. Those whose life of prayer and service had produced the fruits of spiritual maturity were eventually sought out as spiritual parents by those who were newer to the religious life. On some occasions lay people who desired to live more devout and holy lives also sought the spiritual direction of these brothers and sisters. Those entrusted with the care of others' souls were required or expected to be under spiritual direction themselves. Many of the contemplatives, especially the mystics, said that the need to be under direction was of increasing importance the more one matured in the faith. The assumption seemed to be that as one entered more deeply into union with God one became less attached to the mundane realities and more engaged in spiritual warfare. Others were needed to provide a spiritual anchor for that task.

There is no parallel for this tradition within psychology. Psychotherapy is a profession that is characterized by a set of skills and techniques that one can practice and

by an identity and set of values that one can be taught. Even psychoanalytic psychotherapy emphasizes only that the therapist must undergo personal analysis early in
training, not that such analysis must be ongoing. Further, there is no expectation that
only those who have truly matured may be allowed to engage in the practice of psychotherapy. One might argue that if psychotherapy were concerned with such
weighty questions as the eternal state of the soul in union with God, then such safeguards might be warranted. However, because psychotherapy is indeed concerned
with issues of direct relevance to the state of the soul, more safeguards are warranted.

The Centrality of Mourning

At their heart, both psychoanalysis and contemplative spirituality are based on the
foundational importance of mourning in our lives. Psychoanalysis understands the
human quest to be centered in the propelling force of our past and the compelling
force of our longings. Our past has propelled us through the matrix of relationships
that have, either adequately or inadequately, met our relational needs. Our longings
compel us as we seek, through the relational realm, to satisfy what remains unsatis-
fied. Some psychoanalytic writers describe this longing in almost spiritual terms.

In the psychoanalytic tradition the way of maturity goes not around but through
the mourning. The mature adult is the sadder but wiser individual who has learned
to let go of the illusion that our unmet longings can ever truly be satisfied. The illusion of comfort and satisfaction is always a hollow replacement for the truth that
we can never really get what we want.

Those in the contemplative tradition have also emphasized our need to
acknowledge our unmet longings. The theology of the desert does not suggest that
we are searching for the mythical perfect mother (as some psychoanalytic theorists
would suggest). Rather, we are created for an intimate walk with our Creator, but
we are born separated from God, and we have only broken and inadequate
replacements for him. In the desert tradition the way toward union with God is the
way of the abandonment of illusions of comfort and hollow satisfaction.

Alan Jones asserts that both the psychoanalytic tradition and the tradition of
desert spirituality shed light on our reliance on comfortable spiritual illusion rather
than on uncomfortable truth. In the anxiety of our separation from the true object
of our desires, we construct beliefs that ease the ambiguity. "When these two coincide, all is well; but when the 'truth' begins to be at variance with belief, a pattern
of self-deception and lying begins to emerge. Ask Christian believers what they
would do if they had to choose between Jesus Christ and the Truth." Most believers, he suggests, would wiggle out from under the question by insisting that
because Jesus is the truth there can be no conflict. The truth, however, will often be
at variance with our limited perception of who Jesus is.[14]

---

[14]Jones, *Soul Making*, p. 7.

At times I am tempted to keep hold of my distorted illusions of a God with whom I feel comfortable rather than to embrace a God who refuses to be, in C. S. Lewis's image from The Chronicles of Narnia, a tame lion. In a similar vein, French philosopher Simone Weil has urged that "one can never wrestle enough with God if one does so out of pure regard for the truth. Christ likes us to prefer truth to him because, before being Christ, he is truth. If one turns aside from him to go toward the truth, one will not go far before falling into his arms."[15]

Resident Aliens

In the book of Hebrews we are given a picture of the life of the believer as an alien in a strange land:

> All these people were still living by faith when they died. They did not receive the things promised; they only saw them and welcomed them from a distance. And they admitted that they were aliens and strangers on earth. People who say such things show that they are looking for a country of their own. If they had been thinking of the country they had left, they would have had opportunity to return. Instead, they were longing for a better country—a heavenly one. Therefore God is not ashamed to be called their God, for he has prepared a city for them. (Heb 11:13-16 NIV)

In this glimpse of God's desire for us we see an undistorted picture of life. Those who admit that they are aliens and strangers on earth submit themselves to a life of longing for what they cannot yet have. In the psychoanalytic tradition this admission calls for mourning the loss and embracing the longing. In the contemplative tradition it also calls for faith that the longing will ultimately be satisfied in ways we cannot fully imagine.

The contemplative vision of the life of God's children also requires that we forsake the temporary comfort of illusions in favor of the far-off horizon of a homeland. We are to be transients in the truest sense of the word. The desert fathers believed literally that life in the desert was the truest way to remove obstacles to the life of prayer. In the wilderness there can be no illusion of a permanent home. We are revealed to be aliens. In psychoanalysis, the removal of illusions by seeing through the therapist's eyes opens up new vistas of living that had not been available before.

When our journey with God leads to the removal of spiritual illusions, we begin to see that the kingdom actually is at hand; we begin to see through God's eyes. When we see through God's eyes, we will not pretend that the tent we live in today can approximate the mansion in which we are destined to live. We are a people of mourning, created for union with God and longing for the fulfillment of that union. In the psychoanalytic tradition we are called out of the foundationalist illusion that our fallen, human grasping of the truth could ever be free from the pull of our own

---

[15]Simone Weil, *Waiting for God,* trans. Emma Craufurd (New York: Putnams, 1951), p. 69.

desperate longings. That tradition offers no safety from the corresponding despair when we learn that our search for meaning will ultimately find no satisfying conclusion.

The postmodern hermeneutic of suspicion, largely initiated by this psychoanalytic search for the removal of illusion, can be reoriented through the integration of a psychoanalytic psychology and a contemplative theology. In the promise of ultimate satisfaction with God our hermeneutic might be called a hermeneutic of humility and confidence. Such a hermeneutic would reject the foundationalist temptation to assert that we might attain objective knowledge of the truth through human initiative. In this sense it would be a hermeneutic of suspicion. Such humility, however, in no way requires that we slide to the opposite extreme of relativism. Unlike the relativist hermeneutic of nihilism, the faith of the desert contemplative does not assume that humble acknowledgment of our own sinful illusions eliminates the possibility of finding truth. Our confidence, rather, is that though we cannot accurately see the city that has foundations, its architect and builder certainly can. To the extent that we come to know and love that architect and builder our vision will become more fully rooted in truth.

Like the children of Israel we are called out of the city of our bondage and into the wilderness. Christian psychologists must also recognize that while the task of the psychotherapist is not the same as that of the spiritual director, the psychotherapist must never subvert the individual's spiritual pilgrimage. Those who would serve others in their journey into the wilderness and toward the city of God would do well to heed the call of the contemplative spiritual directors through the centuries. If we take their lessons seriously, we must acknowledge that our work of leading others through the painful process of removing illusions and making meaning from pain will be inextricably bound to our own progress on that same journey. As Gregory of Nyssa taught in the fourth century, the role of the spiritual guide mirrors the role of Moses:

> So Moses, who eagerly seeks to behold God, is now taught how he can behold Him: to follow God wherever he might lead is to behold God. His passing by signifies his guiding the one who follows, for someone who does not know the way cannot complete his journey safely in any other way than by following behind his guide. He who leads, then, by his guidance shows the way to the one following. He who follows will not turn aside from the right way if he always keeps the back of his leader in view.[16]

The guide who does not keep God's back in clear view can never lead others through the wilderness.

In the wilderness we will see the heavenly city from afar. We will be tempted to return to the bondage of illusions, but like Moses and Abraham those who confess

---

[16]Gregory of Nyssa, *The Life of Moses*, trans. Abraham J. Malherbe and Everett Ferguson (New York: Paulist, 1978), p. 119.

that they are strangers and aliens on the earth will not settle for a return to their former country. Such believers acknowledge that they long for a better country. Those who engage in the process of leading individuals who are searching for meaning and truth could do no better than to model their work after that of Moses as described by fourteenth-century German Dominican Johannes Tauler:

> Those who renounce the love of the world depart truly out of Egypt; they leave King Pharaoh's service in renouncing pride, vainglory, presumption and all other sins; and those who would go out of the world have great need of finding a Moses who will serve them as conductor—one who will be like the first Moses, full of gentleness and compassion. They need a guide—sweet, kindly and patient—who will make their going forth, which costs so dearly, more easy to them.[17]

Going forth into the wilderness is indeed costly. Those who guide others in that journey must take that cost seriously for themselves and for those they lead. As we pursue the integration of psychology and theology, the voices of spiritual directors through the ages call us to a high standard of accountability and sacrificial leadership.

---

[17]Johannes Tauler, *Sermons and Conferences,* in *Writings on Spiritual Direction by Great Christian Masters,* ed. Jerome M. Neufelder and Mary C. Coelho (New York: Seabury, 1982), p. 28.

9

EXPLORING CLIENTS' PERSONAL SIN IN THE THERAPEUTIC CONTEXT

Theological Perspectives on a Case Study of Self-Deceit

Philip G. Monroe

T HOMAS, A FORTY-YEAR-OLD, SINGLE CHRISTIAN, COMES TO YOU FOR THERAPY because he is struggling with depression and loneliness. He is wondering where his life is headed and why God doesn't answer his prayers. After all, he isn't asking for much—just a little respect from his family and intimacy with a wife.

Given this brief vignette, how would you counsel Thomas? Obviously, you would want more information before making a decision about how to intervene. As any good therapist would do, you would assess the extent, nature and history of the problem; existing resources; and previous attempts to solve the problem. Assessment is the key component in deciding how to act in therapy. But what do you look for? That depends somewhat on your orientation. Some look first at systemic issues; others look at intrapsychic tension; others at biological, psychological, and social interactions and so on. Whatever their orientation, therapists tend to look for factors that may explain or reveal proximal and distal causes of presenting problems.[1] Despite our inability to label particular factors as truly causal, we tend to look for those factors that provide explanation and that give us direction about where to focus our interventions.

---

[1] S. Bruce Narramore, "The Concept of Responsibility in Psychopathology and Psychotherapy," *Journal of Psychology and Theology* 13 (1985): 91-96.

The thesis of this chapter is that the central Christian concept of personal, active (but not necessarily conscious) sin appears to be neglected when we look for salient factors that explain psychological dysfunction. A quick search of articles in the *Journal of Psychology and Christianity* and the *Journal of Psychology and Theology* (n = 1,143) reveals that fewer than four percent (n = 43) deal specifically with the topic of sin (see figure 1). Of the forty-three articles, fewer than 5 percent (n = 2) look at some aspect of the effects of personal sin (see figure 2).[2] The vast majority of our work thus far has been to conceptualize the nature and origin of sin from the viewpoint of various psychological theories. Although these conceptualizations may be helpful, sin does not exist as an abstract theory. Rather, we must involve ourselves in the "study of the *recognition* and *knowledge* of our sin," so as to see its "evil consequences which corrode the whole of our living."[3]

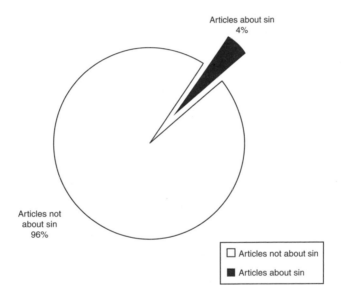

Figure 1. "Sin" in JPC/JPT (figure by Philip G. Monroe)

[2]A Psychlit search of all articles in the *Journal of Psychology and Christianity* and the *Journal of Psychology and Theology* as of the end of 1996, plus a hand search of articles in the *Journal of Psychology and Theology* that were published before 1974 yielded 1,143 articles. Of the 43 articles on sin, 26 focused on the psychological description of the nature and origin of sin, variations on the Christian conception of sin, and differences between psychopathology and sin. Thirteen articles were on a variety of topics such as forgiveness, responsibility and distinguishing between sinful and righteous anger. Two articles discussed treatment-related issues, and two articles focused on the effects of sin (autonomic response to sinful thoughts and sin's effect on attitudes). This type of search will neglect those articles that address sinful behavior (for example, sex offenses) without using a variant of the word *sin*.

[3]G. C. Berkouwer, *Sin* (Grand Rapids, Mich.: Eerdmans, 1971), p. 235, emphasis his.

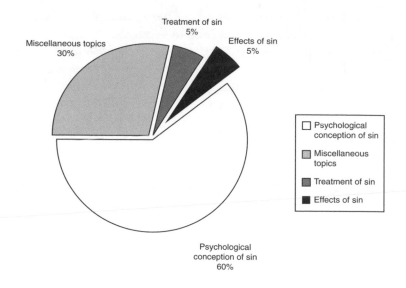

Figure 2. Categories of "sin" articles (figure by Philip G. Monroe)

The purpose of this chapter is to survey some of the possible reasons that our field has neglected research on and discussion of the topic of personal sin, using self-deceit as an example of the impact of sin on one man's life.[4] Thomas has led a difficult life. He has experienced a great deal of pain. Some of his pain has resulted from others sinning against him, and some has resulted from Thomas's own long-practiced responsive sin patterns. Without denying the former we will focus here on the latter because Spirit-led self-examination is the primary path to recognizing the existence and impact of our sinful behavior. To help us along the way, the comments of Puritan and like-minded theologians will be interjected in hopes that their comments will spark interest in exploring their understanding of the human condition.

I believe that it is difficult to identify a one-to-one correlation between personal sin and consequential difficulties in life. Nor is it easy to decipher the true cause of sin itself. In his award winning book on sin, Cornelius Plantinga reminds us that when we look at the context, motives and explanations of sin, they appear to be both connected and disconnected. Despite our best efforts at assessment, "we still do not know why a person succumbs to the [sinful] motive."[5] When we finish exploring all of the variables we must conclude that the heart is mysterious.

---

[4]Thomas is fictional, but his problem represents real problems faced by several clients.
[5]Cornelius Plantinga Jr., *Not the Way It's Supposed to Be: A Breviary of Sin* (Grand Rapids, Mich.: Eerdmans, 1995), p. 63.

Sin Is a Problem, But Should It Be a Focus of Therapy?

We cannot completely untangle the way in which the effects of sin play out in individuals, but we surely agree that sin has a most damaging affect on the whole of creation. Therefore, sin cannot be conceptualized as a mere deficiency. Rather, it is a "power at work in the personal lives of people and in the larger social units."[6] Sin destroys community by creating conflict with God and neighbor. Although we recognize that this enmity exists, we have difficulty seeing its day-to-day impact because we often feel too at home with estranged relationships. It is only when we sense an unusual loss of peace or hear of dramatic evil within families that relational estrangement becomes more salient to us. Many times we are too accustomed to feeling distant from God.

But the loss of communion with God and others brings isolation and increased anxiety, feeding the tendency to turn inward and listen first to our own wisdom, and in turn stirring our lust for things other than God.[7] Sin not only causes external destruction, such as child abuse and adultery, but also metastasizes during character formation. "Dispositions and acts form character, which then forms dispositions and acts."[8] If this weren't bad enough, we tend to make matters worse when we try to evade the reality of the condemnation that we deserve by erecting a "protective wall of self-righteousness."[9] We do so by denying our need for redemption or by comforting ourselves with the belief that we need a little less redemption than our neighbor.

The personal sin of all of our clients will bring devastation and disorientation to their (and others') lives.[10] It penetrates every aspect of emotions and thoughts, leaving no square inch unaffected. Sin is so vile that it causes us to despise the cure of redemption that God has lovingly provided and to search for another cure that we can claim in our own strength.

Some may wonder whether exploring personal sin in the therapeutic environment is necessarily appropriate. Might not such discussions lead deeply troubled clients to wrongly accept false guilt as real or at least encourage them to make a quick and shallow repentance that denies the existence of larger life patterns? Although these outcomes are possible they should not keep us from incisively exploring sin. As we strive to root out false guilt, we should also recognize the equally dangerous problem of false innocence, of "feeling good about the evil we

---

[6]Bernard L. Ramm, *Offense to Reason: A Theology of Sin* (San Francisco: Harper & Row, 1985), p. 109.

[7]Despite sin's power, it ultimately fails to gratify our desires, and it drives us deeper into "more and more extreme perversity" (Anthony Campolo, *Seven Deadly Sins* [Wheaton, Ill.: Victor, 1987], pp. 37-38).

[8]Plantinga, *Not the Way It's Supposed to Be*, p. 70.

[9]C. John Miller, *Repentance and 20th Century Man*, rev. ed. (Fort Washington, Penn.: Christian Literature Crusade, 1980), p. 94.

[10]Although there are other types of sin that affect our thoughts, feelings and behaviors, for the sake of space I am limiting my comments to sins Christians commit against themselves.

have done."[11] Narramore reminds us that objective guilt always lies beneath even the most obvious false guilt. Using the illustration of Nathan's confrontation of David about his commission of adultery and murder, Narramore summarizes the need to expose both sin and its consequences. He says:

> Such careful, consistent, and loving uncovering of our counselee's sinfulness is a prerequisite both for the resolution of unnecessary guilt feelings and for the development of a sense of inner wholeness and constructive sorrow. As long as we are either denying our sinfulness to avoid feeling guilty or punishing ourselves to avoid rejection or punishment from others, we have little time or energy to devote to constructive sorrow or true repentance. [12]

On the other hand, quick confessions to avoid self-examination are usually spotted because they lack the depth of insight and contrition that comes with the recognition that we truly deserve God's wrath.

Some people may see the benefits of dealing with sin but wonder if the language of sin is too offensive to modern ears. But addiction treatments thrive today in spite of their strong vocabulary of sinfulness and their recognition that "I'm *not* okay."[13]

So why do we counsel? Is not Christian counseling distinctly about restoring human hearts and souls? If this is true, then it must minimize neither the repulsiveness of sin nor God's gracious prescription for restoration: a heart understanding of sin that is brought about by his graciousness and leads to confession, a lifestyle of repentance and a growing desire to carry out righteous acts. Any therapy that circumvents repentance or creates an intellectualized parallel (for example, by encouraging clients to give up bitterness because it is not in their best interest) denies clients an opportunity to restore their broken relationship with God and to deepen their experience of grace.

Hindrances to Exploring the Effects of a Client's Personal Sin

Here we arrive at a point of tension: (1) All sin (personal or corporate) causes the destruction of horizontal and vertical relationships, it also causes intrapersonal destruction (in the form, for example, of disordered desires, distorted self-concept and so on).[14] (2) Yet it is difficult to tease out the differences between the effects of personal sin and the effects of the sins of others and the fallen world. (3) Adding to this tension we practitioners in the field of psychology desire to explore systematically and statistically the impact of an assortment of variables on human functioning. So what happens when these three propositions collide? Unfortunately, we may find ourselves drawn to the more vibrant and easily operationalized factors, especially those that are "outside the human heart and its motives."[15]

---

[11]John R. Stott, *The Cross of Christ* (Downers Grove, Ill.: InterVarsity Press, 1986), p. 98.
[12]S. Bruce Narramore, *No Condemnation* (Grand Rapids, Mich.: Zondervan, 1984), p. 251.
[13]Ernest Kurtz and Katharine Ketcham, *The Spirituality of Imperfection: Storytelling and the Journey to Wholeness* (New York: Bantam, 1992).
[14]See Psalm 51 for a poetic description of sin's oppressive impact on the sinner.
[15]Plantinga, *Not the Way It's Supposed to Be,* p. 73.

I see several possible explanations for the paucity of literature on the concept of personal sin, and several reasons that we seldom address the active, personal sin of our clients. First, because we focus on variables that we can isolate and study, we may have a tendency to believe that client behaviors are determined by an external fallen world and clients' subsequent tragic choices rather than seeing clients (and ourselves) as both "ratifiers" and "extenders" of sin.[16] The field of psychology in general has evidenced more interest in describing tangible aspects of human sickness than in identifying personal or corporate sin.[17] As a result, we may treat the sin nature as a background variable that is constant for the entire population. Although this variable is indeed constant across humanity, its expression is unique in every individual. If we gather a group of people who have suffered similar negative environmental influences, we are likely to find a myriad of responsive sin patterns. Unfortunately, we tend to push back constant variables such as the human sin nature so that their impact on our thinking is minimized.[18]

Second, and this reason is similar to the first, Christian psychologists may find that they rely on the larger field of psychology to engage in the most groundbreaking and field-defining research. When this is true, sin will often be neglected. For example, the *Diagnostic and Statistical Manual of Mental Disorders* (DSM-IV) operationally classifies disorders and conditions according to their external symptoms, neglecting the major impact of personal sinful behavior such as fear, idolatry, pride, lust and denial.[19] False presuppositions (for example, about the innate moral goodness of humankind) that we normally reject in light of Scripture may influence Christian psychology—not so much in terms of what we produce, but in terms of what we leave unexplored. A therapist who relies solely on the DSM-IV's classification scheme risks overlooking important etiological factors that are likely foundational in forming the disorder in question. This danger is heightened when therapists feel pressure from managed care organizations to view psychotherapy as an exercise in symptom reduction. Such pressures may cause therapists to neglect the process of long-term spiritual growth.

Third, we may have concerns about the antitherapeutic effects of confronting sin. I imagine that we are concerned about this because we have encountered those who see the removal of sin as a matter of simple behavior change and because we fear that if we address personal sin, we will be placing blame and responsibility solely on the individual. Some people may cringe when they hear Jay Adams say that "personal sin [is] the root and cause of most of the day-to-day counseling problems that arise"

---

[16]Ibid., p. 26.

[17]Mark R. McMinn, *Psychology, Theology, and Spirituality in Christian Counseling* (Wheaton, Ill.: Tyndale House, 1996).

[18]David A. Powlison, personal communication, February 1997.

[19]*Diagnostic and Statistical Manual of Mental Disorders*, 4th ed. (Washington, D.C.: American Psychiatric Association, 1994).

because they believe that the therapy arising from this position is likely to be harsh and unempathetic.[20] Despite our beliefs about and feelings toward Jay Adams and his followers, we must not avoid questioning what needs to be addressed in counseling sinful people just because we believe that others have not always carefully considered how best to intervene. People who deal with more overt sins, such as criminal behavior, may be more aware of ways to name sin patterns. For example, one well-seasoned attorney and forensic psychologist believes that people have an innate desire to confess their "iniquity," even if their goal is to reconstruct reality in order to make it more socially acceptable to themselves and others.[21]

Fourth, some Christian counselors have come out of legalistic Christian communities and have later had their faith renewed by the gospel of grace. They may find that they experience a knee-jerk response to the call to mortify the flesh because it seems to exalt a gospel of works. They may be concerned that focusing on or labeling personal sin during counseling may inculcate legalism and a pull-yourself-up-by-the-bootstraps mentality. However, Scripture makes it clear that both law and grace are necessary components of the gospel of Christ. The law presented in the context of the gospel is necessary to inform us of and reveal our sin.[22] Illegitimate variations of the law and the gospel—legalism and cheap grace—can be avoided if our knowledge of sin positively correlates with our knowledge of God's mercy for sinners. Armed with an understanding of this proper relationship between the law and the gospel, believers can victoriously struggle with their sin and benefit from the "disclosing and revealing function of the law" spoken of in Romans 3:20.[23] I know of no better place than in counseling where someone can let the law and the gospel speak gently but incisively to indwelling sin.

Fifth, in modern times the vocabulary of sin has lost its rich descriptiveness. An analogy may help to explain this problem. In the last few years, the coffee market has exploded here in the Midwest. My father, a life-long coffee drinker, enjoys Maxwell House instant coffee every morning with breakfast. The differences among Starbucks, Caribou and Gavalia coffee, the types of beans and the types of drink are lost on him. However, we "hipper" folks need to decide if we will have latte, cappuccino or espresso. We have developed a rich understanding of the multiple forms coffee can take. At times, our understanding of sin is more like my father's understanding of instant coffee than it is like the coffee connoisseur's understanding of the varieties available at the coffee bar down the street. How much of our time is spent plumbing the depths of Scripture so we will understand the many flavors of sin and their impact on believers and unbelievers?

---

[20]Cited in David Powlison, "Competent to Counsel? The History of a Conservative Protestant Anti-Psychiatry Movement" (Ph.D. diss., University of Pennsylvania, 1996), p. 170.
[21]Eric Ostrov, in-service lecture, Illinois Youth Center, St. Charles, Illinois, April 1997.
[22]Berkouwer, *Sin*.
[23]Ibid., p. 160.

Finally, a more personal note may help to explain some of our hesitancy to explore this topic. As I write on the topic of personal sin, I am at times deeply aware of the weight of my own sin and its consequences. It is then that I realize that this is not a theoretical discussion. Sin does truly affect each and every life. But I find that my heart often revolts against the reality of my own sinful longings and behaviors. Perhaps others have avoided this topic, having experienced the same tension and having recognized their inadequacy to deal fully with the reality of sin in their own lives. I recently discovered a quotation by the Puritan Richard Sibbes, who, it has been said, "exemplified the synthesis between biblical depth and pastoral sensitivity."[24] Sibbes aptly describes this difficulty in focusing on sin:

> It were an easy thing to be a Christian, if religion stood only in a few outward works and duties, but to take the soul to task, and to deal roundly with our own hearts, and to let conscience have its full work, and to bring the soul unto God, this is not so easy a matter, because the soul out of self-love is loath to enter into itself, lest it should have other thoughts of itself than it would have.[25]

Enriching Our Awareness of Personal Sin: Self-Deceit as Exemplar

Given that therapy should function as one part of the process of sanctification, how do we reverse the neglect of personal sin in our field? I believe that part of the answer to this problem is found among the writings of historical and present-day theological elders of our faith. The Puritans, in particular, provide us with the opportunity to engage in a phenomenological observation of the effects of sin on believers and of the healing message of the gospel.[26] The Puritan pastors "who wrote so perceptively about our inclination to hurt others in order to satisfy ourselves and what we must do to change ourselves for the better were profound psychologists."[27]

A reintroduction to these and other like-minded theologians will be beneficial for several reasons. First, it should resensitize us to the concept of personal sin as it impacts ours and others' lives. Second, it will enrich our vocabulary concerning the effects of sin and the process of sanctification. Third, it can warn us of the implications of superficial change without repentance (Jer 3:10). Fourth, it can help bring balance to our conceptions of sin and grace—holding on to one without the other

---

[24]I. Breward, "Puritan Theology," in *New Dictionary of Theology*, ed. Sinclair B. Ferguson, David F. Wright and J. I. Packer (Downers Grove, Ill.: InterVarsity Press, 1988), p. 551.

[25]Richard Sibbes, cited in David A. Powlison, "To Take the Soul to Task," *Journal of Biblical Counseling* 12, no. 3 (1994): 2.

[26]A few examples are Thomas Brooks, *Precious Remedies Against Satan's Devices: With the Covenant of Grace* (1652; reprint [n.p.]: Sovereign Grace, 1960); Jonathan Edwards, *A Treatise on Religious Affections* (1852; reprint, Grand Rapids, Mich.: Baker, 1982); John Owen, *The Works of John Owen* (1850-1853; reprint, Edinburgh: Banner of Truth, 1967), vol. 6; Thomas Watson, *The Mischief of Sin* (1671; reprint, Morgan, Penn.: Soli Deo Gloria, 1994).

[27]Solomon Schimmel, *The Seven Deadly Sins: Jewish, Christian, and Classical Reflections on Human Nature* (New York: Free Press, 1992), p. 4.

distorts the character and meaning of the gospel. Finally, it can reorient our understanding of the role of theology in the discipline of psychology.

William Ames, an English Puritan whose writings in systematic theology are said to have been the first and most important books in the Harvard library, writes that theology is about the "good life whereby we live to God."

> This practice of life is so perfectly reflected in theology that there is no precept of universal truth relevant to living well in domestic economy, morality, political life, or lawmaking [or psychology] which does not rightly pertain to theology. Theology, therefore, is to us the ultimate and the noblest of all exact teaching arts. It is a guide and master plan for our highest end, sent in a special manner from God, treating of divine things, tending towards God, and leading man to God.[28]

In the spirit of the Puritan self-examination, I would like to

Matthew Poncelet, portrayed by Sean Penn, is a murderer and rapist on death row in the 1995 movie *Dead Man Walking*. In this portrayal of a true story, Poncelet defends his innocence to Sister Helen Prejean, claiming to have only been present when the real killer "snapped," raping and killing the young couple parked on the town's lover's lane. Prejean becomes Poncelet's spiritual adviser and listening ear during the last week of his life, as he faces death by lethal injection. At several points, Prejean inquires about the truth of that fateful night many years before. For a long time Poncelet sticks to his story, and his flashbacks portray him as a fearful observer. Prejean lovingly persists, comforting him and yet confronting inconsistencies and his attempts to identify himself as a victim. Each ensuing flashback depicts Poncelet as participating in more of the crime until he finally reaches a watershed and wrenchingly admits his gleeful participation in the gruesome acts. At this moment he finally experiences what he has searched for all his life, forgiveness and love. Although we cannot know the extent to which Poncelet actually deceived himself, it is clear that the effort he expended in maintaining his innocence cost him dearly because he was unable to connect with God or others until the last moments of his life.

explore the implications of self-deceit as just one form of personal (but not necessarily conscious) sin in the lives of believers. Self-deceit does not form a neat package within which to conceptualize all sin patterns, but I have chosen it because it functions as a utility sin that "pursues no particular end but rather serves whatever end [we pursue]."[29] Deceit works by searing the conscience (Rom 1) in order to release us from the knowledge that we are creatures who must revere the Creator. Then we are free to follow our own sinful agenda, which will ultimately be our god. I have also chosen to examine self-deceit because it illustrates that internal heart issues need our attention as much as, if not more than, external sinful behaviors such as lying, cheating or stealing.

[28]William Ames, *The Marrow of Theology* (1968; reprint, Durham, N.C.: Labyrinth, 1983), p. 78.
[29]William F. May, *A Catalogue of Sins: A Contemporary Examination of Christian Conscience* (New York: Holt, Rinehart & Winston, 1967), p. 145.

One of the natural consequences of our fallenness is that we all live in some form of fantasy that exaggerates either our virtues or our vices. Some people, such as habitual sex offenders, deny the reality of their responsibility and the damage to their victims, and their denial is evident to everyone but themselves. With other people—especially mature Christians—self-deceit is much more subtle. In different eras both Gregory the Great and the American Puritan Jonathan Edwards warned readers to be aware that vices can be easily passed off as virtues (for example, sinful anger being passed of as a zeal for justice).[30]

Deceit functions much like the magician David Copperfield, a master of deception and distraction. Copperfield charms his audience by drawing their attention to something seemingly significant while he manipulates reality in front of their eyes. Likewise, our desire uses a grain of truth to engage our attention, then with sleight of hand enjoins us to accept as truth something that we would reject if it were laid out in black and white. Russian novelist Leo Tolstoy confesses that his pursuit of knowledge performed such a deceptive feat in his own life: "Quite often a man goes on for years imagining that the religious teaching that had been imparted to him since childhood is still intact, while all the time there is not a trace of it left in him."[31]

What are the effects of being self-deceived? Sin results in loss of community, increased isolation and fearfulness, and false worship. But, what are the effects of deceit in particular? I will use the case study of Thomas to illustrate the ways in which deception tends to allow us to elevate pride, to blur memory and to misconstrue reality, and how it increases the likelihood that we will engage in other sins.

Thomas is a single, well-educated Christian man. He has a good job and makes a decent salary. He comes to therapy to deal with his mounting depression stemming from an overwhelming sense of emptiness and insignificance. He also mentions that he has amassed a great deal of debt, that he owns a condominium that is now beyond his means to pay for, and that he doesn't know how to get out from under this financial burden. While he is describing his background, he explains that he never felt like he measured up to his father's strict standards. He wasn't athletic enough, he wasn't good enough with his hands, and he certainly wasn't as smart as his older brother. He also felt that he never really received loving attention from his emotionally weak and distant mother.

As Thomas's life story unfolds, you begin to see connections between the verbal abuse he experienced as a child and his tendency to depend heavily on others in order to gain a sense of self. Two powerful and repeating patterns that reveal this dependency emerge from his story. Thomas will do just about anything if he thinks

---

[30]Gregory *Pastoral Care* 7.14; 9.30, trans. Henry Davis (New York: Newman Press, 1950); Edwards, *Religious Affections*.
[31]Leo Tolstoy, *Confession* (1884; reprint, New York: W. W. Norton, 1983), p. 15.

it will bring respect and acceptance. He has slept with and financially provided for women whom he barely knew in the hope of feeling desirable and worthy of respect. He often meets his partners in bars where he goes "to see if I can't talk to someone about Christ." He regularly spends more than he can afford on gifts for friends and family members.

Thomas sees himself as a caring, generous and loving person. He acknowledges that he sometimes goes overboard, but he quickly adds that he is "only trying to be nice." When his attempts to buy respect do not satisfy his deep cravings, he vacillates between rage and depression. In moments of rage, he has made prank phone calls, written "poison" letters to coworkers and shadowed ex-lovers. He even slashed the tires of someone who recently left him. He often ends periods of rage and revengeful behavior by sinking into depression and crying out, "Why won't God answer my prayers? All I want is to feel like I have something to offer, that I'm somebody. What is so wrong with that?"

Self-deceit elevates pride. Self-deceit almost always serves to inordinately increase one's view of oneself or one's achievements. Some people are easily recognized as being full of pride, and in spite of their skyrocketing egoism, their sinful pride appears to have only minimal impact on their day-to-day functioning. The psalmist records his perception that those who are rich and comfortable appear to gain so much comfort that they sneer at God (Ps 73). Similarly, Moses warns the Israelites that satisfaction with God's blessing can create the temptation to grow proud: "When you eat and are satisfied, when you build fine houses and settle down, and when your herds and flocks grow large and your silver and gold increase . . . you may say to yourself, 'My power and the strength of my hands have produced this wealth for me' " (Deut 8:12-13, 17 NIV).

Moses understood that empire builders are in danger of having too much pride, but martyrs may be just as capable of developing self-serving pride. In either case the self, with its stolen glory, becomes the focus of attention. The "good" reasons for taking action become the sole focus, and broken relationships are ignored and trampled on. Where does Thomas fit? Is his manic or depressive pride? At first glance, he does not appear to struggle with sinful pride at all. In fact, many people would believe that he suffers from low self-esteem. But Thomas's life is a textbook example of depressive pride. Thomas is psychologically minded. He recognizes his parents' deficits and believes that he was not given the love and affection that children should receive from their parents. Yet despite his parents' incompetence, he can proudly list his accomplishments: he was the first in the family to get a college degree, he was the youngest senior computer programmer in his company, and now he is able to serve his ailing father without holding a grudge. To soothe that deep ache he feels, he often looks at his strengths and begins his self-talk with "I deserve better than this." Before he knows it, he finds himself indulging in alcohol, spending sprees, pornography and illicit sexual activities.

Self-deceit blurs memory and misconstrues reality. In both the Old and New Testaments, Scripture regularly warns us that we should remember what the Lord has done in the lives of his people. This illuminates the fact that fallen creatures often have short or selective memories.[32]

How might selective memory impact the lives of our counselees? John Owen, arguably the most eminent British theologian, suggests that Christians who do not mortify the flesh often deceive themselves in order to avoid acknowledging habitual, enslaving sin. They may look for some good within themselves to distract themselves from larger problems; they may run too quickly to grace and mercy without sincerely repenting; and they may satisfy guilt by listing the "big" sins they do not engage in, so that they can ignore the "smaller" ones that they have harbored.[33] I would add a fourth possibility: people who are psychologically minded may use honesty about shortcomings and "the fact that they are 'in process' or 'getting in touch with their real selves' as an excuse for irresponsible (sinful) behavior."[34]

Thomas habitually reminds himself of what he has accomplished in the face of great adversity. Unfortunately, his identity of being generous to those who have mistreated him makes it easier for him to ignore the selfishness and sexual sin he engages in to seek respect. In those moments when he cannot escape the reality of his sexual sin, he often runs quickly to grace, claiming God's forgiveness in order to avoid shame and to quell doubts about the health of his faith. From Owen's point of view, this may be his most dangerous behavior. People who are successful in using grace to avoid guilt face grave danger because "sin is never less quiet than when it seems to be most quiet."[35]

Thomas uses God's mercy as something that helps him to escape the reality of his sin, not as something that compels him to hate sin and to desire to put on virtue. This may help Thomas to ignore the painful reality that he needs help, but he is not likely to encounter true forgiveness and the power to change. How dangerous Thomas's false means of comfort can be. "The root of an unmortified course is the digestion of sin without bitterness in the heart. When a man hath confirmed his imagination to such an apprehension of grace and mercy as to be able, without bitterness, to swallow and digest daily sins, that man is at the very brink of turning the grace of God into lasciviousness, and being hardened by the deceitfulness of sin."[36]

During therapy Thomas tends to minimize his sinful behaviors and to maximize his adversities. He does not consider his life to be all that dysfunctional. "Others

---

[32]A classic example of blurred memory is that of Israel asking to return to Egypt. They remember eating onions and leeks, but they forget their torturous enslavement.

[33]Owen, *Works,* 6:43ff.

[34]Narramore, "Concept of Responsibility," p. 95.

[35]Owen, *Works,* 6:11.

[36]Ibid., 6:15.

have debt. . . . Everyone has sex sometimes. . . . That dancer at the bar did have some questions about God. I think I should see her again." When he has fleeting experiences of significance, Thomas may overlook obvious signs that his current partner cares little for his well-being. When he fails to experience love, he tends to rehearse memories of maltreatment by others, neglecting the fact that he often places himself in high-risk situations.

Thomas' treatment might focus on specific problems (for example, inadequate boundaries, unconscious desires to devalue himself) and interventions (such as exploring and developing his sense of self by being appropriately mirrored, decreasing dangerous sexual activity or developing good stewardship of his resources). All of these foci may be useful. However, will these interventions help him to recognize that the deceit of his heart has allowed him to pass off inordinate desires for significance and acceptance as legitimate, and to blame God for not giving him what he believes he rightfully deserves? Treatments that only alleviate his symptoms or focus on exposing the external causes of his behaviors may recondition his idol of love so that it does not exact such a stiff price, but his self-deceit about the legitimacy of his inordinate desire to be respected will remain. Traditional treatments may present an inaccurate reality while God seeks reconciliation and desires to tenderly teach Thomas that although he has an unquenchable desire for meaningful relationships, he is frequently satisfied with too little.[37]

Although Thomas shows many signs of underestimating his depravity, during deep depression he is just as likely to despair that his sin is too great for redemption. How could God forgive him when he knowingly sins? Another Puritan theologian, Thomas Brooks, reminds us that one of Satan's devices is to encourage the hopeless to "mind their sins more than their Savior."[38] As disheartenment increases, desire for repentance decreases because it is perceived as ineffective. Thomas overlooks Scriptures that might place salve on his wounds because he believes that they do not pertain to his sorry state. Instead, he recounts recurring sins as evidence of the lack of redemption. Despair of this kind has led Thomas to repeated salvation attempts and to the brink of denying the Christian faith.

Self-deceit invites other sins. Self-deception allows us to pass off (to ourselves and others) vices as if they were virtues. "Satan knows that if he should present sin in its own nature and dress, the soul would rather fly from it than to yield to it, and therefore he presents it unto us . . . painted and gilded."[39] We may find that we can pass off our greatest liability as one of our greatest strengths. Thomas attempts to pass off his inordinate desire to be respected as a virtue even though it often leads

---

[37]C. S. Lewis, "The Weight of Glory," in *The Weight of Glory and Other Addresses* (Grand Rapids, Mich.: Eerdmans, 1965), p. 2.

[38]Brooks, *Precious Remedies,* p. 91.

[39]Ibid., p. 17.

to risky sexual and financial behavior. As a result of his self-deception, he easily excuses vengeful desires ("After what I've done for her, look how she has treated me!") as normal reactions to being mistreated. In an age when emotions are often considered to be neutral expressions, Thomas is able to gild sinful anger with deceptive mantras ("I'm just being honest; anger is normal; Jesus got angry too!") in order to focus his attention anywhere but on self-examination. Meanwhile, anger eats away at his spiritual and physical health by decreasing his sense of peace and increasing his stress level and his blood pressure.

When a Thomas displays his rage toward others and God, how will we respond? Historically we have emphasized the value of authenticity over the value of suppressing emotion. But therapists must be able to encourage not only authenticity but also self-examination in search of the root of the anger.[40] Jonathan Edwards, a Puritan pastor and evangelist to the Native Americans of Massachusetts, suggests that appropriate self-examination includes looking at the type of angry response (for example, revenge), its "occasion" (kicking the innocent dog), its "purpose," and its "measure" (how severe it was and how long it was held).[41] Edwards uses a number of questions to examine the angry heart: (1) Does it "disturb charity?" (2) Does it "embitter the feelings?" (3) "Does the least touch renew the anger?" (4) "What good has been obtained by it?" (5) How do my faults deserve similar wrath? (6) What impact does it have on my peace with God? (7) How does it keep me from God's service?

Implications for Practice

I propose four foundational questions for all practitioners to ask themselves in order to understand the implications of exploring client sins.

Does my orienting style of practice encourage examination of personal sin? Therapists from different theoretical orientations differ in how likely they would be to encourage self-examination. Strict behavioral or cognitive treatments of anxiety may be more interested in the end result (reduction in anxiety) than in existential or insight-oriented treatments that encourage self-examination. Yet some insight-oriented theories are premised on the belief that the therapist should work only with what the client brings so that only client-generated insights will be of value in changing behaviors or emotions. Proponents of these theories may assume that clients will want to explore their personal sin. Clients are more likely, however, to come to therapy in order to reconstruct reality in a way that makes their sin more palatable.

Do my techniques lead clients to a deeper relationship with God or simply make

---

[40]See Dennis Okholm's chapter in this book for a balanced view of the vice of anger.

[41]Jonathan Edwards, *Charity and Its Fruits: Christian Love as Manifested in the Heart and Life* (London: Banner of Truth, 1969), pp. 199ff.

them self-confident? Therapists are beginning to address confession of shortcomings and sins within the psychotherapeutic context.[42] Confession allows clients the opportunity to explicitly recognize their depravity and leads to a more meaningful understanding of Christ's redemptive work on the cross. Similarly, prayer, Bible reading and the spiritual disciplines can be of tremendous value to counseling. However, any one of these techniques can be used superficially to bring relief of guilt and shame, yet miss their intended purpose. Any techniques that explicitly or implicitly value self-examination outside of the context of the person's relationship to a gracious but righteous God may lead the client to reconstruct reality in order to make it more tolerable.

Am I following fads within psychology or am I educating clients about how to think more biblically about themselves? Western Christians are seldom ignorant of pop psychology fads. Some approach psychology looking for a blessing on their "sickness" and see treatment as an opportunity for "atonement."[43] Other clients are interested in examining themselves but lack the necessary theological backdrop from which to analyze their lives. As therapists, we must ask ourselves if our clients guide how we deal with the topic of sin or if we are willing to take the risk of gently but firmly redirecting their self-centered focus so they will have a more balanced understanding of themselves in relation to God.

Does my life exemplify a life of self-examination? The trite phrase "you can't teach what you don't know" is applicable to this topic. We will be gravely limited in our ability to lead clients to the Puritans' view of self-examination if we have not experienced the overwhelming sense of our own depravity and the joyous power to change that is found in God's redemptive power at work in our lives. Older Christians must not rest on past experiences of grace but need to continually see God's grace as empowering them to persevere in developing the fruits of the Spirit (Gal 5:22-23).

Conclusion

No matter what the therapist's theoretical orientation is, therapy will deal with the sins of clients. But the dominant culture that sets boundaries for appropriate care of persons does not generally consider sinfulness and all of its ramifications as a significant influence on human functioning and behavior. Because we function within the dominant paradigm, we also may be tempted to downplay the effect of sin in our clients' lives, or at least to remove the traditional vocabulary of sin. It is my belief that we must consider the result of the vocabulary we use when we talk about sin. In our effort to contextualize our message to clients, we often use words

[42]See McMinn, *Psychology, Theology, and Spirituality;* Kurtz and Ketcham, *Spirituality of Imperfection.*
[43]Ostrov, in-service lecture.

that are more palatable to their ears. However, does our new vocabulary cause the concept of sin to lose its teeth and meaning because sin's devastation and God-ward orientation are softened? Does the vocabulary of shortcomings and dysfunction direct our eyes away from the destructiveness of sin and God's holiness? Does our vocabulary encourage a lifestyle of self-examination and repentance?

The Puritans may have found the antidote as they vigorously pursued self-examination against the backdrop of the Bible's portrayal of our just and merciful Redeemer.[44] Counseling that builds on their understanding of sin and redemption will encourage self-evaluation that imitates the process of Lent. It will awaken us to the horrific consequences of our sin, it will clarify our need, and it will provide us with the only power and impetus to mortify the flesh and give glory to God. In this way we will see forgiveness not just as repeated mercy for habitual sin, but as the avenue for breaking the power of sin at work in our lives and in the lives of our counselees.[45]

---

[44]Sacvan Bercovitch, *The Puritan Origins of the American Self* (New Haven, Conn.: Yale University Press, 1975).

[45]David A. Powlison, "Idols of the Heart and 'Vanity Fair,' " *Journal of Biblical Counseling* 13, no. 2 (1995): 35-50.

10

AN INTERDISCIPLINARY MAP FOR CHRISTIAN COUNSELORS

Theology & Psychology in Pastoral Counseling

Deborah van Deusen Hunsinger

W HEN I WORKED AS A PASTORAL COUNSELOR, I OFTEN FELT LIKE I WAS traveling in uncharted territory. Sometimes during a counseling session an image would arise spontaneously in my mind of the counselee and me walking through the woods at night. It seemed as if the light I held in my hand were just barely bright enough for us to see a step or two ahead of us on the path. I hoped it was enough to keep us from stumbling into an unexpected pit. The counselee was on an important journey and had invited me along as companion and guide, but where were we headed? To be sure, I had various maps in hand, some constructed by depth psychologists and others drawn up by various theologians and spiritual guides, but how did they all fit together?

If I followed one map only, we might find a clear path on which to travel, but would our destination be the one we had intended? Were all our efforts straining toward the kingdom of God or toward a more modest goal of healing from psychological trauma? Did the counselee long for the communion of saints or simply for relief from depression and loneliness? Were these different ways of conceiving of our destination compatible with each other, or would they take us in different directions? Where was the particular crossroads where the two sets of maps intersected?

Just where do theology and psychology meet when we are interested in that pastoral art called caring for the soul? This is the question that vexed me for years, and my book *Theology and Pastoral Counseling: A New Interdisciplinary Approach* might be seen as the map I drew after a decade of being lost in the woods.[1]

The more I wandered with my counselees, the more urgently I needed an answer to my question. It was confusing to have two sets of maps that charted some of the same territory but in oddly different ways. How could I make sense of them, for myself as well as for the people I was trying to help? As I pondered them over time, I became more and more confused and felt more and more hopeless about ever finding a way through the thicket. And yet the question was urgent because it was at the very heart of my sense of vocation: How do we properly conceive of the relationship between these two disciplines, theology and psychology, in the context of pastoral counseling as a ministry of the church? Both theology and psychology were needed to do the work I was called to do, but how were they related to each other?

What were some of the logical possibilities? Perhaps if I removed myself somewhat from the immediate situation with the counselee and approached the question from a more theoretical standpoint, I might be better able to get an overview, a grasp of the whole. If I did that, how might I conceive of the relationship between theology and psychology?

First, I might view the relationship between psychology and theology as a relationship between promise and fulfillment, or between something that is incomplete and something that is complete.[2] Psychology, then, would be conceived as a map that would take a person only part of the way to the destination. Where it leaves off, theology would take over. Psychology, in other words, would be seen as having certain inherent limits; it would need to be extended or supplemented with theological concepts.

Second, I might see that some aspects of psychology conceptualize the same or similar experiences that theology conceptualizes, only using a different vocabulary. Both languages attempt to give shape and meaning to a particular set of human experiences, but in different ways. Thus, one would be able to translate back and forth between the two idioms.

Third, I might view theology and psychology as complementary, each having a distinct area of expertise and providing reliable guidance in that area. I would not understand them as contradicting each other because they do not describe the same territory.

Fourth, by contrast perhaps I would view theology and psychology as being directly opposed to each other. They do indeed chart the same territory, but the paths they map through the woods lead to decidedly different destinations. Those

---

[1] Deborah van Deusen Hunsinger, *Theology and Pastoral Counseling: A New Interdisciplinary Approach* (Grand Rapids, Mich.: Eerdmans, 1995).

[2] This typology is adapted from George Lindbeck's study of the possible relationships among various religions. Lindbeck also develops an extended cartographic metaphor, in which conceptual theories function as various kinds of maps.

paths might converge for a while, but at certain decisive points they would separate, forcing us to make a choice.

Fifth, perhaps I could best understand the relationship between theology and psychology as the relationship between the coherent and the incoherent or between the authentic and inauthentic. Perhaps there are inconsistencies in one map's charting of a particular patch of woods, but the other map presents the way through that part of the woods consistently so that it becomes comprehensible. Maybe people who authentically pursue a psychologically healthy way of life have a similar moral outlook to that of people who authentically practice the disciplines of the Christian faith. If we conceive of the relationship this way, a committed Christian disciple has more in common with someone who is committed to a discipline of intensive psychotherapy than with a nominal Christian.

Finally, depending on which aspects of theology and psychology I was investigating, I might attain a proper conception of the relationship through a combination of these possibilities.

A Theological Compass: The Chalcedonian Pattern
Rather than sorting through each of these logical possibilities, which are intended to be more suggestive than definitive, I would like to propose a different approach. In the midst of such a bewildering and complex set of possibilities, we need a way of orienting ourselves theologically. We need something more basic than a map; we need a compass. I find such a compass in the church's definition of how the divine and human natures of Jesus Christ are to be conceived and related in the teaching of the church. The church fathers who gathered at the Council of Chalcedon in A.D. 451 confronted many of the conceptual issues that I was facing as I pondered the proper way to conceive of the relationship between theology and psychology. The relevant passage from the Chalcedonian definition of the relationship between Christ's two natures reads as follows:

> Therefore . . . we all with one accord teach people to acknowledge one and the same Son, our Lord Jesus Christ, at once complete in Godhead and complete in manhood, truly God and truly human . . . one and the same Christ, Son, Lord, Only-Begotten, recognized in two natures, without confusion, without change, without division, without separation; the distinction of natures in no way annulled by the union, but rather the characteristics of each nature being preserved and coming together to form one person and subsistence, not as parted or separated into two persons, but one and the same Son and Only begotten God the Word, Lord Jesus Christ.[3]

How did this definition function in its original context? The Council of Chalcedon was called into being after centuries of debate over how to understand the

---

[3]As cited in James E. Loder and W. Jim Neidhardt, *The Knight's Move* (Colorado Springs, Colo.: Helmers & Howard, 1992), p. 83.

claims of Scripture and the early church that Jesus is Lord, the Son of God. The purpose of the council was not to define the faith of the church in any comprehensive or exhaustive sense, but rather to demarcate clear boundaries for orthodox teaching. The council sought on the one hand to rule out various heretical teachings (such as Arianism and Nestorianism), and on the other hand to hold together the partial truths expressed in various competing understandings of Jesus' simultaneous divinity and humanity (such as those of Christians in Alexandria and Antioch).

The Chalcedonian definition evidences more concern about what it rules out than what it rules in. Its focus is that Christ's two natures are related without separation or division on the one hand and without confusion or change on the other. This was the key move. For the formal nature of these defining or relational terms can be abstracted from the Chalcedonian definition and applied to a wide range of other questions.

The compass that finally provided me with a clear theological orientation was what one scholar has called a "Chalcedonian pattern" of thought.[4] The Chalcedonian definition of how properly to understand the incarnation of the Word of God in Jesus Christ became the basis for my thinking about how properly to conceive of the relationship between the disciplines of theology and psychology in the work of pastoral counseling.

Let me be very clear at this point. I am making a crucial distinction between the Chalcedonian pattern and the Chalcedonian definition. It is the pattern, not the definition, that gives me guidance for thinking about the relationship between theology and psychology. The pattern merely provides form, whereas the definition is substantive. And because the pattern is formal, it can be applied to a variety of different relationships, whereas the substantive definition is specific to Christology. The pattern offers a kind of grammar, whereas the definition sets forth a particular statement in which the grammar is exemplified.

There are three formal features of the Chalcedonian pattern. First, two terms are placed in a relationship in which they exist together without confusion or change so that they remain indissolubly differentiated. Second, those terms are related without separation or division so that they coexist in inseparable unity. Finally, one term is considered to be logically prior to the other; it provides a point of normative orientation, or a framework. In cases in which the two terms generate conceptual conflict, the logically prior term is allowed to prevail. This is what Karl Barth has called indestructible order.[5]

To explicate each of these formal or relational features, I will first ask about their substantive use in the Chalcedonian definition itself. How are Christ's two natures

---

[4]George Hunsinger, *How to Read Karl Barth: The Shape of His Theology* (New York: Oxford University Press, 1991), p. 185.
[5]Karl Barth, *Church Dogmatics* 3/2 (Edinburgh: T & T Clark, 1960), p. 437.

properly understood to be related when we ponder the mystery of the incarnation? Second, in each case I will abstract the formal pattern from the definition by asking what clues it provides regarding the relationship between the discipline of theology and that of psychology.

Indissoluble differentiation: without confusion or change. What does this relational grammar require when we ponder the mysterious event of the incarnation of God in Jesus Christ? "Indissoluble differentiation" has to do with the importance of maintaining the clear distinction between Christ's divine and human natures. Jesus Christ is said to have not one but two "natures" that are inconceivably united. Their union is said to be inconceivable because nothing could be more radically incommensurable than to be completely divine and completely human at the same time. God alone is eternal; human beings are mortal. God alone is holy; human beings are fallen and sinful. It would be the utmost error to confuse these two natures or to see them as somehow capable of being interchanged.

Kierkegaard captures this characteristic of the incarnation when he speaks of the "infinite qualitative difference" between God and the human being. Following Barth we might think of this difference as the "ontological divide" that separates divine from human being, and which is overcome only when God graciously crosses it in Jesus Christ. Barth asks: "Will not this being of ours be given over to death? Will it not be so questioned that we can be sure only of its not being? And where then is the comparability between his Creator-being and our creature-being, between his holy being and our sinful being, between his eternal being and our temporal being?"[6]

There is no common mode of being that connects the divine nature and the human nature to one another. Although Jesus Christ is both fully God and fully human, the terms of his deity are not to be confused with the terms of his humanity.

When we abstract the formal pattern and apply it to our conception of how theology and psychology are to be related in the work of pastoral counseling, it would seem first of all that we must recognize the clear differentiation between the two fields. Each discipline has relative autonomy; it can delimit its own sphere of inquiry to secure its self-defined integrity. Each discipline proceeds with the investigation of its subject matter according to the methods appropriate to it. A method of investigation based on God's self-revelation would arguably be quite different from the empirical observation of early childhood interpersonal relationships that forms the basis for theories of psychological development.

Even though both theology and psychology may need to deal with basic issues of love and hate, trust and mistrust, they do so with entirely different contexts of meaning. It would be a mistake to consider them to be somehow interchangeable

---

[6]Barth, *Church Dogmatics* 2/1, p. 83.

or to determine that they are saying essentially the same thing but in a slightly different vocabulary. We are confused if we think that theological and psychological terms and concepts can simply be translated back and forth so that, for example, we see a client's sins and symptoms as virtually equivalent, or believe that salvation and individuation are two different ways of talking about the same thing. If we are committed to maintaining the clear distinction between theology and psychology, we will be careful not to disregard their irreducible differences. We will be alert to the vastly different subject matters, the different methods employed and the distinctive norms; indeed, we will be alert to the wholly different conceptual universe that we inhabit when we dwell in one or the other thought world.

Inseparable unity: without separation or division. When we ponder the mystery of the incarnation, we must also ponder the deep paradox that though Jesus Christ was fully God and fully human, he was not two persons, but one. His two natures were inseparably united in what is called a *hypostatic* union; he has two natures but one *hypostasis*, a single subsistence or person. We cannot conceive of Jesus Christ properly if we separate his divine nature from his human nature. The whole person, Jesus Christ, human and divine, suffered and died on the cross. Therefore, we can affirm the otherwise incomprehensible mystery that God suffered and died. The whole person, Jesus Christ, divine and human, was raised from the dead. Therefore, we can affirm the otherwise incomprehensible mystery that a human being was raised to eternal life. In all of Jesus Christ's actions and passion he was and is both fully human and fully divine. Thus, though Jesus Christ was without sin because of his divine nature, he took on the sin of the world, becoming what Barth shockingly calls "the one great sinner."[7] Jesus Christ, by virtue of taking on our humanity, suffered and died as a sinner.

How might the formal or relational category of inseparable unity illuminate the relationship between theology and psychology? When we look at human beings in the world and try to understand them in their wholeness, we find that we cannot fully separate or divide theological and psychological perspectives from one another. Though they are clearly distinguishable and need to be distinguished according to their different subject matters, methods and norms, in the context of pastoral counseling as a ministry of the church, theology and psychology are inseparable. Everything we do and think and speak and suffer we do and think and speak and suffer as psychological beings.

Yet our ordinary human experience in time and space is the very place where God meets us. God comes into our lives in such a decisive way that in the mystery of divine grace, and whether we recognize it or not, we are called to believe, to become persons of faith. At the very core of our humanity is our relationship to God. Through revelation we know ourselves to be created in God's image, to have

---

[7]Barth, *Church Dogmatics* 4/1, p. 239.

fallen away from God's intentions for our lives, and to have been redeemed through Christ and in him promised a new humanity.

As seen from the standpoint of faith, these psychic and spiritual realities are, in fact, inseparable. We can no more divide them from one another than we can separate our bodies from our souls. We are a psychospiritual unity even as we are also "embodied souls" or "ensouled bodies."[8] If we want to understand human beings in their essential psychospiritual wholeness, we need to perceive them through both sets of lenses, the psychological and the theological.

T. F. Torrance captures this kind of complex unity well, and he shows its basis in the incarnation of Jesus Christ:

> Through the incarnation of God's Word and Truth in Jesus Christ, empirical correlates have an ineradicable place both in the mediation of divine revelation to us and in the theological concepts and statements we are bound to employ in any faithful interpretation of it. These concepts and statements point indefinitely beyond themselves to the ultimate mystery of the Triune God, and must do so if they are to have divine significance and validity, but unless they are correlated with empirical reality in our creaturely world they can have no meaning for us.[9]

Torrance is speaking here not only of the ways in which God uses ordinary human events in time and space to show us his hidden reality, but also of the concepts we need to use to capture those events faithfully. Because Jesus Christ entered fully into human time and space, our strictly theological statements need to find correlations with those statements from other fields that describe ordinary empirical reality; we need to find correlations in history, sociology, political science, anthropology, psychology and other fields. Though we are focusing here on theology's relationship with psychology, the conceptual relationship between theology and the other disciplines would be governed by the same formal pattern.

Indestructible order: Asymmetrical relationship. Now we come to the third formal feature of the Chalcedonian definition, the indestructible order of Christ's two natures. According to Karl Barth, Chalcedon's ordering of Jesus Christ's two natures as fully divine and fully human indicates a kind of logical priority or precedence of his divine over his human nature. Barth is not subordinating the Son to the Father, but rather is ordering the two natures of Christ, divine and human, in relation to each other.

These two natures, completely distinct and yet united in the one person, Jesus Christ, are not united by virtue of some common element or attribute that they share. Their union, though real, is utterly incomprehensible to the human mind. It is not as if there is some neutral category of being that exists by degrees along a

---

[8]Barth, *Church Dogmatics* 3/2, p. 327.
[9]T. F. Torrance, *The Christian Doctrine of God: One Being, Three Persons* (Edinburgh: T & T Clark, 1996), pp. 82-83.

divine-human continuum. According to such a mistaken conception, Christ's humanity would somehow be seen as subordinated to his divine being. But such a conception would fail to take note of the radicalness of the distinction between divine and human reality.

There is no common scale by which God and humanity can be measured. Therefore, Christ's two natures cannot be hierarchically related, for hierarchy presupposes a common standard of measure. The word *asymmetry* more adequately captures the logic of the terms of relationship between Christ's divine and human natures. The preexistent divine Logos, who was with God before the foundation of the world and through whom the world was created, became incarnate as a human being in space and time, as the Jewish rabbi, Jesus of Nazareth, Mary's son. Though Jesus Christ is both fully divine and fully human, the two terms of his person are not equal and reciprocal but are asymmetrically related, with the divine nature having logical priority.

What are the implications of this formal pattern when it is applied to the complex relationship between theology and psychology? When Christian theology is ordered in relationship to psychology, theology is given the place of logical priority. That is, psychological concepts, while retaining their irreducible distinctiveness and autonomy as psychological concepts, are placed properly within a larger overarching context of Christian theology. The implications of the formal pattern of asymmetry are threefold:

1. It is not possible to conceptually integrate theology and psychology because they function on logically different levels.

2. We must not try to translate theological concepts into psychological concepts or vice versa because such translation is possible only with concepts that are symmetrically related.

3. For those who seek to do counseling in the context of Christian ministry, the norms and values internal to faith have logical precedence over all externally derived norms or values, including those of psychology.

I will discuss each of these points in turn.

No Conceptual Integration

It is a mistake to try to integrate Christian theology with any type of psychology at the conceptual level. Just as divine being is ontologically other than human being, so theology is logically other than psychology. Theology and psychology may both be languages that speak of the human condition, but they do so with frameworks and assumptions that are logically diverse. They function conceptually at different levels even when they are intertwined in experience.

Michael Polanyi has elucidated the way in which disciplines may function on different levels and how they may relate to each other in what he calls a stratified hierarchy. In his book *The Tacit Dimension* he investigates the nature of human

knowledge at various levels of comprehensiveness. By using vivid and apt examples, Polanyi describes exceedingly complex relationships so that they can be
apprehended and remembered. One illustration shows clearly what is meant by the
difference in logical levels among various bodies of knowledge. "Take the art of
making bricks," Polanyi writes.

> It relies on its raw materials placed on a level below it. But above the brickmaker there
> operates the architect, relying on the brickmaker's work, and the architect in his turn
> has to serve the town planner. To these four successive levels there correspond four
> successive levels of rules. The laws of physics and chemistry govern the raw material
> of bricks; technology prescribes the art of brickmaking; architecture teaches the build-
> ers; and the rules of town planning control the town planners.[10]

Each successive level relies on the knowledge of those disciplines lower in the
stratified hierarchy. Yet the terms "lower" and "higher" do not denote greater or
lesser value. Each discipline is indispensable to the whole. A house that has poorly
made bricks because of insufficient knowledge of the laws of physics and chemistry is uninhabitable, even if it is architecturally brilliant. While town planners may
have greater power to conceive the total environment of the town, the bricklayers
have power over their own sphere, and competence in their task is an irreplaceable
contribution toward the desired end. Polanyi's idea of stratified hierarchy is a comment on the logic of the relationships among disciplines. Explaining the contours of
this logic, he emphasizes that "the operations of a higher level cannot be accounted
for by the laws governing its particulars forming the lower level."[11]

Perhaps it will be helpful to look at another vivid example. Polanyi notes that
when giving a speech one must have mastery of voice, words, sentences, style and
literary composition. But "you cannot derive a vocabulary from phonetics; you cannot derive a grammar of a language from its vocabulary; a correct use of grammar
does not account for good style; and good style does not provide the content of a
piece of prose."[12] Each level of mastery relies on the level beneath it, but one cannot logically account for the higher level in the terms of the lower: "Comprehensive
entities exist in a peculiar logical combination of consecutive levels of reality. . . .
Each higher principle controls the boundary left indeterminate by the next lower
principle. It relies for its operations on the lower principle without interfering with
its laws. . . . The higher principle is logically unaccountable in terms of the lower."[13]

From the standpoint of faith, theology is obviously higher than psychology on
the scale of Polanyi's stratified hierarchy. Thus, theology controls the boundary left
indeterminate by psychology, but it relies on knowledge gathered by psychology in
its own distinct sphere. Theology does not interfere with the free functioning of

---

[10]Michael Polanyi, *The Tacit Dimension* (Gloucester, Mass.: Peter Smith, 1983), p. 35.
[11]Ibid., p. 36.
[12]Ibid.
[13]Ibid., p. 49.

psychology, but we cannot derive our theology, our ultimate beliefs about God, human beings and the world, from within the sphere of psychological assumptions. Any attempt to understand the essence of theological affirmations in psychological terms is as fruitless as a brickmaker's attempt to explain architecture by means of his knowledge of the physics and chemistry of brickmaking. Polanyi's case against reductionism is impressive. He regards the effort to account for the higher operations in the terms of the lower as "patent nonsense."[14]

Although Polanyi uses the term *stratified hierarchy,* he is not presupposing common standards of measurement among the various disciplines. The skills and knowledge necessary for good brickmaking, for example, are incommensurate with the skills and knowledge required by the architect. Remember that it was the issue of incommensurability that led me to reject the term hierarchy and to instead use the concept of asymmetry. Even though we are using terms differently, I believe that Polanyi's description of stratified hierarchy helps elucidate what I mean by asymmetry.

There is a particularity to theology that Polanyi does not discuss. The peculiar logical status of theology, that which makes it radically incommensurable with any other scientific discipline, has to do with the uniqueness of its subject matter. While theology itself is obviously a human enterprise, the event that theology seeks to describe faithfully and to present conceptually is an event that has no parallel or counterpart in human history, namely, God's crossing of the ontological divide by becoming incarnate in Jesus Christ, by living and dying as a human being in history, and by being raised from the dead. All other disciplines seek to ground their knowledge in empirical reality; only theology speaks of an event that is both empirical and transcendent.

Psychology may responsibly speak of a person's conscious concept of God or unconscious image of God. It may examine one's self-understanding in relation to one's understanding of God. It may even speak of how one interprets experiences that one deems religious. But by virtue of its delimited subject matter, psychology cannot speak of God himself in his relationship with human beings. Only a theology that has God's self-revelation as its methodological point of departure can purport to speak of God. Its framework indicates the very different basis on which theological knowledge is based. From a theological perspective, even our knowledge of human beings is derived from God's revelation of true humanity as we come to know it in Jesus Christ. A theological understanding of human beings therefore functions at a different logical level than our knowledge of human beings that is derived from psychology. Theology and psychology cannot be integrated into one comprehensive system of thought without doing violence to the varying logical levels of meaning.

---

[14]Ibid., p. 37.

No Translation

Because they function on these differing logical levels, theological and psychologi-cal concepts cannot be translated into each other's idioms. As an example let us think about the concept of shame as it functions within these two different con-texts. If we are speaking of the concept of shame from a theological perspective, we cannot assume that a psychological understanding of shame means essentially the same thing. Unlike psychological understandings of shame, biblical understand-ings of shame are always placed in the context of a person's primary relationship with God. Think of the psalmist's preoccupation with his fear of being put to shame. He repeatedly calls on God to rescue him and to save him from shame for the sake of God's honor. The psalmist sees himself as being graciously delivered from shame in the face of his enemies because he has remained true to God. He believes that because he has taken up God's cause and God's honor, he too will be lifted up above his enemies.

Another primary biblical use of the concept of shame is in regard to the shame of being a sinner before God. Thus Peter despairs of his sinful heart when he rec-ognizes the holiness of Jesus as Lord: "Depart from me, for I am a sinful man, O Lord" (Lk 5:8 RSV). The publican recognizes his utter sinfulness and stands in shame before God, not daring to lift his eyes. Unlike the foolish Pharisee, he knows how futile human boasting or attempts at self-justification are in the face of God's holi-ness. While in both of these examples there is a horizontal dimension to the expe-rience of shame (the psalmist is rescued from shame before his enemies, and the publican humbles himself in contrast to the Pharisee, who raises himself up), the primary meaning of the term *shame* is derived from the vertical dimension, from the reality of being a sinner before God. As sinners we throw ourselves on God's mercy and are thereby delivered from shame. God covers our shame with the cloak of his mercy and righteousness.

By contrast, psychology focuses on shame as an effect that arises in the context of human relationships. Feelings of exposure and inadequacy arise whenever there is a rupture in a relationship with a highly valued other person, or as one writer puts it, when there is a "break in the interpersonal bridge."[15] If a child has such experiences again and again, and if the valued other person does not seek to repair the damage done by the rupture, the child will eventually internalize the shame. Over time such internalized shame will bring about enduring feelings of worthless-ness, deficiency or inadequacy. One's whole sense of identity may become bound up with shame. In such circumstances, there is little that enables a person to build a foundation for positive self-esteem. People who are bound up with shame come to believe that they are in fact inferior, defective, inadequate or worthless.

But should such feelings of worthlessness be equated with shame over sin in the

---

[15]Gershen Kaufman, *Shame: The Power of Caring* (Cambridge, Mass.: Schenkman, 1980), p. 11.

theological sense? To equate the two would confuse two universes of discourse that function on different levels of meaning. The meaning of the term *shame* changes when we shift from a theological context to a psychological context. Yet there is a vast amount of literature today that glosses over or confuses these important distinctions. In this literature the language of sin is considered to be harmful to a person's growing self-esteem. New liturgies have even been devised that leave out the confession of sin because it might make people feel badly about themselves. In such cases the creators of liturgy clearly do not understand that the language of sin functions in a radically different context, the context of the gospel as a whole.

In the gospel as I understand it, knowledge of sin and the shame that accompanies it lead to repentance, forgiveness, renewal, vocation and finally joy (2 Cor 7:9-10). Shame is a single moment along a continuum that leads eventually to the lifting up of the sinner, to the recognition that though one is a sinner, one is a forgiven sinner; indeed, that one is a beloved child of God. Known sin is always forgiven sin because one cannot be aware of what sin is apart from a knowledge of what God has already done in Jesus Christ to overcome and defeat sin. As one who belongs to Jesus Christ in life and in death, one is lifted up with a sense of awe at such an honor. I cannot imagine a more stable foundation for true self-esteem than to know that one's most enduring identity is that of being a beloved child of God.

The Logical Precedence of Theology

If we use faith as a means to an end, as a mere method for improving self-esteem, we will be reversing the asymmetrical order between the disciplines. To make faith a means to an end other than faith itself is to assume that the proposed end is of greater value than faith. In our interdisciplinary field, where psychological norms play an important role in diagnosis and treatment, we sometimes fail to see that in subtle ways what we hold to be normative for the life of faith begins to play a subordinate role to the supposedly greater good of mental health.

This shift has begun to occur, for example, when people understand prayer as a resource for healing. Healing is conceived of as the goal toward which all our efforts are straining. If prayer relieves stress and thereby contributes to healing, then it must be used because it is an important resource, the argument goes. Empirical studies have been published that show a positive correlation between the use of prayer and physical and emotional healing. Some people consider such studies to be a good apologetic for prayer, and some have been convinced enough by the studies to engage in daily prayer for the sake of its practical benefits. But the real focus and purpose of prayer as the means of intimate communion with God has been lost. Everything has been turned upside down. Instead of God being at the center of our lives, our emotional or mental health occupies the center. God thus becomes a helpful adjunct to our self-determined goals.

When biblical and theological concepts are put into an overarching psychological framework, this reversal of values takes place. When prayer and confession, Scripture and forgiveness are used as biblical principles and practices to be integrated into psychological counseling, they may subtly begin to serve different ends than those they are meant to serve in the life of faith. They become relativized by their overarching psychological context.

Newton Maloney points out in a recent review of a book that seeks to integrate biblical principles and practices into counseling, "[The author] does not seem to realize that the only legitimate function that any methodology, including spiritual practices, can serve in a counseling situation is to alleviate distress and enhance adaptation to the culture in which a person chooses to live."[16] Maloney's basic assumption is the reverse of my own. He is assuming an asymmetrical relationship between the disciplines, but in the reverse order. He is assuming that the norms and values of psychology set the terms of the overarching context, rather than the reverse. Thus Scripture and prayer would become the means to the end of alleviating distress and enhancing adaptation. By contrast, I am interested in bringing psychological principles and practices to bear on counseling that is set within a biblical and theological context.

The affirmation of Job, "though he slay me, yet will I trust in him" (Job 13:15 KJV), is incomprehensible to people for whom the norms of psychology have priority. Job could only be masochistic to give voice to such an utterance. But Job is affirming faith in the midst of incomprehensible suffering at the hand of an incomprehensible God who is to be loved and feared above all else. No other value has priority, neither health nor family nor honor nor material goods nor even life itself, but only faith and trust in God, even though Job perceives God as his enemy and slayer. To acknowledge the profundity of Job's faith, even if we cannot remotely approach it in our own life, is to understand something of what it means to say that the norms and values internal to faith have logical precedence over all externally derived norms and values. Other norms and values are therefore necessarily relativized whenever they come into conflict with faith in God. Faith, or rather God as the object of faith, is to be placed at the very center of our lives. All other values and relationships are ordered around this central relationship.

Before we turn from the topic of the asymmetrical ordering of the two disciplines, I would like to make a few additional comments, lest I be misunderstood. The asymmetrical ordering of the relationship between psychology and theology follows logically, I believe, from the first commandment, that we must have no other gods before God. But that is not to say that the norms and values of psychology are themselves unimportant. Penultimate values may not be ultimate, but they

---

[16]See Newton Maloney's review of Mark McMinn, *Psychology, Theology and Spirituality in Christian Counseling* (Wheaton, Ill: Tyndale House, 1996), in *Journal of Pastoral Care* 51, no. 1 (spring 1997):119.

are nonetheless extremely valuable. Who among us would scorn the value of emotional health or good communication skills or nurturing parenting? Who among us would easily cast aside the importance of healthy social adjustment for our children and basic acceptance by their peers?

I am affirming that the gospel makes ultimate claims on us, claims that need to be reflected in our theological concepts, but I do not want to be understood as saying that psychology has little or nothing to offer. On the contrary, I have spent my entire adult life studying psychology. I believe that psychology has much to offer Christians who seek to worship God with all their heart, soul, mind and strength and to love their neighbor as themselves. I believe that the study of psychology in relation to theology has the potential to enrich and deepen our life of faith, sometimes in unexpected ways. Although I share many of the concerns expressed by those who are worried about what has been called the "triumph of the therapeutic" in the church, I believe that psychology has much to contribute to the pastoral art of caring for the soul. While I do not want to lose theology's distinctive concepts or collapse them into psychological discourse, I do not believe that the solution that will protect our theological inheritance is to ignore the gifts that psychology can bring to ministry.

Before turning to a discussion of three of the gifts that psychology can bring to ministry, let us find a clearing, hold the light directly over our maps, and assess where we have gone thus far. When we started out, we were lost in the woods, pondering the various maps we had with us and wondering where they all led. We found our theological compass by extracting the formal pattern of thought from the Chalcedonian definition of the relationship between Christ's two natures. We discussed what it means to affirm that Christ's two natures are related without confusion and change on the one hand and without separation or division on the other. We first asked how these affirmations apply substantively to Jesus Christ in the incarnation and then how the formal Chalcedonian pattern might be applied to the relationship between the disciplines of theology and psychology. Finally, we spent some time on the question of asymmetrical order, trying to draw out the implications of saying that theology has logical precedence over psychology. Now we will focus on the gifts that psychology brings to the pastoral art of the care of souls.

I will focus on only three gifts, though many more could be mentioned. We will consider gifts from the tradition that I know best, the one that arises out of the insights of Freud and Jung, though a different and perhaps equally compelling list of gifts could be drawn up by a cognitive or behavioral psychologist or a family systems theoretician. We will look at three fundamental psychological concepts: first, the theory of the unconscious; second, the therapeutic or pastoral relationship as the context for healing; and third, psychotherapy's attention to process. In each case, I will show how theology can rely on insights from psychology to deepen its own art of pastoral care without reducing pastoral care to psychotherapy. Pastoral

care is ministry, and it is appropriately judged by its own intrinsic theological criteria; nevertheless, it can rely on insights from the sister discipline of psychology,
which lies directly below it in the stratified hierarchy.

Psychology's First Gift to Theology: The Theory of the Unconscious

Despite a range of questions and criticisms that have been leveled at modern psychoanalytic theory since it began and that persist into the present day, it seems
unlikely that the idea of the unconscious will ever lose its illuminating power.[17] To
truly love God with all our heart, soul, mind and strength requires that we know
not only something about the object of our love, namely, God, but also something
about the subject, namely, the nature of our heart, soul and mind. The theory of the
unconscious assumes that we know very little about who we actually are. It claims
that most of what motivates us, most of what we feel, think, desire and hope for,
lies outside of our awareness. The theory of the unconscious provides a way for us
to become acquainted with ourselves, with our soul in all its richness, mystery and
complexity.

Both Freud and Jung worked with dreams. Each spent years learning to decipher these strange nocturnal messengers. Anyone who has worked at understanding her dreams over a period of years and has thus mined the depths of her
unconscious processes can attest to the inestimable value of learning about aspects
of herself that she never imagined were there. My teacher Ann Ulanov used to
describe the unconscious as a river of being moving below the surface of consciousness and teeming with life. To fall asleep and to dream is to become present
to all of that vitality, to all of those wishes, longings, fears, hopes, sorrows and joys
that lie outside of our awareness much of the time.

The maps of our inner landscape that have been so carefully drawn up by psychologists of the unconscious can also give us insight into the way in which we
come to imagine God on the basis of our early life experiences with our parents
and other caregivers. We can dismiss such knowledge as a mere projection of our
unconscious desires onto the unknown screen of eternity and call it an illusion as
Freud did, or we can disregard such knowledge because it tells us nothing about
God's actual identity, which can be known only by revelation, as Barth did. But we
would be wiser, I believe, to pay attention to those projected images because the
stuff of our very psyche is hidden in them. Their value lies not in what they tell us
about God (in that I believe that Barth is right), but rather in what they tell us about
ourselves. We must not disregard or disparage these creations of our psyches; we
need to respect them even when they conflict with the way the Bible depicts God's

---

[17]For a thoughtful assessment of recent challenges to Freud's basic discoveries, see Richard
Webster, "The Bewildered Visionary," in *The Times Literary Supplement,* May 16, 1997, pp.
10-11.

identity. If we attend to these idiosyncratic images of God, we may learn much about the deeply-felt needs and wishes, sorrows and longings of our earliest years.

A woman who was abandoned in early childhood, for example, may find herself returning again and again to the contemplation of Christ's moment of utter forsakenness on the cross. A man who was abused as an infant but has repressed all memory of the abuse may find the memory pushing its way into his consciousness by means of his preoccupation with the question of God's trustworthiness. A woman's sense of personal autonomy and agency may have been so undermined because of a traumatic loss at an early stage of her development that she now pictures God as a kind of deus ex machina, as the active partner while she remains passive, dependent and helpless.

These hypothetical examples are not meant to show how God's image can become a veritable Rorschach inkblot test, but rather to suggest that psychology has something to offer Christians as they ponder what they bring into their life with God. Surely we all distort God's identity, for our human imaginings are so meager and paltry and inadequate. To be sure, our human images are sometimes used by God, in spite of their complete inadequacy, to give us knowledge of who God really is. But we cannot test whether this is the case on the basis of the images themselves. Our images must always be tested in the light of what we learn about God in Jesus Christ. And even when our God representations tell us nothing reliable about God, they always tell us a great deal of value about ourselves. Our representations of God represent the human expectations, desires and fears that we bring into our relationship with God.

In some cases a person's conscious understanding of God conflicts with his unconscious image of God. His carefully reasoned theological views may function psychologically as a defense against his very threatening inner image of God. Perhaps you know someone whose theology seems to be a weapon with which to bully those who see things differently. Theological disagreements with him create an emotional atmosphere fraught with tension. I believe that a knowledge of the unconscious might give such a person theoretical and practical tools for self-inquiry. Why is he holding his picture of God so rigidly? Perhaps he is not simply expressing zeal for the Lord. Perhaps he is being threatened from within by an unconscious image of God that contradicts his theologically orthodox, consciously held understanding. He has to defensively uphold his conscious understanding in order to drown out inner voices of self-doubt and fear.

Such a person may consciously love and seek to serve God, but that love might not reach down into his unconscious roots. Hiding underneath the surface might be a powerful image of a sadistic, persecuting God who delights in human misery, or perhaps an abandoning God who doesn't care about human anguish. Whenever people hold theological beliefs defensively, whenever they seem to be greatly threatened by disagreement, we can wonder whether there is a different image of

God threatening them from within. Depth psychology offers us tools for investigating such a hypothesis.

Depth psychology and its understanding of the unconscious also give us conceptual tools for understanding events that cannot be understood from within a theological frame of reference, but that affect the life of faith dramatically. I recently heard a tragic story of a woman in another culture and country whose pastor and church leaders believed that she was demonically possessed. She was hearing voices, and she believed that she was pregnant with Isaac, the child of the promise. Members of her church prayed for her and with her again and again, but nothing seemed to help. Eventually they held prayer meetings for hours at a time and beat her until she was bruised, trying to rid her soul of the destructive powers that were tormenting her. Her brother learned of these events and did everything he could to intervene. Though he lived literally on the other side of the world from his sister, he persevered until he found a Christian psychologist who could help her.

The psychologist learned that the woman was suffering from depression, rage and repressed grief over the seven abortions she had undergone at the instigation of her husband's family. In her culture, as in many of the cultures during biblical times, everything depended on having a son. Each time she had been pregnant, this woman had learned with the help of modern diagnostic tests that the child she carried was a daughter. Her husband was the last male descendent of his ancestral line, and he had insisted that his wife wait until she conceived a son before carrying a child to term and giving birth. He and his family had insisted not once or twice but seven times, until her grief and rage could be repressed no longer and issued forth in extreme symptoms.

I do not use this example to suggest that demonic possession is always a case of psychopathology. I do not understand the mystery of demonic possession, but I suspect that such cases may exist. In this instance, however, I am quite certain that the members of the church were in over their heads. They were not good diagnosticians. They did not investigate the woman's history closely. They used the theological and spiritual tools that were available to them without asking whether other tools would be more fitting and appropriate. They disregarded psychological perspectives or collapsed them into a single theological perspective. They understood everything to be a consequence of sin, and they apparently allowed no room for other possible explanations. Their diagnostic framework was too narrowly theological; it was made to do work it was not equipped to do. Because they did not differentiate the psychological side enough, they effectively silenced any independent points of view that it might have offered.

This case is quite dramatic, but there are perhaps dozens of events in any person's life that could bring tremendous insight and healing if they were interpreted according to the psychology of the unconscious. "What are the blocks that keep me from forgiving my parents no matter how hard I try?" one young woman asks.

Rather than heaping guilt and scorn on herself for not being able to forgive as she has been forgiven, she would do well to investigate whether she has fully uncovered her own unconscious grief and anger. "Why do I keep having sexual fantasies that come into my mind against my will and make me feel degraded?" an older man asks. He could be advised to pray about it, and it would be good for him to do so. But a psychological perspective would begin with the hypothesis that there is an unconscious reason for such fantasies, then would seek their hidden meaning. If the man simply turns in horror from his fantasies and tries harder to repress them, they will return with even more intensity, as repressed contents inevitably do.[18]

In each of these cases understanding and healing may come not primarily by means of theological investigation and its use of the conceptual category of sin, but rather by means of a search for the unconscious threads that the mind has woven into a pattern of meaning outside of awareness. If we confront these issues solely from a theological perspective, separating them from the underlying psychological dynamics that are at work, we are in danger of misapprehending them. We are unable to give real pastoral help if we insist exclusively on diagnosing sin and offering forgiveness, when instead what is needed is careful attention to how the person has been hurt or traumatized. A knowledge of how the unconscious mind uses various defense mechanisms to cope with trauma can be a priceless treasure for people who desire to learn the pastoral art of caring for the soul.

Psychology's Second Gift: The Pastoral Relationship as the Context for Healing
The church has long known of the healing power of relationship, for we are instructed to place every condition of our lives, whether joyful or sorrowful, in the context of our relationship with God. Our identities as human beings are constituted as persons-in-relationship, and the church as a fellowship of believers is a source of lifelong comfort, strength, accountability and companionship. We are continually called into fellowship with God in prayer and into fellowship with one another in marriage, in friendship, in parenting and especially in the church. What particular gift does psychotherapy bring if the church has known the value of relationship all along?

First, let us consider two closely related ideas: the concept of the therapeutic relationship as a *holding environment,* and the phenomenon of transference. Child psychotherapist D. W. Winnicott calls the therapeutic relationship a holding environment, comparing it to the primary mother-infant bond. The infant is understood to be threatened by anxiety because she can neither fend for herself in the outer world nor always cope with intense feelings from within. The mother, or mothering

---

[18]See Ann Belford Ulanov, "The Perverse and the Transcendent," in *The Functioning Transcendent: A Study in Analytical Psychology* (Wilmette, Ill: Chiron, 1996), pp. 52-71, for a fascinating case study on this issue.

person, knows how to help contain this anxiety, first by providing a stable nonanxious presence; second by introducing the world to the child in small, manageable steps; and third by mirroring back the child to herself. The empathetic mother will know how to intervene when anxiety threatens to overwhelm the child.

In an analogous fashion, the empathetic therapist provides a stable environment for a person who is going back and emotionally reliving early anxiety-provoking moments from infancy and early childhood. All of the ritual aspects of psychotherapy as a cultural form—a specific time and place, a reliable and empathetic listener, a set fee, a known way of investigating psychic phenomena—are predictable ways of being and interacting that help to provide a secure and safe structure for the relationship, which is seen as a kind of container for the person's anxiety.

In the life of faith innumerable issues may raise our anxiety, and there are few places where those issues can be explored safely. In many churches any exploration of sexuality provokes intense anxiety. Furthermore, a congregant's questions about what he believes deep down about God, or his fears about whether his beliefs are orthodox or about whether he is saved may be sources of nagging, ongoing concern. Sometimes people experience shame or anguish over their sins or wrongdoings and fear judgment by their fellow believers. In all of these instances, a relationship with a pastoral counselor who is pledged not to exploit counselees' vulnerability and who will explore the consequences of their sin without playing God by standing in judgment may be a container strong enough and safe enough to provide the kind of stability that is needed.

The second, closely related, idea is psychotherapy's concept of transference. "Defined most simply, transference is a phenomenon when one person becomes the carrier for an unconscious content activated in another person. That content carries into the present moment conflicting and unassimilated feelings about figures in the past that distort the perception of the present person or situation."[19] Transference is similar to projection except that it is not so much a matter of a single trait being projected onto someone else as it is matter of a whole complex of issues that belong to a relationship in the past being transferred to a relationship in the present. Transference occurs unconsciously; one consciously thinks that one is accurately perceiving the other in the present.

How might a knowledge of transference phenomena be helpful to those who seek to care for the soul? The skillful pastoral counselor who understands transference phenomena will know how to work with a counselee's intense feelings. First, she will understand that many of the feelings that the counselee has toward her do not belong personally to her, but are instead clues to understanding the counselee's

---

[19]Ann Belford Ulanov, "Transference/Countertransference: A Jungian Perspective," in *The Functioning Transcendent: A Study in Analytical Psychology* (Wilmette, Ill: Chiron, 1996), p. 123.

past relationships, particularly those of early childhood. For painful, unresolved issues from the past become present in the transference. The present relationship thus provides access to issues that would otherwise remain inaccessible. In a very real sense the past is never really past, for it lives on within the unconscious mind. Whatever has not been healed pushes for recognition and attention in the present relationship.

One simple example is so common that it is the subject of rueful humor among therapists: the client's reaction to the therapist's annual vacation. From a conscious standpoint, the fears of abandonment that begin to arise in the counselee when the therapist prepares to go on vacation may seem unreasonable and out of proportion, even to the counselee. Intense, irrational, vivid, there are the fears in all their full-ness, not to be denied. What is going on here? Now that the counselee is in a relationship that provides enough safety, that functions as a protective container for all his repressed anxiety, he can afford to experience the terrors that he felt as a child but that he had to repress at the time. The transference relationship offers him an opportunity to regain lost parts of himself. Those feelings of fear and anger long hidden can now surface and be integrated into his adult ego. Once these feelings become fully conscious, they will lose their determining power over his choices. Whenever feelings that were unconscious are made conscious, the ego is strength-ened.

When Freud generalized about the nature of transference, he emphasized two issues of overriding importance, namely, unresolved feelings of a sexual or aggressive nature. Conflicts about need and dependency, about sexual desire and long-ing, and about power and authority were the kinds of issues that he found to be most often problematic. Untrained counselors who do not understand the nature of these phenomena can easily fall into destructive power struggles on the one hand or destructive sexual acting out on the other. Theology does not have the conceptual resources for working directly with these kinds of unconscious dynamics. Simply labeling aggressive or sexual wishes as sinful and then struggling against them consciously, trying to keep them repressed, actually increases their power because repressed wishes continue to push for expression. By contrast, allowing those wishes into awareness by means of transference, and suffering them consciously, reduces their power.

Psychology's Third Gift: Attention to Process

The third gift that psychotherapy brings to people who are learning the pastoral art of caring for the soul is its detailed attention to process. There are numerous questions of primary importance in the work of counseling that have to do not essentially with content, but rather with process. How do you develop emotional rapport with another human being? How do you ask questions that deepen emotional contact but are not invasive? How do you accurately read the meaning of a person's body language, eye contact or tone of voice? How do you confront someone in a way that maximizes your chances of being heard instead of being dismissed defensively? How do you show a counselee that you have heard her accurately, and how do you communicate your respect for her? How do you tune into your own feelings as a way to help you understand the feelings of the person you are counseling? How do you address transference and countertransference issues in a way that minimizes possible embarrassment and maximizes potential insight? When is it appropriate to use a story from your own life to show a counselee that you have understood him? How do you develop a sense of timing, learning to make interpretations in the right way and at the right time? In all of these ways and many more, psychotherapy has much to teach people who are engaged in the practice of the pastoral arts.

These kinds of issues are addressed by every pastoral-counselor-in-training, every beginning chaplain and every student of clinical pastoral education. Some of us take these issues so much for granted that we lose sight of just how much there is to learn, and how much we have already learned from the field of psychotherapy. But curiously we have not yet fully integrated these insights into our pastoral functioning. Pastors and pastoral counselors seem quite able to function in these ways when they are operating out of a psychological frame of reference, but when they move into their strictly pastoral role, they seem less capable of continuing to pay attention to issues of process. One prominent pastoral theologian writes:

> Prayer and theological reflection are crucial resources to be used in some form within the counseling process. However, much of my praying and theological thinking takes place outside the actual counseling hour and counseling relationship. I offer prayers of intercession for my counselees in the privacy of my own devotional life. The counseling relationship also generates many insights of a spiritual and theological nature, but I do not share them with the counselees because I am reluctant to turn the counseling session into a classroom, fearing that prayer and the sharing of theological insights would disrupt the therapeutic process.[20]

Why should prayer necessarily disrupt the therapeutic process? Why should the sharing of theological insight necessarily turn a counseling session into a classroom? Could the counselor not share a theological insight with the same kind of careful attention to timing, body language and overall process that she would have if she were sharing a psychological insight?

I believe that process skills are best learned through apprenticeship: by undergoing counseling oneself, by observing and imitating one's mentors and teachers, by undergoing supervision of one's counseling work, and by participating in a process group. Pastoral counseling is a process that involves us as whole persons; it is

---

[20]Edward P. Wimberly, *Prayer in Pastoral Counseling* (Louisville, Ky.: Westminster John Knox, 1990), p 15.

not simply a skill that can be mastered. Counseling is not a matter of an expert telling a beginner "how to do it." Sometimes all the counselor can do is provide general guidelines.

When offering a prayer the pastoral counselor must not only be true to the scriptural witness, but also address the particularities of the situation before her. The prayer must be sensitively attuned to all the issues of context, both the wider context and the more immediate interpersonal context. Similarly, the counselor should introduce interpretations using theological concepts in the same manner in which she would introduce interpretations using strictly psychological concepts. She should give the same kind of exquisite attention to the particular situation, need and language of the counselee. In no sense should the counselor turn the counseling room into a classroom. The counselor should always consider the process dynamics of intervention.

In pastoral counseling, every level of the counselor's person is engaged—his thinking, his feeling and his willing. Therefore, though I am very much against the conceptual integration of theoretical categories of interpretation, I am very much for personal integration—intellectually, emotionally and spiritually. The more fluently the counselor speaks the language of faith and understand the concepts of theology from the inside, the better. The more the counselor can integrate skills such as active listening and asking noninvasive questions into his normal way of functioning, the better. The more the counselor becomes a person of prayer and feels at home in taking everything before God, the better. Pastoral counseling is not just a role that one puts on like a lab coat when one goes to work; rather, it needs to be wholly integrated into one's personal way of functioning.

Conclusion

By emphasizing the asymmetrical ordering of theology and psychology, I have sought to illustrate what it might mean to "seek first His kingdom" (Mt 6:33 NASB) in the context of pastoral counseling as a ministry of the church. But as we seek that kingdom together, let us not neglect the conceptual and practical tools that psychology and psychotherapy have given to the church.

When we considered the disciplines of theology and psychology in relation to each other, we affirmed six basic theses:

1. When theology and psychology are used as interpretive frameworks in the context of pastoral counseling, each has autonomy in terms of its distinctive methods, aims, norms and linguistic conventions.

2. When we seek to understand persons in their psychological and spiritual wholeness, it is important not to separate these two conceptual frameworks from each other. Though they are to be clearly distinguished, they are not to be separated from one another.

3. The counselor must conceive of these conceptual frameworks as incommen-

surable languages that function on different logical levels; it would be a mistake to try to integrate them with each other at the conceptual level.

4. The counselor must place psychological discourse into the larger theological framework of meaning, rather than the reverse.

5. People who seek to learn the pastoral art of caring for the soul can study psychology and apply some of its concepts and skills to pastoral counseling, in particular psychology's theory of the unconscious, its understanding of the therapeutic relationship as the context of healing, and its attention to questions of process.

6. Although it is a mistake to strive for systematic or conceptual integration of the theological and psychological modes of discourse, it is crucially important to integrate them in practice at the level of personal integration—intellectually, emotionally and spiritually—so that the skill of using these ways of thinking and speaking becomes a part of who the pastoral counselor is, part of the counselor's ordinary way of functioning.

To do the work of pastoral counseling is one way among others that the church has for seeking to love God with all our heart, soul, mind and strength, and our neighbors as ourselves.

11

HEALING THE WOUNDS OF MEMORY

Theology & Psychology on Salvation & Sin

L. Gregory Jones

WO CLICHÉS ARE OFTEN INVOKED IN RELATION TO SITUATIONS OF UNRESOLVED conflict: *forgive and forget* and *time heals all wounds*. There is a certain measure of folk wisdom in each of these sayings, wisdom that has enabled the sayings to endure and to be passed on from generation to generation. We recognize that there is a danger in claiming to forgive someone, yet remembering the offense so that it can be used against the person in a future argument or conflict. We know of situations and relationships in which we needed to let the past stay in the past because otherwise the past would burden us and prevent us from envisioning a better, more life-giving future. Further, we know that some wounds just take time to heal. Given time, our bodies' wondrous restorative healing power enables them to heal so well that we forget the wounds were even there.

But we also know the limits of these sayings, particularly the latter one. We know that time does not heal all wounds; if it did, we wouldn't need surgeons and psychiatrists. We know that time allows many untreated wounds to become infected and to fester, and we know that the infection can spread throughout our bodies. A more accurate saying would be "Time heals some wounds but causes some untreated wounds to develop an infection that can spread." But that does not sound nearly as pithy.

We are less attentive to the limits of the saying *forgive and forget.* The phrase implies that the real struggle for us is to learn to forgive others; it presumes our power and control. But it is at least as important for us to learn to be forgiven. That is the logic of Matthew 7:1-5, that we are willing to judge and forgive others but rarely see a need for someone to judge and forgive us.

But a deeper problem with the phrase *forgive and forget* is that we have so closely linked the logic of forgiving and that of forgetting that we rarely subject them to scrutiny to see if they belong together in the ways we expect. One issue, of course, is the time required for healing wounds, the timefulness of forgiveness. C. S. Lewis writes of discovering after over thirty years that he had finally forgiven someone. If it takes that long to discover forgiveness in some situations or relationships, how much more might we carry the burden of a memory formed and nurtured over at least that long a time?

Perhaps the second cliché, *time heals all wounds,* helps to minimize the potential danger of equating forgiveness with forgetting. Perhaps if we take a long enough view of the time necessary to heal all wounds, then we can have confidence that eventually—and perhaps only after this life—we will be enabled to link our forgiveness to an ability to forget. However, maybe we neither can nor should forget the sins that we have committed or suffered, sins that exemplify and exacerbate our separation from God and from one another. Could it be that the injunction to forgive and forget actually inhibits our ability to embody God's forgiveness as holy people? I fear that linking forgiveness with forgetting tempts us to worship an uncrucified Christ, rather than Christ who was crucified and has risen.

There are important psychological, moral and theological issues involved in the dynamics of remembering and forgetting in relation to forgiveness. Psychologically, a crucial question is this: can we find ways to forget things that have happened without unhealthily repressing the memories? Morally a crucial question is this: should we try to forget, or does that involve a betrayal of those we have sinned against, of those who have sinned against us, of loved ones who have suffered, and of innocent victims whom we may have never met? Theologically a crucial question is this: what would it mean for us to learn to remember well and, as Miroslav Volf has recently suggested, to receive a divine gift of nonremembering?

My analysis will proceed in three steps. First, I will distinguish several diverse ways in which memory of the past becomes a burden for us, and I will also suggest some of the complexities of memory. Second, I will analyze ways in which forgiveness can be linked to learning to remember the past differently, and therefore well. More specifically I will explore the location of our memory—and our forgiveness—in the wounds of Christ, and I will consider what that entails for how we think about the dynamics of remembering and forgetting. In the third and final section, I will offer some proposals about the important roles theology and psychology can each play in fostering Christian practices that contribute to healing the wounds of memory.

Memory as a Burden

We all know how tricky our memory can be. Some things we want desperately to remember but we seemingly cannot, so we are endlessly searching for the car keys. Other things we would be content to forget, but we seemingly cannot. Those memories are often triggered in unpredictable ways: by dreams, by traveling to a place that stimulates memories we had long forgotten, even by a song playing in an elevator or a shopping mall.

There are, of course, additional issues, some having to do with the physiological make-up of the brain. For example, we are physiologically unable to remember everything we experience. This is both a blessing and a curse: a blessing because the selectivity of our perception prevents us from being overwhelmed by sensory data, a curse because often we become unable to remember that which is most important to us. This selectivity is complicated by age-related differences in the brain. Young children are not able to remember as much as adults can, and as the painful experiences of sufferers of Alzheimer's disease illustrates, many people struggle with the physiological deterioration of memory in older adulthood.[1]

In addition, we know how easy it is for our memory to play tricks on us. We like to think of our minds as neutral data repositories that simply store information, but we also know how easily our memories are distorted by such factors as our selective perception, our emotion, our biases and prejudices, our prior experiences and cultural and gender-related issues. Furthermore, other people can affect or even alter our memories by using the power of suggestion. Most poignantly there is the complex difficulty of repressed memories. We must struggle to discern when people are genuinely recovering memories of events long past and when they are creating new memories through the power of suggestion on the part of therapists or other persons. One of the most famous of these cases involved the late Cardinal Joseph Bernardin. After provoking tremendous publicity and great anguish, Bernardin's accuser acknowledged that the "recovered memory" was inaccurate.

To these physiological and psychological issues involved in remembering and forgetting, we must add the theological complexity of sin. As David Keck rightly suggests, sin is both a cause and effect of forgetting:

> Despite the Deuteronomist's warning to the Israelites to take heed lest they forget the Lord and sin (Deut 8:11), the Israelites were quite proficient at not remembering. Israel's idolatry and ingratitude towards the late Gideon's family is interwoven with the fact that "the people of Israel did not remember the LORD their God" (Judg 8:34). Similar tapestries of forgetfulness and sin are found throughout the prophets (e.g. Neh 9:17). Likewise, the testimonies of our own forgetfulness are legion. The adulterer forgets the spouse, the rich forget the poor, the friend forgets the friend.[2]

---

[1]For a provocative discussion of memory, Alzheimer's and theology, see David Keck, *Forgetting Whose We Are: Alzheimer's Disease and the Love of God* (Nashville, Tenn.: Abingdon, 1996). Keck's analysis has helped me to identify a number of the complexities involved in memory and theology, and I express my indebtedness to this work for much of my analysis in this first section.
[2]Ibid., p. 58.

Sometimes the selectivity of memory comes from learning just to see what we want to see, and forgetting the rest. But it also can come from actively pretending that we have not seen or done what we know we have seen or done. As Augustine writes in his *Confessions*, "I had known it [my iniquity], but acted as though I knew it not—I winked at it and forgot it."[3] We have a remarkable capacity for learning how to forget God and our responsibilities to others; we can also forget our sins so that we can live more comfortably with ourselves.

Given such realities, we are enjoined to remember God and the realities of our lives. To be known by God is also to know oneself and to be remembered. The church has developed practices for learning to remember so that we will be able to testify to the truth and stop forgetting. Christian practices such as baptism, the Eucharist, *lectio divina* and invoking the communion of the saints help to school us as a people of memory.

Such practices are important. But what about those circumstances in which the problem is not our temptation to forget, but the horrifying presence of memories whose power paralyzes us and prevents us from envisioning a better future? How do we cope with those situations in which forgetfulness might help to enable the healing of our psyche and our relationships? This possibility is suggested with particular poignancy in Amos Elon's 1993 essay, "The Politics of Memory":

> I have lived in Israel most of my life and have come to the conclusion that where there is so much traumatic memory, so much pain, so much memory innocently or deliberately mobilized for political purposes, a little forgetfulness might finally be in order. This should not be seen as a banal plea to "forgive and forget." Forgiveness has nothing to do with it. While remembrance is often a form of vengeance, it is also, paradoxically, the basis of reconciliation. What is needed, in my view, is a shift in emphasis and proportion, and a new equilibrium in Israeli political life between memory and hope.[4]

Elon's eloquently expressed perspective addresses some of the most difficult psychological and political issues involved in remembrance's paradoxical dual function as a form of vengeance and the basis of reconciliation. What would it mean for people to discover that "a little forgetfulness might finally be in order" and to suggest, contrary to Elon's position, that forgiveness does have something to do with it?

In order to begin dealing with this issue, we need to disentangle several dynamics that are involved in the discovery of "so much traumatic memory," dynamics that all too often converge in our most difficult psychological, social and political dilemmas: problems in the Middle East, in Bosnia, in Rwanda, racial divisions in the United States, broken and oppressive family relations and so on. Disentangling these will help us to understand the overlapping issues involved in coping with searing memories.

---

[3] Augustine *Confessions and Enchirideon* 8.7, trans. Albert C. Outler (Philadelphia: Westminster Press, 1955).
[4] Amos Elon, "The Politics of Memory," *New York Review of Books* 40 (1993): 5.

First, some people have difficulty in coming to terms with a single individual episode whose horrifying effects are imprinted in their memory: the murder or suicide of a child, a rape or other sexual assault, a devastating betrayal, a bomb that destroyed home and surroundings. Lloyd LeBlanc's son was brutally murdered. (The story is told in Helen Prejean's *Dead Man Walking*.) LeBlanc struggles with memories every day of his life as he prays for the strength to forgive.

Second, some people suffer the horrors of repeated abuse, torture or other violence over time, and the effects perdure in the soul long after the beatings or the emotional assaults or the violence stops (if they stop at all).[5] This is more obviously painful when there are permanent marks or wounds left on the body, but it is no less painful—and the results are perhaps more difficult to identify and treat—when the wounds are imprinted only on the soul.[6]

Third, there are the horrors that have not only assaulted individual people in isolated acts, and others in repeated abuse and violence, but whose effects have so pervaded a culture, a people, that they are passed on from generation to generation. A particular person may not have directly experienced the horrors, but traumatic memories are the legacy of prior horrors that continue to haunt the present.

Finally, there are the horrors that sear our memories not because they have happened to us or to others we love or even to innocent strangers, but because we have been the perpetrators of them ourselves. After the end of World War II Albert Speer, a Nazi architect and Minister of Armaments, genuinely sought to repent for his complicity in the Nazi regime. Even so, he was unable ever to acknowledge the full force of what he was guilty of—most explicitly, his knowledge of the Final Solution—perhaps because he feared that he would have been unable to fully acknowledge it and continue to live.[7]

Obviously, many people may suffer from one or two of these kinds of searing memories without suffering from all four. These diverse forms of memories present different yet overlapping challenges, including the degree to which the memories reside primarily in one's mind (even if they cannot be controlled there, for both physiological and psychological reasons!) or are to be found in social and political traditions or, more generally, in some amorphous place "out there."

Our memories converge in some of our most difficult dilemmas. Their forcefulness is dramatically depicted in Toni Morrison's *Beloved*.[8] The novel focuses on the

---

[5]See the discussion in G. Simon Harak, "Child Abuse and Embodiment from a Thomistic Perspective," *Modern Theology* 11 (1995): 315-40.

[6]For a particularly powerful discussion of these issues, see Elaine Scarry, *The Body in Pain* (New York: Oxford University Press, 1985).

[7]See my analysis of Gitta Sereny's *Albert Speer: His Battle with Truth*, in "Becoming a Different Man: Inside Albert Speer," *Christian Century* 113 (1996): 516-19.

[8]Toni Morrison, *Beloved* (New York: Plume, 1987), p. 163. My discussion here is taken from the beginning of chapter nine of my *Embodying Forgiveness* (Grand Rapids, Mich.: Eerdmans, 1995), pp. 279-80.

246 Care for the Soul

heart-rending brokenness of slavery and its chilling aftermath. Set in rural Ohio several years after the Civil War, the novel chronicles the life of Sethe, a woman who escaped from slavery but is unable to escape from its heritage and its effects. Sethe is haunted by life on every level, from the destructive attacks on her flesh to the imprints of that abuse left on her soul. While a slave, she had been beaten and raped, separated from her husband and other loved ones, and treated like an animal. After she struggled to flee the circumstances of her slavery with her children, Sethe saw some white men coming to take her back. Their arrival is described in apocalyptic terms; there were four men coming on horseback, and they planned to take her back on a borrowed mule. The ominous presence of evil is not hard to detect.

Sethe was unable to face a return to such a life; even more, she refused to return her children to that life. She wants to take them "through the veil, out, away, over there where no one could hurt them."[9] So in order to prevent their return to slavery, Sethe killed her infant by slitting her throat. Once the men saw this, they realized that they had no use for a deranged woman, so they left her alone. But the black folk in the community also were afraid of a woman who would kill her own child, and they left her alone as well.

Sethe is haunted by her past, both by what had been done to her and by what she had done. Her past takes particular form in a young woman who appears out of nowhere. Sethe first sees her sitting on a stump. The young woman seems to be the ghost of her dead child, Beloved. Sethe desperately wants to figure out how to love this girl, and it is clear that the girl wants to "be loved." But the effects of Sethe's past prevent her from being able to imagine any future, much less one different from the past. "To Sethe, the future was a matter of keeping the past at bay."[10] And even that was no easy task because Sethe knows that her brain is devious, and that memories have a way of coming back whether we want them to or not. The memories have a life of their own. So Sethe's life is marked by the endless and unsuccessful task of trying to prevent her memories from working their way into her life. For Sethe every day involves the "serious work of beating back the past."[11]

Sometimes Sethe thinks that she would like to die, except that she knows that death is "anything but forgetfulness." She is "suspended between the nastiness of life and the meanness of the dead." [12] The scars on her body, and the distorted (and distorting) love that compelled her to kill and maim her children rather than see them returned to slavery, have also scarred her soul. All of her energy is

---

[9]Morrison, *Beloved,* p. 163.
[10]Ibid., p. 42.
[11]Ibid., p. 73.
[12]Ibid., p. 34.

spent in trying to keep the past at bay; there are no other options, no sense of tomorrow. She has no room in her brain for the future; she has no time to imagine.[13]

Toward the end of the novel, the pain of that collapsed time comes home to Sethe. Her pain is made clear to her by Paul D, an escaped slave whose own life is marked by physical pain and a scarred soul. He has, the narrator tells us, a "tobacco tin buried in his chest where a red heart used to be. Its lid rusted shut."[14] He tells Sethe, "me and you, we got more yesterday than anybody. We need some kind of tomorrow."[15] But it seems that a sense of tomorrow is what Sethe, Paul D and Beloved are condemned never to have.

Sethe clearly has the burden that Elon addresses: "so much traumatic memory, so much pain." She would agree that "a little forgetfulness might finally be in order," but how is that to be? What can psychology or theology, or both together, contribute to such a task? Does forgiveness have nothing to do with it; is Elon right when he implies that perhaps in this life there are situations and relations for which forgiveness and reconciliation are at best a matter of "hoping against hope"? Or does forgiveness have everything to do with it when forgiveness is understood in the eschatological work of the crucified and risen Christ?

Forgiveness and Memory

Christian living is clearly grounded in and linked to practices of remembering well: remembering God, remembering our forgiven sin as a protection against sin, remembering our vocation and responsibility to love God and neighbor. In this sense our life in God—our commitment to the truth that makes us free, that enables us to stop forgetting—is shaped by the crucified and risen Christ whose forgiveness re-members us as the body. Augustine's comments are instructive:

> See how I have explored the vast field of my memory in search of you, O Lord! And I have not found you outside it. For I have discovered nothing about you except what I have remembered since the time when I learned about you. Even since then I have not forgotten you. For I found my God, who is Truth itself, when I found truth, and ever since I learned the truth I have not forgotten it. So, since the time when I first learned of you, you have always been present in my memory, and it is there that I found you whenever I am reminded of you and find delight in you.[16]

At the heart of learning to remember well is learning to be forgiven by God. Rowan Williams has noted, "God is the agency that gives us back our memories, because God is the 'presence' to which all reality is present." But Williams does not shrink from the harder questions. He asks:

---

[13]Ibid., p. 72.
[14]Ibid., pp. 72-73.
[15]Ibid., p. 273.
[16]Augustine *Confessions* 10.24, trans. R. S. Pine-Coffin (New York: Penguin, 1961), p. 230.

What if the past that is returned or recovered is a record of guilt, hurt and diminution? The memory I have to recover is that of my particular, unalterable past; and if that is a memory whose recollection is unbearably painful, the record of a moral and spiritual "shrinkage" or deprivation, how is it liberating? What of the destructive power of "the bitterness which in human life so often succeeds what at least in memory seems fraught with promise," the "seeds of corruption" sown unseen?[17]

Here we confront the complexities of memory: our tendency to forget, our vast self-deception, the ways in which we wallow in bitterness and anger over hurts suffered, grievances unheard, offenses unforgiven or unforgiving. We struggle with the willingness to accept the diminution of ourselves and others through the refusal to remember well, whether it is the memory of abandonment, such as Mary at the tomb; or of betrayal, such as Peter by the fire; or of a refusal to repent of sin, such as Cain's inability to master the sin lurking at the door; or of hostility because our enemies do repent, such as Jonah pouting outside the city. Whatever the situation and history of our sin, God engages with our particular past, seeking to redeem it for renewed life in the future.

In this sense forgiveness has everything to do with it. As Williams suggests, "If forgiveness is liberation, it is also a recovery of the past in hope, a return of memory, in which what is potentially threatening, destructive, despair-inducing, in the past is transfigured into the ground of hope."[18] This occurs as the risen Christ returns to those who crucified him, bringing a judgment that does not condemn but instead offers the hope found in new life. It is a hope that comes through the return of memory, not its erasure or its denial. Christ redeems the past; he does not undo it. Because of the offer of new life in Christ, the past—whatever it is—can be borne.

Our life in Christ is ritually signified in our dying and rising with Christ in baptism. We die to the old self, to be raised in newness of life. As forgiven sinners, we can learn to tell the story of our life differently, presumably more truthfully, because we are freed of the burdens of telling forgetful or deceptive stories. We need hide the truth about ourselves neither in praise nor in penitence, for we are enveloped in God's grace. Further, as we live into our baptism, perhaps signified from time to time through services of baptismal renewal, we locate our life, our memories and our forgiveness in the grace of the crucified and risen Christ.

Moreover, the Eucharist is the sign of a reconciled fellowship broken by human sin and infidelity. Note Williams's comments about John's and Luke's descriptions of the resurrection meals: in both Gospels the meals

> echo specific occasions of crisis, misunderstanding, illusion and disaster. They 'recover' not only the memory of table-fellowship, but the memory of false hope, betrayal and

---

[17]Rowan Williams, *Resurrection* (New York: Pilgrim, 1982), p. 32. The internal quotation is from D. M. MacKinnon, "Some Notes on the Irreversibility of Time," in *Explorations in Theology* 5 (London: SCM, 1979), pp. 96-97.

[18]Williams, *Resurrection*, p. 32.

desertion, of a past in which ignorance and pride and the rejection of *Jesus'* account of his destiny in favour of power-fantasies of their own led the disciples into their most tragic failure, their indirect but real share in the ruin of their Lord. Yet Jesus, even as he sees their rejection taking shape, nonetheless gives himself to his betrayers in the breaking of bread. The resurrection meals restore precisely that poignant juxtaposition of his unfailing grace and their rejection, distortion and betrayal of it.[19]

So also the practice of reading Scripture, and specifically the *lectio divina*, can help to school us as people of forgiveness and holiness, as people whose memories are nurtured and conformed by the Spirit's uniquely particular grace to the crucified and risen Christ. For ancient and medieval Christians there was nothing so important as our memory, which was understood to be shaped by the habits and practices of attention to God and God's Word.

The practice of confession and, more generally, the care of souls is crucial for learning to attend to the particularities of each person's struggles with the past, and for determining whether and how it can or should be remembered. Here psychological insights, shaped by the larger practices (for example, traditions of spiritual direction) and understandings of salvation, can significantly enrich our understanding of the dynamics of effective practices of confession, counseling and the more general care of souls.

In all of these ways I am suggesting that forgiveness ought to be linked far more closely to remembering well than to forgetting. The church is a people of memory whose practices help us bear the burdens of our own struggles with remembering and forgetting. But what do we do about those situations in which, as Elon suggests, "a little forgetfulness might be in order"? In part this depends on whether we really want our remembering to be the ground of reconciliation or whether we prefer to immerse ourselves in our own wounds, licking them, savoring them, even allowing them to fester for the sake of moral and political mobilization. If we are struggling for reconciliation, for healing, how do we learn to remember well if the day's task really is "keeping the past at bay"? Can we will a little forgetfulness?

In his recent book *Exclusion and Embrace*, Miroslav Volf offers a rich and complex set of suggestions about "the affliction of memory" and the potential significance of forgetting—or, as he more accurately also calls it, a "divine gift of non-remembering." Volf knows well the dangers of forgetting and the importance of learning to remember well as a sign of our forgiveness and reconciliation with God and others. He also knows that the "certain kind of forgetting" that he advocates "assumes that the matters of 'truth' and 'justice' have been taken care of," that "perpetrators have been named, judged, and (hopefully) transformed, that victims are safe and their wounds healed" so that the forgetting can "ultimately take place *only together with* the creation of 'all things new.' " He goes on to suggest that, "if

---

[19]Ibid., pp. 39-40.

we must remember wrongdoings to be safe in an unsafe world, we must also let go of their memory in order to be finally redeemed, or so I want to argue here, and suggest that only those who are willing ultimately to forget will be able to remember rightly."[20]

There is something profoundly right about Volf's analysis. His phrase "the grace of non-remembering" is preferable to the term *forgetting*. In this life, we must be guided by the memory of sin because it provides a shield against sin, by the memory of Christ's wounds that are healing, in solidarity with all victims who have suffered and those who continue to suffer. As Volf insists, we must remember their suffering, and we must allow that memory to be spoken out loud for all to hear. Volf believes this "indispensable remembering" should be guided

> by the vision of that same redemption that will one day make us lose the memory of hurts suffered and offenses committed against us. For ultimately, forgetting the suffering is better than remembering it, because wholeness is better than brokenness, the communion of love better than the distance of suspicion, harmony better than disharmony. We remember now in order that we may forget then; and we will forget then in order that we may love without reservation. Though we would be unwise to drop the shield of memory from our hands before the dawn of the new age, we may be able to move it cautiously to the side by opening our arms to embrace the other, even the former enemy.[21]

Volf's proposal helps us to envision how to understand Elon's plea for a little forgetfulness. Further, his analysis helps us to understand the significance of key biblical passages that refer to God forgetting sin, blotting out Israel's transgressions (Jer 31:34; Is 43:25) or imploring people to "not remember the former things" because he is about to do a new thing (Is 43:18-19; cf. 65:17). But there is a tension in Volf's descriptions *nonremembering* and *forgetting,* tensions that he does not fully resolve and that pose potential dangers.

At points Volf seems to suggest that memory is inextricably, even eschatologically, painful.

> Put starkly, the alternative is: either heaven *or* the memory of horror. Either heaven will have no monuments to keep the memory of the horrors alive, or it will be closer to hell than we would like to think. For if heaven cannot rectify Auschwitz, then the memory of Auschwitz must undo the experience of heaven. Redemption will be complete only when the creation of "all things new" is coupled with the passage of "all things old" into the double *nihil* of nonexistence and nonremembrance.[22]

Volf closes this analysis with a reference to Revelation's vision of the first things passing away, but he curiously says that the Lamb has "taken away the sin of the world"—a biblical phrase—and has "erased their memory."[23]

---

[20]Miroslav Volf, *Exclusion and Embrace* (Nashville: Abingdon, 1996), pp. 131-32.
[21]Ibid., p. 139.
[22]Ibid., pp. 135-36.
[23]Ibid., p. 140.

Yet elsewhere Volf suggests that the task is to be sure that the memories are "fully healed," implying that a memory might be fully healed so that it is no longer painful. This, I think, is a more fruitful way to envision the eschatological final act than is language about forgetting or erasing memories. There are two reasons that this is so.

First, we need to be able to maintain some measure of continuity in the stories of our lives. Though Volf anticipates and responds to this objection in a note, his response is unpersuasive. It is clearly true, as Volf suggests, that we are ourselves even though we don't remember everything, and that we reconstitute our identity daily in response to the dynamics of remembering and forgetting.[24] But equally clearly, for those features of our lives and our relationships—including their horrors, their shattered brokenness—that are central to our definition of our identity in this life, the only way that we can still be identifiably ourselves and can have reconstituted identities and relationships is if our memories are eschatologically fully healed rather than erased or forgotten.

Second, when I read the biblical passages dealing with these issues, including the book of Revelation, the vision of the kingdom is a vision of wounds and brokenness fully healed rather than erased. To erase memories would seem to be much closer to uncrucifying Christ than would healing those memories fully—eschatologically—through the healing wounds of the crucified and risen Christ.

How, then, do I understand the language about God "blotting out transgressions" and "remembering their sin no more?" How do I understand Revelation's vision of the "first things passing away" with the new heaven and the new earth? I believe that these refer to a transformation in which we will learn to remember our histories, even in their ugliness, but in which we will not remember them as sin because they will have been fully healed. Just as in this life time heals many minor wounds so that they recede into a state of nonremembrance, so also in God's kingdom even the most horrifying memories of this life will be healed by the wounds of the crucified and risen Christ, whose unjust suffering and death is the most horrifying thing imaginable. This I take it is the force of Paul's comment: "I consider that the sufferings of this present time are not worth comparing with the glory about to be revealed to us" (Rom 8:18).[25] In this sense, we will discover the passing of forgiveness, and the passing of the first things, because our joy will be complete.

Ultimately, then, my description of the matter would be slightly different from Volf's. Given the reality of sin and evil, there is nothing so whole as a broken and healed heart, nothing so complete as a new creation whose fractures have been

---

[24]Ibid., p. 136 n. 25.
[25]Compare Volf's assessment of the same verse: "If something is not worth comparing, then it will not be compared, and if it will not be compared then it will not have been remembered" (Ibid., p. 138). In my terms, it will not need to be remembered because it will have been fully healed and reconciled, but it will not be forgotten or erased.

fully healed, nothing so hopeful as the promise of the passing of forgiveness through the perfected holiness of disciples washed in the blood of the Lamb. We are given the eschatological divine gift of nonremembrance precisely because we are re-membered as the body of the crucified and risen Christ. But in this life, influenced by the horrifying realities of sin and evil and the time required for forgiveness and healing, we need both Christian theology and, in its modest form, psychology.

I join with Volf in suggesting the importance of vigilance in this life, of standing in solidarity with the memory of those who have suffered and continue to suffer, while nonetheless opening our arms to begin to learn to embrace the other, even the former enemy. A little nonremembrance is in order, but only because that nonremembrance has—contra Elon—everything to do with the forgiveness wrought by Jesus Christ.

The Relationship Between Theology and Psychology

Theology and psychology can each play an important role in fostering Christian practices that contribute to healing the wounds of memory. Each of these five theses points to an important dimension in the relationship between theology and psychology. They would need considerable explication and defense before they would be fully persuasive; however, I identify them here to suggest directions for future conversation and research.

1. Both theology and psychology have important contributions to make to our understanding of the complex dynamics of remembering and forgetting. Both need to be shaped by narrative understandings of human life in relation to God. There are interesting and significant convergences to be found in the work of such theologians and Christian philosophers as Hans Frei, Stanley Hauerwas and Alasdair MacIntyre on the one hand, and such psychologists as Jerome Bruner and Jonathan Lear on the other.

2. Theology has priority in establishing the determinative context in which the relations are understood. It locates our understandings and practices in the context of God's eschatological salvation and our redemption from sin. That is, theology locates our lives in a particular narrative, the narrative of the triune God's dealings with the world and with human beings. That narrative is learned and lived in and through the practices of the church. Consult the recent work of Rowan Williams and Sarah Coakley in this regard.

3. There is much to commend Deborah van Deusen Hunsinger's proposal for a Chalcedonian understanding of the relationship between theology and psychology: without separation or division, without confusion or change, and with theology having conceptual precedence. Hunsinger's proposal preserves the relative autonomy of the disciplines while insisting on the centrality of the desire to know God. The work of such figures as Stanley Leavy and Robert Roberts point in a direction similar to Hunsinger's.

4. Just as Chalcedon, a masterful solution to pressing issues in Christology, did not resolve all christological issues, so Hunsinger's proposal does not resolve all issues in the relationship between the disciplines of theology and psychology. Indeed, just as people's tendency toward either an Alexandrian or an Antiochene position in Christology affects how they assess Chalcedon, so also there will be different emphases in people's assessment of the relative autonomy of each discipline, even within a Chalcedonian pattern. For example, my views are shaped by an Augustinian-Thomist tradition: I believe that while the two disciplines have significant independence, theology transforms psychological investigations. Because of her more Augustinian-Calvinist sensibilities, Hunsinger may give psychology more independence than I do. Debates about John Milbank's proposal in *Theology and Social Theory* can help to illuminate the issues on this point.[26]

5. There is much in the Christian tradition—on the emotions, virtues and vices, the power of habits—that can enrich our understanding of theology and psychology in relation to the practices of Christian living. We ought not allow modernity's construction of disciplines to determine our investigations or to establish the boundaries of texts that might reshape our thinking and living. Recent works by Thomas Oden, Dennis Okholm and Ellen Charry offer rich resources for our thinking.

Many, if not most, of us struggle with the difficulties of remembering and forgetting, particularly in relation to salvation and sin. Some of those difficulties involve memories of horrible brokenness, whether caused by momentous events or by repeated occurrences over time. Even so, by living in Christ, we are enabled to keep the vision of God's eschatological reconciliation—and God's gift of divine nonremembrance—ever before us. And as we discover over and over again, both theology and Christian psychology help us to discover that forgiveness has everything to do with the ways in which, by the power of God's Holy Spirit, all things are being made new.

---

[26]John Milbank, *Theology and Social Theory: Beyond Secular Reason* (Cambridge, Mass.: Blackwell, 1991).

12

RESPONSIBLE HERMENEUTICS FOR WISDOM LITERATURE

Richard Schultz

But in the multitude of counselors there is safety. (PROV 11:14 NKJV)

E RIC JOHNSON ASSERTS IN A 1996 ARTICLE IN THE *JOURNAL OF PSYCHOLOGY AND Theology* that "the Scriptures were given to the church to shed light on its path, even the path of psychologists."[1] Popular publications in Christian psychology naturally turn to the Scriptures for biblical support for their analyses of human psychological problems and their proposed psychotherapeutic solutions, although the specific reasons for doing so seldom are discussed by the authors.

A survey of popular books and journal articles by Christian counselors and psychologists indicates that there are two forms or directions of integration of the Bible and psychology: Sometimes authors cite biblical passages, precedents or principles that parallel contemporary psychological theories and therapies. Less commonly, authors use psychological theory to illuminate biblical narratives (for example, seeking to determine the nature of Job's depression or the causes of Ezekiel's eccentricities) or to identify the emotions and motivations that caused biblical persons to behave as they did. Though these approaches presumably proceed in opposite directions, sometimes they overlap. On the one hand, when scholars turn to the Bible for support of psychological theories, they sometimes reinterpret the biblical text in the light of psychology, imposing a foreign grid or foreign terminology on the Bible. On the other hand, scholars who expressly employ psychological theory as a hermeneutical aid for understanding the Bible often use their psycho-

---

[1]Eric L. Johnson, "The Call of Wisdom: Adult Development Within Christian Community, Part II: Toward a Covenantal Constructivist Model of Post-Formal Development," *Journal of Psychology and Theology* 24 (1996): 94.

logical exegesis to enrich their understanding of some aspect of human psychology. Thus a dynamic relationship between psychology and the Bible can be operative in the integrative process.

The Christian psychology literature reflects three basic attitudes toward the integration of psychology with the Bible. At one end of the spectrum are counselors and psychologists who espouse the dictum, either explicitly or implicitly, that because "all truth is God's truth," genuine psychology is Christian psychology, although secular theory must be filtered through a Christian worldview. Therefore, it is possible to write an entire book on "Christian" psychology without even mentioning the Bible.[2]

At the other end of the spectrum are those Christian counselors and psychologists who demonize all secular psychology as atheistic, humanistic and antibiblical. All knowledge of human psychology and every approach used in counseling should be derived from Scripture. Because they have no desire to integrate secular psychology with the Bible, these counselors make a broader appeal to the biblical message as a whole and to biblical examples of the counselor-counselee relationship, rather than to individual passages.

Mediating between these two positions are Christian counselors and psychologists who pair various key elements of secular theory with what they consider to be corroborating biblical texts. Counselors who take this approach may be convinced that referring to specific texts guarantees that their views are biblical (that is, supported by or in harmony with biblical teaching) or that by referring to specific texts they allay the fears of readers and clients who are skeptical about the use of secular psychological theory to treat the spiritual problems of Christians. This essay will focus on the third approach because it is the dominant approach in popular Christian writings.

Biblical Authority and Responsible Hermeneutics

How should one assess this search for biblical warrants? Admittedly, it is not inherently objectionable for a Christian counselor to use Bible verses to illustrate, clarify or even reinforce elements of psychological theory that are generally accepted as true and compatible with Christian teachings. The technical terminology of any academic subdiscipline is an unfamiliar foreign currency to the average Christian, and it may need to be exchanged for the currency of Canaan. Cashing in the vocabulary of psychology for biblical language simply helps psychology to make more sense to Christian nonspecialists.

Nevertheless, this approach may spring more from an unconscious compulsion than from theological necessity. As long as it can be demonstrated that a particular

---

[2]Edward Hindson, "The Inerrancy Debate and the Use of Scripture in Counseling," *Grace Theological Journal* 3 (1982): 209 n. 10.

psychological theory or therapy does not entail the explicit or implicit rejection of biblical teachings regarding human nature, sin and salvation or the violation of biblical ethics, its use by a Christian psychologist or psychotherapist is unproblematic. However, rather than indicating how their theories relate to foundational biblical teachings, popular authors in the area of Christian psychology often rely instead on a proof-text approach, citing a wide variety of isolated texts whose meanings presumably are self-evident. Unfortunately, the uses that such authors make of specific Bible passages frequently are in violation of sound hermeneutical principles.

Although it is fair to assume that these counselors are motivated by a deep confidence in the veracity and efficacy of the Scripture texts that they cite,[3] the authority of the Bible can be abused when it is invoked in connection with an obviously misinterpreted or misapplied passage. The texts to which these Christian counselors turn sometimes provide, at best, wobbly biblical support for the psychological theories that they advance. The intended "Bible therapy" becomes a mere placebo that makes the client feel better for having ingested a few Bible verses. Not every biblical text will support counselors who seek to take their stand upon it; it is not true that "every promise in the book is mine" if responsible hermeneutics determines that a promise belongs to someone else.

To be sure, some Christian psychologists and counselors are aware of this danger, but they do not appear to understand the true nature and extent of the problem. Dan Allender describes Christians "who have found comfort in Bible passages when the meaning has been twisted beyond comprehension or who have been forced to bear a perspective that was simply not to be found in the verse, yet they were encouraged or convicted as a result of their understanding."[4] John Scanish and Mark McMinn suggest that competent lay Christian counselors must "understand and use Scripture wisely,"[5] but they explain this understanding in terms of an adequate knowledge of Scripture and theology, not in terms of hermeneutical sophistication. One textbook on Christian counseling includes a thirty-five page appendix on "the use of Scripture in counseling"[6] but fails to

---

[3]Ibid., pp. 210, 213. See Hindson's headings: "Thy Word Is Truth: Confidence in the Message" and "Thy Word Works: Confidence in Counseling."

[4]Dan B. Allender and Tremper Longman III, *Bold Love* (Colorado Springs, Colo.: NavPress, 1992), p. 15. Jay Adams writes similarly of those who "bend and warp the Word of God to fit ideas previously found in some pagan book" ("Biblical Interpretation and Counseling," *Journal of Biblical Counseling* 16 [1998]: 7).

[5]John D. Scanish and Mark R. McMinn, "The Competent Lay Christian Counselor," *Journal of Psychology and Christianity* 15 (1996): 31-32.

[6]Clyde Narramore, *The Psychology of Counseling* (Grand Rapids, Mich.: Zondervan, 1960), pp. 237-73. Furthermore, it is not untypical for Christian counselors to criticize another author's exegesis of the Scriptures as "faulty in critical respects" (Leanne Payne, *Restoring the Christian Soul: Overcoming Barriers to Completion in Christ Through Healing Prayer* [Grand Rapids, Mich.: Baker, 1991], p. 215), but to remain unaware of the problems with their own interpretations of Scripture.

acknowledge the possibility that the listed verses can easily be misused in counseling.

Foundational Hermeneutical Principles for the Use of Scripture in Christian Psychology

Most of the flawed interpretation and application of Bible passages in the writings of popular Christian psychology probably is unintentional rather than deliberate. It may be helpful to categorize and illustrate some of the most frequent kinds of errors. It is hoped that a greater awareness of the importance of proper hermeneutics will lead to a more consciously exegetical and more appropriate approach to the Bible by Christian psychologists and counselors, whether they are writing for the church or for their colleagues. The following examples have been selected from popular publications by Christian psychologists or counselors because they represent the kind of literature that is having the greatest impact on the church.[7]

Contextual considerations in interpretation and application. One of the most familiar hermeneutical slogans is "a text without a context is a pretext." Anyone who desires to interpret and apply a specific biblical text accurately must consider its context. The context may include literary, historical-cultural, salvation-historical and theological-thematic aspects.

The significance of an individual puzzle piece is determined not primarily by its combination of colors but by the particular section of the puzzle and the complete picture of which it forms a part. Similarly, the meaning of a given verse is determined not primarily by the meaning of the individual words that it contains but by the immediate and larger literary context that surrounds the verse.

In their book *Boundaries*, Henry Cloud and John Townsend interpret Isaiah 1:18 ("Come now, let us reason together" [NIV]) as teaching that God, "like a real friend, or a real father," wants to hear our side of things and consider changing his mind.[8] But the larger context of Isaiah 1:2-20 indicates that God's indictment of Israel for blatant sins is irrefutable and that the verdict is already certain. Thus God's offer sets before his people the only two options open to them: repentance and forgiveness or further rebellion and destruction (vv. 19-20).

Each Bible author writes from a perspective that is determined largely by the author's personal and corporate historical and cultural background and writes to those who presumably share a common background. That background is presupposed in the literature and accordingly must be understood before the literature can be understood.

---

[7]Most of these examples involve references to the Old Testament both because I am more familiar with this portion of the Bible and because its texts are more prone to misuse.

[8]Henry Cloud and John Townsend, *Boundaries: When to Say Yes, When to Say No to Take Control of Your Life* (Grand Rapids, Mich.: Zondervan, 1992), p. 233.

Leanne Payne encourages people to offer intercessory prayer about the unknown sins of others' families, thereby breaking the power of those sins to further wound the sufferers. She says that she is applying an important principle from the Old Testament prophets and cites the confessional prayers of Daniel (Dan 9:4-19) and Nehemiah (Neh 1:5-11).[9] However, the purpose of Daniel's and Nehemiah's confession of Israel's corporate sin was to acknowledge the justness of the Babylonian exile of God's people, thus laying a foundation for pleading for mercy and restoration. (And incidentally, Nehemiah is not a prophet.) These passages thus offer no warrant for intercessory prayer having the specific effect that Payne suggests.

Because God's plan for humanity is progressively revealed in the course of biblical history, each passage must be interpreted in the light of its place along the continuum of divine revelation and in light of the covenant relationships that are operational in a given period of biblical history.[10] When we are considering matters of application, it makes a difference whether a particular biblical injunction occurs in the Mosaic law, one of the postexilic prophetic books or a Pauline epistle.

In a book on biblical forgiveness, Jay Adams claims that the act of divine forgiveness ensures that although there may be continuing consequences of a sin that serve a beneficial purpose, there will be no further punishment of the sinner. Adams then seeks to show that all potentially conflicting passages support this viewpoint, including Numbers 14:20-23. The divine decree that the entire Exodus generation would die in the wilderness should not be construed as punishment; rather, in the light of 1 Corinthians 10:6, it should be understood as having occurred then "for the benefit of the church in all subsequent ages."[11] This forced interpretation is designed to support a questionable theory that the Israelites dying in the wilderness could hardly appreciate.

If we examine the Numbers text in the context of its place in redemptive history, we observe that every post-Sinai rebellion recorded in Exodus and Numbers results in the punishment of a segment of the people, in keeping with the provisions of the Sinai covenant. The rejection of the promised land by ten of the twelve spies and by the people as a whole marks the central (the fourth out of seven) and climactic rebellion in the book of Numbers. According to Numbers 14 God indeed does forgive the people on the basis of Moses' intercessory prayer, but the punishment that the people thereby escape is the divine threat to destroy the entire nation at once and to turn Moses into a second Abraham (vv. 11-12).

Although the Bible is not a book of systematic theology, individual texts presuppose and contribute to certain foundational theological themes (for example,

---

[9] Payne, *Restoring the Christian Soul*, pp. 69, 92.

[10] A helpful book in this regard is Willem A. VanGemeren, *The Progress of Redemption: The Story of Salvation from Creation to the New Jerusalem* (Grand Rapids, Mich.: Zondervan, 1988).

[11] Jay E. Adams, *From Forgiven to Forgiving* (Wheaton, Ill.: Victor, 1989), pp. 151-53.

regarding the nature of God and his dealings with humanity) and help to develop the theological themes of the canonical book of which they are a part.[12] Thus, when we are interpreting individual texts, we should examine how their key themes are used elsewhere within the same canonical book.

In a discussion of the causes of depression, Frank Minirth and Paul Meier quote Isaiah 43:8 ("Lead out those who have eyes but are blind" [NIV]). They observe that God continually refers to human blindness and conclude that "all of us humans have blind spots."[13] Probably everyone would agree that their conclusion is an accurate assessment of the human condition and is therefore not unbiblical. However, their implicit claim that this conclusion is taught by the book of Isaiah (and elsewhere in the Bible) bestows upon their observation a "biblical" status. Unfortunately, when they cite Isaiah 43:8 in this manner, they fail to acknowledge that blindness, which encompasses both physical and spiritual blindness (and is basically limited to Isaiah and quotations of Isaiah in the New Testament), represents a major theme within the book of Isaiah (note especially Isaiah 42:7, 16, 18-19).[14] In Isaiah 43:8 the motif clearly refers to Israel's profound spiritual insensitivity and its inability to carry out its divinely appointed task, not merely to blind spots. Therefore it should not be cited in support of Minirth and Meier's generalization.

Generic considerations. Each literary genre possesses certain distinctive elements so that it communicates its message in a unique way. The label that we attach to a given book or text will largely determine how we interpret and apply it. For example, if we view the Song of Songs as an allegory about divine love or the Genesis creation account as a myth, this will influence our interpretation.

Gary Smalley and John Trent devote an entire book to the importance of parental blessing, and it is based on the model of the patriarchal blessing. To their credit, its authors correctly acknowledge the unique place the patriarchal blessing played in redemptive history: it was reserved for one special occasion, it was irrevocable and prophetic, and it was based on God's sovereign choice of the biological line of divine blessing. However, Smalley and Trent are convinced that these passages not only portray patriarchal actions, but also teach the importance of parental blessing. They even specify five essential elements of the blessing: giving a meaningful touch, delivering a spoken message, attaching high value to the one being blessed, picturing a special future for the one

---

[12]For a detailed discussion of the significance of the theological context of a text, see Richard L. Schultz, "Integrating Old Testament Theology and Exegesis: Literary, Thematic, and Canonical Issues," in *New International Dictionary of Old Testament Theology and Exegesis,* ed. Willem VanGemeren (Grand Rapids, Mich.: Zondervan, 1997), 1:188-98.

[13]Frank B. Minirth and Paul D. Meier, *Happiness Is a Choice: A Manual on the Symptoms, Causes, and Cures of Depression* (Grand Rapids, Mich.: Baker, 1978), p. 97.

[14]See Kenneth T. Aitken, "Hearing and Seeing: Metamorphoses of a Motif in Isaiah 1—39," in *Among the Prophets. Language, Image and Structure in the Prophetic Writings,* eds. Philip R. Davies and David J. A. Clines (Sheffield, U.K.: JSOT, 1993), pp. 12-42.

being blessed, and being actively committed to helping to fulfill the blessing.[15]

Smalley and Trent's approach reflects a basic misunderstanding of how biblical narratives communicate spiritual truth. To move properly from the descriptive to the prescriptive when interpreting a narrative, it is important, first of all, to identify the narrative's place within the larger biblical story of redemption, keeping the focus on God and his involvement in history, not on the deeds of biblical heroes and heroines (or villains). We should avoid deriving theological or procedural paradigms directly from narrative description because such texts "often illustrate what is taught directly and categorically elsewhere."[16] Instead, we should examine the way in which the narrative selection and ordering of its details point toward a message regarding the nature of genuine faith and obedience in the interplay between divine sovereignty and human responsibility.

The dominant theme of the book of Genesis is God's sovereign election, preparation and preservation of a covenant family in order to counteract the devastating effects of sin. The covenant family will serve as a channel of divine blessing to the nations. When he blessed a son, a patriarch was simply acknowledging what God had already determined and promised to do, but a patriarch could be tricked, or he could be swayed by his own prejudices. The fact that only one son per family (and never a daughter) was singled out to receive the blessing hardly suggests that this offers a paradigm for Christian parenting. Nor can a patriarch who offers a death-bed blessing be described as someone who was actively committed to seeing the blessing fulfilled.

The fact that there is no indication that Abraham officially blessed his son Isaac and that there is not a single paternal blessing recorded in the Old Testament outside of the book of Genesis suggests that the patriarchal blessing was a unique, pre-Sinai ceremony rather than a model for us. That the closest parallel to the patriarchal blessing is Moses' blessing of the tribes of Israel (Deut 33) indicates that God's means of passing on the divine blessing may have already changed by Moses' day. The fact that the book's authors turn to the psalms and proverbs for sample blessings suggests that the prayers, encouragement and optimistic wishes of present-day Christian parents have little in common with the patriarchal blessing. The use of proverbs in contemporary blessings also may reflect genre-related confusion: biblical proverbs should not be understood as divine promises but merely as probabilities, spiritual results that frequently occur when a person follows the way of wisdom.[17]

---

[15]Gary Smalley and John Trent, *The Blessing* (Nashville: Thomas Nelson, 1986), pp. 22-24.

[16]Gordon D. Fee and Douglas Stuart, *How to Read the Bible for All Its Worth: A Guide to Understanding the Bible* (Grand Rapids, Mich.: Zondervan, 1993), p. 82.

[17]A related instance of genre confusion occurs when Cloud and Townsend (*Boundaries*, p. 41) misunderstand the proverbial principle "a man reaps what he sows" (Gal 6:7; cf. Prov 22:8) to be a divine law that no one (including a parent) should interrupt by preventing the expected consequences from occurring.

Semantic considerations. The meaning of an individual word is determined primarily by its discourse usage in a given context, not by its historical derivation (its so-called basic meaning), its possible meanings elsewhere in the Bible or its usage in contemporary society. The literature of Christian psychology frequently ignores discourse usage, and errors in application are often the result. Two types of semantic fallacies will be noted here: the root fallacy and semantic anachronism.[18]

The root fallacy can be seen in *The Masculine Journey,* in which Robert Hicks seeks to correlate secular research by Daniel Levinson[19] with six Hebrew nouns that are used to refer to the male gender on the basis of their etymologically derived basic meaning: (1) the creational male—*'ādām,* (2) the phallic male—*zākār,* (3) the warrior—*gibbôr,* (4) the wounded male—*'ĕnôš,* (5) the mature man—*'îš,* and (6) the sage—*zāqēn.* Hicks presents his word studies as "what the Scripture has to contribute" to an understanding of the male life cycle,[20] though it is doubtful that the words that comprise this semantic field can be viewed as presenting a chronological sequence.

Hicks fails to explain his omission of two additional common Hebrew words that belong to the same field: son—*bēn* and young man—*na'ar.* More problematic, however, is the fact that etymology has little to do with contextual meaning: a pineapple neither grows on a pine tree nor looks or tastes like an apple; to call a person "nice" is not an insult, even though the English word *nice* is derived from Latin *nescius,* meaning "ignorant."

To return to Hicks's examples, the derivation of the noun *'ĕnôš* from a verb meaning "to be weak or sickly" is uncertain; one standard Hebrew lexicon suggests that it derives from a verb meaning "to be friendly or social," in which case the author could suggest a new stage: *'ĕnôš*—the well-connected man. But even if his posited etymology is correct, Hicks makes an incorrect assumption about the word's usage. It is incorrect to assume that the Old Testament authors used the word *'ĕnôš* whenever they wanted to emphasize a man's weakness—or *'îš,* which in many texts is better translated as "person,"—to emphasize his maturity. (In fact, *'ĕnôš* is used in its Aramaic form *'ĕnāš* in Daniel 7:13 to designate the one like the Son of Man who comes on the clouds to receive authority over the eternal kingdom of God—hardly a picture of weakness!) It is equally unlikely that the biblical writers understood these terms as referring to distinct stages in the journey that every male must take, thus warranting Hicks's book-length map of masculinity.

Several Christian psychologists and therapists demonstrate semantic anachro-

---

[18]For a fuller discussion of word-study fallacies, see Donald A. Carson, *Exegetical Fallacies,* 2nd ed. (Grand Rapids, Mich.: Baker, 1996), chap. 1.

[19]Robert Hicks, *The Masculine Journey: Understanding the Six Stages of Manhood* (Colorado Springs, Colo.: NavPress, 1993); Daniel J. Levinson, *The Seasons of a Man's Life* (New York: Knopf, 1978).

[20]Hicks, *Masculine Journey,* p. 19.

nism when they read the modern concept of the Christian psychologist back into Old Testament usage. One author asks: "Who is the greatest psychologist and clinician that has ever lived?" and answers, not surprisingly, "Jesus the Christ," referring to Isaiah 9:6 for support. In their book on depression Minirth and Meier cite Proverbs 11:14 ("Where there is no guidance, the people fall, but in abundance of counselors there is victory" [NASB]) as a biblical endorsement of professional Christian psychotherapy.[21] But the Old Testament adviser *(yôʿēṣ)* fulfilled a societal role that was very different from that of the present-day Christian counselor; the advisor often served as a high-ranking official in the royal court of Israel or Judah, as indicated in 1 Chronicles 27:32-33.

Guidelines for Employing Old Testament Wisdom Literature in Christian Counseling

After presenting and illustrating some basic hermeneutical principles, I will examine Old Testament wisdom literature in greater detail because Christian caregivers frequently turn to it. We will discuss both the dangers and the possibilities that this genre presents for integrating psychology with biblical teachings. The wisdom genre is usually considered to include the books of Proverbs, Ecclesiastes, Job and Song of Songs; select Psalms, such as chapters 1, 37, 49, 73 and 119; and several apocryphal books, including Sirach, or Ecclesiasticus, and the Wisdom of Solomon.

Wisdom literature is often wrongly denigrated as ahistorical, secular, humanistic, purely pragmatic and individualistic, and is viewed as being virtually indistinguishable from other ancient Near Eastern or even from modern wisdom collections. It is thus considered to be of lesser value than those books that focus on Israel's covenant history and obligations. However, wisdom literature is attractive precisely because of its unique rhetoric and themes.[22]

Wisdom literature is winsome. Wisdom's scope and literary forms are universal and timeless. Wisdom literature's use of vivid comparisons and generalized observations help it to transcend the boundaries of ancient Israelite society. Its character-

---

[21]George Scipione, "The Wonderful Counselor, the Other Counselor, and Christian Counseling," *Westminster Theological Journal* 36 (1973-74): 174-97; Minirth and Meier, *Happiness Is a Choice*, p. 98. (Minirth and Meier cite the NASB; its translation of Proverbs 11:14 is more amenable to their interpretation than is the NIV's "advisers.")

[22]Helpful introductions to Old Testament wisdom literature include C. Hassell Bullock, *An Introduction to the Old Testament Poetic Books*, 2nd ed. (Chicago: Moody Press, 1988); Fee and Stuart, *How to Read the Bible*, chap. 12; Graeme Goldsworthy, *Gospel and Wisdom: Israel's Wisdom Literature in the Christian Life* (Carlisle, U.K.: Paternoster, 1987); Derek Kidner, *The Wisdom of Proverbs, Job, and Ecclesiastes: An Introduction to Wisdom Literature* (Downers Grove, Ill.: InterVarsity Press, 1985); William E. Mouser, *Getting the Most out of Proverbs* (Grand Rapids, Mich.: Zondervan, 1991); and D. Brent Sandy and Ronald L. Giese Jr., eds., *Cracking Old Testament Codes: A Guide to Interpreting the Literary Genres of the Old Testament* (Nashville: Broadman & Holman, 1995), chaps. 12-13.

istic literary forms are found in many cultures throughout the world. Wisdom literature includes proverbs (Prov 10:1—22:16), allegory (Prov 5:15-18; Eccles 12:1-7), parable (Eccles 9:13-16) and dialogue or disputation (Job 3—27).

Wisdom literature has both intellectual and practical appeal. Proverbs are "for learning about wisdom and instruction, for understanding words of insight" (Prov 1:2). Wisdom is the thinking person's literature; it calls for analysis, reflection and rumination. According to Andrew Hill, "non-proverbial wisdom literature invites the inquisitive, the curious, the cerebral, and the risk-taker to probe the mysteries of the way of God's wisdom. Such exploration is not for everyone."[23] Wisdom, especially proverbial wisdom, addresses every-day topics such as work (commerce, money and possessions), speech (lies, promises and quarrels), interpersonal relationships (marital sexual harmony and infidelity, child-rearing, friendship and neighbors), moral behavior (wisdom and folly, righteousness and wickedness), authority and government, and food and drink. Nonproverbial wisdom, as found in Ecclesiastes and Job, also ponders the paradoxical nature of reality and probes the divine mysteries of suffering, injustice and human limitations.

Wisdom literature invites, encourages, admonishes and illustrates rather than directly commanding. The law thunders from Sinai, the prophetic voice boldly proclaims in the royal courts, "Thus says the LORD," but Lady Wisdom lifts her voice on the crowded street corners (Prov 1:20-21; 8:1-4) and appeals to her listeners' life experience and common sense. It is therefore not surprising that Christian counselors are naturally drawn to these rich biblical resources as they seek to address the daily concerns and vexing problems of those who turn to them for help.

Characteristics of wisdom literature. Lest the unique features of wisdom among biblical writings and its striking similarities to extrabiblical sapiential literature lead to the practical misuse of this genre, it is necessary to discuss the characteristics of wisdom theology before moving on to some practical guidelines for its use.[24]

Biblical wisdom is the ability, both divinely bestowed (Prov 2:6; 30:5-6; Job 28:20-28; Eccles 12:11-12; cf. 1 Kings 3:12; 4:29) and acquired through a life-long process (Prov 1:5; 2:1-6), to make and carry out decisions that are pleasing to God and ultimately socially and personally beneficial. Biblical wisdom, therefore, cannot be reduced to mere skills for mastering or coping with life,[25] although its acquisi-

---

[23]Andrew Hill, quoted in Sandy and Giese, *Cracking Old Testament Codes*, p. 255.
[24]For a more complete discussion of wisdom theology, see Richard L. Schultz, "Unity or Diversity in Wisdom Theology? A Canonical and Covenantal Perspective," *Tyndale Bulletin* 48 (1997): 271-306; Richard L. Schultz, "Ecclesiastes," in *New Dictionary of Biblical Theology,* ed. T. Desmond Alexander et al. (Downers Grove, Ill.: InterVarsity Press, 2000), pp. 211-15; also Alan W. Jenks, "Theological Presuppositions of Israel's Wisdom Literature," *Horizons in Biblical Theology* 7 (1985): 43-75, and Goldsworthy, *Gospel and Wisdom*, chap. 10.
[25]James L. Crenshaw, *Old Testament Wisdom: An Introduction* (Louisville, Ky.: Westminster John Knox, 1998), p. 111: "Thematically wisdom comprises self-evident intuitions about mastering life for human betterment."

tion obviously assists us in this task. Thus wisdom literature is an ideal source for principles to appropriate in Christian counseling.

Because of the strikingly similar extrabiblical parallels to Old Testament wisdom writings,[26] the gnomic "everyday" nature of proverbial wisdom and its posited source in human experience and observation, wisdom literature often is viewed as exclusively derived from general revelation. According to John Goldingay, "The nature of wisdom literature is such as to maximize the potential of human reflection in the context of our life before God in the world. The approach of Proverbs and Ecclesiastes is to seek to discover truth from the world and from life rather than to expect it to be supernaturally revealed."[27] However, the book of Job clearly demonstrates that human participants were unable to offer an accurate explanation for Job's suffering.

To be sure, Proverbs affirms repeatedly that wisdom can be gained through instruction by a parent or a sage, through personal experience, and even through the close observation of ants and other lowly creatures (Prov 6:6; 30:24-28). Nevertheless, this acquisition of wisdom occurs in the context of the Israelite's faith[28]— the covenantal name for God, Yahweh, occurs eighty-seven times in Proverbs and repeatedly in the narrative sections of Job—and of the acknowledgement of God as Creator (Prov 8:22-31; 14:31; 17:5; 20:12; 22:2; 29:13; Eccles 3:11; 12:1,7; Job 38— 40). Thus the acquisition of wisdom is dependent on prior special revelation. Furthermore, many individual proverbs are highly theological, emphasizing God's standards and ultimate judgment, which often are seemingly contradicted by everyday experience (for example, see Prov 28:13-14, 25, 27; Eccles 8:11-13). This suggests a source other than human observations of patterns of life within society. Thus wisdom literature cannot be viewed as offering a clear warrant for expecting divine revelation through the social sciences, even though these disciplines may discover much about human beings as God's creation.

Wisdom's theological foundation is therefore twofold: it is creational and covenantal. It is creational in its affirmation that God created a world that is orderly and

---

[26]It has even been claimed, though never compellingly demonstrated, that Proverbs 22:17— 24:20 was extensively plagiarized or adapted from the Egyptian "Instruction of Amenemope." See John Ruffle, "The Teaching of Amenemope and Its Connection with the Book of Proverbs," *Tyndale Bulletin* 28 (1977): 29-68.

[27]John Goldingay, *Models for Scripture* (Grand Rapids, Mich.: Eerdmans, 1994), pp. 362-63. Similarly, Bruce K. Waltke, "Theology of Proverbs," in *New International Dictionary of Old Testament Theology and Exegesis,* ed. Willem VanGemeren (Grand Rapids, Mich.: Zondervan, 1997), 4:1079, states: "God did not speak to the sages face to face. . . . Rather, he spoke to them principally through their observations of the creation and of human behavior and their godly reflections, informed by faith, on what they saw." See also James B. Hurley and James T. Berry, "The Relation of Scripture and Psychology in Counseling from a Pro-Integration Position," *Journal of Psychology and Christianity* 16 (1997): 329-35, 340-42.

[28]Proverbs 29:18 asserts that the fabric of society unravels when there is no revelation (*ḥāzôn*) of the divine will through a prophet or lawgiver.

good (Prov 3:19-20; Eccles 3:11; 7:29) and thus reflects his wisdom. Wisdom involves both the celebration of creation's goodness as a gift of the Creator (Eccles 2:24-26; 9:7) and the acknowledgement of creation's fallen state, which Ecclesiastes aptly characterizes as "utterly transient" *(hebel).*[29] Wisdom offers a biblical warrant for the genuine enjoyment of God's everyday gifts—food, companionship and work—under the sovereign hand of God (Eccles 11:9) and thus resists our categorization of life experiences as either secular or sacred. At the same time, it recognizes that suffering is an integral and valuable part of the human experience (Eccles 7:2-3, 13-14, cf. the book of Job).

Rooted also in Israel's covenantal faith, wisdom presupposes a dynamic relationship with the one true God, which it calls "the fear of the LORD," the foundational principle of biblical wisdom. The phrase occurs eighteen times in Proverbs, five times in Ecclesiastes and ten times in Job, along with several related expressions, including those in Proverbs 1:29; 8:13; 31:30; Job 1:1, 8-9; 2:3 and Ecclesiastes 12:13, and others throughout the Old Testament (for example, Gen 22:12; 42:18; Ex 1:21; 14:31; Lev 19:14, 32; 25:17; Deut 4:10; 5:29; 6:2, 13, 24; 8:6; 10:12, 20; Josh 4:24; 24:14; 1 Sam 12:14, 24; 2 Sam 23:3; 1 Kings 8:43; 18:12; Ps 2:11; 128:1), though not always with the same nuance.[30]

Wisdom makes the same ethical demands as the Mosaic law,[31] and accordingly it makes the same promises and threats as the Sinai covenant,[32] while focusing on the individual rather than the nation. The wisdom teacher claims that covenant blessings are available to those who walk in the fear of the Lord, even if the nation as a whole is apostate. Conversely, because God graciously may delay the ultimate punishment of a nation, wickedness may evoke divine wrath on individuals "before your time" (Eccles 7:17 NIV; cf. 8:8). This understanding of wisdom's theological foundations suggests that wisdom principles cannot be applied effectively to the life of an individual who does not accept the biblical teaching that humans are created by and dependent on God.

Growing in wisdom is a central aspect of godly character formation. According

---

[29]This basic translation is defended persuasively by Daniel C. Fredericks in *Coping with Transience: Ecclesiastes on Brevity in Life* (Sheffield, U.K.: JSOT, 1993). According to Proverbs the wise and the righteous are constantly afflicted by the sinful actions of the foolish and wicked.

[30]Joachim Becker has argued that the fear of God in the Old Testament can be numinous, cultic, ethical or nomistic, *Gottesfurcht im Alten Testament* (Rome: PBI, 1965).

[31]These include the warnings against dishonesty in commerce (Prov 11:1; 16:11; 20:10; Deut 25:13-16; cf. Lev 19:35-36) and moving boundary stones (Prov 22:28; 23:10; Deut 19:14; 27:17) and the commands to honor parents (Prov 13:1; 15:5; 19:26; 20:20; 28:24; Deut 5:16; 21:18-21; 27:16) and avoid adultery (Prov 22:14; Deut 5:18; 22:22).

[32]Wise behavior leads to long life (Prov 3:1-2; 4:10-13; 8:32-36; Deut 5:16; 30:15-18) and to possession of the land (Prov 2:20-22; Deut 5:32-33; 30:15-18), but folly brings death, and disobedience brings judgment.

to William Brown, "the instrumental virtues of discretion and good sense are intimately bound up with the welfare of the community. The prudent lifestyle is profiled *relationally*, beyond the perspective of the efficient and successful attainment of individual goals."[33] On the one hand, the various wisdom terms (cleverness, discipline, discretion, insight, knowledge, prudence) represent complementary skills for living so that growth in breadth and depth can occur over the course of a lifetime. On the other hand, the various terms for fool (or folly) have meanings ranging from "naive" or "simpleton" to "fool" (*ʾeʾwîl, keʾsîl nāḇāl*) and "scoffer" (*lēṣ*), portraying varying degrees of personal culpability for foolishness, of receptivity to wisdom's voice, and of the likelihood of reform.[34]

According to Gerhard von Rad, "the word 'folly' does not describe a particular intellectual defect. . . . Folly is a disorder in the centre of a man's life."[35] The fool is one who has made the ultimate wrong decision, excluding God and his standards from the control center of life (*lēḇ;* Ps 14:1-3; 53:1-3), and thus is said to literally "lack heart" (Prov 6:32; 7:7; 10:13, 21; 11:12; 12:11; 15:21; 17:16, 18; 24:30); the result is a lifetime of bad decisions. Because wisdom clearly has a moral and not only a pragmatic dimension—it involves doing what is right, just and fair (Prov 1:3; 2:9)—folly is interchangeable with wickedness (and wisdom with righteousness). The fool takes sin lightly (Prov 10:23; 14:9) and rages against God (Prov 19:3); the wise fear the Lord and turn away from evil (Prov 14:16). Thus wisdom literature gives guidelines for lifelong moral development, not just tips for successful living.

The wisdom contained in the books of Job and Ecclesiastes differs in form and emphasis from that in Proverbs. It is more dialogical and disputational than proverbial. It focuses on the limitations rather than on the great benefits of human wisdom. However, this does not justify the frequent scholarly claim that Job and Ecclesiastes reflect a postexilic "crisis in wisdom," a protest against the rosy-viewed confidence of Proverbs.

According to David Hubbard, "Proverbs seems to say, 'These are the rules for life; try them and find that they will work.' Job and Ecclesiastes say, 'We did, and

---

[33]William P. Brown, *Character in Crisis: A Fresh Approach to the Wisdom Literature of the Old Testament* (Grand Rapids, Mich.: Eerdmans, 1996), 35. See also Daniel J. Estes, *Hear, My Son: Teaching and Learning in Proverbs 1—9* (Leicester, U.K.: Inter-Varsity Press, 1997), and Deryck Sheriffs, *The Friendship of the Lord: An Old Testament Spirituality* (Carlisle, U.K.: Paternoster, 1996), chap. 6. Sheriffs views wisdom as presenting "a genuine spirituality of the secular," because "the mundane is incorporated within Yahweh's domain" (p. 158).

[34]The best studies of these respective semantic fields are Michael V. Fox, "Words for Wisdom," *Zeitschrift für Althebräistik* 6 (1993): 149-69, and his "Words for Folly," *Zeitschrift für Althebräistik* 10 (1997): 4-15; see also Derek Kidner's helpful character sketches in *Proverbs,* Tyndale Old Testament Commentary (Downers Grove, Ill.: InterVarsity Press, 1964), pp. 36-43.

[35]Gerhard von Rad, *Old Testament Theology,* vol. 1, *The Theology of Israel's Historical Traditions* (New York: Harper & Row, 1962), p. 429.

they don't.'"[36] However, there is nothing that the latter books state regarding the relative value and limitations of wisdom and righteousness or regarding divine freedom, justice and inscrutability that cannot be found in the former, though these ideas are expressed less prominently therein.[37] Thus Job and Ecclesiastes serve as a check against an overly dogmatic and self-assured application of wisdom teaching, and Proverbs affirms that the exceptions to wisdom principles that Job and Ecclesiastes observe do not invalidate the general truths that they express. Job and Ecclesiastes emphasize the fact that whether or not one experiences divine justice or seeming injustice in the present is a matter of God's sovereign timing. Waiting for God to respond to his complaints was as painful for Job as his physical maladies. Together these wisdom books help us to find and maintain a balance between optimism and pessimism.

Interpreting Specific Wisdom Books

What implications do these literary features and theological themes have for how we interpret wisdom texts and apply them to contemporary life situations? Because of the diversity of the individual wisdom books I will discuss the books one at a time.[38]

Proverbs. The basic form of wisdom literature is the proverb, which Ted Hildebrandt defines as "a short, salty, concrete, fixed, paradigmatic, poetically-crafted saying."[39] This combination of features makes individual proverbs notoriously difficult to translate and interpret; therefore, they are easily misused by those who are unfamiliar with the characteristic vocabulary and ethos of wisdom sayings. In the words of George Schwab, "Proverbs is too often treated as a proof-text source to sanction psychological theories" without due attention being paid to "the deep structure and central message of the book."[40] This problem is illustrated vividly by Proverbs 22:6 ("Train children in the right way, and when old, they will not stray,"

---

[36]David A. Hubbard, "The Wisdom Movement and Israel's Covenant Faith," *Tyndale Bulletin* 17 (1966): 6.

[37]See Schultz, "Unity or Diversity?" pp. 281-89.

[38]George M. Schwab Sr. has authored the most helpful series of articles in this regard: "The Proverbs and the Art of Persuasion," *Journal of Biblical Counseling* 14 (1995): 6-17; "Cultivating the Vineyard: Solomon's Counsel for Lovers," *Journal of Biblical Counseling* 15 (1997): 8-20; "Ecclesiastes and Counsel Under the Sun," *Journal of Biblical Counseling* 15 (1997): 7-16; "The Book of Job and Counsel in the Whirlwind," *Journal of Biblical Counseling* 17 (1998): 31-43. However, his approach is weakened by his analysis of the Song of Songs as an anthology of love songs rather than as a unified composition and by his overly negative view of the message of Ecclesiastes. See also John W. Hilber, "Old Testament Wisdom and the Integration Debate in Christian Counseling," *Bibliotheca Sacra* 155 (1998): 411-22. In this essay, I will emphasize Proverbs before commenting briefly on the other books.

[39]Ted A. Hildebrandt, "Proverb," in Sandy and Giese, eds., *Cracking Old Testament Codes*, pp. 234-37.

[40]Schwab, "Proverbs and the Art of Persuasion," p. 17.

Care for the Soul

a favorite of Christian family counselors. Christian psychologists' and counselors' interpretations of this familiar proverb indicate clearly the extent to which their counseling theory influences their interpretation. How many heartaches are needlessly caused by counselors who promise parents that if they train their children in the way they should go, their children will not abandon that way when they grow up?

This traditional understanding of Proverbs 22:6 nearly becomes Paul Meier's motto on parenting, especially regarding the first six years of life.[41] However, it is highly unlikely that the noun *na'ar*, sometimes translated "child," refers primarily to preschoolers. It is more accurate to translate *na'ar* as "young man" in Proverbs, because the person to whom the book is addressed is old enough to study the proverbs (Prov 1:4) and to be seduced by an adulteress (Prov 7:7). Henry Cloud and John Townsend offer another interpretation: "The verse actually means 'the way God has planned for him (or her) to go,'" that is, "what God intended for them."[42] This is not likely to be the meaning of *way* in this context. Smalley and Trent suggest translating this verse "according to his bent," so that we are to take a personal interest in each child when training (or blessing) him or her because we know each one's unique set of needs.[43] However, it is unlikely that such a modern emphasis on a tailor-made upbringing that is sensitive to the idiosyncrasies of each individual would have a place in the community-oriented ethic of the sage. Robert Hicks argues that the verse instead encourages parents to give children varied initiatory "experiences in the way of wisdom."[44]

Ted Hildebrandt, an Old Testament scholar who authored a two-volume doctoral dissertation on Proverbs, points out that especially in the light of the proverbs' historical-cultural background, all of these interpretations overlook the more restrictive meanings of the key terms in Proverbs 22:6, including that of the verb *hānak*, "to initiate." After reviewing numerous possible interpretations, Hildebrandt argues that the most probable paraphrase would be: "A squire's status is to be recognized and his experience, training, and subsequent responsibilities are to reflect that high status, for this will be his status for his entire life."[45] The often elliptical and generalizing language of Proverbs lends itself to a wide range of suggested translations,

---

[41]Meier cites Proverbs 22:6 seven times in his book *Christian Child-Rearing and Personality Development* (Grand Rapids, Mich.: Baker, 1977), pp. 18, 45, 92, 123, 151, 159, 160.

[42]Cloud and Townsend, *Boundaries*, pp. 62-63.

[43]Smalley and Trent, *Blessing*, p. 103.

[44]Robert Hicks, *In Search of Wisdom: Timeless Insights for the Practice of Life* (Colorado Springs, Colo.: NavPress, 1995), p. 120-22.

[45]Ted Hildebrandt, "Proverbs 22:6a: Train Up a Child?" *Grace Theological Journal* 9 (1988): 3-19. Understanding *way* as the "way of divine wisdom," the way in which every young person should be directed by his or her parents, also could be defended in light of the reference to the "fear of the LORD" in 22:4 and the depiction of "thorns and snares" besetting the "way " (same Hebrew word) of the perverse in 22:5.

but a counselor's particular theory of child-rearing should not determine his or her choice of a translation. In order to counter this danger, it is helpful to compare several published translations of a given proverb and to consult a commentary or two regarding interpretive options.

Proverbs 1—9 serves as a hermeneutical key (or primer) for understanding wisdom. The general and seemingly secular proverbs that constitute the collections that begin in Proverbs 10 should be read against the backdrop of the highly theological characterization of proverbial wisdom in the first nine chapters (and the theologically explicit proverbs that are scattered throughout the collections). Proverbial sayings can be expressed as imperatival admonitions or prohibitions followed by motivating promises or threats (for example, Prov 3:1-12) or as indicative statements (for example, Prov 3:13-20), and both types should be viewed as equally authoritative. Their authority is based on their source rather than on their form. According to Hildebrandt, it is helpful if interpreters seek to analyze proverbs using the "topic/comment method," identifying the subject or theme of each saying and what is said about it, using the following categories:[46]

Character	→	Consequence	(Prov 10:1, 4, 6)
Character	→	Act	(Prov 10:12, 23, 32)
Character	→	Evaluation	(Prov 10:11a, 20)
Act	→	Evaluation	(Prov 10:5; 29:5)
Act	→	Consequence	(Prov 10:9, 17)
Item	→	Evaluation	(Prov 10:2a, 15)

Hildebrandt's approach helps us to focus on the core movement of the proverb rather than on a peripheral element of it. For example, in the case of Proverbs 10:12 ("Hatred stirs up strife, but love covers all offenses"), the use of the category "character → act" rather than "character → consequence" keeps us from concluding wrongly that love *compensates for* rather than *overlooks* shortcomings.

Despite the seemingly atomistic nature of individual proverbs, recent studies suggest that they are often carefully arranged to form short thematic units, with a basic element consisting of a proverbial pair, such as Proverbs 18:10-11: "The name of the LORD is a strong tower; the righteous run into it and are safe. / The wealth of the rich is their strong city; in their imagination it is like a high wall." Proverbs 26:1-12 is a good example of a thematic unit that describes the nature and danger of folly. It contains the familiar proverbial pair in verses 4 and 5: "Do not answer fools according to their folly, or you will be a fool yourself. / Answer fools according to their folly, or they will be wise in their own eyes." It is important that the interpreter examine the surrounding context of any given proverbial statement (not only

---

[46]Hildebrandt, "Proverbs," p. 236.

in Prov 1—9) for related proverbs that might help in the interpretation and application process.[47] The proverbial pair in Proverbs 26:4-5 also reflects the situational
nature of proverbs: the discerning person will know which proverb (or action, v. 4a
or 5a) is appropriate in a given situation (v. 4b or 5b), and that application is sometimes indicated in the immediate context.

Douglas Stuart has offered a helpful set of guidelines for the correct use of proverbs:[48]

1. Proverbs are often parabolic; in other words, they are figurative, pointing
beyond themselves.

2. Proverbs are intensely practical, not theoretically theological.

3. Proverbs are worded to be memorable, not technically precise.

4. Proverbs are not designed to support selfish behavior—just the opposite!

5. Proverbs strongly reflecting ancient cultures may need sensible "translation"
so we do not lose their meaning.

6. Proverbs are not guarantees from God, but poetic guidelines for good behavior.

7. Proverbs may use highly specific language, exaggeration, or any of a variety
of literary techniques to make their point.

8. Proverbs give good advice for wise approaches to certain aspects of life, but
they are not exhaustive in their coverage.

9. Wrongly used, proverbs might justify a crass, materialistic lifestyle. Rightly
used, proverbs provide practical advice for daily living.

If interpreters heed Stuart's guidelines and examples, many abuses of proverbial
wisdom will be avoided. Though they are formulated absolutely, proverbs merely
offer divinely inspired generalizations regarding spiritual probabilities. They are
true with regard to one slice of life but reflect only that one aspect of reality; we do
not seek to synthesize theology from sound bites.

Ecclesiastes and Job. It is crucial to pay attention to the unique features of the
particular literary form or genre of Ecclesiastes and Job. Ecclesiastes combines auto-
biographical reflections with direct instruction, while Job combines a narrative
framework with disputational dialogues and monologues. Each reflects the per-

---

[47]John Goldingay, "The Arrangement of Sayings in Proverbs 10—15," *Journal for the Study of
the Old Testament* 61 (1994): 75-83; Raymond C. Van Leeuwen, *Context and Meaning in
Proverbs 25—27* (Atlanta: Scholars Press, 1988); Ted Hildebrandt, "Proverbial Pairs:
Compositional Units in Proverbs 10—29," *Journal of Biblical Literature* 107 (1988): 207-24.
Most recent commentaries give some indication of thematic groupings of or intertextual links
between adjacent proverbs. Jay Adams offers an excellent example of how giving attention
to literary context will correct the misuse of Prov 23:7 ("As he thinketh in his heart, so is he"
[KJV], also a questionable translation, reducing "a philosophical principle" to a "practical
warning" regarding table manners) ("Biblical Interpretation and Counseling, Part 2," *Journal
of Biblical Counseling* 17 [1998]: 26-27).
[48]Fee and Stuart, *How to Read the Bible,* pp. 225-26.

sonal circumstances, experiences and observations of its speaker/author and makes no absolute claims for the universal validity of its statements. We may or may not, therefore, be able to identify easily with the perspectives expressed in specific passages, especially as they wrestle intellectually and spiritually with the paradoxical and often inscrutable nature of reality.

Accordingly, we must interpret individual verses (which may contain proverbs) in the light of the whole (the literary context and the overall message). We should be aware that we may encounter radically opposing views of Ecclesiastes's message in Bible commentaries. R. N. Whybray describes the speaker as a "preacher of joy" who affirms God's creational everyday gifts, while Scott characterizes him as a rationalist, agnostic, skeptic, pessimist and fatalist who disputes the benefits of wisdom and the meaningfulness of life.[49] From Ecclesiastes 12:9-14 one can conclude that Qoheleth's (the speaker's self-designation) words are ordered, reliable, and authoritative. Because everything under the sun is utterly temporary (*hebel*, a word that occurs thirty-eight times in the book, for example in Eccles 1:2 and 12:8), he sets out to analyze and assess the various activities of life in order to determine what has lasting value (*yitrôn*, or "profit," used fifteen times) in such a world (Eccles 1:3). He considers human achievements and wisdom (Eccles 1:12-2:26), social relationships (Eccles 4:1-16) and wealth (Eccles 5:10-6:9). Ecclesiastes thus offers an excellent resource for responding to a society that desperately seeks life's meaning and happiness in all the wrong places and to a church that sometimes denigrates the enjoyment of everyday ("secular") activities (Eccles 2:24; 3:12-13, 22; 5:18-19; 8:15; 9:7-9).

In a very different manner, the book of Job seeks to answer the accuser's question ("Does Job fear God for nothing?" [Job 1:9]) by demonstrating that genuine faith does exist and that it survives, even though God's promised benefits and rewards are not experienced continually or immediately. The search for the ultimate explanation for Job's suffering leads to many statements that are patently false in Job's particular situation (Job 42:7), though generally true enough that Paul can affirmatively quote Eliphaz's words (from Job 5:13) in 1 Corinthians 3:19. Job is exemplary in his perseverance in the face of suffering (Jas 5:10-11), if not in all that he says. His story can be a great source of encouragement for those who are encountering severe and unexplainable suffering.

In light of the larger purposes or messages of these books, it is easier to understand why one verse or statement often qualifies (or even contradicts) the verses that precede it. This is especially frequent in Ecclesiastes, and we must sustain the

---

[49]Roger N. Whybray, "Qoheleth, Preacher of Joy," *Journal for the Study of the Old Testament* 23 (1982): 87-98; similarly Martin A. Klopfenstein, "Kohelet und die Freude am Dasein," *Theologische Zeitschrift* 47 (1991): 97-107; Robert B. Y. Scott, *Proverbs, Ecclesiastes* (Garden City, N.Y.: Doubleday, 1965), p. 192.

tension created by the juxtaposition of such contrary verses rather than resolve the tension by affirming the one and rejecting the other. Achievement brings delight and disappointment (Eccles 2:10-11). Wisdom is beneficial and futile (Eccles 2:12-16). The certainty of death leads to madness and hope (Eccles 9:3-5). Ecclesiastes 7:1-2 offers a striking example of a shocking proverbial statement that can be clarified by that which follows it: "A good name is better than precious ointment, and the day of death, than the day of birth. / It is better to go to the house of mourning than to go to the house of feasting; for this is the end of everyone, and the living will lay it to heart" (NASB). Similarly, in Ecclesiastes and Job absolute-sounding claims often reflect strong emotional responses to the speaker's situation and experiences. Thus Qoheleth hates life (Eccles 2:17) and Job curses and wishes to blot out his day of birth (Job 3:1-5). Therefore, it is essential that no verse from either of these books be considered apart from its conceptual and literary context.

Unfortunately Job not only suffered greatly at the hands of Satan but also has suffered at the hands of Christian counselors.[50] There are two basic approaches to Job in the psychological literature. One approach is to psychoanalyze Job, his friends and even God as they are portrayed in the book. The second approach is to derive principles on effective counseling from the book. There is no inherent reason why we should not seek to derive principles from a narrative text, but we must ask whether Job is an appropriate source for learning counseling techniques.

Why call the three friends and Elihu Job's four "counselors," as Hulme does, when the book never describes them as such? According to Elihu's assessment in Job 32:3, the three friends, who originally gathered to try to comfort Job by their mere presence, were unable to refute Job's arguments and thus condemned Job. They were thus self-appointed apologists for a rigid retributional theology. Elihu also cannot be viewed as a counselor, for he speaks out of anger rather than in compassion and there is no indication in the text that Job heeded or responded to Elihu's words. One author even views Job's silence as proof of Elihu's effectiveness as a pastoral counselor because there is "no line of demarcation between Elihu's ministry to Job and Job's encounter with God."[51] As an example of the nonproverbial disputation genre of wisdom literature, the central section of Job resembles a debate more than it does a counseling session. At best, Job powerfully illustrates

---

[50]See James R. Beck, "Patient Job as a Patient," book review of I. J. Gerber, *Job on Trial: A Book for Our Times*, in *Journal of Psychology and Theology* 12 (1984): 136-17; William E. Hulme, "Pastoral Counseling in the Book of Job," *Concordia Journal* (1989): 121-38; Jeannette P. Maas, "A Psychological Assessment of Job," *Pacific Journal of Theology* 2 (1989): 55-68; Peter W. Nimmo, "Sin, Evil and Job: Monotheism as a Psychological and Pastoral Problem," *Pastoral Psychology* 43 (1994): 427-39; James H. Reynierse, "Behavior Therapy and Job's Recovery," *Journal of Psychology and Theology* 3 (1975): 187-94; James M. Siwy and Carole E. Smith, "Christian Group Therapy: Sitting with Job," *Journal of Psychology and Theology* 16 (1988): 318-23.
[51]Hulme, "Pastoral Counseling," p. 136.

how we should *not* respond to someone who is suffering intensely.

The Song of Songs. The Song of Songs may appropriately be called wisdom literature because of its verbal and conceptual parallels with Proverbs 5:15-20 and its didactic conclusion (Song 8:6-7). Like Job and Ecclesiastes, The Song of Songs can be viewed as a unified, artistic and well-planned composition—it is the *Song,* not the *Songs,* of Solomon—although there are scholars who reject this assessment with regard to each of the wisdom books.

In the Song of Songs we can identify a literary context, two main characters and a loose plot centering on the developing relationship of two married lovers (the wedding ceremony and wedding night are clearly indicated in Song 3:6—5:1). Thus it is a song of longing with a biographical point of reference. Its lyrical world is a world of images, comparisons and metaphors that have striking parallels in Egyptian love songs. Repetition is prominent: there are repeated images (for example, the vineyard, 1:6; 8:11-12), phrases ("I am faint with love," 2:5; 5:8), scenes (dreams, 3:1-4; 5:4-7) and refrains (2:7; 3:5; 8:4). Once again, it is inappropriate to focus on individual verses as though they teach something specific about dating or marital relationships without understanding their contribution to the development of the book as a whole.

Although it is hardly a manual on overcoming sexual dysfunction,[52] The Song of Songs appears to have a didactic purpose. It addresses young women (the "daughters of Jerusalem") in a manner similar to the way in which Proverbs addresses young men. The value of chastity and fidelity and the delights of marital sexuality are vividly described through speech and image, offering a message that our present-day society, marked by temporary and self-serving relationships between men and women, desperately needs to embrace: "Many waters cannot quench love, neither can floods drown it. If one offered for love all the wealth of his house, it would be utterly scorned" (Song 8:7).

Wisdom as a Way of Knowing

Lest this essay leave the impression that I consider all efforts at integrating theology (or biblical teachings) with the social sciences, especially psychology, to be seriously flawed, I will conclude by looking at several general discussions of the value of wisdom for such integration of faith and learning.

Eric Johnson explores analogies between wisdom and adult postformal development, such as its recognition of the limitations of human thought, its nonpassive, reconstructive, communal and covenantal nature, and of the nonnecessity of a "crisis of doubt." Gladson and Lucas argue that wisdom is suitable as a basis for psy-

---

[52]This is the impression given by Joseph C. Dillow, S*olomon on Sex* (New York: Thomas Nelson, 1977). S. Craig Glickman, *A Song for Lovers* (Downers Grove, Ill.: InterVarsity Press, 1976) offers a much more exegetically satisfying and holistic practical exposition of the book.

chotheological dialogue because it does not distinguish rigidly between perception and apperception or between religious and nonreligious and because it has an experiential and anthropocentric orientation. They clearly contrast wisdom's approach with psychology's empirical, naturalistic approach, but they note several similarities in wisdom's and psychology's respective epistemologies. They seek common ground between wisdom and the theories of Frankl and Adler, such as the resilient "will to meaning" and the emphasis on "social responsibility." [53]

Richard Wells identifies a parallel between wisdom and Christian psychology in the latter's emphasis on "theologically interpreted experience," though one hardly can characterize wisdom as a quest for holiness when the basic Hebrew root for "holy" (*qādôš*) occurs only three times in the book of Proverbs, two of these instances being in a divine title. Wells also contends that wisdom offers a corrective to psychological theory because the former emphasizes character as a therapeutic goal and upholds the "paradox of disorder." Edward Curtis seeks to relate general revelation to the special revelation in wisdom as a model for faith-learning integration; he writes that the general revelation is possible "because God has created order and regularity in this world." Finally, George Schwab seeks to derive principles from Proverbs on the "art of persuasion" that are applicable to the counseling process; he views the proverbs as "a seamless source of wisdom." [54]

These essays share several features in common. Their authors seek a proper approach for integrating theology with psychology or counseling: They seek to understand wisdom or proverbial wisdom as a whole rather than citing individual verses, they make thorough use of current Old Testament scholarship, they candidly acknowledge the differences between biblical wisdom and psychology, and in their conclusions they are suggestive rather than prescriptive, exploratory rather than dogmatic. These efforts are to be welcomed and applauded even though the one or the other author may depend too much on historical-critical reconstructions, give inadequate attention to the uniqueness of Old Testament wisdom within its ancient Near Eastern context, or ignore Old Testament wisdom's covenantal roots, this-worldly focus or claim to special revelation.

Concluding Recommendations

One may be tempted to dismiss the critical analysis in this essay as the nitpicking of a biblical scholar. However, similar concerns have been expressed by leading Christian counselors. Jay Adams states the matter quite bluntly: "A person who can't

---

[53] Johnson, "Call of Wisdom," pp. 93-103; Jerry Gladson and Ron Lucas, "Hebrew Wisdom and Psycho-Theological Dialogue," *Zygon* 24 (1989): 357-76.

[54] C. Richard Wells, "Hebrew Wisdom as a Quest for Wholeness and Holiness," *Journal of Psychology and Christianity* 15 (1996): 58-69; Edward M. Curtis, "Old Testament Wisdom: A Model for Faith-Learning Integration," *Christian Scholars Review* 15 (1986): 213-227; Schwab, "Proverbs and the Art of Persuasion," pp. 6-17.

interpret the Word of God properly can't counsel biblically. . . . To use the Bible in a shallow, simplistic fashion that in many cases misrepresents what God is saying in the passage to which one refers is inexcusable."[55]

If continued progress is to be made in the integration of psychology and theology, several concrete steps need to be taken. First, the foundation must be laid by a series of thorough, synthetic studies of biblical genres and themes similar to those just cited on wisdom, and psychologists and counselors must be on the lookout for good models of integrative work to follow. Second, individual biblical texts should be cited only after they have been interpreted in a hermeneutically responsible manner, with consultation of several reputable commentaries to validate the interpretation. Third, Christian counselors and psychologists should read more widely in biblical and systematic theology and in Christian ethics in order to gain a clearer framework for evaluating secular psychological theory. Biblical scholars interested in integrative work must also become more familiar with the standard psychological literature. Fourth, required courses in theology and biblical hermeneutics should become an integral part of the training of Christian psychologists and counselors. Some Christian therapists may find it necessary to pursue advanced degrees in theology. Fifth, psychologists and theologians must redouble their efforts to partner together and learn from one another. The collaborative efforts of Tremper Longman III and Dan Allender are exemplary in this regard.[56]

May we go forward together. "Do your best to present yourself to God as one approved by him, a worker who has no need to be ashamed, rightly explaining the word of truth" (2 Tim 2:15).

---

[55]Adams, "Biblical Interpretation and Counseling," pp. 5-9; "Biblical Interpretation and Counseling, Part 2," pp. 23-30. The quotation is from the opening paragraph of the first article. Adams follows his criticisms with a brief summary of interpretive procedure in which he distinguishes four analytical steps: literary-rhetorical, historical-grammatical, systematic-biblical-theological, and telic (How did the Holy Spirit want people to change as a result of this passage?).

[56]Dan B. Allender and Tremper Longman III, *Intimate Allies* (Wheaton, Ill.: Tyndale House, 1995); Allender and Longman, *Bold Love*.

13

BIBLICAL HERMENEUTICS
& CHRISTIAN PSYCHOLOGY

Bryan N. Maier & Philip G. Monroe

SUPPOSE YOU ARE SUPERVISING A DOCTORAL STUDENT IN PSYCHOLOGY. AS YOU watch through a one-way mirror, your trainee introduces himself to a new client and says, "How can I help you?" The client gives his name and says he is single. When he draws a breath to go on, your student interrupts and proclaims, "You have not successfully negotiated your phallic stage and you have many unresolved, affect-laden negative self objects that are causing your problems."

It would be outrageous to treat a client this way, but sometimes Christian psychologists treat the Word of God no better. Clinicians spend years studying the hermeneutics of the client so that they will feel competent to make judgments about diagnosis and treatment plans. Competent Christian clinicians should pay at least the same respect to Scripture by preparing themselves to interpret its message.

Almost twenty years ago, John Carter and Bruce Narramore warned that two of the barriers to integration would be "proof-texting" and "attempting to press the data of Scripture onto psychology or vice versa in a way that is inappropriate."[1] Their warning is still valid today, yet very little is written about the importance or methods of biblical hermeneutics in psychology. Several years later, Narramore again wrote about the danger of clients using poor interpretations of Scripture as defense mechanisms.[2] John Gartner and Robert Carbo, in their response to Narramore's article, point out that counselors cannot always assume that they are cor-

---

[1]John Carter and Bruce Narramore, *The Integration of Psychology and Theology* (Grand Rapids, Mich.: Zondervan, 1979), p. 30.
[2]Bruce Narramore, "Dealing with Religious Resistances in Psychotherapy," *Journal of Psychology and Theology* 22 (1994): 249-58.

rect and that their clients are wrong.[3] In the same issue of the *Journal of Psychology and Theology*, David Cranmer and Brian Eck, emphasizing the use of hermeneutical tools, assume that the therapist is more qualified than the client to make accurate interpretations.[4] If Christian psychologists are properly trained in the biblical side of their discipline, it is plausible to expect their reading of Scripture to be superior to that of their clients. But the *if* is a big one.

Christian therapists sometimes pay lip service to the importance of biblical hermeneutics, but little is done to promote its study in the field of Christian psychology. We will argue that the study of biblical hermeneutics is one of the most important tasks of a Christian psychologist, for both theory development and practice. It is important both because of the nature of Scripture and because of the use of Scripture in Christian psychology. In the first major section of this paper we will address three characteristics of Scripture that have clear implications for Christian psychology: First, Scripture is God's special revelation to his image-bearers. Second, because God is its author, Scripture is authoritative in all that it addresses. And finally, God's Word promises power. In the second major section of the paper we will address how Scripture is used in Christian psychology.

The Nature of Scripture

"All Scripture is inspired by God and profitable for teaching, for reproof, for correction, and for training in righteousness" (2 Tim 3:16 RSV).

Scripture is special revelation. The Bible warrants careful and rigorous interpretation because it is the clearest revelation of God and his will. In theological usage the term *revelation* is restricted to God's communication to us of what we would not otherwise know; ultimately, anything we know about God is a result of revelation.[5] "God can be known only because and so far as he reveals Himself."[6] Our conception of revelation will affect our understanding of everything else. All revelation is from God, but we usually divide it into two categories according to content. The first category, general revelation, contains what can be known about God through creation and nature; the second category, special revelation, contains what can be known about God through his direct speech to humans, through the incarnation of Christ and through inspired Scripture.

The creation accounts in Scripture tell the story of the glory of the Creator.[7] This

---

[3]John Gartner and Robert Carbo, "Serving Two Masters? Commentary on 'Dealing with Resistances to Psychotherapy,'" *Journal of Psychology and Theology* 22 (1994): 259-60.

[4]David Cranmer and Brian Eck, "God Said It: Psychology and Biblical Interpretation, How Text and Reader Interact Through the Glass Darkly," *Journal of Psychology and Theology* 22 (1994): 207-14.

[5]Lewis S. Chafer, *Chafer's Systematic Theology* (Dallas: Dallas Seminary Press, 1975), vol. 1.

[6]Benjamin B. Warfield, *Revelation and Inspiration* (Grand Rapids, Mich.: Baker, 1981), p. 37.

[7]Psalm 8:1-2 and 19:1 explicitly tell us that creation glorifies God.

message is so clear and obvious that those who "suppress" this truth are "without excuse" (Rom 1:18—2:1 RSV). Everything that can be perceived gives evidence of the power and majesty of the Creator. Especially important are the data we humans perceive when we look at ourselves; for all of us give evidence of being created in the image of God (Gen 1:26).

Even with all of the information that general revelation provides, God in his wisdom decided to reveal more of himself than what could be learned in nature. In addition to the revelation of his awesome power and glory as Creator, he revealed his ethical, or holy, character and his love in a very special way. First, he actually spoke with Adam and Eve. Genesis 1:28 says that he blessed them and explained to them their role: to rule the rest of creation under him. He also gave them the concepts that they needed in order to make moral decisions. Morality was defined as doing what God allows and not doing what he forbids (Gen 2:16-17). God communicated all of this directly and in propositional form. After the Fall, God continued to reveal himself in this special way through prophets and through the Scriptures. The subject of the revelation was the remedy God would provide for Adam's sin. The Scriptures particularly reveal God as the author, initiator and completer of the process of salvation (Eph 1:4-12; Jn 6:44; Rom 8:28-30; Phil 1:6). This revelation culminated in the incarnation of Christ. Now all special revelation relates to Christ and what he accomplished (Heb 1:1-2). This special revelation has been preserved for us in Scripture.

It is imperative that we understand the relationship between these two forms of revelation. God is the author of both, having created the universe and having authored Scripture, so there can be no contradiction between them. In addition, God is the subject of both forms of revelation. We can properly understand neither nature nor Scripture unless we see God as the main character in both stories, as the one whose nature and purposes are revealed. Finally, both forms of revelation are directed at human beings. Humanity, created in the image of God, is the intended recipient of both special and general revelation. We have been given the capacity to process what God reveals.

In spite of the similarities between these two kinds of revelation, general revelation has one key limitation: it is inadequate for salvation. Even before the Fall, God considered it necessary to communicate with his image-bearing creatures more than what was obvious in nature, so he spoke to Adam and Eve. Natural revelation cannot tell the whole story about God. It can tell us that we are creatures and that the Creator is infinitely powerful, intelligent and glorious, but it cannot tell us the purpose for which God created us. It took a special, verbal communication from the Creator to inform the creature about what is pleasing to God and what is not.

After the Fall the situation became much worse. Now humanity could not even interpret general revelation accurately. We suppressed much that nature in general and our own nature told us about being creatures or image-bearers (Rom 1:18-20).

Humankind has "cemented colored glasses to his eyes which he cannot remove."[8] God responded to this tragedy by planning a way for us to be redeemed. Christ came to earth and paid the price for sin so that we could be restored to the intimate relationship with God for which we were created. The focus of special revelation was now to communicate this plan to humanity. This is the overarching theme of Scripture. However, our blindness is so complete that merely confronting us with the truth of God's plan of redemption is not enough. A supernatural change of heart orchestrated by the Holy Spirit (Jn 6:44; 1 Cor 2:14) is necessary. Exposure to special revelation accompanied by the illuminating influence of the Holy Spirit results in regeneration.

Why is an understanding of special revelation important to Christian counselors? Without special revelation, fallen image-bearers cannot interpret anything correctly in an ultimate sense.[9] God has spoken about many (and in principle all) of the issues that psychologists deal with. The Scriptures say much about the heart in its natural state, about the nature of persons and about how people change and grow. Finally, they address our final destiny.

Christian practitioners often go to one of two unhelpful extremes here. Some take the position that Scripture answers every psychological question, more or less in the manner of a counseling handbook. They think that each particular kind of problem with which twentieth-century clients come to therapy is directly addressed by Scripture, so that the counselor need only find the texts (instructions) that are applicable to the client's presenting problem and then induce the client to follow the instructions. This is too simple a view of the relation between Christian psychology and the Bible. Even where Christian psychology does not involve the integration of insights or techniques from secular psychologies, it is a creative and systematic endeavor in which the psychologist, starting from Scripture, makes applications of biblical psychology that may not be made in the Bible itself. After all, many of our psychological ailments are peculiar to our period of history and so are not addressed in the Bible.[10]

Proponents of the other extreme view recognize how different the biblical documents are from twentieth-century and more recent works of scientific and clinical psychology and infer from this that Scripture can play only a very minor role in theory formation or psychotherapeutic practice. According to this view, we are warranted in using Scripture as ethical motivation for our psychological work and as

---

[8]Cornelius Van Til, *The Defense of the Faith* (Philadelphia: Presbyterian & Reformed, 1955), p. 94.

[9]Hendrik G. Stoker, "Reconnoitering the Theory of Knowledge of Prof. Dr. Cornelius Van Til," in *Jerusalem and Athens: Critical Discussions on the Theology and Apologetics of Cornelius Van Til*, ed. E. R. Geehan (Phillipsburg, N.J.: Presbyterian & Reformed, 1980), pp. 25-71.

[10]See Philip Cushman, *Constructing the Self, Constructing America: A Cultural History of Psychotherapy* (Reading, Mass.: Addison-Wesley, 1995).

food for our own spiritual growth, and this has an indirect impact in our counseling. But we cannot hope to derive much of anything in the way of substantive psychological insight or guidance on practice from the Bible. This view fails to recognize the psychological depth of Scripture (e.g., the psalms, the teachings of Jesus, and the writings of the apostle Paul).[11]

Scripture is authoritative. A second reason that sound hermeneutics is important to Christian psychology is that we often use Scripture to authenticate our psychological models. Yet we continue to struggle to understand the extent to which the Bible speaks authoritatively about psychology or about the issues to which psychological inquiry is directed. And even when we have some inkling of how the Bible might be used, we face the monumental task of understanding how we are to go about interpreting biblical texts in our postmodern context, which seems to undermine the authority of all texts.

Christians believe that Scripture is the authoritative Word of God. It was passed on to us by prophets "as they were carried along by the Holy Spirit" (2 Pet 1:21 NIV). However, Christian counselors have questioned whether or to what extent an orthodox understanding of this doctrine means that Scripture supplies the frame for psychology. Over the years we have heard individuals needlessly debate whether the Bible is a textbook for counseling.[12] Even when we avoid polarizing the issues ("The Bible has nothing to say to psychology" versus "The Bible is the only source of data for counseling") we are often left wondering what the Bible does have to say authoritatively concerning psychological theory and practice.

If you were to listen in on a random sample of Christian counselors discussing what psychological data can be gleaned from the Bible, what would you hear? Most likely a discussion of the nature of persons, including a long conversation about the meaning of being God's image-bearers. They would also discuss the impact of sin and suffering on humans, God's design for healing communities and God's plan for redeeming broken and hurting people. Each of these discussions would be valuable; however, it is our perception that Christian counselors often discuss broad themes found in the Bible (for example, sin and grace) rather than detailed biblical data that are relevant to psychology. At times we seem to believe that Scripture speaks deeply about our condition as sinners and about God's plan for redemption, but rather simplistically about how we live healthy lives here on earth.

Scripture does indeed reveal the way of salvation, but also, by way of teaching, rebuking, correcting and training (2 Tim 3:15-16), it equips believers to live righteous lives. Peter writes that God's revelation gives us "everything we need for life

---

[11]For an example of deriving psychology from Scripture without treating Scripture as a handbook of psychology, see Robert C. Roberts's chapter about Pauline psychotherapy in this volume.

[12]See Philip G. Monroe, "Building Bridges with Biblical Counselors," *Journal of Psychology and Theology* 25 (1997): 28-37.

and godliness" (2 Pet 1:3). The Westminster Confession summarizes this point well: "The whole counsel of God, concerning all things necessary for his own glory, man's salvation, faith, and life, is either expressly set down in Scripture, or by good and necessary consequence may be deduced from Scripture."[13]

The Bible gives us everything we need to live out our destiny as regenerate image-bearers. Questions about living and about all the pain, confusion and meaning that goes with it—questions that every client implicitly or explicitly brings to therapy—are addressed deeply by the authoritative Word of God.

Does this mean that Scripture sets forth a prescription for curing all mental health problems or physical diseases? We do not find in the Bible a means to cure schizophrenia or prostate cancer, but let us not be afraid to say that Scripture does give direction on how to avoid psychological difficulties (for example, hopelessness and despair, which might lead to depression, and anxiety, which might lead to phobias and anxiety disorders). Scripture speaks clearly about human functioning, about the temporal and eternal impact of living a sinful life (and thus about the psychological manifestations of sin), and about how to mortify indwelling sin. God reveals how we can fulfill our purpose in life—to glorify God and enjoy Him forever[14]—despite our mental or physical limitations.

Even though we accept that the Bible is special and authoritative and speaks to issues that are central to psychotherapy, we face difficult questions about discovering its meaning. How are we to approach God's Word in a postmodern world? We are aware of a growing anxiety among educated and thoughtful Christian counselors about their ability to interpret Scripture correctly. They are usually quite willing to list possible meanings and interpretations, but they are much less likely to say, "to the best of my understanding, here is what God is actually saying." This hesitancy to interpret will surprise no one who has wandered through the aisles of a Christian bookstore and seen shelves of books laced with enough Scripture to justify a confusing array of cockeyed and mutually incompatible views and practices. Further, there are numerous examples of bad interpretation of Scripture in every era of our ecclesiastical history. So when postmodern thought tells us we cannot consider any scientific or literary data except through the filter of our culture or our individual biases, it is not hard for us to see the point. But instead of despairing of the possibility of interpreting Scripture correctly, we should ask how we can interpret it correctly and undertake to gain the skills to do it.

Christian psychologists would do well to know something about the history of the theory of biblical interpretation. Early hermeneutic scholars tended to speak of extracting the author-intended meaning from the text (some said that this should be

---

[13]Confession 1.6 in *The Confession of Faith and Catechisms* (Atlanta: Presbyterian Church in America, 1986).
[14]Ibid., Larger Catechism, question 1.

done by literal interpretation, others that it should be done by spiritualizing), but they were not very aware of the cultural lenses through which they viewed the text. Current hermeneutic theorists, intensely aware that all readers bring their own cultural lenses to the text, sometimes go so far as to deny that we have any interpretive access to the author's intentions; instead, each reader imposes her own meaning on the text.[15]

We suggest that, far from paralyzing us with obsessional postmodern tentativeness, a knowledge of the history of hermeneutics, may help to relativize the relativizers for us, and thus free us for interpretive self-confidence. In the light of this history we need not aim for a nebulous compromise between what the text itself says and the meanings that we breathe into it with our readings. We hope, rather, that a historically and literarily informed reading of a biblical text, combined with a self-critical awareness of our own biases, will enable us to confidently declare what the text is saying.

In a social climate in which the influence of reader bias is sometimes exaggerated to the point of convincing us that we can find nothing in texts except our biases, it is natural that a tendency should arise of limiting ourselves to asking questions of Scripture rather than arguing for particular interpretations of it. This ironic, noncommittal attitude toward Scripture is often convenient for psychological reasons. In *The Gagging of God*, Donald Carson suggests that Christians sometimes

> appeal to postmodernism to justify their . . . sometimes bitter reactions against the unnecessary dogmatisms and legalisms of a previous generation, without asking if they are sometimes in danger of throwing out the baby with the bath water. They give the impression that they feel there is a specially high place in the spiritual sphere reserved for those who ask questions and say they don't know, and only low places for those who write and preach "so that you may know the certainty of the things you have been taught" (to use the words of Luke 1:4).[16]

Carson's point is well-taken. We must not let those who are contentious about the gospel take from us our birthright of faith-based knowledge, nor must we let our personal developmental issues work in us an exaggerated receptivity to the psychological comforts of postmodern irony. As an aside, Carson cites a second

---

[15]A number of theologians have written on the philosophical movements in literary criticism. In *The Hermeneutical Spiral: A Comprehensive Introduction to Biblical Interpretation,* Grant Osborne nicely traces the movement of modern interpretation from its early focus on the author-intended meaning of the text to more recent deconstructionism theory, which holds that the reader creates the text's meaning during the act of reading (Downers Grove, Ill.: InterVarsity Press, 1991). See also Dan McCartney and Charles Clayton, *Let the Reader Understand: A Guide to Interpreting and Applying Scripture* (Wheaton, Ill.: Bridgepoint, 1994); Donald A. Carson, *Exegetical Fallacies,* 2nd ed. (Grand Rapids, Mich.: Baker, 1996); and Donald A. Carson, *The Gagging of God: Christianity Confronts Pluralism* (Grand Rapids, Mich.: Zondervan, 1996).

[16]Carson, *Gagging of God*, p. 91.

psychological reason we may hesitate to offer interpretations. Many evangelicals are biblically illiterate. They focus more on the feeling of grace than on teaching the doctrine of grace. Being less knowledgeable than we should be of the structure and themes of different books of the Bible, we feel anxious and vulnerable when we offer definite interpretations.

Those who believe that Scripture is God's Word to us (2 Tim 3:16) will reject the most radical postmodern hermeneutics. However, we must not deny the power of reader bias. Those who are unaware of their own system of interpretation may ignore the historical context and stray quite close to the deconstructionist prediction of purely projective reading. This frequently happens in private Bible study that asks only, "How does this relate to my situation?"[17] McCartney and Clayton succinctly spell out an evangelically defensible position in their summary of the interpretation and application of Scripture: Readers do not need to deny either what they bring to the interpretive task or what God's distinct meaning of the text is. "We postulate that God, the inventor of language, provides the basis for interpretation which is at once both truly objective and truly subjective."[18] God, who is faithful throughout the history of his church, has provided the modern Christian with the opportunity to benefit from the history of interpretation. Christian counselors who know this history and who understand the possible influence of their own concepts, biases and concerns on their reading of texts can faithfully pursue biblical foundations for the care of souls.

Scripture is powerful. The third reason biblical hermeneutics is important to Christian psychology is that the Bible is more than just a book of propositions about God. It also carries power. "For the word of God is living and active. Sharper than any double-edged sword, it penetrates even to dividing soul and spirit, joints and marrow; it judges the thoughts and attitudes of the heart" (Heb 4:12 NIV). The context of this passage deals with God's ability to expose the heart of humankind in all of its evil and hypocrisy. Nothing can be hidden from God, not even the deepest part of the human heart. The Word of God is compared to the most effective sword in the weaponry of the author's day. A double-edged (literally: double-mouthed) sword pierced more easily and went in deeper.[19] It cut to the deepest part of an enemy, and nothing could impede its progress. The author of Hebrews claims that the Word of God is sharper than such a sword. However, this sword is used not for destructive purposes, but as a scalpel for productive surgery. The divine surgeon is able to penetrate any part of the human soul to expose a malignancy and treat it. The Word of God cuts to the thoughts (literally, deliberations) of a person and to the intentions of the heart from which they emerge.

---

[17]Osborne, *Hermeneutical Spiral*, p. 384.
[18]McCartney and Clayton, *Let the Reader Understand*, p. 283.
[19]Albert Barnes, *Barnes Notes: Hebrews to Jude* (Grand Rapids, Mich.: Baker, 1983), p. 102.

The power of God's Word is not dead and static, but living and dynamic. The Bible is meant to be used as an powerful organic instrument to penetrate and expose the inner workings of the human heart. No psychological assessment tool can claim such diagnostic power. Nor can any therapeutic technique produce such results. Other passages that speak of the Scriptures' power (Jer 23:29; 1 Thess 2:13; Eph 6:17) identify it as the only offensive weapon in the armor of God.

If the Scriptures possess such power, the role of hermeneutics becomes even more critical. If we lack knowledge of the tools needed to interpret the Scriptures responsibly, the sharp, piercing scalpel becomes for us nothing more than a ceremonial butter knife. It accents the place setting but is rarely used. It becomes safe and impotent.

As we attempt to construct a Christian psychology, we must not ignore biblical hermeneutics. Rather than adopting a simplistic cookbook approach or relegating the Bible's truths to the arena of spiritual life, we can study hermeneutics so that we can use the Scriptures as the powerful tool they are intended to be. Hermeneutics will not supply all the answers; nor will it result in perfect agreement about the meaning of specific texts. But it does continually challenge us to pursue the meaning of a text in its fullness and context without simplistically proof-texting or committing projective eisegesis.

The Use and Misuse of Scripture in Christian Psychology

A correct hermeneutic is important not only because it respects the exalted nature of Scripture as an authoritative and powerful special revelation of God, but also because it guides the Christian in the proper use of Scripture, and thus in practices of life that are informed by it. With the growth of the integration movement the interpretation of Scripture is no longer just the task of the pastor or seminary professor. Christian psychologists regularly use Scripture in their thinking about psychological issues and in the practical guidance of their clients in therapy. Although traditionally psychologists have not been trained in biblical hermeneutics, it seems to us that hermeneutics is an essential part of training in Christian psychology.

Christian psychologists, as well as pastors and theologians who are concerned with psychological issues, exhibit a number of distinguishable ways of reading Scripture. Some of these methods fall short by orthodox Christian standards. If someone who is well-informed about the fields of hermeneutics, psychology and theology, wrote a book on biblical hermeneutics tailored specifically for the use of psychologists, it would be a great service to the church. In the absence of any such book, we offer a sketch of five unpromising ways to read the Bible as a psychologist, followed by an outline of four more-promising approaches.

Five Ways Not to Read the Bible

[This section and the following were developed by our teacher Dr. Robert C. Roberts and are used in his classroom.][20]

Psychological translation. This hermeneutic consists in starting with a thoroughgoing commitment to a non-Christian psychological model of proper psychic and relational functioning and its corresponding diagnostic scheme and therapeutic interventions, and then reinterpreting the Scriptures so that they seem to endorse this psychology of choice. I call this a translation hermeneutic because practitioners of the psychological translation treat particular words of Scripture as synonyms for crucial terms in the psychological model. Thus a "translation" of Scripture using Carl Rogers's psychology might treat the biblical term *sin* as equivalent to the Rogerian expression "incongruence with self." Similarly, *grace* becomes a synonym for "unconditional positive regard," *redemption* is "translated" as "the process of becoming congruent with oneself through the unconditional positive regard of another human being" and so forth.[21]

This hermeneutic has the effect of substituting a non-Christian psychology for the understanding of persons, their problems and their transformation that is contained in Scripture. I have placed the word *translate* in quotes to indicate that no real translation is going on here, but rather a substitution of one conceptual system (a biblical view of persons) by another (e.g., the Rogerian view of persons). *Sin* and *incongruence* are analogous terms, not synonyms, as they would have to be for a genuine translation. They are analogous inasmuch as *sin* is the chief biblical word for dysfunction and *incongruence* is the chief Rogerian word for dysfunction. But the concept of sin necessarily makes reference to God (sin is by definition always an offense against God), while the Rogerian concept of incongruence makes no such reference. So *sin* and *incongruence* cannot be synonyms, and therefore any such "translation" is bogus and misleading.

The method of correlation. Paul Tillich, an influential theologian during the middle years of the last century, was concerned that the biblical message seemed to be increasingly irrelevant to the lives of modern people. To rectify this situation, he proposed that theologians and pastors interpret Scripture and the Christian tradition by listening very carefully to the culture to determine which "existential questions" the culture is asking, then determining how Scripture and tradition offers answers to those questions. Tillich posits a mutual influence of questions and answers:

---

[20]We wish to thank Dr. Robert C. Roberts for writing this material and for allowing us to use it in our chapter. However, the primary authors share final responsibility for how it fits into our overall argument.

[21]For an example, see Thomas Oden, "The Theology of Carl Rogers," in *Kerygma and Counseling* (New York: Harper & Row, 1978), pp. 83-113. Oden's translation hermeneutic is discussed in Robert C. Roberts, *Taking the Word to Heart: Self and Other in an Age of Therapies* (Grand Rapids, Mich.: Eerdmans, 1993), pp. 31-34.

"Symbolically speaking, God answers man's questions, and *under the impact of God's answers* man asks them. Theology formulates the questions implied in human existence, and theology formulates the answers implied in divine self-manifestation under the guidance of the questions implied in human existence."[22]

The correlation method need not be an inappropriate hermeneutical strategy, especially if it is hedged in by the mutuality of influence of Scripture and culture and if it is practiced very carefully. But it is fraught with the danger that the culture will be allowed to set the agenda for the church. It is likely that the questions the culture is asking ("How can I make more money, faster?" "How can I get out of relationships that cramp my creativity, and do so with a minimum of guilt?" "How can I get more perfectly in touch with my inner self?" "How can I learn to indulge myself more?" "How can I start liking myself better?" "How can I have a wilder sex life, without danger of disease or pregnancy?") are not quite the questions the Christian tradition is in the business of answering. Part of the right strategy of speaking to our culture is trying to induce members of the culture to ask the right questions, the questions to which our faith has some answers.

An example of reading the Bible with an unsophisticated correlation method would be to accept the diagnostic categories of the *Diagnostic and Statistical Manual* (DSM)[23] or some secular psychotherapeutic model, and then to try to determine how, according to the Bible, one would treat people who fall into these categories. A more Bible-honoring approach would be to rethink the diagnostic categories in biblical terms (as psychiatrist A. A. Howsepian has recommended)[24] to get the questions right, and then to devise therapies to address the pathologies so conceived. Howsepian encourages us to rethink psychotic delusion in theological terms. Psychosis is not just a matter of distorted beliefs, but of distorted passions (concerns, loves, commitments); and it is not a rare phenomenon, for we are all psychotics in that we experience as most real what is not real, failing to notice what is most important in life. If psychologists think of the question posed by psychosis in these terms, we are more likely to find answers in the Bible that are authentically biblical.[25]

---

[22]Paul Tillich, *Systematic Theology* (Chicago: University of Chicago Press, 1951), 1:60, italics added.
[23]*Diagnostic and Statistical Manual of Mental Disorders*, 4th ed. (Washington, D.C.: American Psychiatric Association, 1994).
[24]A. A. Howsepian, "Sin and Psychosis," in *Limning the Psyche: Explorations in Christian Psychology*, ed. Robert C. Roberts and Mark R. Talbot (Grand Rapids, Mich.: Eerdmans, 1997), pp. 264-81.
[25]Because the strategy that Howsepian proposes starts with the DSM's categories and offers a Christian interpretation of them, his approach is what I [Robert C. Roberts] call "integration." See my chapter on Pauline psychotherapy in this volume, specifically the section titled "Integration and Christian Psychology." A more radical approach is exemplified by my paper as a whole: I propose to construct a diagnostic scheme directly out of the biblical materials. One may wonder, however, whether the latter approach is not unduly restrictive or awkward in the face of the presenting problems of people whom the DSM would classify as psychotic.

Symbolic interpretation. Carl Jung and his followers treat biblical themes and stories as expressions of events occurring in the unconscious of individuals and of the human race. To interpret biblical stories as actual historical happenings is not always false in their view, but is a falsification of the real significance of the stories as psychological projections, or "symbols of psychic transformation." In other words, it is possible, in principle, that a story—say, the story of Jesus' resurrection from the dead—is historically true; but even if it is, this is not relevant to the story's psychological and religious meaning. Jung interprets the Bible using the same interpretive pattern that he uses to interpret world mythologies, dreams and especially classical alchemy, in which

> figures and laws were dimly perceived and attributed to matter although they really belonged to the psyche. Everything unknown and empty is filled with psychological projection: it is as if the investigator's own psychic background were mirrored in the darkness. What he sees in matter, or thinks he can see, is chiefly the data of his own unconscious which he is projecting into it.
>
> Had the alchemist succeeded in forming any concrete idea of his unconscious contents, he would have been obliged to recognize that he had taken the place of Christ—or, to be more exact, that he, regarded not as ego but as self, had taken over the work of redeeming not man but God. He would then have had to recognize not only himself as the equivalent of Christ, but Christ as a symbol of the self.[26]

We distort the central message of the Bible if we read it as though its stories are all really about things that are happening in the unconscious of humankind and that their historical significance is of only secondary importance, at best. An acceptable, though still somewhat "symbolic" way to read the Bible is suggested by C. S. Lewis, who encourages us to think of pre-Christian myths of dying and rising savior figures as "a divine hinting in poetic and ritual form at the same central truth which was later focussed and (so to speak) historicized in the Incarnation."[27]

The Bible as a facilitator of self-discovery. Our first three perverse hermeneutics are the special domain of professional psychologists and theologians. The present one is more often found among lay people who have been influenced by self-help books or by the psychological spirit of our age. When we read the Bible as a facilitator of self-discovery, we pretty much ignore its content—what it "objectively says"—and treat it instead as a stimulus for self-exploration. In other words, practitioners of this approach treat the Bible as though it were a Rogerian therapist or a dream in the hands of a Jungian analyst. I asked some pastors the question, "What influences of humanistic psychology do you see in your congregation?" and one of the pastors remarked:

---

[26]Carl Jung, *Psychology and Alchemy*, trans. R. F. C. Hull (Princeton, N.J.: Princeton University Press, 1968), pp. 128, 355.

[27]C. S. Lewis, "Religion Without Dogma?" in *God in the Dock: Essays on Theology and Ethics*, ed. Walter Hooper (Grand Rapids, Mich.: Eerdmans, 1970), p. 132.

> There is a move to say "Let's get together for a Bible study and *no one read a commen-tary.* No one do a lot of study, but let's just read scripture and share what it means *to us.*" I appreciate people wanting to apply scripture to themselves, but if they don't have any disciplined way of studying it, it just becomes part of the process of self-understanding, and has no meaning independently of what we feel we need. Whatever it says to me at this moment, that's what it means.[28]

The last sentence of this quotation is a hermeneutical principle, and it is a perverse one because it strongly disinclines us to read the Bible in such a way that God and his message can stand in judgment on us or issue an upward call to us and thus bless us in a truly powerful way.

"Biblical" reductionism. This interpretive approach is motivated by a resistance to the integration of secular psychology into the work of the church. It rests on the premise that no extrabiblical resources are needed in dealing with psychological and relational problems. Pure biblical counseling is taken to be a more powerful method of achieving psychological healing than any secular or integrative approach. I applaud this approach insofar as it evinces a high respect for Scripture, but I call it reductionistic for two reasons.

First, psychology is like other fields of human inquiry such as astronomy, nutrition and medicine. It is true that the Bible has more to say about psychology than about these other subjects, but it is reasonable to suppose that the methods of careful observation that have been developed since biblical times have yielded some insights into the human psyche that are not to be found in the Bible and that may be very useful in helping people. So the Bible is not the only source of psychological insight and intervention.[29]

Second, this approach is reductionistic in the way its practitioners typically read the Bible. Pure biblical counselors tend to correctly attribute all human dysfunction to sin. However, they typically contend that the sins that cause psychological and relational problems are the particular sinful actions of the person who is suffering with the problems. This interpretation of sin is not warranted by the Bible. On the contrary, it is more biblical to suppose that many personal problems are the result not of the sins of the sufferer but of the sins of others, including perhaps nonhuman agents or even of the general sinfulness that pervades our life in this world. The reduction of the concept of sin is just one liability of this orientation to the Bible. We can imagine analogous reductions of the concepts of God, salvation and Christian virtues. Any biblical interpretation that oversimplifies a biblical concept in such a way as to cripple the understanding and practice of the Christian is an example of "biblical" reductionism.

---

[28]Roberts, *Taking the Word to Heart*, pp. 35-36.
[29]It is important to note that many who call themselves biblical counselors do not believe that the Bible is the only source of data about the human psyche.

Four More-Promising Ways to Read the Bible

There are better ways to read the Bible.

Traditional, sound hermeneutical practice. The above interpretive strategies are deficient because in one way or another each of them fails to let the biblical text have its own voice. Texts that originate in cultural settings as different from our own as the settings in which our Scriptures were written have to be treated with special care because of the cultural distance. The principles of traditional general hermeneutics are designed to help insure the Bible's independence from our own agendas and from the influences of our culture. Several traditional rules of interpretation should be observed by the psychologist who reads Scripture.

1. Know the historical setting as well as possible. For example, when we read the letters of Paul, it is important to take into consideration the issues being dealt with in the churches to which Paul addressed his letters.

2. Read the passage in context. Sometimes Bible readers pull verses out of their immediate context and treat them as separate aphorisms that can stand entirely on their own. But the "verses" of Scripture were written not as verses but as parts of narrative or argument or poetry. So verses should be read within the context of the immediately surrounding verses. They should also be read within the setting of the whole book (for example, Paul's letter to the Romans), and within the setting of the other works of the same author (for example, all the letters of Paul). As Christian interpreters we have an even larger context, that of the canon (the whole Bible), and we will want to read texts in that context as well.

3. Be aware of the pitfalls of translation. The meanings of some ancient words are not known even to scholars; translations of such words are conjectural. More often, scholars know the meaning of words in Greek and Hebrew, but those words do not have perfect equivalents in modern English. The meaning of other words is ambiguous, thus enabling alternative translations, and thus alternative readings, of a given passage. If we are reading the Bible to inform our psychology, we will want to be aware of such problems insofar as they impinge on our interpretation.

4. Know the genre of the text. The Bible contains literature of many different types—history, saga, liturgical text, law, apocalypse, prophecy, lament, praise, parable, epistle, moral exhortation and so on. We can make mistakes of interpretation by failing to take genre into account.

5. Be aware of the distinction between reporting what a text says and extrapolating from the text. As psychologists we will certainly do some extrapolating in the course of theory building and imaginative application, but we must be self-critical and clear about when we are reporting what the text says and when we are moving beyond it in a way that we think is faithful to it. Naive readers often fail to make this distinction, so they pass off their "interpretation" as being "what the text says."

6. Be aware of personal bias and the psychological "need" to read the text in

one way or another. We should constantly monitor our readings by asking to what extent they are influenced by such factors.

Thematic interpretation. In this approach we start with a question that any psychology (say, personality theory) might attempt to answer, and then we read the Bible in an effort to determine what it says in answer to that question. I have employed this method of interpretation in an article titled "Parameters of a Christian Psychology."[30]

Following Salvatore Maddi[31] I determined that personality psychologies tend to answer two kinds of questions: "What are the basic tendencies (needs, agendas) of the psyche?" and "What are the psychological structures by which these tendencies are realized or satisfied (or perhaps frustrated) in human development?" Reading the Bible with these questions in mind, I identified nine parameters of a Christian psychology: three tendencies (Godwardness, fellowship and stewardship) and six structures (verbivorousness, agency, inwardness, attachment, self-association and self-dissociation and permeability). If this is a correct reading of Scripture, then a biblical psychology will be a development and defense of these nine attributes and will elaborate them in terms of the maturity and development of personality, the diagnosis of personality failures, and the therapy for such failures. It will also offer evidence, clinical and experimental, for the propriety of the attributions.

Thematic interpretation might seem to be one form of the correlation method. Are we not allowing the culture (in the form of the professional psychological community) to set the questions that the Bible is to answer? Of course we are. These questions do arise out of the culture of modern psychology. But I think the method is relatively safe from the distortions that usually beset the correlation method because of the great generality of the questions. In contrast with the psychological translation method, thematic interpretation does not commit us to any particular psychological theory (Maddi attempted to formulate questions that could be addressed by *any* personality theory). And besides this, the correlation method is not necessarily bad, as long as we allow the Bible to reframe the initial questions in a way that makes them biblically answerable.

Looking for differences. The problem with the psychological translation hermeneutic is not that it recognizes similarities between the biblical psychology and the non-Christian psychology that it uses as home base. There are indeed similarities between secular psychologies and the biblical one. The problem with the psychological translation hermeneutic is that it systematically misses the differences between the two psychologies and is therefore systematically blind to what

---

[30]Robert C. Roberts, "Parameters of a Christian Psychology," in *Limning the Psyche: Explorations in Christian Psychology*, ed. Robert C. Roberts and Mark R. Talbot (Grand Rapids, Mich.: Eerdmans, 1997), pp. 74-101.

[31]Salvatore Maddi, *Personality Theories: A Comparative Analysis* (Homewood, Ill.: Dorsey, 1980).

is distinctive about the Christian psychology. Something similar is true of the correlation method, symbolic interpretation, and the Bible as a facilitator of self-discovery.

When psychologists who read the Bible carefully are interacting with a non-Christian psychology, they look for differences between the biblical view of persons and the view embodied in whatever non-Christian psychology is under consideration. To take the Rogerian psychology as an example, the biblical psychologist will ask pointedly, "How does sin differ from incongruence? How does biblical grace differ from unconditional positive regard? How does the transformation that a client undergoes in ideally effective Rogerian therapy differ from the process of sanctification? How do the Christian virtues differ from Rogerian congruence?" This hermeneutic might seem unfriendly and negative, but we tend not to see what we are not looking for, and it is essential for the Christian psychologist to be alive to what is distinctive about the biblical psychology.

Wisdom and judgment. In the final analysis, neither having the right hermeneutical techniques nor avoiding wrong ones will give a therapist the psychological insights into the Bible that the Christian psychologist cherishes. All the techniques and warnings might be best thought of as an indirect description of a person who reads the Bible sensitively and discerningly. We can become hidebound about rules like those of the hermeneutical methods I have commended, so that they end up standing in the way of penetrating and insightful reading of Scripture rather than facilitating it. Wisdom is a spiritual condition that allows us to be so in tune with God and his ways that we are able to make surprising, deep and creative judgments about God's Word. The most fundamental principle of intelligent biblical interpretation is thus Christian character, a full and deep and thoughtful devotion of one's entire self to the purposes of Christ. To have Christian character is to take to heart the apostle's injunction: "Present your bodies as a living sacrifice, holy and acceptable to God, which is your spiritual worship. Do not be conformed to this world, but be transformed by the renewing of your minds, so that you may discern what is the will of God—what is good and acceptable and perfect" (Rom 12:1-2).

Discernment is, after all, the chief goal of our hermeneutical discipline. Acquiring wisdom is not a private transaction between an individual and God; rather, it occurs in the communal life of Christian action and worship. And for the purpose of Christian wisdom, it is important that the communion of saints extend not just laterally, to members of our own generation and culture, but also historically and across cultures. For this reason the study of older and other cultural interpretations of Scripture—those of the early church fathers, medieval Christians, pastors of the Reformation and Counter Reformation, African and Asian and Latin American Christians—can deepen and enrich and make more flexible the Christian psychologist's readings of Scripture.

Conclusion

Given the nature of Scripture, its practical impact on the work of Christian psychologists and its potential to be misused, the importance of biblical hermeneutics is clear. We conclude with two additional reasons for psychologists to study hermeneutics, then we offer some practical suggestions.

If we study the Bible at all regularly, we will have a way of doing so, whether that way is intelligently selected and consciously developed into a skill, or is merely haphazard, fallen into and absorbed unconsciously from our social environment. A recent study suggests that personality plays a key role in hermeneutical style, but the hermeneutical style determined by our personality may be almost totally outside of our awareness unless we study hermeneutical methods as a way of searching our self-understanding.[32] The danger in not being aware of our style of interpreting Scripture is that we may be innocently using an unreliable method instead of practicing the more careful methods that have been commended historically in the church. The study of hermeneutics forces us to be aware of how we are reading Scripture and strongly encourages us to take an intelligent and informed approach.

We noted earlier that recent decades have seen the dominance of a view according to which the reader virtually creates the meaning of the text without reference to what the text itself is saying. And we have argued that such projective eisegesis is frequently practiced by psychologists, many of whom are, notwithstanding, virtually innocent of hermeneutical theory. We have also argued that such reader-centered exegesis nearly guarantees that we will not learn what the Bible has to teach us about psychology and that it is a sure way for the Christian community to remain in thrall to the psychological systems that dominate our society, forestalling any possible biblically inspired corrective. We propose that psychologists study biblical hermeneutics as an avenue of liberation from the spirit of our age.

Another advantage of psychologists' learning to interpret Scripture in a careful and responsible manner is that it increases the possibility of fruitful dialogue with our colleagues in theology and biblical studies. Psychologists may get away with sloppy exegesis if they communicate only with their colleagues in psychology, but such insularity only begets a befuddled complacency in the psychologists and contempt in the theologians who read or hear them. We should encourage collegial interchange between professional psychologists and professional theologians in the interest of mutual enrichment and the well-being of the larger church. We can hardly blame theologians for withholding their respect from our integrative work when it is based on readings of Scripture that, from their point of view, are naive and incompetent. It would be fruitful for the body of Christ if more theologians

---

[32]Rodney Bassett, Kayrn Mathewson and Angela Gailitis, "Recognizing the Person in Biblical Interpretation: An Empirical Study," *Journal of Psychology and Christianity* 12 (1993): 38-46.

contributed work to publications like the *Journal of Psychology and Christianity* and the *Journal of Psychology and Theology*. If psychologists demonstrated a higher level of hermeneutical sophistication, such contributions would be more frequent, and professional dialogue between psychologists and theologians would be richer and more intense.

We recommend that Christian graduate programs in psychology include a class in biblical hermeneutics, preferably one pitched to psychological interests. Some graduate schools seek to promote integration by requiring theology courses such as biblical theology, systematic theology, historical theology, theological anthropology and spirituality. These classes give the student important help in understanding theology. But without a class in hermeneutics the student does not have the opportunity to see how Christian theological and psychological claims may be supported or undermined by reference to Scripture. To people who are already practicing counselors we recommend auditing a class in biblical hermeneutics at a local evangelical seminary. In addition, the counselor may seek to build a mentoring relationship with a professor or pastor who is skilled in exegesis.

14

WHEN THE WOUNDING RUNS DEEP

Encouragement for Those on the Road to Forgiveness

Myrla Seibold

THE ANGUISH BEHIND THE WORDS CAUGHT ME BY SURPRISE. I HAD NO IDEA THAT he struggled with forgiveness, especially this many years later. He was still hurting. He was embarrassed to acknowledge it, but he was courageously addressing it in the hope of finding some answers. I will let him tell his story in his own words:

> My first wife had an affair with a good friend of ours (who was also married), and they ended up getting married soon after both divorces were final. I was hurt, humiliated and angry. I finally buried the hatchet and discussed it with both of them. Because we still had one thing in common, my young daughter's best interests, we got along and even have had a congenial relationship over the years. I often stopped to talk to my ex-wife's new husband when we met on the street, and I even had coffee with him on occasion when we met.
>
> My ex-wife's husband died unexpectedly recently. From the moment I heard the news, I have been confronted with a variety of strange and unexpected emotions. I thought I had dealt quite well with all of this and yet my latest thing is I am so angry for the time with my daughter that was stolen from me. We probably spent more time with each other than the majority of divorced fathers and daughters and probably a lot more than a lot of intact-family fathers and daughters. But it hit me at the holidays that I had to lose part of every holiday season with my daughter since she was five years old, and I am resenting it after all these years. Years that I thought I had handled everything. Was I fooling myself all those years? Was I just coping? Or is it normal to have this happen like this? It seems so convoluted, but it is real.

My friend's questions poignantly illustrate the fact that when there has been deep wounding, forgiveness is a process, a journey, often down a very long road. My friend does not say so, but I wonder if he is struggling with the issue of forgiveness because of the incongruence between his experience and what he has been taught about forgiveness.

In recent years both psychologists and theologians have had much to say on the subject of forgiveness. Sermons, articles and even entire books, workshops and retreats focus on this topic. All sorts of people fancy themselves to be experts and offer advice on how to extend forgiveness in order to heal oneself from emotional wounding. While their advice may be sound for some, I generally have felt misunderstood and inadequate when I have attempted to apply the advice of many of these forgiveness experts to my own life.

Inadequacies of Current Views of Forgiveness

Current views of forgiveness need to be refined by a careful understanding of psychology and theology so that they will better meet the needs of Christian communities and of individual Christians who have experienced deep wounding. Rather than offering compassion and concern to deeply wounded persons, the Christian church often generates more distress for these individuals by making harsh demands for rapid forgiveness of the offender and for resumption of a normal life. Forgiveness is neither irrelevant nor impossible, but in many cases of deep wounding forgiveness can be considerably more complex and laborious than some Christians proclaim.

Christians tend to discuss forgiveness in a disembodied way, separated from reference to context, circumstances and personalities. It is presented as something that is normative and expected in each and every situation[1] and is held out to be the key to healing from traumatic events.[2] Some authors state unequivocally that if wounded people do not offer forgiveness, they will never heal, and in fact, they will jeopardize their spiritual state.[3] Wounded people are left with the distinct impression that they had better forgive, and the sooner the better.

Forgiveness is often presented as a global, amorphous concept, and there is little agreement about what it means operationally to forgive. Many discussions give the

[1]Jay E. Adams, *From Forgiven to Forgiving* (Wheaton, Ill.: Victor, 1989).

[2]Donald Hope, "The Healing Paradox of Forgiveness," *Psychotherapy* 24 (1987): 240-44; Jared P. Pingleton, "The Role and Function of Forgiveness in the Psychotherapeutic Process," *Journal of Psychology and Theology* 17 (1989): 27-35; Franklin C. Shontz and Charlotte Rosenak, "Psychological Theories and the Need for Forgiveness: Assessment and Critique," *Journal of Psychology and Christianity* 7 (1988): 23-31.

[3]Adams, *From Forgiven to Forgiving;* Harold Wahking, "Spiritual Growth Through Grace and Forgiveness," *Journal of Psychology and Christianity* 11, no. 2 (1992): 198-206.

impression that forgiveness consists of overlooking the wrong, acting like it never happened or pretending like it is not a big deal. Many Christians describe forgiveness as a once-and-for-all event that resolves the issue from that moment on. They define forgiveness as an "act of the will" that one chooses to perform regardless of one's feelings.[4]

Contemporary discussions of forgiveness do not adequately acknowledge the victim's personhood and experience. This is particularly significant because the victim is often exhorted to recognize the offender's personhood and the life experience that contributed to the offender's hurtful behavior. There has not been adequate recognition of the long-term suffering of the deeply wounded individual who must endure ongoing pain, loss and other consequences of the offense. Furthermore, the victim is told that forgiveness means "not using the past against the offender," and the victim is instructed not to bring up the event and accompanying issues anymore. Some authors define forgiveness as the absence of all negative feelings toward the offender or as never bringing up the event again to someone else, to oneself or to God.[5] This counsel requires victims to keep silent about what has happened to them and gives them the impression that no one cares about their pain, that their concerns do not matter.

Serious wounding and victimization in our society is usually inflicted on those with lesser power, namely, women, children, the poor and people of color. I question whether much of the literature on forgiveness adequately addresses the real issues of people who, already disempowered and oppressed, experience serious wounding. Too often the writing on forgiveness comes from a stance of power and of distance from the offense. Many victims possess neither.

Forgiveness is frequently defined as "not taking revenge" against the offender.[6] But for many victims revenge is not an option anyway, or it would be of minimal impact compared to the magnitude and scope of the offense.

The struggle to define forgiveness in the real world was dramatically illustrated in South Africa when Archbishop Desmond Tutu and former president Nelson Mandela offered amnesty to perpetrators of violence in exchange for their confession of

---

[4]Neil T. Anderson, *Victory over the Darkness* (Ventura, Calif.: Regal, 1990); Meiryls Lewis, "On Forgiveness," *Philosophical Quarterly* 30 (1980): 236-45; Frank B. Minirth and Paul D. Meier, *Happiness Is a Choice: A Manual on the Symptoms, Causes, and Cures of Depression* (Grand Rapids, Mich.: Baker, 1978); Wahking, "Spiritual Growth."
[5]Norvin Richards, "Forgiveness," *Ethics* 99 (1988): 77-97; Adams, *From Forgiven to Forgiving.*
[6]John M. Brandsma, "Forgiveness: A Dynamic Theological and Therapeutic Analysis," *Pastoral Psychology* 31 (1982): 40-50; Richard P. Fitzgibbons, "The Cognitive and Emotive Use of Forgiveness in the Treatment of Anger," *Psychotherapy* 23 (1986): 629-33; Hope, "Healing Paradox"; Lewis, "On Forgiveness"; Pingleton, "Role and Function of Forgiveness"; Shontz and Rosenak, "Psychological Theories"; Wahking, "Spiritual Growth."

the truth about their deeds. William Raspberry speaks for many when he questions: "What would be justice for the survivors of thousands of black South Africans who were killed or savaged by the regime during the period the commission is investigating?"[7] Clearly, forgiveness in the case of deep wounding is, in my friend's words, "convoluted."

Psychology's Contributions to the Understanding Forgiveness

Among psychologists there has been an explosion of interest in the subject of forgiveness in recent years. McMinn points out that the period from the early 1980s to the early 1990s saw a 300 percent increase in the number of articles on forgiveness published in psychology journals.[8] These articles evidence a wide range of viewpoints. For example, some authors argue that repentance is necessary in order for forgiveness to occur;[9] others contend that repentance is definitely not required[10] or that repentance does not mandate forgiveness.[11] Generally speaking, the professional psychology literature that addresses forgiveness falls into three basic categories: (1) arguments that forgiveness is completely inappropriate in cases of serious offenses and abuse,[12] (2) arguments that forgiveness is a great idea and should be considered a viable therapeutic technique,[13] and (3) attempts to define and operationalize forgiveness.[14]

---

[7]William Raspberry, "Tutu Leads Extraordinary Effort to Forgive, Forget Racial Wrongs," *St. Paul Pioneer Press,* February 21, 1997.

[8]Mark R. McMinn, *Psychology, Theology, and Spirituality in Christian Counseling* (Wheaton, Ill.: Tyndale House, 1996).

[9]William R. Domeris, "Biblical Perspectives on Forgiveness," *Journal of Theology for Southern Africa* 54 (1986): 48-50; Michael E. McCullough, Steven J. Sandage, and Everett L. Worthington, "Charles Williams on Interpersonal Forgiveness: Theology and Therapy," *Journal of Psychology and Christianity* 14, no. 4 (1995): 355-64; John Wilson, "Why Forgiveness Requires Repentance," *Philosophy* 63 (1988): 534-35.

[10]Educational Psychology Study Group, "Must a Christian Require Repentance Before Forgiving?" *Journal of Psychology and Christianity* 9, no. 3 (1990): 16-19; Human Development Study Group, "Five Points on the Construct of Forgiveness Within Psychotherapy," *Psychotherapy* 28, no. 3 (1991): 493-96; Lewis, "On Forgiveness."

[11]F. Clark Power, "Commentary," *Human Development* 37 (1994): 81-85; Richards, "Forgiveness."

[12]Ellen Bass and Laura Davis, *The Courage to Heal* (New York: Perennial Library, 1988); Susan Forward with Craig Buck, *Toxic Parents* (New York: Bantam, 1989); McCullough et al., "Charles Williams."

[13]H. H. Bloomfield and L. Felder, *Making Peace with Your Parents* (New York: Ballantine, 1983); R. E. Kahrhoff, *Forgiveness: Formula for Peace of Mind* (St. Charles, Mo.: Capital Planning Corporation, 1988); Christina E. Mitchell, "A Model for Forgiveness in Family Relationships," *Family Therapy* 22 (1995): 25-30; S. B. Simon and S. Simon, *Forgiveness: How to Make Peace with Your Past and Get on with Your Life* (New York: Warner Books, 1990); Everett L. Worthington and Frederick A. DiBlasio, "Promoting Mutual Forgiveness Within the Fractured Relationship," *Psychotherapy* 27 (1990): 219-23.

[14]Human Development Study Group, "Five Points"; Peter A. Kirkup, "Some Religious Per-

Some of the most helpful discussions of the complexities of forgiveness are the studies by Robert Enright and his colleagues.[15] These authors acknowledge the necessity of actively processing anger, of adopting reasonable cautions about reconciliation and of viewing forgiveness as a long journey in some cases. Glenn Veenstra links confusion about forgiveness to an insistence on dichotomous thinking and simple solutions: "Either they pardon the offender or they punish the offender. . . . Either victims avenge their wrongs, or they absolve the offender. . . . Rather than doing the difficult work of confronting the offender, people invoke a form of forgiveness such as overlooking, excusing or condoning that seems to short circuit the process but really does not resolve it."[16] Norvin Richards argues that it is "sometimes wrong to forgive, sometimes wrong not to forgive, and sometimes admirable to forgive but acceptable not to do so,"[17] a view some Christians may reject as too relativistic.

Some other themes in the psychological literature are relevant to a discussion of forgiveness, but to my knowledge they have not yet been brought to bear on this topic. These relate to the importance of affirming one's life story in its totality as a way of expressing one's place and worth in the world. I am thinking in particular of two views: silencing-the-self theory and narrative theory.

Dana Jack has studied the connection between depression in women and what she terms "silencing the self."[18] She points out that not expressing her feelings and needs requires a woman to deny whole parts of herself, especially her negative feelings. The net result is self-condemnation, inner division and depression. Women are socialized to respond to external expectations and to ignore their own needs and feelings. Too often, declares Jack, women exhibit an outward conforming self while hiding an inner self who is angry and resentful, and quite hopeless about the whole dilemma.

spectives on Forgiveness and Settling Differences," *Mediation Quarterly* 11, no. 1 (1993): 79-94; Lewis B. Smedes, *Forgive and Forget: Healing the Hurts We Don't Deserve* (San Francisco: Harper & Row, 1984); Glenn J. Veenstra, "Psychological Concepts of Forgiveness," *Journal of Psychology and Christianity* 11, no. 2 (1992): 160-69.

[15]For example, on the problems people encounter when they attempt to forgive one another see Robert D. Enright and Robert L. Zell, "Problems Encountered When We Forgive One Another," *Journal of Psychology and Christianity* 8, no. 1 (1989). On the differences of opinion concerning forgiveness as articulated by those in the helping professions see Robert D. Enright et al., "Interpersonal Forgiveness Within the Helping Profession: An Attempt to Resolve Differences of Opinion," *Counseling and Values* 36 (1992). On forgiveness from a developmental perspective see Robert D. Enright, Elizabeth Gassin, and Ching-Ru Wu, "Forgiveness: A Developmental View," *Journal of Moral Education* 21, no. 2 (1992).

[16]Veenstra, "Psychological Concepts," p. 168.

[17]Richards, "Forgiveness," p. 82.

[18]Dana J. Jack, "Silencing the Self: The Power of Social Imperatives in Female Depression," in *Women and Depression: A Lifespan Perspective,* ed. R Formanek and A. Gurian (New York: Springer, 1987), pp. 161-81; Dana J. Jack, *Silencing the Self: Women and Depression* (Cambridge, Mass.: Harvard University Press, 1991).

There is a disparity between what a woman sees and knows from her experience and what she is told she should think and feel. Many women struggle to reconcile "a morality of goodness that condones the destruction of their authenticity."[19] This is precisely what happens when we are pressured into a premature stance of forgiveness without having had a chance to express our pain adequately. Marie Fortune has eloquently described the position I wish to advance:

> Forgiveness . . . is a means of restoration to wholeness. It should be viewed from the experience of the victim and understood as only one aspect of the healing process. . . . For many victims . . . the longing or obligation to forgive is superseded by the subjective sense of not feeling forgiving. . . . Even though they may speak words of forgiveness, they cannot forget; they know very well that popular piety and platitudes are not enough; they know that nothing has changed for them.[20]

Narrative theory in both psychology and theology emphasizes the importance of telling our life stories. "To remember is the opposite of dismember," states D. John Lee.[21] According to narrative theory, we need all parts of our history to be fully ourselves.[22] To shut out some of our past in the name of forgiveness is to fragment ourselves rather than to bring healing. One writer proclaims, "The narrative metaphor proposes that people live their lives by stories. It suggests that these stories shape people's lives and have real rather than imagined effects on them."[23]

Contrary to the view of those who believe we should never bring up our past to others, ourselves or God, narrative theory affirms the centrality of our stories in their entirety as "witnesses to the mysterious paradoxical nature of God, which is both creative and providential."[24] While Lee does not write specifically to address the issue of forgiveness, he offers a relevant and compassionate view on the subject: "Sometimes God is silent. Sometimes nothing we do or say can alleviate the suffering of our present experience. In the midst of our pain, autobiography can be an invitation to God to be present with us, to remind us of the Resurrection and the Hope."[25]

In short, telling our stories is not incompatible with forgiveness. In fact, God chose historical narrative as the primary way to reveal himself in the Bible. We can forgive and still tell the story—God does! Indeed, I believe affirming our story is a vital component of the journey on the road to forgiveness.

---

[19]Jack, "Silencing the Self: The Power of Social Imperatives," p. 180.

[20]Marie M. Fortune, "Forgiveness: The Last Step," in *Abuse and Religion*, ed. A. L. Horton and J. A. Williamson (Lexington, Mass.: Lexington, 1988), p. 215.

[21]D. John Lee, *Storying Ourselves* (Grand Rapids, Mich.: Baker, 1993), p. 296.

[22]See, for example, R. A. Neimeyer, "The Role of Client-Generated Narratives in Psychotherapy," *Journal of Constructivist Psychology* 7 (1994): 229-42.

[23]Beth Johnson, "The Anti-Depression, Anti-Suicide Group," *Journal of Child and Youth Care* 9, no. 2 (1994): 88.

[24]Lee, *Storying Ourselves*, p. 297.

[25]Ibid., p. 298.

Some Theological Considerations

Paul Tournier has said, "Religion can crush instead of liberate."[26] Nowhere does this seem more true than in the case of forgiveness. Individual Scripture texts are often reified, and contrasting and even contradictory passages are casually ignored. It would be beyond the scope of this paper to delve into a comprehensive theological and hermeneutical analysis of forgiveness. However, there are two main areas that need greater clarification and deeper exploration from the perspective of the wounded individual: (1) Does a too-rapid readiness to forgive deprive wounded persons of the validation and comfort needed for healing? and (2) Does Scripture intend to convey the message that salvation is contingent on one's ability to forgive others? In other words, does one have to earn salvation by being sufficiently forgiving?

Additionally, the concept of covenant is a neglected biblical perspective in the discussion of the process of forgiveness. The entirety of biblical history, from Genesis through Revelation, is tied together by the theme of covenantal relationship. God is revealed as a Being who desires relationship and who makes relationship possible through the vehicle of covenant, which is a call for two parties to live in trust and faithfulness to each other. It is a mutual contract, requiring equal vulnerability from each party. God promises blessings to those who keep covenant and curses and death to those who break covenant. Judgment for covenant breaking is a necessary component of covenant so that covenant can be taken seriously.

In many instances in biblical history (for example, the events following the Israelites' worship of the golden calf), God outlines conditions for re-establishing covenant when it has been broken, and it seems that God's renewed offers of covenant are affected by past human failures.[27] Repentance for how one has broken covenant is a precondition for restored relationship. True repentance entails a soul-felt desire to change (metanoia) and the belief that God will equip one with the power and ability to make the change. The Bible tells us that there is a counterforce, Satan, that is intent on destroying our covenant relationships. Human beings' unique endowment with free will sets the stage for a cosmic drama: God's gracious creation of unlimited love in which humans are invited to participate versus Satan's ruthless destruction of that love. Herein lies the genius and beauty of forgiveness.

Forgiveness creates the possibility for justice, mercy and grace to meet. It is the

---

[26]Paul Tournier, *Guilt and Grace* (New York: Harper & Row, 1962), p. 23.

[27]This is a complex theological position that merits development to an extent that is beyond the scope of this chapter. I am indebted to Paul Eddy for his illumination of the covenant perspective. For further explication of Covenant theology, see Jakob Jocz, *The Covenant* (Grand Rapids, Mich.: Eerdmans, 1968), and William J. Dumbrell, *Covenant and Creation* (Nashville: Thomas Nelson, 1984). For particular focus on the relationship between covenant and forgiveness, see Jerry Gladson, "Higher Than the Heavens: Forgiveness in the Old Testament," *Journal of Psychology and Christianity* 11, no. 2 (1993): 125-35.

mysterious wedding of hope and love that gives birth to the possibility that something beautiful will arise from the ashes of devastated covenant. God cannot force us to love, or we would not be free beings. But we have been created to function optimally in relationship with God and with each other. Therefore we need a mechanism to help us to love consistently, to keep our covenants, and to restore covenants when we break them. Forgiveness is that mechanism for restoration. Jesus Christ is the means of salvation—that is, the restoration of each individual's relationship with God. He has made atonement for our sins, thereby providing a way for God to maintain justice while offering mercy. Jesus Christ, then, is the embodiment of forgiveness. Furthermore, the Holy Spirit is given to us as grace (charisma) to empower us to stop breaking covenants and instead to keep our covenants with God and with each other.

Toward a More Compassionate Understanding of Forgiveness

Why seek to forgive? Forgiveness flies in the face of our normal desire to see the wicked pay for their destructiveness and to see the righteous be rewarded for their good deeds. Why would we want to give up our right to revenge?

Forgiveness has social value. This can be seen throughout biblical history. People began by inflicting all-out massive destruction to avenge their hurts. This was gradually modified to "an eye for an eye, a tooth for a tooth" so that whole groups of innocent people wouldn't be slaughtered in response to an offense. But even that ethic gave license to a great deal of so-called justified violence. In our modern-day world with its mind-boggling nuclear weapons and chemical warfare capabilities, it makes sense to cultivate a method of responding to assaults that minimizes the escalation of violence and aggression. Forgiveness offers a way to defuse hatred and its accompanying destruction.

More and more we see mainstream psychologists touting the benefits of forgiveness. An example is Cloe Madanes[28] in her work with sex offenders and victims. When people decide not to forgive, psychologists tend to view it as a case of unfinished business at best, and as the harboring of bitterness at worst. Some writers claim that forgiveness can improve one's physical well-being, and that conversely, unforgiveness can contribute to physical illness.[29] However, empirical proof that forgiveness reduces negative affect or improves one's sense of well-being is not well-established.[30]

---

[28]Cloe Madanes, *Sex, Love, and Violence: Strategies for Transformation* (New York: W. W. Norton, 1990).

[29]B. H. Kaplan, "Social Health and the Forgiving Heart: The Type B Story," *Journal of Behavioral Medicine* 15 (1992): 3-14; W. Klassen, *The Forgiving Community* (Philadelphia: Westminster Press, 1966); Frank Minirth et al., *How to Beat Burnout* (Chicago: Moody Press, 1986).

[30]Michael E. McCullough and Everett L. Worthington, "Encouraging Clients to Forgive People Who Hurt Them: Review, Critique, and Research Prospectus," *Journal of Psychology and Theology* 22 (1994): 3-20.

What exactly is forgiveness? Despite the large number of "forgiveness experts" who describe forgiveness as a once-and-for-all discrete event, most writers on the subject hold the common-sense view that forgiveness in the case of deep wounding is a process that unfolds over time (sometimes a long time). In my opinion the parameters of the process of forgiveness in such cases should always be defined by the situation of a particular individual in a particular set of circumstances. Elizabeth Gassin and Robert Enright have described at length the numerous components of the forgiveness process, and their work has spawned a number of studies that attempt to empirically examine forgiveness.[31] But the construction of an accurate definition of forgiveness in cases of deep wounding has been elusive. Donald Hope has summarized it succinctly: "How does one accept the unacceptable? How does a person let go of a major disappointment, injustice, humiliation, victimization, or assault in order to live more productively in the present?"[32] One thing is clear: some groundwork must be laid before a wounded person can even start down the road to forgiveness.

Beginning the journey toward forgiveness. First and foremost, one cannot begin to think about forgiveness until one's very survival is secure. This is not a merely pedantic point. Forgiveness is not a major issue when one is dealing with minor affronts that can be overlooked readily. Forgiveness becomes a struggle only when one has been seriously, severely wounded. For many people that wounding may threaten their physical survival or mental well-being. To counsel an individual in such a position to focus on forgiving the person who has done (and may still be doing) such extensive damage is not only insensitive, it is the height of arrogance.

The establishment of both emotional and physical safety is of top priority. Enormous fear frequently accompanies trauma. The wounded person will likely be terrified that the assaults will continue. Situations of abuse that the victim cannot escape are particularly damaging and often give rise to a residual haunting fear that continues long after the threat has been diminished or removed. It is absolutely essential to establish a climate of safety in order to begin to address the fear. As long as an individual must channel emotional energy into protecting the self from ongoing or future threats, it is not possible to lay a foundation for forgiveness. And to counsel a person in this stage to forgive is itself abusive.[33]

After some semblance of safety has been established, good, consistent self-care of the whole person is necessary. Patience with oneself and acceptance of one's condition and situation are prerequisites to being able to turn one's attention to forgiveness. Needless to say, the establishment and the maintenance of general heal-

---

[31]Elizabeth Gassin and Robert D. Enright, "The Will to Meaning in the Process of Forgiving," *Journal of Psychology and Christianity* 14, no. 1 (1995): 38-49.
[32]Hope, "Healing Paradox," p. 241.
[33]See McCullough and Worthington, "Encouraging Clients," on this point.

ing may take a protracted period of time. Trying to circumvent this stage by hurrying to get to forgiveness in the hope of more rapid healing will only delay the ability to truly forgive and move on.

Thorny issues along the way. The road to forgiveness becomes particularly rocky when one begins to grapple with issues of justice and repentance. It is infinitely easier to forgive when the offender is genuinely remorseful and when there is no threat of further assault.

Marie Fortune argues that justice must be accomplished, if only in a limited way, as a precondition for forgiveness:

> Prior to justice, forgiveness is an empty exercise. . . . Forgiveness before justice is "cheap grace" and cannot contribute to authentic healing and restoration to wholeness for the victim or for the offender. It cuts the healing process short and may well perpetuate the cycle of abuse. It also undercuts the redemption of abusers by preventing them from being accountable for their abusive behavior.[34]

Citing Luke 17:3-4, Fortune defines several elements of justice:

1. Acknowledgment that harm has been done by one person to another. ("To be confronted . . . is to be called to accountability for unjust acts. To confess is to acknowledge responsibility for harm done.")[35]

2. Repentance, not just remorse. Repentance requires metanoia, fundamental change (Ezek 18:30-32). Repentance requires time, hard work and engagement in treatment or therapy of some sort.

3. Restitution wherein the offender is responsible to offer something materially to those who have been harmed, representing a concrete effort to do something about what has been damaged.

Fortune acknowledges that the offender may not be willing or available to practice these steps. In that case she suggests that the church, the legal system, family, friends and counselors may help facilitate justice for victims. Four ways the wider community can help include (1) truth telling: acknowledgement of the harm done to the victim (communicating belief and sharing in the victim's outrage), (2) deprivatization: breaking the silence (balancing privacy with the need to break out of the isolation of silence), (3) deminimization: hearing the whole story and validating the victim's experience, and (4) protection of the vulnerable (the victim and any others at risk for harm by the offender).

Fortune cautions that offenders may view forgiveness as a quick way to be relieved of their guilt for their hurtful behavior. Remorse without concrete acts of repentance means little, and it should not be used as the basis for pressuring the victim to feel obligated to extend blanket forgiveness. As one author puts it, "Forgiveness requires that a wrong not be disregarded, overlooked or dismissed."[36]

---

[34]Fortune, "Forgiveness," p. 216.
[35]Ibid.
[36]Joanna North, "Wrongdoing and Forgiveness," *Philosophy* 62 (1987): 502.

Glenn Veenstra observes that pardoning and holding accountable are not necessarily mutually exclusive.[37] Forgiveness does not absolve the offender of responsibility to ease the suffering of the victim. Restitution has value not just for the victim, but also for the offender. It signifies sincerity, awareness of the deep impact of the hurt and authentic remorse. Absolution without restitution may enable and even foster continued hurtful behavior. Awareness of the harm one has caused is an essential component of personhood. Its absence indicates severe psychopathology or spiritual deterioration. Gerald Sittser writes that he would not want to trade places with the driver of the car that killed his wife, mother and young daughter because the driver must have been "either tormented by guilt or hardened to all feeling."[38]

Even when there is visible evidence that the offender is trying to make restitution, forgiving does not require that the victim trust the offender or try to restore the relationship to what it was before. This position is in stark contrast to that of some authors who state that forgiveness has taken place only when there is a full openness to complete reconciliation.[39] Marie Fortune writes that "trust that has been so savagely broken can be regained only over time, *if at all*. The return to a relationship is entirely dependent on trust: Can the survivor genuinely trust this person not to abuse her again? The choice to forgive should not be tied to these decisions."[40]

Much damage is done to victims who are counseled that forgiveness requires them to attempt to restore the relationship with the offender. By definition relationship requires mutuality, trust, respect and commitment (the elements of covenant), and the fact that the victim has extended forgiveness does not mean that those key ingredients will now be present in the relationship. The purpose of forgiveness is healing, not the subjection of the victim to more harm. In some instances the process of establishing justice and the victim's readiness and willingness to offer forgiveness may indeed bring forth reconciliation. But we must not presume to expect this in each and every case.

Trust and forgiveness are not synonymous. Neither are reconciliation and forgiveness. I disagree with North's assertion that forgiveness means "accepting back into our heart a person who is responsible for having hurt and damaged us."[41] Some deep wounding is perpetrated by persons who choose to remove themselves from our heart; surely it is an exercise in futility to try to put back into our heart someone who has rejected and abandoned us. Doris Donnelly has explicated a similar position, arguing that forgiveness does not always mean turning the other cheek. She goes on to state that a forgiving spirit and a confrontational approach can be compatible.[42]

[37]Veenstra, "Psychological Concepts."
[38]Gerald Sittser, *A Grace Disguised* (Grand Rapids, Mich.: Zondervan, 1996), p. 128.
[39]Adams, *From Forgiven to Forgiving;* North, "Wrongdoing and Forgiveness."
[40]Fortune, "Forgiveness," p. 218 (emphasis mine).
[41]North, "Wrongdoing and Forgiveness," p. 505.
[42]Doris Donnelly, "Forgiveness and Recidivism," *Pastoral Psychology* 33, no. 1 (1984): 15-24.

Repentance on the part of the offender smooths the road to forgiveness. But is repentance a prerequisite for forgiveness? Robert Enright and his colleagues[43] and others[44] have argued persuasively that a victim's ability to forgive should not be contingent on the offender's repentance; otherwise, victims will forever be held hostage by attitudes and behavior beyond their control. But when no repentance is forthcoming, the victim will need exceptional sources of support and encouragement to advance along the road toward forgiveness.

The Church's Role in Healing and Forgiveness

The Christian church can either promote the ability of Christians to offer forgiveness or it can foster even greater damage to persons who are already severely injured. Much depends on whether the Christian community is a place of compassion or judgment. Are we willing to come alongside wounded persons in solidarity, entering into their pain and seeking to understand the magnitude of the issues with which they struggle? Or will we stand apart in the safety of our own intactness, preaching sterile words of obligation?

Deep wounding and the extension of forgiveness. If the most powerless people in society are the most often called on to exercise forgiveness, how are they to acquire the ability to forgive? Some psychologists theorize that when people see it will benefit them to forgive, they will naturally want to do something that will be self-beneficial.[45] I agree that even when there has been great loss and devastation, and even in the face of great injustice, awareness of the good that can come from suffering can spur people to seek to be forgiving. But I am doubtful that this knowledge alone would ordinarily be sufficient motivation. After all, people are constantly resisting exhortation to behave in ways that will be beneficial to them, and oftentimes those positive behaviors are significantly less painful and difficult than forgiving. It is naive to presume that people will make a decision to forgive on the basis of self-interest alone.

Christianity uniquely equips people to offer forgiveness, but discussions of forgiveness often ignore two points that should be emphasized for deeply wounded people. First, deeply wounded people should look out and up to God; they should see with the eyes of faith God's glory and their own future glory. This is the position often advanced by Paul in the New Testament as his way of coping with the difficulties and abuse he faced (see, e.g., 2 Cor 4:16-18). This viewpoint does not in any way minimize evil or the extent of the damage done to an individual; rather, it

---

[43]Educational Psychology Study Group, "Must a Christian Require Repentance"; Human Development Study Group, "Five Points."

[44]For example, Lewis, "On Forgiveness."

[45]Kenneth Cloke, "Revenge, Forgiveness, and the Magic of Mediation," *Mediation Quarterly* 11 (1993): 67-78; Robert Hemfelt, Frank B. Minirth and Paul D. Meier, *Love Is a Choice* (Nashville: Thomas Nelson, 1989); Hope, "Healing Paradox."

proclaims that evil is minuscule in comparison to the richness and immensity of God's full presence.[46] As we meditate on the glory of God and the riches in Christ that are available to us, we can begin to appreciate how miserly it would be not to extend forgiveness to those who have harmed us. We offer forgiveness then out of a profound sense of the treasure we have found in eternal life, and out of a generosity that naturally flows from that realization.

Second, the power of the indwelling Holy Spirit furnishes Christians with the potential to forgive. When we have a sense of God's indwelling presence, we recognize that because of this mystery of incarnation, God has suffered fully what we ourselves have experienced. There is a clear awareness that we have not suffered alone, that Jesus Christ has been present and has suffered exactly the pain that we have suffered. We look then to Jesus to live out in us his forgiveness of the offender. We do not have to muster feelings of forgiveness on our own or manufacture the ability to forgive; it flows directly from Christ who is alive in us.[47] As Tournier puts it, "Our real failing is to have sought to direct our own affairs—albeit, by good principles, by principles even drawn from the Bible—instead of letting ourselves be directed by God, and opening our eyes and ears to the personal inspiration He grants."[48]

What if we do not feel like forgiving? What if this lofty sense of God's glory and indwelling presence is not forthcoming? Distance from the offense and time increase the likelihood that we will be more amenable to forgiving, but in some instances the offender keeps on with the hurting and there is no way of escape. When the wounding runs deep and the natural means of healing found through distance and time are not available, a particularly compassionate understanding of forgiveness is called for.

A compassionate definition of forgiveness. The most useful definition of forgiveness I have uncovered was formulated by Peter Kirkup: "Forgiveness is a positive response to wrongdoing, in both intention and deed. Wrongdoing refers to an action that harms or humiliates another person, whether deliberately or accidentally. A positive response is one that is neither abusive nor neglectful, but loving."[49]

Forgiveness is about learning how to live again without being overwhelmed by self-pity or driven by a passion for revenge. It is facing life soberly and realistically without repression, denial or escape/avoidance behaviors. Forgiveness is about telling my story—not to impress others with my victimization or to smear the reputa-

---

[46]For a marvelous explication of this view, see C. S. Lewis, *The Great Divorce* (New York: Macmillan, 1946).

[47]I am here combining the incarnational theologies of Karl Barth and Dietrich Bonhoeffer with the contemplative tradition as represented by Henri Nouwen, Thomas Merton and Brennan Manning.

[48]Tournier, *Guilt and Grace,* p. 169.

[49]Peter A. Kirkup, "Some Religious Perspectives," 79.

tion of the offender, but simply to affirm that I am my story, that I am a person of dignity and value, worthy of respect. Forgiveness allows for outrage at injustice on behalf of whoever is suffering, even if the suffering person is myself.

Forgiveness means seeking to be civil even when we want to explode with rage because the alternative is to let violence escalate in a never-ending spiral. Forgiveness does not pretend that something didn't happen; nor does it require us to put on a phony smile. No one would suggest that a person wounded with a gun or a knife should not be experiencing pain or that awareness of the pain is unspiritual and evidence of a lack of faith. I am perplexed by the prejudice against allowing people to feel the pain of emotional wounding.[50] Rage, hate, fear and confusion are normal human reactions to emotional wounding just as throbbing and aching are reactions to physical wounding.[51]

Forgiveness is letting go of the past, but not in the sense of forgetting what happened or disconnecting myself from the pain. Forgiveness is refusing to allow the past to be the sole determinant of my life's course. It is being open to allowing the past to be redeemed so that my life story can still be good and fulfilling. Forgiveness is a radical statement to the world that there is more to the story, that the ending has yet to be told.

We must never tell people what they *must* do in order to heal. Such talk is the last thing a deeply wounded person needs. A harsh, insistent command to forgive will surely dehumanize even further a human being who is struggling to regain a sense of dignity and worth. Severe trauma creates a profound sense of alienation; the sufferer experiences events that fall far outside the realm of the ordinary course of life. To insist in the name of forgiveness that the sufferer disregard that trauma is to push the sufferer even farther outside the realm of ordinary human experience. It is to subject the sufferer to overwhelming feelings of abandonment and ostracism.

When we have been deeply wounded, someone has acted unlovingly toward us. The antidote is to be bathed in love until we are so filled up with love that we can begin to imagine letting some love flow out into forgiveness. Forgiving must flow from love, and forgiving is a form of loving. When we are sufficiently full of love—love that we are receiving and love that we are giving—we will naturally be drawn to offer forgiveness. However, we start not by loving the offender, but by loving people and receiving love from people who will rebuild the broken self, people who are safe and trustworthy. There is no need to force love toward the offender or to "will" forgiveness. The love, and hence the forgiving, will come with time, gently, the way winter melts into spring. This love flows from the soul. For-

---

[50]See, for example, the discussion of Kahrhoff *(Forgiveness: Formula for Peace of Mind)* in Enright, Gassin and Wu, "Forgiveness: A Developmental View."

[51]In "Forgiveness" Norvin Richards offers a strong exposition of this view.

giveness is not merely an act of the will, a phenomenon of the mind or a releasing
of emotion. It is perhaps one of the most uniquely integrative experiences available
to human beings, for it involves the interconnection of mind, body, heart and will,
all of which must be given their due while they are guided and coordinated by
human spirit in union with the Holy Spirit.

The Christian church offers a unique environment for wounded people to practice receiving and extending love. In worship services, in small groups, and in the
many opportunities for advancing God's kingdom in the company of other believers, broken people begin to find healing, hope and new strength. It is a great mystery, but when we choose to go forward in our life of faith, our ability to forgive
becomes manifest in a way that may have eluded us when we sought to focus
exclusively on our attempt to forgive.

To the wounded one whose heart cries out for vengeance, God offers something more wondrous than just the capacity to forgive. He offers his own heart, a
heart that flows with compassion to the poor and the broken. We can know paradoxically that we have been kept safe in the Lord, not safe in the temporal sense—
indeed the exact opposite has been the case—but safe in the eternal sense. Our
soul has been kept safe, it has been carefully guarded, and most amazing of all, it
has flourished. Any forgiving, any snippet of a desire to forgive, is a gift of grace. It
is a sign of hope, evidence of faith that our God is a redeeming God who can and
does make all things new. Forgiveness is not a destination, but a journey, often
along a convoluted route. Forgiveness lies somewhere in the territory between
denying what has happened and obsessively dwelling on it.

Why forgive? To move toward freedom from the hatred and bitterness that can
keep us from living life with joy and enthusiasm. To know more fully what it means
to share in Christ's suffering, to unite our spirit with his. To give God more opportunity to work in the world—in the victim's life, in the offender's life, and in the
lives of everyone they touch. And finally, we forgive because these light and
momentary troubles are minimal compared to the glory we shall someday share
with Jesus Christ our Lord.

15

THINKING OF OURSELVES MORE HIGHLY THAN WE OUGHT

A Psychological & Theological Analysis

Stephen K. Moroney

W HAT IS THE RELATIONSHIP BETWEEN THEOLOGY AND PSYCHOLOGY? WHEN evangelical Christians ask this question, what they usually mean is, "How should we relate the teachings of the Bible to the most influential secular theories of counseling?" When evangelicals speak of psychology, their focus is typically limited to clinical, or counseling, psychology or, less often, to developmental psychology.[1] These areas have been the main focus of the evangelical integrationist movement,[2] as well as of the fundamentalist and evangelical critiques of the integrationist enterprise.[3]

This chapter serves as an alternative to the concentrated interest in clinical, or

---

[1]This usage is not limited to laypersons but may also be found among professional psychologists, as in J. R. Fleck and J. D. Carter, eds., *Psychology and Christianity: Integrative Readings* (Nashville: Abingdon, 1981). Its general title notwithstanding, at least thirty-one of the thirty-four chapters in the book (over 90 percent) address some aspect of clinical/counseling or developmental psychology, and a similar percentage of the contributors to the volume report that their primary specialization is in one of these two areas, with the heaviest emphasis clearly on clinical/counseling psychology.

[2]John Carter and Bruce Narramore, *The Integration of Psychology and Theology: An Introduction* (Grand Rapids, Mich.: Zondervan, 1979); Gary R. Collins, *Christian Counseling*, rev. ed. (Dallas: Word, 1988); C. Stephen Evans, *Preserving the Person* (Grand Rapids, Mich.: Baker, 1982); Stanton L. Jones and Richard E. Butman, *Modern Psychotherapies: A Comprehensive Christian Appraisal* (Downers Grove, Ill.: InterVarsity, 1991).

[3]Jay E. Adams, *Competent to Counsel* (Grand Rapids, Mich.: Baker, 1970); Dave Hunt and T. A. McMahon, *The Seduction of Christianity* (Eugene, Ore.: Harvest House, 1985); Martin Bobgan and Deidre Bobgan, *Psychoheresy: The Psychological Seduction of Christianity* (Santa Barbara, Calif.: Eastgate, 1987); John MacArthur, *Our Sufficiency in Christ* (Dallas: Word, 1991).

counseling, psychology by investigating the less frequently explored relationship of theology to social psychology, the subdiscipline within psychology that "seeks to understand how we think about and interact with others."[4] This essay has two theses. First, from an evangelical perspective social psychology has something valuable to offer Christian theology, and second, from an evangelical perspective Christian theology has something valuable to offer social psychology. To illustrate this reciprocal offering, I examine what these two disciplines contribute to our understanding of self-serving cognitive distortions—the ways in which we think of ourselves more highly than we ought.[5]

What Social Psychology Has to Offer Theology

Key figures from the early church (Augustine), the medieval church (Aquinas), the Reformation church (Calvin) and the American church (Edwards) have observed that sin distorts our thinking. This phenomenon is sometimes referred to as the noetic effect of sin.[6] More recently, Abraham Kuyper and Emil Brunner have formulated detailed models of how sin corrupts our thinking.[7] All of this work has been conducted by theologians, and all of it predates both the emergence in the past half century of social psychology as a prominent academic discipline and the explosion in the past quarter century of research on social cognition. Hence, none of these thinkers was able to take into account the recent empirical research by social psychologists on the foibles of human thinking.

The Christian Scriptures make it plain that the thinking of unregenerate sinners is fallen (2 Cor 4:4; Col 1:21) and that even the thinking of Christians needs to be renewed (Rom 12:2; Eph 4:23-24). What the Scriptures do not tell us is exactly how our thinking is fallen and in what ways it is in need of renewal. This is analogous to the way in which the Bible acknowledges the presence of physical sickness ever since the Fall, but does not explain the medical particulars of how specific illnesses are contracted or the ways in which they attack the body.

The first part of this chapter aims to establish that because recent social psychological research specifies how and where our thinking is fallen, it represents a tre-

---

[4]Robert A. Baron and Donn Byrne, *Social Psychology*, 7th ed. (Boston: Allyn & Bacon, 1994), p. 8.

[5]Not all cognitive distortions are self-serving. Some common fallacies in human thinking (for example, denying the antecedent, affirming the consequent, wrongly inferring causation from correlational data and so on) may simply be instances of logical errors that are not necessarily self-serving. The present essay focuses specifically on the subset of cognitive distortions that are self-serving.

[6]Stephen K. Moroney, "The Noetic Effects of Sin: A Historical and Contemporary Exploration of How Sin Affects Our Thinking (Lanham, Md.: Lexington Books, 2000), especially appendix 2.

[7]Stephen K. Moroney, "How Sin Affects Scholarship: A New Model," *Christian Scholar's Review* 28 (1999): 432-51.

mendous resource available to Christian theology. Although social psychology is largely untapped by Christians, it offers many helpful insights into how we slip into self-serving cognitive distortions and into the ways in which those distortions are most commonly manifested in our lives. Social psychology identifies two main types of self-serving distortions: self-serving attributions and self-serving comparisons.[8]

Self-serving attributions. Social psychologists have consistently found that we attribute our successes mostly to our own effort and ability (internal factors), but we attribute our failures to the difficulty of a task or the impossibility of a situation (external factors).[9] This attributional pattern is found in both children[10] and adults.[11] Examples of this phenomenon abound. For instance, athletes tend to attribute their victories to ability and other internal causes, but not so their failures.[12] Students who do well on an exam attribute their achievement more to ability and effort, but those who do poorly attribute their performance more to the difficulty of the test.[13] Ministers accept more responsibility for positive outcomes, but attribute negative outcomes more to external circumstances.[14] After a divorce both partners typically see themselves as less responsible for the breakup than their ex-spouse.[15] When we are members of successful groups, we claim more responsibility for total group performance than when we are members of groups that have failed.[16] This is true even when reports of group success and failure are fictitiously fabricated for experimental purposes.[17]

---

[8]Although I find this twofold schema to be heuristically valuable, I acknowledge that "any taxonomy of illusions is, to some extent, arbitrary" (Shelley E. Taylor and Jonathon D. Brown, "Illusion and Well-Being: A Social Psychological Perspective on Mental Health," *Psychological Bulletin* 103 [1988]: 194). My initial acquaintance with much of the literature of social psychology came from references scattered throughout chapters two and three of David G. Myers, *Social Psychology,* 5th ed. (New York: McGraw-Hill, 1996).

[9]J. E. R. Luginbuhl, D. H. Crowe, and J. P. Kahan, "Causal Attributions for Success and Failure," *Journal of Personality and Social Psychology* 31 (1975): 86-93.

[10]B. F. Whitley and I. H. Frieze, "Children's Causal Attributions for Success and Failure in Achievement Settings: A Meta-Analysis," *Journal of Educational Psychology* 77 (1985): 608-16.

[11]B. F. Whitley and I. H. Frieze, "Measuring Causal Attributions for Success and Failure: A Meta-Analysis of the Effects of Question-Wording Style," *Basic and Applied Social Psychology* 7 (1986): 35-51.

[12]B. Mullen and C. A. Riordan, "Self-Serving Attributions for Performance in Naturalistic Settings: A Meta-Analytic Review," *Journal of Applied Social Psychology* 18 (1988): 3-22.

[13]M. H. Davis and W. G. Stephan, "Attributions for Exam Performance," *Journal of Applied Social Psychology* 10 (1980): 235-48.

[14]R. Nauta, "Task Performance and Attributional Biases in the Ministry," *Journal for the Scientific Study of Religion* 27 (1988): 609-20.

[15]J. D. Gray and R. C. Silver, "Opposite Sides of the Same Coin: Former Spouses' Divergent Perspectives in Coping with Their Divorce," *Journal of Personality and Social Psychology* 59 (1990): 1185.

[16]B. R. Schlenker, "Group Members' Attributions of Responsibility for Prior Group Performance," *Representative Research in Social Psychology* 6 (1975): 96-108.

[17]Ibid. See also B. R. Schlenker and R. S. Miller, "Egocentrism in Groups: Self-Serving Biases or Logical Information Processing?" *Journal of Personality and Social Psychology* 35 (1977): 755-64.

It appears that both cognitive factors and motivational factors contribute to our attributional biases.[18] Kunda views motivation as "cognitively mediated." Motivation provides "an initial trigger for the operation of cognitive processes that lead to the desired conclusions."[19] In support of this view there is strong evidence that our "cognitive-processing mechanisms impose filters on incoming information that distort it in a positive direction."[20]

The accumulated data has seriously altered many social psychologists' view of what the typical human being is like, so that "instead of a naive scientist entering the environment in search of the truth, we find rather the unflattering picture of a charlatan trying to make the data come out in a manner most advantageous to his or her already-held theories."[21] In order to support a positive view of ourselves we will not only ignore but also fabricate social reality.[22]

However, we do not always employ this same charitable standard in our attributions to others.[23] We excuse our own failures by blaming them on situational causes, but we typically blame others' failures on their enduring personality traits. This is a manifestation of the fundamental attribution error that Myers defines as "the tendency for observers to underestimate situational influences and overestimate dispositional influences upon others' behavior."[24] We do not give enough weight to situational constraints on others' behavior.[25] When I fail, it is because I

---

[18]Richard M. Sorrentino and E. Tory Higgins, "Motivation and Cognition: Warming Up to the Synergism," in *Handbook of Motivation and Cognition*, ed. Richard M. Sorrentino and E. Tory Higgins (New York: Guilford, 1986), pp. 3-19. See also P. E. Tetlock and A. Levi, "Attributional Bias: On the Inconclusiveness of the Cognition-Motivation Debate," *Journal of Experimental Social Psychology* 18 (1982): 68-88.

[19]Ziva Kunda, "The Case for Motivated Reasoning," *Psychological Bulletin* 108 (1990): 480, 493.

[20]Taylor and Brown, "Illusion and Well-Being," p. 193.

[21]Susan T. Fiske and Shelley E. Taylor, *Social Cognition* (Reading, Mass.: Addison-Wesley, 1984), p. 88.

[22]G. R. Goethals, "Fabricating and Ignoring Social Reality: Self-Serving Estimates of Consensus," in *Relative Deprivation and Social Comparison: The Ontario Symposium*, ed. James M. Olson, C. Peter Herman and Mark P. Zanna (Hillsdale, N.J.: Erlbaum, 1986), 4:135-57.

[23]As per note 5, this is not to say that all of our attributions to others are skewed. Baron and Byrne observe that attribution is often "a highly rational process in which individuals seeking to identify the causes of others' behavior follow orderly cognitive steps" (*Social Psychology*, p. 63). However, most of us consistently demonstrate biases in our attributions toward others, and these biases are the focus of this section of the paper.

[24]Myers, *Social Psychology*, p. 80. The fundamental attribution error is also known as "correspondence bias" or "dispositionalism," in other words, "the tendency to overestimate the extent to which human behavior is governed by and reflective of broad personal dispositions and the corresponding tendency to underappreciate the power and subtlety of situational control" (D. Dunning, et al., "The Overconfidence Effect in Social Prediction," *Journal of Personality and Social Psychology* 58 [1990]: 569).

[25]E. E. Jones and V. A. Harris, "The Attribution of Attitudes," *Journal of Experimental Social Psychology* 3 (1967): 1-24. Note, however, the exception that "people in happier relationships blame outside forces or unusual circumstances, not their spouse" (J. C. Pearson, "Positive

was in an impossible situation, but when others fail, it is because that is just the sort of people they are.

The tendency to attribute the behavior of others to their enduring personal characteristics appears to be especially strong for conservatives,[26] people who belong to relatively privileged social groups[27]ee and those who are reared in individualistic Western cultures.[28] Zebrowitz-McArthur has suggested that "the bias to perceive behavior as caused by stable [internal] dispositions, which has been called the 'fundamental attribution error' in U.S. research, reflects a culturally transmitted view of people, rather than some fundamental human perceptual or cognitive process."[29] In some cultures where collective coping is more common, such as that of Japan, self-serving attributions may be less pronounced.[30] However, in other collectivist cultures, such as that of India, self-serving attributions are clearly present.[31] On the other hand, Fletcher and Ward's review of the cross-cultural literature led them to conclude that "research has shown a surprising degree of similarity in achievement attributions across cultures."[32]

Clearly there is a need for more cross-cultural research on self-serving attribution. Nevertheless, the studies to date indicate that although the phenomenon may be especially prevalent in the more individualistic West, the phenomenon also exists in the more collectivist East. Similarly, while the self-serving bias surfaces more prominently for males in the area of academic achievement and more prominently for females in the social arena, it is plain that both sexes take more personal responsibility for positive outcomes than they do for negative outcomes.[33]

Distortion: 'The Most Beautiful Woman in the World,'" in *Making Connections,* ed. Kathleen M. Galvin and Pamela J. Cooper [Los Angeles: Roxbury, 1996], p. 176).

[26]G. S. Zucker and B. Weiner, "Conservatism and Perceptions of Poverty: An Attributional Analysis," *Journal of Applied Social Psychology* 23 (1993): 925-43.

[27]Jean-Léon Beauvois and N. Dubois, "The Norm of Internality in the Explanation of Psychological Events," *European Journal of Social Psychology* 18 (1988): 299-316.

[28]J. G. Miller, "Cultural Influences on the Development of Conceptual Differentiation in Person Description," *British Journal of Developmental Psychology* 5 (1987): 309-19. See also L. S. Newman, "How Individualists Interpret Behavior: Idiocentrism and Spontaneous Trait Inference," *Social Cognition* 11 (1993): 243-69.

[29]Leslie Zebrowitz-McArthur, "Person Perception in Cross-Cultural Perspective," in *The Cross-Cultural Challenge to Social Psychology,* ed. Michael Harris Bond (Newbury Park, Calif.: Sage, 1988), p. 254.

[30]Y. Kashima and H. C. Triandis, "The Self-Serving Bias in Attributions as a Coping Strategy: A Cross-Cultural Study," *Journal of Cross-Cultural Psychology* 17 (1986): 83-97.

[31]T. A. Chandler et al., "Multiattributional Causality: A Five Cross-National Samples Study," *Journal of Cross-Cultural Psychology* 12 (1981): 207-21.

[32]G. J. O. Fletcher and C. Ward, "Attribution Theory and Processes: A Cross-Cultural Perspective," in *The Cross-Cultural Challenge to Social Psychology,* ed. Michael Harris Bond (Newbury Park, Calif.: Sage, 1988), p. 235.

[33]H. L. Mirels, "The Avowal of Responsibility for Good and Bad Outcomes: The Effects of Generalized Self-Serving Biases," *Personality and Social Psychology Bulletin* 6 (1980): 299-306.

Moreover, our self-serving attributions cannot be explained merely as a matter of public posturing, as though for social purposes we present ourselves as better than we know ourselves to be.[34] Not only do we present to others a self that is too good to be true, but we also actually believe that we are the too-good self.[35] In fact, the attributions that we make under private conditions may actually be more self-enhancing than those we make under public conditions.[36] Our self-serving attributional bias seems to be "at least as much in the service of maintaining private self-regard as it is in the service of one's public image."[37] Individuals appear to "have a need to present a positive image to themselves as well as to others."[38] Put simply, the evidence suggests that we are truly self-deceived in the attributions we make.[39]

To summarize, social psychologists have consistently found that we display a strong penchant for attributional egotism, "taking credit for good outcomes and denying blame for bad ones in order to enhance or preserve self-esteem."[40] We are not so charitable in our evaluations of others, and we are

---

[34]J. Greenberg, T. Pyszczynski and S. Solomon, "The Self-Serving Attributional Bias: Beyond Self-Presentation," *Journal of Experimental Social Psychology* 18 (1982): 56-67. See also D. Frey, "Reactions to Success And Failure In Public And Private Conditions," *Journal of Experimental Social Psychology* 14 (1978): 172-79.

[35]A. G. Greenwald and S. J. Breckler, "To Whom Is the Self Presented?" in *The Self and Social Life,* ed. Barry R. Schlenker (New York: McGraw-Hill, 1985), pp. 126-45.

[36]G. Weary et al., "Self-Presentation and the Moderation of Self-Serving Attributional Biases," *Social Cognition* 1 (1982): 140-59. See also Barry R. Schlenker, J. R. Hallam, and N. E. McCown, "Motives and Social Evaluation: Actor-Observer Differences in the Delineation of Motives for a Beneficial Act," *Journal of Experimental Social Psychology* 19 (1983): 254-73.

[37]Greenwald and Breckler, "To Whom Is the Self Presented?" p. 129.

[38]J. Greenberg, T. Pyszczynski, and S. Solomon, "The Causes and Consequences of a Need for Self-Esteem: A Terror Management Theory," in *Public Self and Private Life,* ed. Roy F. Baumeister (New York: Springer-Verlag, 1986), p. 195.

[39]Some people who have commented on this chapter have suggested that most people suffer from low self-esteem and that their inflated estimates of themselves are merely defense mechanisms to guard them against their deeper feelings of inferiority. Hypothetically this is possible, though this view appears almost ideological in the sense that it does not allow any evidence that would count against it. When people are self-denigrating in their attributions or comparisons (as a small minority of people are), this is accepted as face-value support for the inferiority hypothesis. When people are self-eulogizing in their attributions or comparisons (as most people are), this is explained as a defense mechanism that still supports the inferiority hypothesis. Undoubtedly some people do suffer from low self-esteem, underestimate their abilities and fail to realize their value as persons created in God's image. Furthermore, a subset of these persons may display illusions of grandiosity in an effort to compensate for their deeper sense of inadequacy. However, unless social psychological research is interpreted through lenses that reverse its straightforward findings, studies indicate that most humans suffer from pride rather than from low self-esteem. The second part of this chapter will show that Christian theology offers the same diagnosis of our human condition. That is why the Bible does not warn us against thinking of ourselves more lowly than we ought, but instead warns us against thinking of ourselves more highly than we ought.

[40]M. L. Snyder, W. G. Stephan and D. Rosenfield, "Attributional Egotism," in *New Directions in Attribution Research,* ed. John H. Harvey, William John Ickes and Robert F. Kidd (Hillsdale, N.J.: Erlbaum, 1978), 2:113.

more likely to blame their failures on their enduring personality traits. Our attributions betray a strong self-serving bias. As the next section will demonstrate, the same self-serving bias is present when we compare ourselves with others.

Self-serving comparisons. When we compare ourselves with others on socially desirable traits, most of us report that we are better than average (an aggregate statistical impossibility).[41] Our self-ratings are especially exaggerated on broad ambiguous traits (for example, we proclaim how "sensitive" or "sophisticated" we are), perhaps because in the absence of hard data (for example, "I scored in the forty-eighth percentile on math achievement") we are free to use self-serving idiosyncratic criteria to exaggerate our self-assessments.[42] In other words, "people want to see themselves as better than others and use constructive social comparison to do so unless a clear reality makes such self-perceptions dissonant with the facts."[43]

For example, most of us, especially Americans and also Swedes, believe that we are safer and more skillful drivers than others.[44] Business executives consistently report themselves to be more ethical than average.[45] The Educational Testing Service conducted a college-board survey, asking nearly one million high school students to compare themselves with their peers. "Seventy percent rated themselves as above average in leadership ability whereas only 2% judged themselves as below average." Even more amazingly, in the same survey, "when asked to judge their ability to get along with others, all students rated themselves as at least average, 60% placed themselves in the top 10%, and 25% placed themselves in the top first percentile."[46] Lest professors think ourselves exempt from

---

[41]David G. Myers and J. Ridl, "Can We All Be Better Than Average?" *Psychology Today* (August 1979), pp. 89-98. As per notes 5, 23 and 39, I recognize that not all of us always compare ourselves favorably in relation to others. In some social comparisons we find ourselves to be lacking desired qualities, attributes or relationships that others possess, and at times this leads to envy (P. Salovey, "Social Comparison Processes in Envy and Jealousy," in *Social Comparison: Contemporary Theory and Research,* ed. Jerry Suls and Thomas Ashby Wills [Hillsdale, N.J.: Erlbaum, 1991], pp. 261-85). Nonetheless, the data reviewed in this section of the paper suggest that most of us usually compare ourselves favorably in relation to others.

[42]D. Dunning, J. A. Meyerowitz, and A. D. Holzberg, "Ambiguity and Self-Evaluation," *Journal of Personality and Social Psychology* 57 (1989): 1082-90.

[43]G. R. Goethals, D. M. Messick and S. T. Allison, "The Uniqueness Bias: Studies of Constructive Social Comparison," in *Social Comparison: Contemporary Theory and Research,* ed. Jerry Suls and Thomas Ashby Wills (Hillsdale, N.J.: Erlbaum, 1991), p. 172.

[44]O. Svenson, "Are We All Less Risky and More Skillful Than Our Fellow Drivers?" *Acta Psychologica* 47 (1981): 143-48.

[45]S. N. Brenner and E. A. Molander, "Is the Ethics of Business Changing?" *Harvard Business Review* (January-February 1977): 64-66.

[46]Dunning, Meyerowitz and Holzberg "Ambiguity and Self-Evaluation," 1082. Original results reported in College Board, *Student Descriptive Questionnaire* (Princeton, N.J.: Educational Testing Service, 1976-1977).

ng comparisons, it should be noted that when asked to rate the quality
eaching, less than 1 percent of us rate our teaching as poor, 1 percent
rate it as acceptable, 10 percent as average, 64 percent as above average, and 25
percent as superior.[47]

The belief that our performance is above average has been found to exist for a
variety of roles in life, as indicated in the following results from a major study of
representative Australians conducted by Headey and Wearing.[48]

Role	% Above Average	% Below Average	Average
Main Job	85.9	13.1	1.0
Parent	78.3	20.2	1.7
Spouse/Partner	77.9	19.7	3.5
Friend	76.1	22.2	1.7
Money Manager	64.7	26.0	9.3
Keeping Fit and Healthy	56.0	32.5	11.5
Main Spare-Time Activity	49.8	43.2	7.0

Very rarely do we perceive ourselves to be below average as workers, parents,
spouses or friends. In fact, the vast majority of us believe ourselves to be above
average in all these areas of life. Headey and Wearing found that "differences
between men and women, young and old, higher and lower status people, were
slight" and concluded aptly that "a sense of relative superiority is the usual state for
most people."[49]

It should be noted that the "better than average effect" is attenuated when we
are asked to compare ourselves with specific people with whom we have had personal contact rather than with a hypothetical average peer.[50] It may be that "when
people are given a vague comparison target, such as the average person or the
average student, they are able to engage in downward comparisons, thereby comparing themselves with someone who is worse off and more at risk."[51] Apparently
people often "increase their subjective well-being through comparison with a less

---

[47]R. T. Blackburn et al., "Are Instructional Improvement Programs Off-Target?" *Current Issues in Higher Education* 1 (1980): 37. One study found that "an amazing 94 percent rate themselves as above-average teachers, and 68 percent rank themselves in the top quarter in teaching performance" (K. P. Cross, "Not *Can* But *Will* College Teachers Be Improved?" *New Directions for Higher Education* 17 [spring 1977]: 10).

[48]B. Headey and A. Wearing, "The Sense of Relative Superiority—Central to Well-Being," *Social Indicators Research* 20 (1988): 503. I am uncertain why the data on the role of spouse/partner total 101.1 percent.

[49]Ibid., pp. 497, 499.

[50]M. D. Alicke et al., "Personal Contact, Individuation and Better Than Average Effect," *Journal of Personality and Social Psychology* 68 (1995): 804-25.

[51]L. S. Perloff and B. K. Fetzer, "Self-Other Judgments and Perceived Vulnerability to Victimization," *Journal of Personality and Social Psychology* 50 (1986): 505.

fortunate other."[52] And even when we are asked to make comparisons with specific others, we are often still self-congratulatory.[53]

In order to support our opinions, we overestimate others' agreement with our views (the false consensus effect). That is, "people distort others' opinions in the direction of seeing more agreement with their own than actually exists."[54] For example, we often overestimate the percentage of the general population that agrees with our political views, leading us to irrationally predict favorable outcomes for our preferred political party.[55] In matters of opinion it appears that consensus is desirable; perhaps others make good company for us by assuring us that we are right.[56] We also wrongly cling to a false consensus in areas where we are low in ability or performance, viewing our shortcomings as rather commonplace. As Wood and Taylor observe, "when one has an unfavorable characteristic, one may self-enhance by reminding oneself of others who are similarly flawed."[57] Here misery truly does love company. However, we seem to prefer less company when our performance or abilities are favorable, so that we overestimate the sui generis character of our virtues (the false uniqueness effect).[58] This is true for grade school children, high school students and middle-management bankers alike.[59]

As Rosenblatt puts it, "there is an enormous discrepancy between how 'good'

---

[52]Thomas Ashby Wills, "Downward Comparison Principles in Social Psychology," *Psychological Bulletin* 90 (1981): 245. See also the literature review by Thomas Ashby Wills, "Similarity and Self-Esteem in Downward Comparison," in *Social Comparison: Contemporary Theory and Research,* ed. Jerry Suls and Thomas Ashby Wills (Hillsdale, N.J.: Erlbaum, 1991), pp. 51-78. Downward comparison may make us feel better about ourselves, but upward comparison may help us to make positive concrete changes in our lives (P. Brickman and R. J. Bulman, "Pleasure and Pain in Social Comparison," in *Social Comparison Processes: Theoretical and Empirical Perspectives,* ed. Jerry M. Suls and Richard L. Miller [Washington, D.C.: Hemisphere, 1977], pp. 149-86).

[53]After conducting a series of seven experiments that differentiated between "hypothetical" and "real" comparisons, Alicke et al. found that the better-than-average effect "persevered across a wide range of comparison conditions" and may therefore be described as "a pervasive and robust phenomenon" ("Personal Contact," p. 822).

[54]J. D. Campbell, "Similarity and Uniqueness: The Effects of Attribute Type, Relevance, and Individual Differences in Self-Esteem and Depression," *Journal of Personality and Social Psychology* 50 (1986): 281.

[55]E. Babad, M. Hills, and M. O'Driscoll, "Factors Influencing Wishful Thinking and Predictions of Election Outcomes," *Basic and Applied Social Psychology* 13 (1992): 461-76. See also Donald Granberg and Sören Holmberg, *The Political System Matters: Social Psychology and Voting Behavior in Sweden and the United States* (Cambridge: Cambridge University Press, 1988).

[56]G. Marks, "Thinking One's Abilities Are Unique and One's Opinions Are Common," *Personality and Social Psychology Bulletin* 10 (1984): 203-8.

[57]J. V. Wood and K. L. Taylor, "Serving Self-Relevant Goals Through Social Comparison," in *Social Comparison: Contemporary Theory and Research,* ed. J. Suls and T. Wills (Hillsdale, N.J.: Erlbaum, 1991), p. 31.

[58]Marks, "Thinking One's Abilities Are Unique," pp. 203-8.

[59]Goethals, Messick, and Allison, "Uniqueness Bias," pp. 149-76, especially 166-68. Interestingly, these researchers found that "men consistently think that they are smarter than their peers," but women "claim more for themselves than men in the moral domain" (p. 169).

Americans think they are personally and how 'bad' they think their countrymen are."[60] Our false sense of moral superiority to others is abundantly clear in the results of a national survey of Americans' estimation of their own and others' compliance with the Ten Commandments: [61]

Who Follows the Ten Commandments?	Americans Who Say They . . .	Americans Who Say the Majority of Others . . .
Do not curse or use profanity	64%	15%
Go to church, synagogue or mosque on holy days	64%	22%
Respect your parents	95%	49%
Do not commit murder	91%	71%
If married, do not have a sexual relationship with someone other than your spouse	86%	45%
Do not steal	90%	54%
Do not say things that aren't true about another person	88%	33%
Do not envy the things another person has	76%	23%
Do not covet another person's husband/wife	84%	42%
Worship only the one true God	81%	49%

Plainly we think of ourselves as better than others. We also construe our futures as better than others'; we head into the unknown of tomorrow with unrealistic optimism. New car buyers believe that they are much less likely to be killed or injured in a car crash than are other people similar to themselves.[62] College students "tend to believe that they are more likely than their peers to experience positive events and less likely to experience negative events." Students consistently report that they are more likely than their classmates to enjoy their postgraduation job, to own their own home, to have a high starting salary and to travel to Europe. [63]

Conversely, college students believe they are less likely than their peers to have a drinking problem, to attempt suicide, to divorce after a few years of marriage, to have a heart attack before the age of forty, to contract a venereal disease, to be fired from a job, to contract lung cancer, to be sterile, to drop out of college or to be unable to find a job for six months.[64] In comparison to the average student or the average person, college students view themselves as less vulnerable to hyper-

---

[60]R. Rosenblatt, "The 11th Commandment," *Family Circle*, December 21, 1993, p. 30.

[61]Ibid., p. 30. Note the paraphrasing (for example, mosque attendance qualifies as keeping the sabbath day holy). Note also that in Myers's summary of Rosenblatt's data more than half of the reported figures are erroneous (*Social Psychology*, p. 58).

[62]L. S. Robertson, "Car Crashes: Perceived Vulnerability and Willingness to Pay for Crash Protection," *Journal of Community Health* 3 (1977): 136-41.

[63]N. D. Weinstein, "Unrealistic Optimism about Future Life Events," *Journal of Personality and Social Psychology* 39 (1980): 818, 810.

[64]Ibid., p. 810.

tension, cancer, heart attack, drinking problems, divorce, venereal disease and mugging.[65] When they compare themselves to same-sex peers at their institution, students believe they are much less at risk for drug addiction, suicide, venereal disease, epilepsy, alcoholism, lung cancer, obesity, hepatitis, kidney infection, multiple sclerosis and a host of other health problems and causes of death.[66]

In short, we consistently display an unrealistic optimism about the future, perhaps because we overestimate our control over it,[67] and perhaps because we have an egocentric tendency to neglect careful consideration of others' actual circumstances.[68]

Moreover, we consistently exhibit more confidence than accuracy in our prognostications about the future. In fact, it is precisely when we are most confident in our predictions about the future that the gap between our confidence level and the accuracy of our predictions is at its greatest.[69] We think that we know much more about what the future holds for ourselves and others than we actually do.[70] We demonstrate a predisposition to believe with undue confidence that bad things will more often happen to others, but that good things will more often happen to us. Even when we experience a negative event, such as an earthquake, we maintain our unrealistic optimism concerning our overall health, and we soon see ourselves as less vulnerable than average others to the very disaster we have just encountered.[71] As Taylor and Brown explain, "Most people seem to be saying, 'The future will be great, especially for me.' "[72] It appears that hope does spring eternal in the human heart.

Our predilection for self-serving comparisons is present not only at the individual level, but also at the group level.[73] We display a strong in-group ("us") favorit-

---

[65]Perloff and Fetzer, "Self-Other Judgments," p. 504. Interestingly, the "illusions of unique invulnerability were primarily observed when subjects rated themselves and the average person or the average college student. These illusions largely disappeared when subjects rated themselves and their friends or family" (ibid.).

[66]N. D. Weinstein, "Unrealistic Optimism about Susceptibility to Health Problems," *Journal of Behavioral Medicine* 5 (1982): 447.

[67]Ibid., pp. 441-60.

[68]N. D. Weinstein and E. Lachendro, "Egocentrism as a Source of Unrealistic Optimism," *Personality and Social Psychology Bulletin* 8 (1982): 195-200.

[69]Dunning et al., "Overconfidence Effect," pp. 572-76. Of those predictions of which subjects were 100 percent confident, less than 80 percent were true (ibid., p. 574).

[70]R. Vallone et al., "Overconfident Prediction of Future Actions and Outcomes by Self and Others," *Journal of Personality and Social Psychology* 58 (1990): 582-92.

[71]J. M. Burger and M. L. Palmer, "Changes in and Generalization of Unrealistic Optimism Following Experiences with Stressful Events: Reactions to the 1989 California Earthquake," *Personality and Social Psychology Bulletin* 18 (1992): 39-43.

[72]Taylor and Brown, "Illusion and Well-Being," p. 197.

[73]R. Luhtanen and J. Crocker, "Self-Esteem and Intergroup Comparisons: Toward a Theory of Collective Self-Esteem," in *Social Comparison: Contemporary Theory and Research,* ed. Jerry Suls and Thomas Ashby Wills (Hillsdale, N.J.: Erlbaum, 1991), pp. 211-34.

ism and out-group ("them") discrimination.[74] Researchers have found that "even in the absence of conflict or competition over resources, people are motivated to show ingroup bias in intergroup comparisons,"[75] perhaps in order to enhance our self-esteem. In fact, even in new groups that are formed by random selection and that involve minimal interaction, we tend to view our own group as better than other groups.[76] Collective pride in our group is almost instantaneous, and it is manifested in sexism, racism and nationalism, and at any time we wrongly perceive a group to which we belong as superior to others.[77]

We are ingenious in the many ways we bolster ourselves by comparing ourselves with others. Selective and revised memories about ourselves help to feed our self-serving comparisons.[78] Moreover, with both self-serving attributions and self-serving comparisons, cognitive distortion appears to be closely tied to biases in our information processing.[79] One way in which our information processing is skewed is the manner in which we give credence to incoming data. We are more likely to view as valid those sources of information that provide us with flattering feedback than those that provide us with critical feedback. This is true of the credence we give to both scientific research[80] and tests.[81] It is even true of the credence we give to horoscopes: skeptics of astrology who received flattering horoscopes "perceived the descriptions as extremely accurate and, as a result, significantly changed their opinions about astrology in a favorable direction."[82]

Finally, it should be noted that the predisposition for self-serving bias is not lim-

---

[74]M. B. Brewer, "Ingroup Bias in the Minimal Intergroup Situation: A Cognitive-Motivational Analysis," *Psychological Bulletin* 86 (1979): 307-24. See also S. Hinkle and J. Schopler, "Bias in the Evaluation of In-Group and Out-Group Performance," in *Psychology of Intergroup Relations,* ed. Stephen Worchel and William G. Austin, 2nd ed. (Chicago: Nelson-Hall, 1986), pp. 196-212.

[75]Luhtanen and Crocker, "Self-Esteem and Intergroup Comparisons," p. 214.

[76]Ibid. See also H. Tajfel and J. C. Turner, "The Social Identity Theory of Intergroup Behavior," in *Psychology of Intergroup Relations,* ed. Stephen Worchel and William G. Austin, 2nd ed. (Chicago: Nelson-Hall, 1986), pp. 7-24.

[77]David G. Myers, *The Inflated Self* (New York: Seabury, 1980), p. 37.

[78]W. Klein and Ziva Kunda, "Maintaining Self-Serving Social Comparisons: Biased Reconstruction of One's Past Behaviors," *Personality and Social Psychology Bulletin* 19 (1993): 732-39. Klein and Kunda conclude that "people may convince themselves that they are superior to others either by biasing their beliefs about others or by biasing their beliefs about themselves" (p. 737).

[79]N. A. Kuiper et al., "Self-Schema Processing of Depressed and Nondepressed Content: The Effects of Vulnerability to Depression," *Social Cognition* 3 (1985): 77-93.

[80]Kunda, "The Case for Motivated Reasoning," pp. 489-90.

[81]T. Pyszczynski, J. Greenberg and K. Holt, "Maintaining Consistency Between Self-Serving Beliefs and Available Data: A Bias in Information Evaluation," *Personality and Social Psychology Bulletin* 11 (1985): 179-90.

[82]P. Glick, D. Gottesman and J. Jolton, "The Fault Is Not in the Stars: Susceptibility Of Skeptics and Believers in Astrology to the Barnum Effect," *Personality and Social Psychology Bulletin* 15 (1989): 580.

ited to American college students but is widespread across many cultures. Myers cites research that has found a self-serving bias at work "among Dutch high school university students, Belgian basketball players, Indian Hindus, Japanese drivers, Australian students and workers, Chinese students, and French people of all ages."[83] Social psychological research has shown that "there exists a pervasive tendency to see the self as better than others."[84] In fact, the self-serving bias extends even to believing that the research on self-serving bias does not apply to us because we are less self-serving than others. Even when we are informed about the pervasiveness of the self-serving bias, we continue to be "conceited in our perceptions of our own humility." We "see ourselves as somewhat better than average at not thinking ourselves to be better than average."[85]

In the first part of this paper I have documented recent social psychological research that has uncovered numerous ways in which humans engage in self-serving, erroneous thinking about themselves and others. These findings of social psychology can illumine an evangelical understanding of the specific cognitive mechanisms by which humans distort their thinking in self-serving ways. Theologians have long recognized that sin has a corrupting influence on our reason, but social psychologists help theologians to understand some of the particular ways in which the noetic effects of sin are manifested, for instance, through our tendency to engage in self-serving attributions and self-serving comparisons. Does theology have a reciprocal gift for social psychology? Establishing an affirmative answer to this question is the task of the second part of this paper.

What Theology Has to Offer Social Psychology

Christians have approached the relatively new, popular and influential discipline of psychology in a variety of ways. John Carter and Bruce Narramore have set forth perhaps the best-known typology of Christian responses to psychology, following the general outline proposed in H. Richard Niebuhr's *Christ and Culture*.[86] Carter

---

[83]Myers, *Social Psychology,* p. 69.
[84]Taylor and Brown, "Illusion and Well-Being," p. 195.
[85]J. Friedrich, "On Seeing Oneself as Less Self-Serving Than Others: The Ultimate Self-Serving Bias?" *Teaching of Psychology* 23 (April 1996): 107.
[86]H. Richard Niebuhr, *Christ and Culture* (New York: Harper & Row, 1951). Carter and Narramore explicitly acknowledge their dependence on Niebuhr in *Integration of Psychology and Theology,* p. 72 n. 2. Because my focus here is on Christian responses to psychology, my comments will center on the "sacred" versions of the models proffered by Carter and Narramore. It should be noted that two of Carter and Narramore's approaches, the Against model and the Of model, are more relevant to the arena of psychotherapy than to the field of social psychology. I am unaware of Christians who reduce Scripture to social psychology or press all of Scripture into the cookie-cutter mold of social psychology (the "Of" model). Similarly, proponents of the Against model have typically aimed their criticisms at what they understand to be the anti-Christian speculations of secular therapists such as Freud, Rogers and so on, not at social psychologists. Because the argument of the first half of this paper has

and Narramore's typology is closely echoed by the typologies set forth by Larry Crabb,[87] and by Stan Jones and Rich Butman.[88] Within these typologies the two Christian approaches most pertinent to the study of self-serving cognitive distortions are the "Parallels" model of the perspectivalists, and the "Integrates" model of the Christianizers. The two models agree that theology has something of value to offer psychology, but disagree about the exact nature of this offering.

The Parallels model (perspectivalism). Carter and Narramore describe the Parallels model as follows:

> Psychology and Christianity are two separate spheres of knowledge. The two spheres have their own sources of truth (scientific method and revelation), their own methods of investigation (experimentation and exegesis), and their own data (psychological principles and facts, and biblical principles and facts). Integration consists of finding the concepts that are parallel (equivalent) in the other discipline (sphere).[89]

Both Christianity and psychology can be embraced without fear of conflict because they operate in different spheres. Where we find areas of relationship and overlap, we view these more as interesting parallels than as indicators of a deeper or broader unifying set of truths that could conceivably embrace both disciplines.[90]

Larry Crabb calls this model the "separate but equal" approach. Jones and Butman call it perspectivalism, a belief that "scientific/psychological views and religious understandings complement but don't really affect each other."[91] This is the dominant approach of David Myers, who is arguably the most prominent Christian social psychologist.[92]

Myers explicitly acknowledges his preference for the Parallels model (perspectivalism),[93] and it is exemplified in much of his work, perhaps most clearly in his

---

been that social psychology has valuable insights to offer Christian theology, I will discuss neither the Of model nor the Against model in further detail in the present essay.

[87]Larry J. Crabb Jr. "Biblical Counseling: A Basic View," *CAPS Bulletin* 4 (1978): 1-6. In my view, Crabb's categories of (1) Separate but Equal, (2) Spoiling the Egyptians, (3) Nothing Butterists, and (4) Tossed Salad roughly correspond to Carter and Narramore's (1) Parallels, (2) Integrates, (3) Against, and (4) Of models. For reasons explained in the previous note, the latter two categories will not be explored in detail in the present paper.

[88]Jones and Butman, *Modern Psychotherapies*, pp. 17-38. In my view, the perspectives that Jones and Butman label (1) "perspectival integration" and (2) "humanizer or Christianizer of science" are essentially equivalent to Carter and Narramore's (1) Parallels model and (2) Integrates model, respectively. Jones and Butman's third category of ethical integration (in other words, practicing high Christian moral standards as a psychologist) is not directly relevant to the questions raised in this section of the paper, so I will not discuss it in further detail here.

[89]Carter and Narramore, *Integration of Psychology and Theology,* p. 99.

[90]Ibid., p. 98.

[91]Jones and Butman, *Modern Psychotherapies,* p. 20.

[92]See Myers, *Social Psychology,* p. 7; and David G. Myers and Malcom A. Jeeves, *Psychology Through the Eyes of Faith* (San Francisco: Harper & Row, 1987), p. 9.

[93]Myers and Jeeves, *Psychology Through the Eyes of Faith,* p. 17.

article "Yin and Yang in Psychological Research and Christian Belief."[94] Myers applies his perspectivalism to the issue of cognitive distortion and discovers (1) an example of self-justifying bias in the Pharisee of Luke 18:11-12; (2) an assumption of self-serving comparison in Paul's corrective admonishment in Philippians 2:3 to "regard others as better than yourselves" (3) an assumption of self-love in the words of Paul (Eph 5:28-33) and Jesus (Mt 22:39);[95] and (4) hope for overcoming our cognitive conceit, as exemplified by the psalmist (Ps 131) and Paul (Phil 3:9).[96]

In addition to using the Scriptures cited by Myers, perspectivalists could illustrate the tendency to engage in self-justification also by pointing to the expert in the law in Luke 10:25-29 and to the Pharisees in Luke 16:14-15. It could be argued that 1 Corinthians 3:18 and Galatians 6:3 anticipate the human propensity to deceive ourselves with an inflated self-view, to think of ourselves as wise when we are foolish, or as something when we are nothing. Echoes of our self-serving attributions might also be found in Proverbs 16:2; 21:2 and 30:12, which describe how we deceive ourselves by wrongly thinking that we are pure and innocent.

Based on Myers's claims regarding levels of analysis, it also seems possible for perspectivalists to argue that psychology is mainly descriptive, while theology is often prescriptive. It certainly is striking that the social psychological literature on self-serving cognitive distortions offers such a helpful detailed description of the problems in human thinking but very little accompanying prescription focusing on the need to overcome these problems or the manner in which to do so.[97] Kauff-

---

[94]David G. Myers, "Yin and Yang in Psychological Research and Christian Belief," *Perspectives on Science and Christian Faith* 39 (1987): 128-39. It should be noted, however, that portions of Myers, *The Inflated Self,* and Myers and Jeeves, *Psychology Through the Eyes of Faith,* move beyond the Parallels model to more interactive, integrative work. In personal correspondence of May 12, 1997, Myers indicated that he "didn't set out to articulate or represent any particular model, but rather simply to ask how psychological research squares with biblical and theological ideas (insofar as both have some things to say about human nature)."

[95]Myers and Jeeves, *Psychology Through the Eyes of Faith*, pp. 134-35. Myers alludes to the same Scriptures in "Yin and Yang," (p. 137) with the addition of Psalm 19:12.

[96]Myers, "Yin and Yang," pp. 137-38.

[97]The little empirical evidence we have suggests that mere knowledge of cognitive biases often does not eliminate these biases. At present, social psychology provides a helpful diagnosis of our cognitive woes, but provides little in the way of cures. On this see the following studies: J. S. Croxton and N. Morrow, "What Does It Take to Reduce Observer Bias?" *Psychological Reports* 55 (1984): 135-38; J. T. Johnson et al., "Causal Attribution and Dispositional Inference: Evidence of Inconsistent Judgments," *Journal of Experimental Social Psychology* 20 (1984): 567-85; J. S. Croxton and A. G. Miller, "Behavioral Disconfirmation and the Observer Bias," *Journal of Social Behavior and Personality* 2 (1987): 145-52; G. D. Reeder, G. J. O. Fletcher and K. Furman, "The Role of Observers' Expectations in Attitude Attribution," *Journal of Experimental Social Psychology* 25 (1989): 168-88; J. Krueger and R. Clement, "The Truly False Consensus Effect: An Ineradicable and Egocentric Bias in Social Perception," *Journal of Personality and Social Psychology* 67 (1994): 596-610; and Friedrich, "On Seeing Oneself as Less Self-Serving," pp. 107-9.

mann observes that "the research findings of social psychologists are primarily descriptive," and "psychologists engaged in this type of research seldom make connections with prescriptive criteria; that is, they do not presume to indicate what behaviors *should* take place in the particular setting under study."[98] The Christian Scriptures, by contrast, contain many implicit and explicit prescriptions concerning the need to oppose self-serving cognitive distortions.

In Matthew 22:39 Jesus stresses the importance of the commandment first found in Leviticus 19:18, that we love our neighbors as ourselves. Certainly an implicit application of this command is that we love our neighbors with our minds as we do ourselves. We should strive to think rightly about our neighbors and give them a fair shake in our attributions of why they act as they do, rather than applying harsher attributions to them than to ourselves. Along similar lines, Matthew 7:12 records Jesus' golden rule that we should do to others what we would have them do to us. Again an implicit application is that we should not be lax in our self-attributions while we are critical toward others; we should not engage in wrongful self-serving comparisons of ourselves with others because we would not wish others to do so to us.

Romans 12:3 is even more explicit in opposing our inflated views of ourselves: "I say to everyone among you not to think of yourself more highly than you ought to think, but to think with sober judgment, each according to the measure of faith that God has assigned." Second Timothy 3:2 lists improper love of self as characteristic of the terrible times in the last days and antithetical to authentic Christianity. Finally, Matthew 7:1-5 records Jesus' unmistakably direct prescription against our tendency to look first to the shortcomings of others rather than to our own faults, and against our inclination to judge others with a more severe standard than that with which we judge ourselves:

> Do not judge, so that you may not be judged. For with the judgment you make you will be judged, and the measure you give will be the measure you get. Why do you see the speck in your neighbor's eye, but do not notice the log in your own eye? Or how can you say to your neighbor, 'Let me take the speck out of your eye,' while the log is in your own eye? You hypocrite, first take the log out of your own eye, and then you will see clearly to take the speck out of your neighbor's eye. (NRSV)

In sum, according to the Parallels model of the perspectivalists, psychology

---

[98]D. Kauffmann, "Belief and Behavior: Social Psychology and Christian Living," *Journal of Psychology and Christianity* 15 (1996): 47. In my view, Christian social psychologists should move beyond mere descriptive studies that document noetic errors to creative experimental investigation into the possibilities and mechanisms for guarding against and reducing our self-serving biases. Sappington is right that, "a true understanding of self-deception will involve a challenge that has not been met as yet by mainstream psychology—how can accurate perception be increased?" (A. A. Sappington, "Psychology for the Practice of the Presence of God: Putting Psychology at the Service of the Church," *Journal of Psychology and Christianity* 13 [1994]: 8).

offers theology parallels, support, reinforcement, echoes and enlivening modern examples. Theology in turn offers religious anticipations, counterparts and examples of modern psychological principles.[99] According to this view, theology and psychology do not often interact directly. However, when the two fields do address common subject matter (as in the case of self-serving cognitive distortions), their varying perspectives represent different, complementary levels of analysis, as illustrated by theological prescription and psychological description.

The Integrates model (the Christianizers' perspective). Carter and Narramore appreciate the Parallels model, but they also believe that it is unduly limited in its ability to generate a genuine integration of theology and psychology. The Parallels model, they write, "is based on the assumption that we are dealing with two separate entities that can at best be lined up to find common meaning, and this assumption precludes true and comprehensive integration. This is its most basic fault. It cannot produce the broader unifying principles that are necessary for true integration because of its artificial separation of sources of truth."[100]

Due to this limitation of the Parallels model Carter and Narramore prefer what they call the Integrates model, which they describe as follows:

> Believing in the unity of truth, proponents of the Integrates model do not look at psychological and theological understandings as distinct fields of study that are essentially unrelatable. Instead, they assume that since God is the Author of all truth, and since He is the Creator of the entire world, there is ultimately only one set of explanatory hypotheses. While the methods and data of psychology are frequently distinct (and the distinctions need to be maintained), followers of the Integrates model are looking for unifying concepts that will broaden the understanding that would come from either psychology or theology in isolation.[101]

Jones and Butman similarly favor the Christianizer approach "that involves the explicit incorporation of religiously based beliefs as the control beliefs that shape the perception of facts, theories and methods in social science."[102] Proponents of this outlook allow theological and psychological concepts to interact much more directly than do proponents of the Parallels model. The two fields are conceived not as separate but equal but rather as mutually informative and reciprocally critical. Psychology may at times challenge fallible theological concepts or Scriptural interpretations, and theology may at times correct erroneous psychological claims. In the remainder of this chapter I will illustrate the Integrates model by arguing that

---

[99]Myers, "Yin and Yang," pp. 135-39.

[100]Carter and Narramore, *Integration of Psychology and Theology*, p. 100.

[101]Ibid., p. 104. Quoting Carter and Narramore in personal correspondence of May 12, 1997, Myers notes that it may be unfair to contrast Perspectivalists and Integrators, or Christianizers, in this way because "we're all operating from the assumption that 'since God is Author of all truth, and since He is the Creator of the entire world, there is ultimately only one set of explanatory hypotheses.' "

[102]Jones and Butman, *Modern Psychotherapies*, p. 20.

theology offers important correctives of recent psychological claims concerning self-serving cognitive distortions. First I will set forth the psychological claims; then I will offer the theological correctives.

The psychological claims. Self-serving attributions and self-serving comparisons have been found in a wide spectrum of people: young and old, male and female, low status and high status, Eastern and Western. However, some researchers have found that one group of people does not engage in this sort of self-serving cognitive distortion, at least not to the same degree as the rest of us. This group comprises people who are mildly depressed. Their more sober self-understanding is commonly referred to as depressive realism, which is explained by prominent theorist and researcher Shelley Taylor:

> Normal people exaggerate how competent and well liked they are. Depressed people do not. Normal people remember their past behavior with a rosy glow. Depressed people are more evenhanded in recalling their successes and failures. Normal people describe themselves primarily positively. Depressed people describe both their positive and negative qualities. Normal people take credit for successful outcomes and tend to deny responsibility for failure. Depressed people accept responsibility for both success and failure. Normal people exaggerate the control they have over what goes on around them. Depressed people are less vulnerable to the illusion of control. Normal people believe to an unrealistic degree that the future holds a bounty of good things and few bad things. Depressed people are more realistic in their perceptions of the future. In fact, on virtually every point on which normal people show enhanced self-regard, illusions of control, and unrealistic visions of the future, depressed people fail to show the same biases. "Sadder but wiser" does indeed appear to apply to depression.[103]

Taylor's summary may be an oversimplification of the literature on the cognition of depressed persons, as she herself notes.[104] Though some people with depression are realists, others display the optimistic positive illusions common to most of us, and still others exhibit the opposite cognitive distortion of pessimistic negative biases.[105] Also it is not entirely clear whether negative thinking causes depression or

---

[103]Shelley Taylor, *Positive Illusions: Creative Self-Deception and the Healthy Mind* (New York: Basic Books, 1989), p. 214. In the final sentence Taylor is referring to a phrase coined in the pioneering study by L. B. Alloy and L. Y. Abramson, "Judgment of Contingency in Depressed and Nondepressed Students: Sadder but Wiser?" *Journal of Experimental Psychology: General* 108 (1979): 441-85.

[104]Taylor, *Positive Illusions*, p. 215. See also Shelley E. Taylor and Jonathon D. Brown, "Positive Illusions and Well-Being Revisited: Separating Fact from Fiction," *Psychological Bulletin* 116 (1994): 22.

[105]See K. Dobson and R. Franche, "A Conceptual and Empirical Review of the Depressive Realism Hypothesis," *Canadian Journal of Behavioural Science* 21 (1989): 419-33; D. Dunning and A. L. Story, "Depression, Realism, and the Overconfidence Effect: Are the Sadder Wiser When Predicting Future Actions and Events?" *Journal of Personality and Social Psychology* 61 (1991): 521-32; and R. Ackerman and R. J. DeRubeis, "Is Depressive Realism Real?" *Clinical Psychology Review* 11 (1991): 565-84.

results from it.[106] Be that as it may, Taylor and her colleague Jonathon Brown argue that in conjunction with many other pieces of evidence, the literature on depressive realism raises important questions about the historically dominant view that an accurate perception of reality is essential to mental health.[107]

Taylor and Brown argue that "the mentally healthy person appears to have the enviable capacity to distort reality in a direction that enhances self-esteem, maintains beliefs in personal efficacy, and promotes an optimistic view of the future."[108] Depressed persons lack precisely this "enviable capacity to distort reality" in self-serving ways. As Baumeister puts it, "seeing self and world too accurately is depressing; indeed, part of the problem in depression may be the loss of one's rose-colored glasses that make things look better than they are."[109]

If the realists are depressed, then perhaps proponents of the traditional view are wrong to laud the virtues of an accurate perception of reality.[110] Taylor suggests that "in many ways, the healthy mind is a self-deceptive one."[111] After all, the cognitive distorters are the ones who appear happy, well-adjusted and normal.[112] So Taylor and Brown argue that certain types of self-serving illusions should actually be viewed as "adaptive for mental health and well-being."[113] Admittedly, major cognitive distortions may be problematic when they collide with reality, resulting in the unpleasant disconfirmation of our illusions.[114] However, mild self-serving distortions do not carry these same risks, which leads Baumeister to hypothesize that "it may be most adaptive to hold a view of self that is a little better than the truth—neither too inflated nor too accurate."[115]

According to the view promoted by Taylor and Brown and echoed by Baumeister, self-serving cognitive distortions are not something to be shunned or overcome; instead, they are something to be actively cultivated. Rather than to "help people form more realistic judgments about themselves," Taylor suggests, "the goal of therapy might better be to help people develop cognitive illusions so that they can think more positively about themselves, the world, and the future, employing the mildly inflated biases that normal people characteristically use."[116] Taylor and

---

[106]See the argument for bidirectional causation and the related literature review in Myers, *Social Psychology,* pp. 174-77.

[107]Taylor and Brown, "Illusion and Well-Being," p. 197.

[108]Ibid., 204.

[109]Roy F. Baumeister, "The Optimal Margin of Illusion," *Journal of Social and Clinical Psychology* 8 (1989): 184.

[110]Taylor, *Positive Illusions: Creative Self-Deception and the Healthy Mind,* p. 46.

[111]Ibid., ix.

[112]Ibid., 49.

[113]Taylor and Brown, "Illusion and Well-Being," p. 193.

[114]Ibid., 204. See also Baumeister, "Optimal Margin," pp. 177-81.

[115]Baumeister, "Optimal Margin," p. 184. See also Taylor, *Positive Illusions,* p. 244.

[116]Taylor, *Positive Illusions,* p. 220.

Brown conclude that our self-serving cognitive distortions are neither problems to be counteracted nor sins of which we should repent. Just the opposite, "the capacity to develop and maintain positive illusions may be thought of as a valuable human resource to be nurtured and promoted, rather than an error-prone processing system to be corrected."[117]

Taylor and Brown's proposal has not gone without criticism from fellow psychologists. Colvin and Block have questioned the logic and the empirical evidence that Taylor and Brown adduce in support of their view.[118] Shedler, Mayman and Manis have likewise offered alternative explanations of the data, arguing that "people who are prone to distort also give distorted responses to mental health scale items, and their scores simply cannot be taken at face value."[119] These critics, however, see themselves as being in the minority. They believe that Taylor and Brown's position "has gained currency among academic researchers"[120] and has met with "seemingly widespread acceptance."[121] Even Myers seems persuaded that "there may be some practical wisdom in self-serving perceptions," such that in comparison to the depressive explanatory style, "self-serving illusions are adaptive."[122]

It is precisely at this point in the debate over cognitive distortions that Christian theology represents a helpful resource. Specifically, Christian theology offers five antidotes that may be beneficial in counteracting our propensity to engage in self-serving cognitive distortions.

First, Christian theology offers a clear corrective to the mistaken notion that self-serving cognitive distortions should be encouraged and cultivated. The Scriptures contain repeated implicit and explicit prescriptions concerning the need to oppose self-serving cognitive distortions. That is, despite self-serving cognitive distortions' apparent temporary benefits for mental health or adjustment, Christian theology names cognitive conceit (thinking more highly of our-

---

[117]Taylor and Brown, "Illusion and Well-Being," p. 205.

[118]C. R. Colvin and J. Block, "Do Positive Illusions Foster Mental Health? An Examination of the Taylor and Brown Formulation," *Psychological Bulletin* 116 (1994): 3-20. See also Taylor and Brown's response and Colvin and Block's rejoinder that immediately follow in the same issue of the *Psychological Bulletin*: Taylor and Brown, "Positive Illusions and Well-Being Revisited," pp. 21-27; J. Block and C. R. Colvin, "Positive Illusions and Well-Being Revisited: Separating Fiction from Fact," *Psychological Bulletin* 116 (1994): 28.

[119]J. Shedler, M. Mayman and M. Manis, "The *Illusion* of Mental Health," *American Psychologist* 48 (1993): 1128. See also the response and rejoinder appearing one year later: Shelley E. Taylor and Jonathon D. Brown, " 'Illusion' of Mental Health Does Not Explain Positive Illusions," *American Psychologist* 49 (1994): 972-73; J. Shedler, M. Mayman and M. Manis, "More Illusions," *American Psychologist* 49 (1994): 974-76.

[120]Shedler, Mayman and Manis, "The *Illusion* of Mental Health," p. 1128.

[121]Colvin and Block, "Do Positive Illusions Foster Mental Health?" p. 4.

[122]Myers, *Social Psychology,* p. 62, 174. See also Myers's annotation on Taylor and Block's *Positive Illusions: Creative Self-Deception and the Healthy Mind*: "The ancient wisdom to 'know thyself' notwithstanding, mental health may instead reflect the art of being well deceived" (ibid., p. 70).

selves than we ought) as sin that is not acceptable for Christians.[123] For Christians psychological utility is not the final standard, and self-reported happiness is not the ultimate authority. Realistic thinking, like conviction of sin that leads to repentance, may be uncomfortable, even painful or temporarily depressing, but ultimately it is in our best interests (2 Cor 7:8-11; cf. Jas 4:9-10).[124] Theology teaches us to see our proclivity to engage in self-serving cognitive distortions as a sinful tendency that must be confessed and opposed. That tendency is not, as Taylor and Brown propose, "a valuable human resource to be nurtured and promoted."[125]

Second, Christian theology offers three means of counteracting our sinful tendency to think of ourselves more highly than we ought. The history of Christian theology contains numerous, though frequently unheeded, admonishments for followers of Christ to be self-critical, open to criticism from others and humble. Self-critique that is illumined by the Holy Spirit and the Word of God may serve as a helpful starting point for detecting our cognitive distortions.[126] However, our ability to see our own errors is limited, so we also need to be open to criticism from others.[127] As Proverbs 27:17 puts it, "As iron sharpens iron, so one man sharpens

---

[123]Myers and Jeeves observe that "for the heroes of the Bible, good adjustment—thinking well of oneself and feeling positive about the world—was not the aim of life" (*Psychology Through the Eyes of Faith,* p. 148).

[124]Thanks to Mark McMinn (personal correspondence of July 10, 1997) for raising an important question about whether the call for Christians to think accurately about themselves is "a life sentence for depression." Dr. McMinn speculates that perhaps "Christians who understand grace can afford to think of themselves realistically without depression," so that we need not conclude "that the best Christians are inevitably depressed." Dr. McMinn's suggestions, which are closely related to my third and fourth antidotes, may find some support in research that has found a positive correlation between religious commitment and happiness (see D. Myers, *The Pursuit of Happiness* [New York: William Morrow, 1992], especially pp. 183, 261). Beyond this empirical literature, there are numerous scriptural indications that God's people will experience joy not only in the life to come, but often in this life as well (1 Kings 1:40; 1 Chron. 12:40; 2 Chron 30:26; Ezra 6:22; Neh 12:43; Esther 8:16-17; Ps 16:11; Jn 15:11; Acts 13:52; Rom 15:13; 1 Thess 3:9; 1 Pet 1:8-9). In fact, the Bible teaches that joy is to be part of the normal Christian experience of the fruit of the Spirit (Gal 5:22-23), which is possible even in the midst of troubles in this life (Lk 6:20-23; Rom 5:3-5; 2 Cor 8:2; 1 Thess 1:6; Jas 1:2-4; 1 Pet 1:6-7). Within a single chapter of Scripture, Paul indicates that by God's grace Christians can both think of themselves with "sober judgment" (Rom 12:3 NIV) and "be joyful" and "rejoice" (Rom 12:12, 15 NIV).

[125]Taylor and Brown, "Illusion and Well-Being," p. 205.

[126]Søren Kierkegaard, *Attack upon "Christendom"* (1855; reprint, Princeton, N.J.: Princeton University Press, 1968); R. Montgomery, "Bias in Interpreting Social Facts: Is It a Sin?" *Journal for the Scientific Study of Religion* 23 (1984): 278-91; S. Mott, "Biblical Faith and the Reality of Social Evil," *Christian Scholar's Review* 9 (1980): 225-40.

[127]R. Clark and S. Gaede, "Knowing Together: Reflections on a Holistic Sociology of Knowledge," in *The Reality of Christian Learning,* ed. H. Heie and D. L. Wolfe (Grand Rapids, Mich.: Eerdmans, 1987), pp. 55-86; W. Swartley, *Slavery, Sabbath, War, and Women* (Scottdale, Penn.: Herald Press, 1983).

another" (NIV).[128] Even Peter and Barnabas needed Paul to show them the error of their ways (Gal 2:11-14).

Theology also reminds us of our need to be humble.[129] When "we see ourselves as gullible creatures who can be seduced readily into accepting social fictions, self-deceptions, and distortions of the truth,"[130] we realize our need for humility. A humble attitude could serve us well within the body of Christ, as well as in our relationships with unbelievers. To the extent that we follow the exhortations to "clothe yourselves with humility toward one another" (1 Pet 5:5 NIV) and "show true humility toward all men" (Tit 3:2 NIV), we will be less prone to engage in all-too-common self-serving attributions and self-serving comparisons.[131]

Third, Christian theology offers us the hope of eternal bliss in heaven, which may reduce our need to seek happiness in an inflated view of our earthly future. We are not called to adjust to our culture, or to seek our ultimate happiness in this life. Rather we are commanded: "Do not conform any longer to the pattern of this world, but be transformed by the renewing of your mind" (Rom 12:2 NIV). The Scriptures remind us that this world is not our home, but that we are "aliens and strangers in the world" (1 Pet 2:11 NIV) whose final citizenship is in heaven (Phil 3:20). To the extent that we place our ultimate hope in Christ's return and in the bliss of eternal fellowship with God, our Creator and Redeemer, we will have less need to fabricate unrealistically optimistic views of our earthly future (see Lk 12:18-20; Jas 4:13-16).

Fourth, Christian theology offers us grace, forgiveness and a new identity in Christ, which may reduce our need to engage in self-serving attributions and comparisons with others. The gospel teaches that we need not earn our acceptance with God through our performance or our superiority to others. Rather, our salvation is the gracious gift of God that we receive by faith in Christ (Eph 2:8-9). Everyone who is in Christ is a new creation, reconciled to God and made righteous in God's sight because of Christ's substitutionary atoning death (2 Cor 5:17-21). When we meditate on our equality at the foot of the cross (Rom 3:22-23) and our equality in Christ (Gal 3:26-28), we may become less prone to self-enhancement through

[handwritten marginal note: Taking yourself out of the world.]

---

[128]See also Burwell's observation on "the value of intersubjectivity as an antidote to error and deception" (R. Burwell, "Epistemic Justification, Cultural Universals, and Revelation: Further Reflections on the Sociology of Knowledge," in *The Reality of Christian Learning,* ed. H. Heie and D. L. Wolfe [Grand Rapids, Mich.: Eerdmans, 1987], p. 96).

[129]M. D. Doss, "Humility in Theology: The Way of the Cappadocian Fathers," *Epiphany* 7 (1987): 57-62.

[130]Clark and Gaede, "Knowing Together," p. 80.

[131]Thanks to a Christian friend from the Orthodox tradition for suggesting that in addition to my scriptural reflections, a further antidote to self-serving cognitive distortions may be found in the practice of Christian liturgy. For instance, humility may be inculcated in us through repeating the prayer, "Lord have mercy," or through examining ourselves as part of participating in the Lord's Supper (1 Cor 11:27-29).

social cannibalism, to building ourselves up by rating ourselves more highly than others. The writers of the New Testament never encourage downward social comparison (2 Cor 10:12; Gal 6:4-5), but only upward imitation of godly models (Phil 3:17; Heb 13:7) and ultimately of the Lord Jesus himself (1 Cor 11:1; 1 Thess 1:6).

Fifth and finally, Christian theology offers us a compelling motivation to strive for holiness in our thinking, to seek what might be called noetic sanctification. The Scriptures repeatedly call us to pursue truthful, wholesome thinking in accordance with the mind of Christ (Rom 12:3; 2 Pet 3:1). In imitation of the One who called us, Christians are to aspire to be holy in all that we do (1 Pet 1:15-16); presumably this includes striving for holiness in our thinking about ourselves and others. Non-Christians may not have compelling reasons to abandon self-serving attributions and comparisons. Jesus Christ, however, is full of grace and truth (Jn 1:14)—indeed he is the truth (Jn 14:6)—and Christ's followers, who are indwelt by the Spirit of truth (Jn 14:16-17), are called to truthful thinking. This, at least in part, is what it means to love the Lord our God with all our minds (Mt 22:37).

Summary

This chapter has explored an infrequently traversed terrain: the intersection between Christian theology and social psychology. It provides a reminder that psychology is not reducible to counseling, but consists of many subdisciplines with which Christians may interact. I have also argued that social psychology sheds important light on some of the specific cognitive mechanisms by which humans display the noetic effects of sin. Often we think of ourselves more highly than we ought by engaging in self-serving attributions and self-serving comparisons.

I have further attempted to establish that Christian theology offers something of value to social psychology. For perspectivalists (proponents of the Parallels model) theology offers religious counterparts and examples of psychological principles. For Christianizers (proponents of the Integrates model) theology offers correctives and challenges to erroneous psychological claims. Theology corrects the mistaken notion, recently proposed by some social psychologists, that we should actively cultivate creative self-deceptions that enhance our lives. Theology teaches us instead to name our self-serving cognitive distortions as sins that should be confessed and opposed through the pursuit of humble, truthful, gospel-enlightened thinking about ourselves and others.

16

KNOWING AS PARTICIPATION

Toward an Intersection Between Psychology & Postcritical Epistemology

David Alan Williams

Thought is the child of action. (BENJAMIN DISRAELI, *VIVIAN GREY*, 1826)

V ERY OFTEN IN A DIALOGUE IN WHICH PEOPLE TRY TO INTEGRATE TWO DISCI-plines we find those in one discipline telling those in the other discipline how their own insights could be used to help the other. We have a type of posturing in which participants want to talk but are less interested in listening. I want to stand against that trend. As a philosopher and theologian I want to listen to psychology to gather insights into my own discipline. I want to listen to psychologists with the belief that they have something that we theologians need to listen to. So I have written this chapter mainly to theologians and philosophers about insights I think we need to glean from psychology.

In this chapter I will explore the language used in philosophy to talk about knowledge. I will begin with a discussion of what philosophers usually mean by *knowledge*. Paying special attention to the language that is used to talk about knowing, I will unpack this understanding of knowing and illustrate how it has impacted theological discourse. Next, I will discuss several findings in contemporary psychology that I believe call into question the adequacy of this understanding of knowledge. I will argue that these findings suggest the need for a reconceptualization of what we mean when we say "to know." I will then suggest what this new conceptualization of knowledge might look like and suggest ways in which it might be beneficial to theological discourse.

Knowing as Mirroring

Richard Rorty, in *Philosophy and the Mirror of Nature*, argues that throughout the western philosophical tradition the predominant metaphor for understanding the mind has been that of a mirror: philosophy's task is to attempt to gain a proper image of how the world is. That is, the world is out there and our link to it is the ability to have a proper image of it inside our minds.

We usually speak of this reflection in terms of knowledge. Mirroring is knowing. We know the world when our claims about the world correspond to the way the world is. An unbiased, objective reflection of how reality actually is functions as the standard by which all claims to truth are judged, because everyone who sees properly will know the same reality. The problem, of course, is that our mirror is hindered by all kinds of biases and distortions that make it difficult to have an accurate (objective) knowledge of the world rather than a knowledge of the world that is of our own creation (subjective).

When we cannot substantiate the correspondence between a claim and the way the world is, we hold the claim at arm's length and call it a mere belief. If the claim clearly does not correspond to the way the world is, then we say the claim is false. Within this metaphor the task of language is to serve as a conduit between the internal world of our private minds and the more public external world. Thus, language provides verbal linguistic referents to the pictures of reality created in our minds.

The evidence for Rorty's claim that a mirror is the predominant metaphor for understanding the mind is probably as familiar to you as your Introduction to Philosophy class in college. What do you think of when you think of knowledge? Most people who have had a first-year philosophy class can tell you that the standard definition of knowledge is "justified true belief." In philosophy class we learn that before one can claim to "know," one must first have a "belief." Of course simply having a belief does not count as knowledge; the belief must be "justified." For the past two hundred years philosophy has focused primarily on the question of how knowledge can be justified, but for most philosophers a "justified belief," although it is close to what we would call knowledge, is still inadequate. For one to have bona fide knowledge, not only must one's belief be justified, but that belief must also be true.

Knowledge must be preceded by belief. By definition, therefore, before we can claim to know something, we must be able to say what we think we know. That is, we must be able to articulate a cognitive belief before that belief can achieve the status of knowledge. This approach to knowledge implies that we can always say what we know. If we know it, we can say it; if we cannot say it, we cannot know it. In short, knowledge is always propositional.

When we treat knowledge essentially as a cognitive belief, we become involved in the sticky problem of meaning.[1] For if a belief, or proposition, is going to be useful at all it must be understood. This leads us into a study of how language works, or what philosophers call a philosophy of language or a theory of meaning. The earliest discussions on language centered around the issue of whether language is grounded in the way reality is, or whether language is merely a human convention.[2] But with the coming of the modern period there was much more interest in epistemology, which eventually led to what Richard Rorty calls the linguistic turn.[3]

If we read the history of philosophy with an eye to understanding how philosophers use language and understand meaning, we see that the most prominent philosophical understanding is what has recently been called representationalism.[4] The basic idea of representationalism is that language functions primarily as a means of description. This is true for both the rationalist tradition and the empiricist tradition. In the rationalist tradition words are taken to represent ideas in the mind that refer to objects in reality.[5] In the empiricist tradition words represent the data of experience or combinations of sensory input. Essentially then, words represent. What and how they represent is much debated, but in the end they represent either objects or subjects.

Closely connected with the referential theory of meaning[6] is the correspondence theory of truth: For knowledge to be true it must correspond to the way things are. For example, if I say that "the house is red," once we are clear about what object I am referencing by saying "the house" and what color I am referencing by saying "red," then we can simply look at the house and see if it is red. If it is beige then I have made a false statement: "the house is red" does not correspond to the way the house really is; the house is beige. It is important to note that only descriptions of states of affairs—propositions—can be true or false. Words can be misunderstood (when the referent is not known) or ambiguous (when the referent points to two or more objects), but words cannot be false. Because only propositions can be false, then only propositions can be true. The correspondence theory of truth has had a

---

[1] For a good survey of the history of philosophy of language, particularly as it relates to religious language, see Dan Stiver, *The Philosophy of Religious Language: Sign, Symbol, and Story* (Oxford: Blackwell, 1996).

[2] For an interesting survey of the early philosophers see Vincent Brummer, *Theology and Philosophical Inquiry* (Philadelphia: Westminster Press, 1982).

[3] Richard Rorty, ed., *The Linguistic Turn* (Chicago: University of Chicago Press, 1967).

[4] For a defense of this, see Janet Rumfelt, "Biblical Narrative, the Christian Form of Life: A Study of the Inadequacy of a Representationalist Philosophy of Language and of the Primacy of a Performative Philosophy of Language" (master's thesis, Denver Seminary, 1995).

[5] For example, as Descartes says, "Some of my thoughts are as it were the images of things, and it is only in these cases that the term 'idea' is strictly appropriate—for example, when I think of a man, a chimera, or the sky, or an angel, or God." René Descartes, *Descartes: Selected Philosophical Writings*, trans. John Cottingham, Robert Stoothoff and Dugald Murdoch (Cambridge: Cambridge University Press, 1988), p. 88.

[6] Although technically representationalism is a particular form of referentialism, in this chapter I will use them interchangeably.

long and illustrious career in Western philosophy, but it has been primarily since the Enlightenment that philosophers have attempted to be more cognizant of language itself.

The Gap Between Knowing and Reality

In referential theory (and in correspondence theory as well), there is a gap between knowledge and reality. On one side of the gap we have the description, the words or ideas; on the other side of the gap we have the objects that those words or ideas represent.

The epistemological task is to bridge the gap between the internal picture and the external reality. If our knowledge is like an internal picture of an external reality, then how can we be sure that the picture is accurate? How can we be sure it is not distorted, or even worse, a creation of our own imagination? Not only was solving the dilemma of connecting the world inside with the world outside a concern for seventeenth-century philosophers; it is also a concern for current thinkers. There are numerous creative illustrations of the problem, from Descartes's "evil genius," and John Pollock's "Brain in the Vat" scenario to *Star Trek: The Next Generation* episodes, and Arnold Schwarzenegger's *Total Recall*. The major epistemological drive can be seen in terms of the attempt to bridge the gap between the picture inside the mind and the world outside.[7]

I am recounting this bit of intellectual history to call attention to the language we use to talk about knowledge, particularly as it relates to Rorty's claim about the mirror metaphor. In summary: First, the primary metaphor for knowledge is that of a "mirror." Knowing is mirroring. Our mirroring is articulated by the use of words that describe reality for us. This understanding of language as description leads to the implication that we must always be able to say what we know. Second, we consider knowledge true when the reflection is accurate and false when the reflection is inaccurate or distorted. And, third, inherent in this conception of knowledge is a gap between our knowledge and the reality that it purportedly reflects. This gap has caused great difficulty for modern thinkers and eventually led to two different responses. Some thinkers believed that the gap had been bridged and that knowledge is grounded in the objective character of external reality; others argued that the gap had not been bridged and that we are left only

---

[7]It is beyond the scope of this paper to survey the proposed solutions to this dilemma. In brief it was once thought that the gap could be bridged if we could find a truth or group of truths that simply had to be true. That is, if knowledge was based on something that could not be false, then we could have confidence that the gap had been bridged. The second task (after finding that certain foundation for knowledge) was to find the proper method for making valid inferences based on those certain truths. If we could not be guaranteed that our inferences were sound, then we could be led into error. Thus the task of epistemology was to discover foundational truths and the proper method of inference.

with our own private and communal constructions of knowledge.

The Impact of This Intellectual Tradition on Theology

This intellectual tradition has significantly influenced theological formulations.[8] This is certainly the case with evangelical theology.[9] Pick up almost any evangelical theology book and you will notice the way theological knowledge takes the form of description. For example, the doctrine of the Trinity is a description of the ontological nature of God. Orthodox Christology emphasizes the proper description of Christ's two natures and how they interrelate, and the proper description of what Christ did (both objectively and subjectively) in the atonement. The influence of the intellectual tradition has been particularly significant recently as theologians have wrestled with the doctrine of revelation in general and the doctrine of Scripture in particular.

For example, many thinkers believe that the referential theory of meaning has fueled much of the debate during the last two centuries about Scripture, and particularly the recent inerrancy debates. On the one side of the debate are those who believe that Scripture is divine communication of propositional truth, divine description of the way things really happened. Proponents of this position respond with dismay to the idea that any of the descriptions given within Scripture might not be perfectly accurate. Because Scripture is God's knowledge communicated to humans, it cannot be anything other than perfect truth, that is, a perfect description of the events it narrates. To call into question historical, scientific, geographical or any other aspects of this description is to call into question God's revealed knowledge. "Obviously, if God be admitted as the Author of Scripture, error in the original text becomes unthinkable, lest the very character of God be impugned."[10]

On the other side of the debate are liberals who believe that there is no way to harmonize the historical, scientific and geographical discrepancies among the texts of Scripture with the true findings of historians, archeologists and scientists. Scriptural writings, they argue, reflect the same kinds of prejudices and historical inaccuracies as any other literature of their day. But that is okay because it is erroneous to conceive of God's revelation as propositional truth. Instead these theologians understand revelation in terms of "some basic experience that constitutes the essence of religion; religious language gives expression to that experience." Scripture is not communication from God but an expression of how we have experi-

---

[8]For a more general discussion of these and related issues see George Lindbeck, *The Nature of Doctrine: Religion and Doctrine in a Postliberal Age* (Philadelphia: Westminster Press, 1984); Ronald Thiemann, *Revelation and Theology* (Notre Dame, Ind.: University of Notre Dame Press, 1984); and Nancey Murphy, *Beyond Fundamentalism and Liberalism: How Modern and Postmodern Philosophy Set the Theological Agenda* (Valley Forge, Penn.: Trinity, 1996).

[9]See Stanley J. Grenz and John R. Franke, *Beyond Foundationalism: Shaping Theology in a Postmodern Context* (Louisville, Ky.: Westminster John Knox, 2000).

[10]Everett F. Harrison, "The Phenomena of Scripture," in *Revelation and the Bible*, ed. Carl F. H. Henry (Grand Rapids, Mich.: Baker, 1958), p. 237.

enced God's working in the community of faith. "According to Schleiermacher," Nancey Murphy writes, "the doctrine of creation does not describe God's acts in creating the universe but expresses that Christian's awareness of the dependence of all things upon God." [11] Those who hold the liberal position value Scripture not because it accurately tells of historical events but rather because it serves as a record of our subjective experiences with God.

The way that we understand knowledge has a significant impact on theology, and particularly on how we understand knowledge that comes from God. When our primary metaphor for knowledge is a mirror, we see Scripture primarily in terms of description: description of objects such as historical events or description of subjects such as a particular people's experiences with God. The problem, of course, is that there are elements of truth in both perspectives.

Psychological Findings on Perception and Knowing

Although the mirror metaphor is intuitively appealing for many people, in the end it is misleading. This conclusion is supported by the findings of psychological research on perception. Research has borne out that it is not that simple.

It is a well-known fact that not everything that is received by a particular sense organ can be perceived by the brain. There are simply too many stimuli coming our way. We cope by selecting certain stimuli to attend to and ignoring the rest. Psychologists call this focal attention, and we exercise it every time we look at the world.

People who have raised children are aware firsthand of a particularly frustrating aspect of this process. I can remember times when my wife and I took our son to the park to play for the afternoon. After what we thought was a sufficient amount of play time, we would call to him to let him know it was time to go home. Our son, who was no more than thirty yards from us, showed no signs of response. We would call again: "Matthew, it's time to go home," this time a bit louder and with more urgency in our voices. Then having failed to make ourselves heard, we would begin to pick up our things, and my wife would mention to me that we had nothing at home for supper and would suggest that we stop at McDonald's on the way home. With that our son would jump out of the swing and come running toward us with all the enthusiasm he could muster, proclaiming that he too would like to go to McDonald's for supper. To what can we attribute this remarkable increase in hearing ability? Like the rest of us, Matthew hears what he wants to hear. At a very young age we all learn to block out sounds that we deem unimportant (particularly the voices of our parents). Eating at McDonald's is important to Matthew, and he can pick out the *M* word at amazing distances.

We are all doing the same thing right now. As you read this chapter you are

---

[11] Murphy, *Beyond Fundamentalism,* p. 46.

probably completely unaware of the hum of the fluorescent lights, the sound of shuffling papers and the noises out in the hallway. What you hear is related in part to what is important to you. You are attending to the words of this chapter, and if I have kept your interest then you have blocked out all of those noises. However, if you are bored with my comments, or if you are more interested in something else, you may have a hard time continuing to read this and you may allow many different outside noises to distract you.

In nonprofessional terminology you might say that we hear what we want to hear. This is not to say that we make up what we hear, but rather that we filter out what we think is important to us and ignore the rest. This process, however, is not absolute. We can be trained to hear what we at first do not want to hear. For example, we had to train Matthew to hear us anytime we spoke. We told him that we would always speak loudly enough for him to hear but that he was responsible for what we said regardless of whether he heard us or not. It was amazing to us how attentive he became to the sound of our voices.

This is nothing new in psychology. Selective perception has been recognized for a long time. William James stated in his 1890 book *Principles of Psychology:*

> Millions of items . . . are presented to my senses which never properly enter my experience. Why? Because they have no *interest* for me. *My experience is what I agree to attend to.* . . . Everyone knows what attention is. It is the taking possession by the mind, in clear and vivid form, of one out of what seem several simultaneously possible objects or trains of thought. Focalization, concentration of consciousness are of its essence. It implies withdrawal from some things in order to deal effectively with others.[12]

The process of selective perception has been put to detailed scientific study, and psychologists have gained a wealth of information about the many factors involved in perception. They have learned that perception can be affected by physical conditions:[13] people will "see" images of food in ambiguous drawings when they are hungry,[14] and semistarved peoples can order their whole world

[12]Quoted in Eric Kendel, James Schwartz and Thomas Jessell, *Essentials of Neural Science and Behavior* (Norwalk, Conn.: Appleton & Lange, 1995), p. 403, emphasis in the original.

[13]An extreme form of this phenomenon is illustrated in a *Star Trek: The Next Generation* episode called "Chain of Command." Captain Picard is captured by the Cardassians and undergoes a form of torture designed to totally restructure his identity. Throughout the episode Picard is commanded to tell his captor how many lights he sees shining on him. Although the audience can see that there are four lights, the "correct" response to end the torture is "five." Picard stubbornly holds out until he is finally rescued, proclaiming all the time that he sees four lights. In the epilogue, Picard seeks help from Troi, the ship's counselor. His concern is that at the very end of his torture, just before he was rescued, he believed that he saw five lights.

[14]R. Levine, I. Chein and G. Murphy, "The Relation of the Intensity of a Need to the Amount of Perceptual Distortion: A Preliminary Report," *Journal of Psychology* 13 (1942): 283-93.

around food.[15] Research has also demonstrated that people who are hungry tend to perceive food items as larger than people who are not hungry perceive them.[16] We have the tendency to block out perceptions that we find particularly intolerable: threatening or taboo words, or memories of tragic events.[17]

Perception is also related to what we expect to experience. Research shows that we see what we expect to see, or what others expect us to see. The creation of perceptual norms by social groups is a well-known and well-studied phenomenon. The tendency to conform one's perceptions to the expectations or perceptual norms of the group is also a well-established phenomenon. In a classic study Solomon Asch demonstrates the power of group conformity. Asch asked seven students at a time to compare the lengths of a series of lines.[18] The real subject in each group was unaware that the six other "subjects" were in league with the experimenter and were giving a false judgment. Asch found that about one-third of all the subjects conformed to the group.

Perception is not only susceptible to social forces, but also significantly influenced by culture. For example, "Since the 1900s, it has been known that people in industrialized societies are far more susceptible to the Muller-Lyer illusion than are people in nonindustrialized societies."[19] The latter tend to see the lines as equal or nearly equal more often than do people in industrialized societies. Other studies have found that cultures demonstrate differing degrees of ability to perceive depth in pictures.[20]

Perception, then, is not something that happens to the passive mind; it is a process that allows individuals to actively participate with the world in which they live.

---

[15]Ancel Keys et al., *The Biology of Human Starvation* (Minneapolis: University of Minnesota Press, 1950).

[16]D. C. McClelland and J. W. Atkinson, "The Projective Expression of Needs. 1: The Effect of Different Intensities of the Hunger Drive on Perception," *Journal of Psychology* 25 (1948): 205-22.

[17]J. S. Bruner, and L. Postman, "Emotional Selectivity in Perception and Reaction," *Journal of Personality* 16 (1947): 16, 69-77; E. McGinnies, "Emotional and Perceptual Defense," *Psychological Review* 56 (1949): 56, 244-51.

[18]Solomon E. Asch, "Effects of Group Pressure upon the Modification and Distortion of Judgments," in *Groups, Leadership, and Men*, ed. H. Guetzkow (Pittsburgh: Carnegie University Press, 1951).

[19]Don H. Hockenbury and Sandra E. Hockenbury, *Psychology* (New York: Worth, 1997), p. 137. See also, M. H. Segall, D. T. Campbell and M. J. Herskovits, "Cultural Differences in the Perception of Geometric Illusions," *Science* 139 (1963): 139, 769-71; M. H. Segall, D. T. Campbell and M. J. Herskovits, *The Influence of Culture on Visual Perception* (Indianapolis: Bobbs-Merril, 1966). The Muller-Lyer illusion involves the perceived length of two lines. Connected to each line are two arrows, one at each end. On one line the arrows are pointing inward, on the other the arrows are pointing outward. Even though the two lines are of equal length, the line with the arrows pointing inward appears to be longer.

[20]J. B. Deregowski, "Pictorial Perception and Culture," *Scientific American* 227, no. 5 (1972): 82-88.

It is often said that we construct the world that we perceive.[21] This construction is influenced not only by the "hardware" with which we are created, but also by our past experiences, our values, our culture and our expectations.[22]

One common metaphor for visual perception is that of viewing the eye as a camera. There are certainly similarities between the way the eye works and the way a camera works, but psychologists who study perception agree that the metaphor is misleading. Kendel, Schwartz and Jessell state that

> Until recently, visual perception was often compared with the operation of a camera. Like the lens of a camera, the lens of the eye focuses an inverted image onto the retina. This analogy breaks down rapidly however, because it misses what vision actually does, which is to create a three-dimensional perception of the world that is different from the two-dimensional images projected onto the retina. It fails to capture the importance of our visual system—that we are able to recognize an object as the same even though the actual image on the retina varies widely under different light conditions. . . . The degree to which visual perception is transformational and therefore creative has been fully appreciated only recently.[23]

Thus to a significant degree the world we see is a world of our own making. Our perceptive abilities are transformative, and they create the world of our experience. But this recognition creates havoc with the traditional understanding of knowledge. It seems to make it unlikely that we can ever bridge the gap between the real world and the picture of the world inside our minds. If we construct our images of the world rather than receive them from reality, then knowledge is lost and all we have is the abyss of subjectivity and relativism. This is a common conclusion that has lead to a significant degree of skepticism in our contemporary context, but I believe that the conclusion is unwarranted. It has missed the most significant insight of the psychology of perception: the fact that perceiving is an activity. Because it is an activity, perception is a way of interacting with the world. I suggest that we think of knowing not in the passive terms of cognitive belief that mirrors reality, but in the active terms of an activity that is a way of participating in the world.

---

[21]The idea that we construct the world we see is not new in either epistemology or psychology. Immanuel Kant initiated the epistemological emphasis on construction in his *Critique of Pure Reason* (trans. Norman Kemp [New York: St. Martin's, 1965]). He postulated that the mind molds the perceptions we receive from the noumenal world. This created what is now a well-recognized continuum between objectivist and constructivist views of knowledge. See Stanley J. Grenz, *A Postmodern Primer* (Grand Rapids, Mich.: Eerdmans, 1996), pp. 40ff. The same continuum is manifested in the range of views on perception. Older objectivist views, grounded in the British empiricism of Locke and Berkeley, were replaced with constructivist views. A constructivist theory in psychology was first articulated by German psychologists who founded the Gestalt school of psychology.

[22]For a fascinating, yet tragic, account of the way neurological disorders affect perception, see Oliver Sacks, *The Man Who Mistook His Wife for a Hat and Other Clinical Tales* (New York: Summit, 1985).

[23]Kendel, Schwartz and Jessell, *Essentials,* p. 388.

Knowing as Participation

Michael Polanyi argues in several of his works on epistemology that knowing is a participation with the world.[24] He argues that because we have neglected the participatory nature of knowledge and have submitted to the tendency to think of knowledge only in terms of cognitive belief, we have been misled epistemologically, and with disastrous results. Several aspects of Polanyi's epistemology are relevant to our discussion.

Polanyi challenges the traditional understanding of knowledge. He believes that we always know *more* than we can say.[25] To support his argument Polanyi makes a distinction between explicit knowledge and tacit knowledge. To make sense of this distinction we need to discuss a couple of other distinctions. The first is the distinction between focal awareness and subsidiary awareness.[26] As Jerry Gill explains, "In any given cognitive context there are some factors of which the knowing subject is aware because he is directing his attention to them. Such awareness is termed *focal.* In the same context there are also factors of which the knower is aware even though he is not focusing on them. This is termed *subsidiary* awareness."[27]

For example, when you see the word *cat* in the sentence "The cat is on the mat," you are focally aware of the meaning of *cat* and subsidiarily aware of the letters *c-a-t.* Obviously this distinction is a relative one. You can choose to attend to that which was previously subsidiary. You can shift your focal awareness back and forth from the meaning to the letters, but the two types of awareness are mutually exclusive.[28] That is, you cannot at the same time be both focally and subsidiarily aware of the same thing. Similarly, when you are typing, you can focally attend to the words you are typing and things go along relatively well. But if you begin to attend to what your fingers are doing, to that which was previously only in your subsidiary awareness, your typing will become confused and you may have to stop altogether.

Focal awareness always requires some subsidiary awareness. That is, I recognize the word *cat* because it comprises the letters *c-a-t.* If I shift focal awareness to the letters, I recognize the *c-a-t* because of a subsidiary awareness of the curves and lines that make up the letters. My subsidiary awareness creates the context so that focal awareness can happen. Polanyi asserts that subsidiary awareness is logically prior to focal awareness. I always attend "from" subsidiary awareness "to" focal awareness.

Gill suggests that awareness occurs along a continuum between the two poles of

---

[24]See Michael Polanyi, *Personal Knowledge* (Chicago: University of Chicago Press, 1958), and his *The Tacit Dimension* (Gloucester, Mass.: Peter Smith, 1983).
[25]Polanyi, *Personal Knowledge,* p. 95
[26]Ibid., pp. 55-57.
[27]Jerry Gill, *On Knowing God* (Philadelphia: Westminster Press, 1981), p. 92.
[28]Polanyi, *Personal Knowledge,* p. 56.

focal and subsidiary awareness. I think that contemporary neuropsychology would dispute this claim. If focal and subsidiary awareness correspond to what psychologists call implicit and explicit awareness, then they are not on a continuum at all. Indeed, they are functions of different parts of the brain.[29] Regardless of whether or not the two forms of awareness form a continuum, Polanyi contends that the distinction between focal and subsidiary awareness is real and that it is important to how we understand knowing.

Polanyi makes a second distinction, between different types of human activity. Human activity is on a continuum between bodily activity and conceptual activity.[30] A bodily activity is something like swimming or riding a bicycle, and a conceptual activity is something like reading a book or solving a problem in statistics. The bodily nature of riding a bike is obvious. To learn how to ride one needs very little other than time to learn the skills of pedaling, keeping one's balance and finding a safe place to fall. Trying to conceptualize what one is doing not only is unnecessary but gets in the way. Bodily activities are most often spoken of in terms of skills that are developed with practice and with the mentoring of a skilled master, what Polanyi refers to as connoisseurship.[31]

Reading a book requires bodily activity as well. The ability to move the eyes across the page, to focus on certain groups of letters and so on. Polanyi argues that conceptual activities require bodily activity, but bodily activities do not require conceptual activity. Few of us could say conceptually what it takes to keep one's balance, for example, but most of us do it very well. Bodily activity is logically prior to conceptual activity. All human activity requires some bodily activity. Even conceptual activity such as adding numbers requires a whole complex of neurological activity, not to mention the skills developed in math class.[32]

Once we understand these two distinctions we can understand what Polanyi means by explicit and tacit knowledge. Explicit knowledge is conceptual activity combined with focal awareness. Tacit knowledge is bodily activity combined with subsidiary awareness. Because the movement is always from subsidiary awareness to focal awareness, and because bodily activity always grounds conceptual activity, Polanyi argues that explicit knowledge always comes from tacit knowledge. Thus the knowledge that can be stated, explicit knowledge, always rests on knowledge that cannot be stated, tacit knowledge.

The implications of this view of knowledge are significant. In terms of epistemology, the gap that philosophers have spent centuries trying to bridge simply dis-

---

[29]I owe this insight to my colleague Dr. Gayle Brosnan-Watters.
[30]The language here is Jerry Gill's; Polanyi writes of muscular and intellectual activity (see Polanyi, *Personal Knowledge*, p. 90).
[31]Polanyi, *Personal Knowledge*, p. 54.
[32]A significant portion of *Personal Knowledge* is made up of Polanyi's demonstration of the ways in which math and the natural sciences require bodily activity. See chapters 1-3.

solves. There is no gap between our knowledge and reality because knowledge is not a mirror. The gap is an illusion created by a metaphor. Reality is not what our knowledge mirrors; rather, reality is that with which our knowledge participates. It is the context for participation.

Another implication is that explicit knowledge can never stand alone. It grows out of a way of acting in the world. That which can be articulated can never be complete because the explicit always comes from the tacit. Thus, we always know more than we can say. What we say is always grounded in ways of being in the world, in skills learned in order to inhabit the world and to function effectively in it.

Theological Implications of Knowing as Participation

This understanding of knowledge as participation can have a significant impact on how we think of theology. The cognitive aspects of theology (explicit knowledge) are not the most important aspects, but rather are outgrowths of the tacit components. This is not to say that the cognitive aspects are unimportant; certainly they are, but they do not ground everything else. What we say in terms of our theological formulations are outgrowths of the way in which we live and function in the world. It is our being in the world that gives stability and meaning to our explicit formulations. But often in evangelical theology the cognitive aspects of knowledge are given a privileged status. Too often when we read theology we get the idea that if we just get our thinking right (explicit knowledge) all the rest will follow. Of course we do not verbalize this, but it is evidenced, for instance, in the way we separate theology from ethics, giving priority to the former, particularly in the training of pastoral leaders.[33]

In the first volume of his systematic theology, titled *Ethics,* James McClendon makes much of this tendency in the broader theological arena. He notes that Ron Sider once said that it is all too typical for theologians to save ethics till last, and then to leave it out.[34] The postcritical approach implies that what one thinks grows out of what one does. Thus, formation in godly practices takes precedence over articulation of proper cognitive belief.[35]

I suggest that rather than thinking of theology as our generalizations from God's

---

[33]For example, at my alma mater, Denver Seminary, an M.Div. student is required to take four quarters of systematic theology, but until recently the ethics courses were purely elective.

[34]James W. McClendon Jr., *Systematic Theology: Ethics* (Nashville: Abingdon, 1986), p. 42.

[35]Support for this conclusion can also be found in what is taken as common knowledge in the field of social psychology. Social psychologists have long known that there is a bidirectional interplay between thought and action. For example, in a standard college text (*Social Psychology*) David G. Myers gives significant attention to the way in which behavior affects attitudes. "The attitude-action relation also works in the reverse direction: We are likely not only to think ourselves into action but also to act ourselves into a way of thinking. . . . We not only stand up for what we believe, we also believe in what we have stood up for" (p. 143).

descriptions of reality, we should think of theology as a set of tools to train us to be in the world in particular ways. Then we might see Scripture not so much in terms of what it is trying to tell us as in terms of what it is trying to do to us. The first question we come to the text with would not be "What does this mean?" but "How is this embodied?"[36] This is particularly true for the narrative portions of Scripture. So often we get hung up in debates about when and where Jesus did something or if he really did it as the Bible records until we forget that the goal for us is to become like Christ, to take on the story of Christ and make it our story. We are to be in the world in such a way that our lives look like his life.

Our explicit knowledge of Scripture is an outgrowth of the way the Scripture is embodied in our lives. In his book *Uses of Scripture in Recent Theology* David Kelsey draws fascinating correlations between the ecclesiastical practices of well-known theologians and their views of Scripture. He argues that what we say about the nature of Scripture is a function of the way we use Scripture. If he is correct, and I believe he is, then many debates about the nature of Scripture are misguided. We can resolve such debates only by joining together in shared practices.

This is not to neglect or to undervalue what God might want to tell us in Scripture. Certainly God's message to us is an important aspect of God's revelation, but what we understand Scripture to be teaching is embedded in particular practices. If we do not attend to the proper practices (for evangelicals the so-called histori-cal-grammatical method) what we derive from the Scriptures is not guaranteed to be the Word of God. Of course, theologians debate about what constitutes proper interpretative practice. For example, Stanley Hauerwas, building on the work of Hans Frei and others, points out that the communal practices that justify the histor-ical critical interpretative method are not only alien to the gospel but are in fact det-rimental to it.[37] Much is at stake. Even if God tells us things through Scripture, we must first be trained in certain reading practices.

This view of knowledge has implications for evangelism as well. If it is true that what we know is an outgrowth of the types of skills, habits and activities we embody, and if these activities ultimately give the support necessary for explicit knowledge, then we must recognize that a change in others' cognitive beliefs requires a change of their way of being in the world. At the very least this would imply our active engagement with them. Our engagement might take many differ-ent forms, such as being present with someone in a time of suffering, or confront-ing someone about wrongdoing. What is most important is that we recognize the

---

[36]For an interesting account of what embodiment might look like, see Stephen Fowl and L. Gregory Jones, *Reading in Communion* (Grand Rapids, Mich.: Eerdmans, 1991). See particularly their chapter on Dietrich Bonhoeffer.

[37]See Stanley Hauerwas, *Unleashing the Scriptures: Freeing the Bible from Captivity to America* (Nashville: Abingdon, 1993); and Stanley Hauerwas, *A Community of Character* (Notre Dame, Ind.: University of Notre Dame Press, 1981), particularly chaps. 2, 3, 5.

necessity of such an engagement. For people to see the truth of Christianity requires that they participate to some degree in an alternative way of being in the world. They begin with the practices and activities from which their explicit knowledge emerges.

Basic psychological insights can be very suggestive for epistemology and can thus provide important insights for theology. In light of those insights I am arguing that it would be very fruitful for us to think of knowing as a way of being in the world rather than as a way of mirroring the world. When we do so, we will not need to worry about bridging the gap between our knowledge and the world because we will see that the gap is an illusion. This view of knowledge has significant theological implications. Instead of misleadingly giving priority to cognitive belief, we will give greater priority to the way in which we inhabit the world.

17

FAMILY BROKENNESS

A Developmental Approach

Cynthia Neal Kimball

I N OUR EVANGELICAL WORLD WE HEAR TWO COMMON AND CONTRASTING RESPONSES
from troubled families:

> Every therapist and pastor we went to communicated either explicitly or implicitly that
> we were the sources of our son's acting out. Our guilt is overwhelming. We thought
> we'd done our best. Did we fail to love him enough, did we spank too hard or too often,
> did we push for too much or too little school achievement? If we had just done things
> right, he would have turned out happy. He would be working hard and loving God.

or

> Our daughter is willful and rebellious. She has turned from God and disobeys us. We
> need help getting her under control. We need to find a therapist or pastor who will
> support our authority (as the Bible asserts it) and show her the error and potential
> destruction of her ways.

These views of the parental responsibility for children's outcomes are inadequate. They miss essential features of what it means to parent children. Parenting
is not about a recipe for parents that, if followed, produces good outcomes. It is
not about breaking a child's will as John Wesley argued: "Break their will that you
may save their souls,"[1] or as George Whitefield observed: if parents "would but
have resolution to break their (children's) wills, thoroughly when young, the

---

[1]John Wesley, "On Obedience to Parents," *The Works of the Rev. John Wesley* (London: Thomas
Cordeux, 1811), 7:103, quoted in Philip Greven, *The Protestant Temperament: Patterns of
Child-Rearing, Religious Experience, and the Self in Early America* (Chicago: University of
Chicago Press, 1977), p. 35.

work of conversion would be much easier, and they would not be so troubled with perverse children when they are old."[2]

In this chapter I will demonstrate that parents cannot serve as the only vehicle of God's grace, especially parents who have received little grace in their early developmental histories. I will present the developmental argument that parenting is a matter of passing on our developmental histories to our children. For adults who have suffered neglect or abuse in their developmental past, parenting is either about passing on their developmental wounds (passing the sins of the parents down to the fourth generation, Num 4:18) or about recognizing and finding healing for those wounds. And in spite of intentional and careful parenting, pervasive external influences can and do serve as stumbling blocks that, unfortunately, shape our children's view of themselves and of the world. Jesus calls the church to play a critical familial role in healing and supporting parents and children, a role that was lost for evangelicals beginning in the seventeenth century.

Historical Context

Historical analysis can help us to understand some of the reasons that churches are ill-equipped to handle family nurturance and pain. Historically, adults in evangelical families governed with absolute authority. Children were required to respond with unquestioning obedience and submission. Numerous writings of evangelicals from the seventeenth century forward express these themes about discipline and family governance.[3] The ideal evangelical families consisted only of parents and their children, over whom they had exclusive control. These households were isolated and self-contained, and it was recognized that authority and love were found in the parents. Parental control was so absolute that grandparents were often suspected of indulgences that would undermine parental authority. John Wesley warned mothers that

> Your mother, or your husband's mother, may live with you; and you will do well to shew her all possible respect. But let her on no account have the least share in the management of your children. She would undo all that you have done; she would give them their own will in all things. She would humour them to the destruction of their souls, if not their bodies, too. . . . In four-score years I have not met with one woman that knew how to manage grand-children. Give up your will to hers. But with regard to the management of your children, steadily keep the reins in your own hands.[4]

---

[2]George Whitefield, *George Whitefield's Journal*, p. 146, quoted in Greven, *Protestant Temperament*, p. 35.

[3]Greven, *Protestant Temperament*. For further reading on the historical context of early evangelical families see also Gerald F. Moran and Maris A. Vinovskis, *Religion, Family, and the Life Course* (Ann Arbor: University of Michigan Press, 1992); and Edmund S. Morgan, *The Puritan Family* (Westport, Conn.: Greenwood, 1966).

[4]John Wesley, "Sermon on the Education of Children," *Works of the Rev. John Wesley*, 10:205-19, quoted in Philip Greven, *Child-Rearing Concepts, 1628-1861* (Itasca, Ill.: F. E. Peacock, 1973), p. 64.

Another early evangelical, John Witherspoon, advised absolute submission on the part of children. Like-minded parents must enact very early an unmitigated and total authority over their children:

> I would have it early . . . that it may be absolute, and absolute, that it may not be severe. If parents are too long in beginning to exert their authority, they will find the task very difficult. Children, habituated to indulgence for a few of their first years, are exceedingly impatient of restraint; and if they happen to be of stiff or obstinate tempers, can hardly be brought to an entire, at least to a quiet and placid submission; whereas, if they are taken in time, there is hardly any temper but what may be made to yield, and by early habit the subjection becomes quite easy to themselves.[5]

Thus the emerging will must be controlled and broken in the early years of life. Why was breaking the will of children so important? John Wesley went on to say:

> A wise parent . . . should begin to break [the child's] will, the first moment it appears. In the whole art of Christian education there is nothing more important than this. The will of a parent is to a little child in the place of the will of God. Therefore, studiously teach them to submit to this while they are children, that they may be ready to submit to his will, when they are men.[6]

Breaking the child's will was not just about the child's submission but also about the child's conformity. Parental control over all habits of life, from their children's diet and dress to their children's manners, mattered acutely to the evangelical parent. One's outward behavior was observed, then judgment was made about one's inner values. The church was able to assess how well parents were doing by observing their children's behavioral display. Wesley was clear in his rebuke of parents who permitted their children to deviate from their model. "Whenever . . . I see the fine-dressed daughter of a plain-dressed mother, I see at once the mother is defective either in knowledge or religion. . . . In God's name why do you suffer them to vary a hair's breadth from your example?"[7]

It is not difficult to imagine how intimidating it would be to bring family problems to this kind of church. One's character was judged by how one's children behaved, dressed and asked questions, just as it is today. We have not progressed very far in our judgments about parents and families. It should not be surprising that even today families are reluctant to bring their problems and failures to the church.

The early evangelicals brought a new idolatry to North America. Evangelical parents considered themselves to be next in line after God. Parents were to "be God" for their children so that they could turn their children to God. They were seriously called to shape the child's conscience, often through the use of guilt and shame

[5]John Witherspoon, *The Works of John Witherspoon, D.D.* (Edinburgh: J. Ritchie, 1805), 8:165-89, quoted in Greven, *Child-Rearing Concepts,* 89.
[6]John Wesley, "Sermon on the Education of Children," 10:205-19, quoted in Greven, *Child-Rearing Concepts,* pp. 59-60.
[7]Wesley, *Works,* 10:228-229, quoted in Greven, *Protestant Temperament,* p. 45.

and the withdrawal of love. Cotton Mather explained:

> I first beget in them an high Opinion of their Father's Love to them, and of his being best able to judge, what shall be good for them.
>
> Then I make them sensible, tis a Folly for them to pretend unto any Witt and Will of their own; they must resign all to me, who will be sure to do what is best; my word must be their Law.
>
> I cause them to understand, that it is an *hurtful* and a *shameful* thing to do amiss. I aggravate this, on all Occasions; and let them see how *amiable* they will render themselves by well doing.[8]

Eighteenth-century English evangelist John Wesley advised:

> If you are not willing to lose all the labour you have been at to break the will of your child, to bring his will into subjection to yours that it may be afterward subject to the will of God, there is one advice which, though little known, should be particularly attended. . . . It is this; never, on any account, give a child anything that it cries for. . . . If you give a child what he cries for, you pay him for crying: and then he will certainly cry again.[9]

Jonathan Edwards, Wesley's American counterpart, used analogous language when issuing warnings about child rearing. This repressive style of advice certainly has implications for the quality of the attachment relationship.

The threat of disownment was the ultimate weapon against disobedient children. Disownment left the child bereft of support and isolated.

> When their wills could only exist in conformity to the wills of their parents, who alone could decide 'what shall be good for them,' evangelical children left on their own and disapproved of by their parents could feel utterly devastated and destroyed. The loss of love left only fear. The options presented to children were clear and simple: either obey the wills of parents, or be cast away—left alone without other wills to guide and sustain them. For children whose wills had been broken early, such punishment—which focused upon their inner need to obey without deviation—indeed would be severe. What ultimately guaranteed their obedience was their inability to resist comfortably on their own. Conscience therefore provided them with internalized rules, which mirrored their parents' wishes and wills more faithfully than even parents might have thought possible. The methods of discipline most favored by evangelicals therefore had their most profound impact upon the moral conscience of evangelical children. For the rest of their lives, they would never be entirely freed from the pangs of guilt and the embarrassments of shame implanted within them during their earliest years.[10]

Cotton Mather spoke strongly about the powerful effect of parents on children's spiritual development, leaving very little need for the church to play a role. He asserted that if parents would conscientiously do their duty to their children, the

---

[8]Cotton Mather, *Diary of Cotton Mather 1681-1724,* ed. Worthington Chauncey Ford (Boston: Collections of the Massachusetts Historical Society, 1911-1912), pp. 534-37, quoted in Greven, *Protestant Temperament*, p. 52.

[9]Moran and Vinovskis, *Religion, Family, and the Life Course*, p. 114.

[10]Greven, *Protestant Temperament,* pp. 54-55.

children would automatically be brought to God. If the parents would instill in their children the fear of God, then the pastors could go about the church's business of instructing and confirming. It was generally agreed that "saintly children almost always sprang from the loins of saintly parents."[11] Consider the implications. When a child was seduced by external stumbling blocks, the parents were blamed and their spirituality was brought under suspicion. But Jesus suggested something else: Parents cannot provide all that a child needs, anymore than spouses can provide all that their partners need. We need the full church family to support us.

What role did the early North American evangelical church play in the lives of troubled youth? Frequent sermons preached from Puritan pulpits railed against sexuality and vanity and expressed concern about bad friends and peer pressure. "Since youths were by nature fickle and unstable, it was easy for them to be lured into sin by bad companions, especially considering their innate desire for peer approval. One of the greatest obstacles to religious conversion, young people were told, was bad friends."[12]

Some historians state that religious educators tried to provide children with moral training and guidance, but there is little evidence available other than records of classroom teaching, youth tracts and burning sermons. Reformers in the nineteenth century believed that there were environmental causes for trouble during youth. Youths who were in trouble had flawed character as a result of parental loss or neglect.[13]

This nucleated household provided the setting for isolation that continues today. The church did not play the necessary role in the nurture of families and is ill-equipped to do so now. Through the past several centuries we have left the work of nurturing children and families to two or, all too often, one person. In the presence of so many external distracters, it is clear that our children need the community, the church family, to guide, nurture, correct and love them. Developmental theory can prove instrumental in helping the church return to a strong ecclesiology.

Biblical Context

God wants to bring families back together. The last two verses in the Old Testament herald that hope: "Lo, I will send you the prophet Elijah before the great and terrible day of the LORD comes. He will turn the hearts of parents to their children and the hearts of children to their parents, so that I will not come and strike the land with a curse" (Mal 4:5-6).

I am intrigued by the idea that God will turn the hearts of parents and children toward each other. But what will that look like and how will he accomplish it?

[11]Moran and Vinovskis, *Religion, Family, and the Life Course*, p. 17.
[12]Ibid., p. 148.
[13]Ibid.

There is very little specific instruction in the New Testament about raising children. Evangelicals often refer to the obvious passages where we find promises and commands concerning parenting and children. Children are called to obey their parents, and parents are called to encourage rather than provoke their children; clearly there is a dual expectation. "Children, obey your parents in everything, for this is your acceptable duty in the Lord. Fathers, do not provoke your children, or they may lose heart" (Col 3:20-21). "Children, obey your parents in the Lord, for this is right. 'Honor your father and mother'—this is the first commandment with a promise: 'so that it may be well with you and you may live long on the earth.' And, fathers, do not provoke your children to anger, but bring them up in the discipline and instruction of the Lord" (Eph 6:1-4).

True to my Mennonite tradition and hermeneutic, we will begin with the Gospels. Here Jesus speaks strongly and poignantly about the care of children:

> At that time the disciples came to Jesus and asked, "Who is the greatest in the kingdom of heaven?" He called a child, whom he put among them, and said, "Truly I tell you, unless you change and become like children, you will never enter the kingdom of heaven. Whoever becomes humble like this child is the greatest in the kingdom of heaven. Whoever welcomes one such child in my name welcomes me.
>
> If any of you put a stumbling block before one of these little ones who believe in me, it would be better for you if a great millstone were fastened around your neck and you were drowned in the depth of the sea. Woe to the world because of stumbling blocks! *Occasions for stumbling are bound to come, but woe to the one by whom the stumbling block comes!* (Mt 18:1-7; see also Mk 9—10; Lk 9)

> Take care that you do not despise one of these little ones; for, I tell you, in heaven their angels continually see the face of my Father in heaven. What do you think? If a shepherd has a hundred sheep, and one of them has gone astray, does he not leave the ninety-nine on the mountains and go in search of the one that went astray? And if he finds it truly I tell you, he rejoices over it more than over the ninety-nine that never went astray. *So it is not the will of your Father in heaven that one of these little ones should be lost.* (Mt 18:10-14)

Jesus acknowledges that stumbling blocks will be present to our children, but he renounces those who present the stumbling blocks, not the children who fall under their seduction. He is speaking to the apostles, the next leaders of the church, not the parents. It appears that he is addressing the church's responsibility to the young.

Numerous times Jesus deliberately blurs the line between family and church.

> While he was still speaking to the crowds, his mother and his brothers were standing outside, wanting to speak to him. Someone told him, "Look, your mother and your brothers are standing outside, wanting to speak to you." But to the one who had told him this, Jesus replied, "Who is my mother, and who are my brothers?" And pointing to his disciples, he said, "Here are my mother and my brothers! For whoever does the will of my Father in heaven is my brother and sister and mother." (Mt 12: 46-50)

> While he was saying this, a woman in the crowd raised her voice and said to him, "Blessed is the womb that bore you and the breasts that nursed you!" But he said, "Blessed rather are those who hear the word of God and obey it!" (Lk 11:27-28; see also Mk 3:31-35; Lk 8:19-21)

Jesus paints a portrait of a family that is the larger body of Christ. He contends that our spiritual development and commitment to him will guide how we respond to our family within the body of Christ.

Correspondingly, Paul describes how the body should function together as the community where we learn and grow in our priesthood:

> As God's chosen ones, holy and beloved, clothe yourselves with compassion, kindness, humility, meekness, and patience. Bear with one another and, if anyone has a complaint against another, forgive each other; just as the Lord has forgiven you, so you also must forgive. Above all, clothe yourselves with love, which binds everything together in perfect harmony. And let the peace of Christ rule in your hearts, to which indeed you were called in the one body. And be thankful. Let the word of Christ dwell in you richly; teach and admonish one another in all wisdom. (Col 3:12-17)

I believe that Paul is talking about how we should respond to all members of the body, including the children. This is easily seen in Jesus' words about the treatment of children. Therefore all members of the church, not only the parents, should respond to children in this light.

Jesus says that stumbling blocks will always be present. Why are we surprised when we fail or our children fail? Why do we so easily cast blame on parents when their children fail? Why do we think parents can keep children from failing when God (our heavenly Parent) has not kept us (his holy priesthood) from failing? Where is the church in our failing families? How might we so build a church community that hurting families feel safety and support when they are in pain?

Contributions from Contemporary Developmental Theory

I began with scripture to demonstrate that psychology is not the guiding force behind the church's need to play a critical role in the healing of our wounded families. Now I will introduce two specific developmental theories to assist us with some of our questions. These developmental theories merely reinforce what God has been clear about all along.

Attachment theory. All infants are born with the need for attachment. The attachment system as defined by John Bowlby is a psychological organization that is so constituted that feelings of security and actual conditions of safety are highly correlated. The system's goal is felt security. The mere knowledge that an attachment figure is available and responsive provides an individual with a powerful and ubiquitous feeling of security and so encourages the individual to value and continue the relationship with the attachment figure. The attachment system has a distinct internal motivation and serves the biological function of protecting the attached individual from physical and psychological harm. Bowlby identifies attachment behavior as

> any form of behavior that results in a person attaining or maintaining proximity to some other clearly identified individual who is conceived as better able to cope with the world. It is most obvious whenever the person is frightened, fatigued, or sick, and is assuaged by comforting and care giving. At other times the behavior is less in evidence. Nevertheless for a person to know that an attachment figure is available and responsive gives him a strong and pervasive feeling of security, and so encourages him to value and continue the relationship. . . . The biological function attributed to it is that of protection. To remain within easy access of a familiar individual known to be ready and willing to come to our aid in an emergency is clearly a good insurance policy—whatever our age.[14]

The quality of the attachment relationship is built on the generalized expectation that the child acquires from the accumulation of failed or successful interactive experiences with caregivers. Differing organizations of the relationship develop on the basis of differing interactive events. The view of the self, that which is carried over into other interactions, emerges out of the view of the relationship. Hence, the quality of the early relationships we have with caregivers gives birth to our early self-concept.

Attachment behaviors become increasingly focused on primary figures who respond to the infant's needs and who engage the infant in social interaction. Once securely attached, infants are able to use attachment figures as a secure base for exploring their world while at the same time having the reassurance of a safe haven. How effectively the attachment figure can serve in these roles depends on the quality of social interaction—especially the attachment figure's sensitivity to the infant's signals. Through early primary relationships or attachments, the infant forms representational models of others and self, models that not only strongly influence the way the child relates to others, but also determine the child's expectations regarding self and the attachment figure.

Children with secure attachments internalize representational models of attachment figures as available, responsive and helpful, and correlative models of themselves as at least potentially lovable and valuable persons. Hence, these children tend to grow up valuing the self, and the data indicate that apart from external and unexpected trauma they tend to develop similar relationships with both marital partners and children.[15]

---

[14]John Bowlby, *A Secure Base: Parent-Child Attachment and Healthy Human Development* (New York: BasicBooks, 1998), pp. 26-27.

[15]For an excellent compilation of studies examining various components of attachment, see Inge Bretherton and Everett Waters, "Growing Points of Attachment Theory and Research," *Monographs of the Society for Research in Child Development* 50, nos. I-Z (1985); and Michael B. Sperling and William H. Berman, *Attachment in Adults: Clinical and Developmental Perspectives* (New York: Guilford Press, 1994).

However, when security needs are not met, there are many negative consequences. Bowlby writes, "of the many types of psychological disturbances resulting from [parental] deprivation, the effects on one's ability to nurture and parent are potentially the most serious."[16] Children whose parents are, for whatever reason, unavailable or nonresponsive have a distorted view of self, and their view of others' ability to meet their needs becomes compromised. Consequently their ability to parent the next generation is terribly handicapped. When children who view themselves as nonvaluable and the world as nontrustworthy grow up and become parents, they have a difficult time understanding and responding to their children's cues that communicate the need for love and intimacy. They may distrust kindnesses shown and needs expressed by their children, and they may even project on their children evil motives.

Therefore, it is incumbent upon those who are interested in supporting and helping families that are wounded and suffering psychologically to recognize the importance of the parents' developmental history and its effects on their ability to nurture and care for their own young. Our developmental history, and particularly our attachment relationships, affect our psychological resources positively or negatively, most often in a manner that is outside our awareness.

Attachment clinicians write of the "ghosts in the nursery":

> In every nursery there are ghosts. They are the visitors from the remembered past of the parents; the uninvited guests at the christening. . . . The intruders from the past have taken up residence in the nursery, claiming tradition and rights of ownership. They have been present at the christening for two or more generations. While no one has issued an invitation, the ghosts take up residence and conduct the rehearsal of the family tragedy from a tattered script. . . . The parent, it seems, is condemned to repeat the tragedy of his childhood with his own baby in terrible and exacting detail.[17]

Alice Miller writes, "You can drive the devil out of your garden but you will find him again in the garden of your son." [18] Unless awareness and change happens, we pass the developmental torch to the next generation.

Attachment theory helps us to understand how wounded parents bring their ghosts into parenting. It provides one explanation of the way in which the "sins of the parents are passed down unto the fourth generation" (Num 14:18). We need the church family to reparent us and to help us find our value, so that we as parents might better help our children see their value. And the church's concern must go beyond simple dyadic (mother-child, father-child) relationships. God calls the church

---

[16]John Bowlby, "Attachment and Loss: Retrospect and Prospect," *American Journal of Orthopsychiatry* 52 (1982): 675.

[17]S. Fraiberg, E. Adelson and V. Shapiro, "Ghosts in the Nursery," *Journal of the American Academy of Child Psychiatry* 14 (1975): 387-88.

[18]Alice Miller, *The Drama of the Gifted Child: The Search for the True Self* (New York: Basic Books, 1981), p. 27.

to participate in the nurturing and parenting of our children. This is a direct response to God's call for the church family to be a holy, loving community (Col 3:12-17).

Lev Vygotsky's developmental perspective. Lev Vygotsky's cognitive developmental theory explains that children are not merely mirrors of their parents' training but are agents who have internalized the processes of the relationship. This is how we pass on healthy values or relational sins: we pass on not merely information but also forgiveness, humility and compassion; or conversely, lapses in empathy, an unforgiving spirit, intolerance, rigidity and lack of humility. Our children internalize the processes of our interactions with them, and those processes evolve into our children's new representations of healthy values or relational sins. The same phenomenon occurs with all of the significant people in our children's lives.

Vygotsky was a Soviet developmental psychologist who wrote during the early 1920s, and he challenges our Western notions of independent, autonomous individuation as the process of becoming mature individuals. He asserts that human nature can be understood only in a sociocultural context. Humans are not independent of their environment; they are part of their environment. They are agents-in-context. A child is an active, inherently social organism in a broad system of interacting forces. A child's knowledge is shaped and organized by and has meaning through communal acts. Therefore, development can be understood only as embedded within a sociohistorical context. According to Vygotsky, attempting to explain child development by separating it from the social context distorts our understanding of the nature of the child and the community.

> Two essentially different modes of analysis are possible in the study of psychological structures. . . . The first method analyzes complex psychological wholes into elements. It may be compared to the chemical analysis of water into hydrogen and oxygen, neither of which possesses the properties of the whole and each of which possesses properties not present in the whole. The student applying this method in looking for the explanation of some property of water—why it extinguishes fire, for example—will find to his surprise that hydrogen burns and oxygen sustains fire. These discoveries will not help him much in solving the problem.[19]

An organizing theme in Vygotsky's developmental theory is that cognitive development can be understood as the transformation of basic, biological processes into higher psychological functions. According to the theory, each child enters the world with biological processes that include perceptual, attentional and memory capacities. These basic processes become transformed through the social world, the onset of language and formal education, ultimately giving birth to higher psychological functions. Whereas the biological processes are primarily regulated by the immediate stimulus fields, the transformation to higher psychological functions occurs through the increasing self-regulation of the individual. For example, primi-

---

[19]L. S. Vygotsky, *Thought and Language* (Cambridge, Mass.: MIT Press, 1962), p. 3.

tive memory processes gradually come under voluntary control, resulting in the strategic use of mnemonic devices; the capacity for selective attention emerges from the early ability to distinguish salient stimulus features, such as facial features; arousal and habituation patterns develop into the capacity for vigilance, concentration and sustained attention.[20]

How does this transformation occur? Vygotsky contends that the transformation of basic processes into higher psychological functions occurs within the child's social interactions and through the use of culturally determined tools and symbols, such as speech, written language and the mastery of symbols to solve problems. This view is in sharp contrast to Piaget's stage theory. Specifically, Vygotsky suggests that the care-giving adult negotiates and coordinates the child's communion with his or her immediate environment. The shared processes are subsequently internalized by the learner. Hence, individual differences in cognitive processing can be understood and explained by the social milieu in which the child interacts. Higher psychological functions have social origins.

Vygotsky introduced an operating principle known as the zone of proximal development. "What children can do with the assistance of others might be in some sense even more indicative of their mental development than what they can do alone."[21] The difference between the actual development and the development achieved when working with a competent teacher is called the zone of proximal development. "The zone of proximal development defines those functions that have not yet matured but are in the process of maturation, functions that will mature tomorrow but are currently in an embryonic state. These functions could be termed the 'buds' or 'flowers' of development rather than the 'fruits' of development."[22]

A person who is more competent than the child collaborates with the child to help the child move from where she or he is now to where she or he can be with help. Wertsch and Rogoff have conceptualized the zone of proximal development as

> that phase in development in which the child has only partially mastered a task but can participate in its execution with the assistance and supervision of an adult or more capable peer. Thus, the zone of proximal development is a dynamic region of sensitivity to learning the skills of culture, in which children develop through participation in problem solving with more experienced members of the culture.[23]

---

[20]For further readings about Vygotsky's theory see L. S. Vygotsky, *Mind in Society: The Development of Higher Psychological Processes* (Cambridge, Mass.: Harvard University Press, 1978); Cynthia Neal, "Power of Vygotsky," in *Nurture That Is Christian: Developmental Perspectives on Christian Education,* ed. James C. Wilhoit and John M. Dettoni (Wheaton, Ill.: Victor, 1995); and Barbara Rogoff and James Wertsch, *Children's Learning in the "Zone of Proximal Development"* (San Francisco: Jossey-Bass, 1984).
[21]Vygotsky, *Mind in Society,* p. 85.
[22]Ibid., p. 84.
[23]Rogoff and Wertsch, *Children's Learning,* p. 1.

Ideally, the more experienced adult builds on the capabilities the child already has and presents the child with activities that support a level of competence slightly beyond where the child is at present.

The zone of proximal development is an important concept. It embodies the notion that because the human infant is immersed from birth in a sociocultural environment, learning is first a shared act, an interpersonal phenomenon. Hence, when we consider development from a Vygotskian perspective we must consider first of all that learning is a social phenomenon before it is an individual one; second, that development occurs in a cultural context; and third, that development occurs within a child's zone of proximal development.

Vygotsky did not believe that internalization was solely a matter of shifting knowledge or skills that were first shared with a more competent teacher. He believed that the very tools of the joint educational process are internalized, transforming old cognitive capacities and producing new ones.[24] The learner internalizes the process and is subsequently transformed by it. The functional objective is not for the learner to become just like the teacher. "The focus . . . is not on transferring skills, as such, from those who know more to those who know less but on the collaborative use of mediational means to create, obtain, and communicate meaning."[25]

I believe that Vygotsky has discerned a part of the imago Dei, that relational aspect that images God and the discipling role we play in each other's lives. According to Vygotsky, "an individual is formed through the internalization of activities carried out in the bosom of society and through the interaction that occurs within the zone of proximal development."[26] This imagery captures the beauty and instrumentality that God intends as our children develop within the bosom of our church family. The emphasis, then, would be on the collaboration of the apprentice mediated by the mentor with the expressed goal of helping the novice "obtain and express meaning in ways that would enable them to make this knowledge and meaning their own."[27] Children are essentially "scaffolded" by mentors and parents who provide assistance within the child's zone of proximal development. A strong ecclesiology would assume the church's participation in this collaborative, scaffolding role.

---

[24]L. S. Vygotsky, *Sociohistorical Psychology and Its Contemporary Applications* (New York: Plenum, 1991).

[25]Luis C. Moll, ed., *Vygotsky and Education* (Cambridge: Cambridge University Press, 1990), p. 13.

[26]A. Rosa and I. Montero, "The Historical Context of Vygotsky's Work: A Sociohistorical Approach," quoted in *Vygotsky and Education,* ed. Luis C. Moll (Cambridge: Cambridge University Press, 1990), pp. 59-88.

[27]Rosa and Montero, "Historical Context," p. 14.

Relating Theory to Ecclesiology

There are several ways to relate the concepts of attachment and the zone of proximal development to the church family. Unfortunately, we often equate discipleship or mentoring of our children in their faith development with curricular concerns rather than relational concerns. In other words, more time is often spent in choosing the curriculum for the Sunday school than on identifying ways in which the church family will build faith relationships with the children. Therefore, we miss the opportunity to provide key supports that would help our children develop ownership of their faith.

The children must be part of the faith community and share in its life. When we leave discipling to the traditional Sunday school setting, we displace faith from life experience. Faith primarily means to believe, to trust in, to rely on, to be persuaded by.[28] As a verb *faith* is always relational and dynamic; it is an active mode of being and committing. Christians' faith is an active faith in Jesus Christ, a living faith that guides who we are and the meaning we bring to our world. I am not convinced that our current Sunday school programs have worked out the most effective way to invite children to become a part of the faith community. We are not connecting truth and biblical knowledge with lived and shared experiences.

Too often it is a tragic reality that the church community is out of touch with the child's life outside the Sunday school classroom. The church community never sees how or whether her faith understanding has an impact on her world or guides her behavior. Unfortunately, too many churches relegate responsibility for the faith development of the children to the Sunday school teachers. This is in direct contrast to the scriptural understanding of faith. Fostering an evolving faith community requires the union of biblical doctrines and creeds with the collaborative sharing of our faith experiences.[29]

Through relationships our homes and churches impress on us how faith is lived. If we are people in relationship with others and if we learn from our relationships with others, then our narratives, our stories of faith, must be an integral part of church life. It is within these communal relationships that the zone of proximal development functions. The mature members of the church proactively recognize the developmental level already achieved by each child and individually facilitate those abilities that will mature tomorrow. We recognize not just the fruits of our children's development but encourage the buds that have yet to mature. We invite the novice to participate in activities and skills that are beyond those that he is capable of handling independently.

---

[28]Henry G. Liddell and Robert Scott, eds., *A Lexicon: Abridged from Liddell and Scott's Greek-English Lexicon* (Oxford, N.Y.: Clarendon, 1974).

[29]Parker J. Palmer, *To Know As We Are Known: A Spirituality of Education* (San Francisco: Harper & Row, 1983).

In our church all of the adolescent children are encouraged to choose adult mentors to spend time with outside the church setting. Both the children and their mentors have benefited tremendously from these relationships. A variety of activities are shaped by the individual dyads, and occasional corporate programs include all the dyads.

My own children's lives have been powerfully impacted when people in our church family have tapped them on the shoulder and suggested that their input on a particular matter would be important. When my son is asked to play the piano so that others can worship, he sees his involvement as contributing to the worship experience of our community. My daughter has been invited to participate on the worship committee as well as on the board of the self-help store. I cannot begin to describe to you how important the adults who involve them have been in their lives. As a parent I can play a particular role that is important but is also tainted by my own fallenness. When others recognize and value my children's contribution, it means more in their lives than what I can impart.

The value of mentors is without dispute in the developmental research. Adolescents who "do well" despite terrible odds consistently identify one adult who served as a mentor. The research on resiliency in children indicates several protective factors that appear to enable children to mature into individuals who have high self-esteem and thoughtful values that guide their lives. Longitudinal studies examining childhood resilience identify several factors within families of origin and outside the family circle that buffer or mediate the stresses of poverty, mental illness of parents, abuse and so on.

Some of the factors are congenital, for example, temperamental characteristics, alertness, health and so on.[30] Environmental factors, however, play a more interesting and controllable role. Resilient children tend to have a close bond with at least one nonparental adult from whom they receive positive attention. This nurturing adult can be a member of the family, such as a grandparent, aunt, uncle or older sibling. However, the substitute parent often comes from outside the family circle: a baby sitter, neighbor, church member, youth leader or minister. Many resilient kids rely on these external sources of support for counsel in times of stress and crisis. "With the help of these support networks, the resilient children developed a sense of meaning in their lives and a belief that they could control their fate. Their experience in effectively coping with and mastering stressful life events built an attitude of hopefulness that contrasted starkly with the feelings of helplessness and futility that were expressed by their troubled peers."[31] When we mentor, we create new zones of proximal development within which to work.

Children are not the only ones in need of mentoring. Families need mentors. As

---

[30]Emmy Werner, "Children of the Garden Island," *Scientific American* 260 (1989): 106-11.
[31]Ibid., p. 110.

children are born into a family, new demands and stresses emerge. Mothers and fathers are faced with multiple priorities and often have serious questions about child rearing. In our transient society, we rarely live near extended family that might otherwise provide the support and encouragement we so desperately need. When children become adolescents, new questions and fears arise, both for the adolescents and for their parents. Receiving nourishment and guidance from family mentors who have gone before can renew a struggling family's strength and vision.

Greg Ogden calls the church to "unleash the sleeping giant and see the ministry returned to the people of God." He argues that we should eliminate the language of clergy and laity from our vocabulary. Too often these terms represent a hierarchical notion of roles and expectations that can inhibit the needed ministering of the priesthood of believers. Ogden is determined to redefine the word *minister* to describe all members of Christ's body: each member of the church is a minister, not merely those who are paid.

> One day I was almost caught in my own trap. I was visiting a deputation site where our high school youth were serving. At dinner that evening I was asked by a youth with whom our team worked, "How many ministers do you have at your Church?" Eavesdropping on our conversation was one of the adult leaders serving as a counselor for the week. I was about to stumble into the traditional answer when Dave saved me: "Yes, Greg, how any ministers *do* we have?" Catching his tone and myself, I said, "We have close to six hundred." I came perilously close to reinforcing the old-wineskin perspective and thereby undermining the new vision that Dave and others had already adopted.[32]

Ogden reminds us that "no individual was ever meant to show the fullness of Christ to the world. We are meant to do that through redeemed communities."[33] These redeemed communities—the body of Christ—need to take seriously this role of ministry, beginning within our own families. Perhaps "equipping the saints" needs to be a more proactive equipping beginning with the discernment of gifts and strengths within the body. Taking ministry seriously requires that the saints are prepared for service based on giftedness. The other side of this, of course, is that ministers need to be ministered to. Too often when we send the saints out we forget that they need nourishment for strength and vision.

Summary
Vygotsky asks the epistemological and moral question: How do we collectively come to know and make sense of our world? He concludes that we create meaning initially by learning the shared meanings of others around us. Collectively people construct shared meanings, and these shared meanings are passed down from gen-

---

[32]Greg Ogden, *The New Reformation: Returning the Ministry to the People of God* (Grand Rapids, Mich.: Zondervan, 1990), p. 74.
[33]Ibid., p. 75.

eration to generation. We develop understanding and expertise through mentoring or apprenticeship with more knowledgeable learners. When we are allowed to participate and are assisted in our participation, we are enabled to discern more about our world and to develop increasing skills. The family and the church should be more intentional about serving as the child's first apprenticeship partners.

The church is a community of disciples and is a necessary witness today. The secretary of the World Council of Churches expressed in 1937:

> The main task of the Christian community, and the greatest service which it can render to the world, is . . . to be the Christian community. For the real tragedy of our time is that we have on the one hand an incoherent mass of individual Christians and on the other hand powerful impulses towards new forms of community, but no Christian community. Christians today do not form a new community; and the communities which shape the new world are not Christians. The present-day task of the Christian community is, therefore, not to enter more deeply into the world but to rediscover itself. It must learn to understand again what Christian community means before it can go out and change the world around it.[34]

In his book *Life Together* Dietrich Bonhoeffer reminds us that Christian community is a divine reality, not an ideal. This community, lived in and through Jesus Christ, "springs solely from the Biblical and Reformation message of the justification of man through grace alone; this alone is the basis of the longing of Christians for one another."[35]

Our children desperately need and long for numerous attachment figures who will provide perspective on the multiple distractors in their world. As Bonhoeffer argues, "the Christian needs another Christian who speaks God's word to him. He needs him again and again when he becomes uncertain and discouraged, for by himself he cannot help himself without belying the truth. . . . He needs his brother solely because of Jesus Christ."[36]

Jesus consistently called the church community to be the family. He was adamant with the apostles about the importance of caring for the souls of the young. The community brings vision for each of us, helps us to forgive and to receive forgiveness and sees our value and worth before we are able to see it for ourselves. These processes, in addition to the community's commitment to nurturing our young, will serve as a primary vehicle for healing the souls of our families.

I challenge the church of the new millennium to practice a strong ecclesiology and to rediscover the how of discipling or mentoring, and I challenge us to begin with our families and children. Can we conceive of nurturing and raising children

---

[34]Franklin H. Littell, "The Anabaptist Concept of the Church," in *The Recovery of the Anabaptist Vision: Twenty-Three Essays by Contemporary Scholars,* ed. Guy F. Hershberger (Scottdale, Penn.: Herald, 1957), pp. 127-28.
[35]Dietrich Bonhoeffer, *Life Together* (New York: Harper, 1954), p. 23.
[36]Ibid.

by using the principle of discipleship or apprenticeship rather than by merely practicing discipline? This would require the entire church to take seriously the nurture
of its children, much as it promises to do when it recites any of the baby dedication
or baptism litanies.

The church has a dual role: to mentor parents in their important role but without
abdicating its own equally important role of caring for the children. "Take care that
you do not despise one of these little ones; for, I tell you, in heaven their angels
continually see the face of my Father in heaven. . . . *So it is not the will of your
Father in heaven that one of these little ones should be lost"* (Mt 18:10, 14).

In sum, both attachment theory and Vygotsky's developmental theory argue that
as relational creatures, we need disciplers or mentors to care for us, to walk with
us, to believe that we can go on to the next developmental level even when we
doubt ourselves. Our children need multiple mentors in their lives. Families need
caregivers. Developmental theory has much to offer as it relates to the dynamics of
family brokenness. The doctrine of forgiveness and grace, and a renewed view of
ecclesiology can provide nurture and care for the souls of our hurting families. Lest
we forget, human history is a story of fallenness. Understanding family brokenness
may enable our churches to become places of healing where lives can be restruc-
tured according to God's plan.

Editors & Contributors

EDITORS

Mark R. McMinn, Ph.D., is Rech Professor of Psychology at Wheaton College, where he teaches in the doctoral program in clinical psychology and oversees the Center for Church Psychology Collaboration. He is a licensed clinical psychologist with Alliance Clinical Associates in Wheaton, Illinois. His most recent book is *Psychology, Theology, and Spirituality in Christian Counseling.*

Timothy R. Phillips, Ph.D., was associate professor of theology at Wheaton College, where he was instrumental in starting and organizing the annual Wheaton College Theology Conference. Along with coediting several scholarly books, he was coauthor (with Dennis L. Okholm) of *Welcome to the Family: An Introduction to Evangelical Christianity.*

CONTRIBUTORS

Jeffrey H. Boyd, M.D., is chairman of psychiatry and chairman of ethics at Waterbury Hospital, Connecticut, and an ordained pastor. He has published more than a dozen articles and three books on the biblical concept of the soul, and is one of the authors of the DSM-IV diagnostic system used in mental health.

Ellen T. Charry, Ph.D., is the Margaret W. Harmon Associate Professor of Systematic Theology at Princeton Theological Seminary. She is the author of many scholarly and popular articles and is editor of *Theology Today.* Her most recent book is *Inquiring After God: Classic and Contemporary Readings.*

Deborah van Deusen Hunsinger, Ph.D., is associate professor of pastoral theology at Princeton Theological Seminary. Author of *Theology and Pastoral Counseling: A New Interdisciplinary Approach,* she is interested in the relationship between Christian theology and psychotherapeutic theory and practice.

L. Gregory Jones, Ph.D., is dean of the Divinity School and professor of theology at Duke University in Durham, North Carolina. His major areas of interest are theology and ethics. He is the author, most recently, of *Embodying Forgiveness.*

Stanton L. Jones, Ph.D., is provost and professor of psychology at Wheaton College. His recent books include *Homosexuality: The Use of Scientific Research in the Church's Moral Debate* (coauthored with Mark A. Yarhouse), and *Psychology & Christianity: Four Views* (coedited with Eric L. Johnson). His major interests are integration of faith and learning, and sexuality.

Cynthia Neal Kimball, Ph.D., is associate professor of psychology and chair of the psychology department at Wheaton College. She has written numerous articles and chapters pertaining to integration of developmental psychology and Christianity.

Bryan N. Maier, Psy.D., is assistant professor of pastoral counseling and psychology at Trinity Evangelical Divinity School, Deerfield, Illinois. His major area of interest is the integration of psychology and theology with a specific interest in historical aspects of integration.

Michael Mangis, Ph.D., is associate professor of psychology at Wheaton College, where he is the master's program coordinator in the psychology department. He practices as a clinical psychologist in Elburn, Illinois, and has authored various articles pertaining to the integration of contemplative Christian spirituality and psychoanalytic psychology.

Philip G. Monroe, Psy.D., is assistant professor of counseling and psychology and director of the master's in counseling program at Biblical Theological Seminary. He is also in private practice as an associate at Diane Langberg, Ph.D., & Associates in Jenkintown, Pennsylvania.

Stephen K. Moroney, Ph.D., is associate professor of theology at Malone College in Canton, Ohio, where he has been recognized with the distinguished faculty award for teaching. He is the author of *The Noetic Effects of Sin: A Historical and Contemporary Exploration of How Sin Affects Our Thinking.*

Dennis L. Okholm, Ph.D., is professor of theology at Wheaton College, an ordained minister in the Presbyterian Church (USA), and an oblate of a Benedictine monastery (Blue Cloud Abbey, SD). He has coauthored and coedited several books, including *Welcome to the Family: An Introduction to Evangelical Christianity* (coauthored with Timothy R. Phillips).

David Powlison, Ph.D., edits the *Journal of Biblical Counseling,* teaches at Westminster Seminary, and counsels at Christian Counseling & Educational Foundation. He has written numerous articles about Christian counseling, and about how Christian faith and practice relate to the faiths and practices of the modern psychologies.

Robert C. Roberts, Ph.D., is distinguished professor of ethics at Baylor University. He was formerly professor of philosophy and psychological studies at Wheaton College, where he worked on integration aspects of clinical psychology. Author of numerous books and articles, he is currently completing a volume on the moral psychology of emotions.

Richard L. Schultz, Ph.D., is professor of Old Testament and Armerding Chair of Biblical Studies at Wheaton College. He has written various articles on Old Testament wisdom literature, was part of the New Living Bible translation team for Proverbs and maintains a scholarly interest in biblical hermeneutics.

Myrla Seibold, Ph.D., is professor of psychology at Bethel College in St. Paul, Minnesota. A licensed psychologist, she provides psychotherapy and supervision in the student counseling center, teaches undergraduate and graduate courses, is clinical director of the M.A. program in counseling psychology, and serves on the state of Minnesota Board of Psychology.

Brett Webb-Mitchell, Ph.D., is assistant professor of Christian nurture, Duke Divinity School, Duke University, and an ordained pastor in the Presbyterian Church (USA). He has written numerous books and essays, and has given presentations nationally and internationally regarding people with disabilities in the church. His book *Christly Gestures* is to be published in 2001.

David Alan Williams, Ph.D., is professor of philosophical theology and ethics at Colorado Christian University in Lakewood, Colorado. His major area of interest is in constructive engagements between evangelical theology and postmodern thought.